16⁹⁵

Nature in Asian Traditions of Thought

D0573189

SUNY Series in Philosophy and Biology

David Edward Shaner, editor
Furman University

Nature in Asian Traditions of Thought: Essays in Environmental Philosophy

edited by

J. Baird Callicott
and
Roger T. Ames

State University of New York Press

Santa Fe Community
College Library
6401 Richards Ave.
Santa Fe, NM 87508

Published by
State University of New York Press, Albany

© 1989 State University of New York

All rights reserved

Printed in the United States of America

No part of this book may be used or reproduced
in any manner whatsoever without written permission
except in the case of brief quotations embodied in
critical articles and reviews.

For information, address State University of New York
Press, State University Plaza, Albany, N.Y., 12246

Library of Congress Cataloging in Publication Data

Nature in Asian Traditions of Thought.

(SUNY series in philosophy and biology)
Includes index.
1. Ecology—Philosophy. 2. Natural history—
Philosophy. 3. Philosophy, Oriental. I. Callicott,
J. Baird, 1941– II. Ames, Roger T., 1947–
III. Series.
QH540.7.E58 1989 179'.1'095 88–16003
ISBN 0–88706–950–9
ISBN 0–88706–951–7 (pbk.)

10 9 8 7 6 5 4 3 2

For our children—
Burton, Anthony, Anna, Jason, and Austin
—each one of them in his and her insistent particularity

Contents

Preface   ix

Foreword
    Eugene C. Hargrove   xiii

Introduction: The Asian Traditions as a Conceptual Resource for
    Environmental Philosophy
    J. Baird Callicott and Roger T. Ames   1

I
The Ecological World View: A Basis for Engagement

Pacific Shift
    William Irwin Thompson   25

Biology as a Cosmological Science
    Harold J. Morowitz   37

The Metaphysical Implications of Ecology
    J. Baird Callicott   51

II
The Chinese World View

The Continuity of Being: Chinese Visions of Nature
    Tu Wei-ming   67

Human/Nature in Nietzsche and Taoism
    Graham Parkes   79

On Seeking a Change of Environment
    David L. Hall   99

Putting the *Te* back into Taoism
    Roger T. Ames   113

Units of Change—Units of Value
    Robert C. Neville   145

III
The Japanese World View

The Japanese Concept of "Nature"
  Hubertus Tellenbach and Bin Kimura   153

The Japanese Experience of Nature
  David Edward Shaner   163

Saigyō and the Buddhist Value of Nature
  William R. LaFleur   183

IV
The Buddhist World View

The Jewel Net of Indra
  Francis H. Cook   213

Environmental Problematics
  Kenneth K. Inada   231

Toward a Middle Path of Survival
  David J. Kalupahana   247

V
The Indian World View

A Metaphysical Grounding for Natural Reverence: East-West
  Eliot Deutsch   259

"Conceptual Resources" in South Asia for "Environmental Ethics"
  Gerald James Larson   267

Epilogue: On the Relation of Idea and Action
  J. Baird Callicott and Roger T. Ames   279

Notes   291

Index   325

Preface

Nature in Asian Traditions of Thought: Essays in Environmental Philosophy grew out of discussions begun at the first Institute for Comparative Philosophy held at the University of Hawaii in Honolulu in the summer of 1984. We, its editors, are J. Baird Callicott and Roger T. Ames— respectively, an environmental philosopher and a comparative philosopher. The former was an Institute fellow and the latter a member of the faculty.

At one of the initial Institute sessions, Callicott strongly averred that Ames was making a straw man of Plato—a phony foil for his Confucius. With eight weeks to go and an opportunity for mutual growth at stake, each of us came immediately, but independently, to the conclusion that we had better seek common ground both personally and philosophically. Ames was motivated by an oriental sense of appropriateness (*yi*) and ritual deference (*li*), and Callicott by an ecological attitude of synergy and symbiosis.

It turns out that we had more in common than at first appeared—even on the question of the right way to read Plato. During daily mid-day runs through the ti leaves and bougainvillaea of lush Manoa valley, site of the University of Hawaii campus, we talked through our differences and reflected on our roles in the future directions of our profession.

Western philosophy is currently in a state of transition, as even some of its most well-established and celebrated exponents profess. Early in the present century, Western philosophers became enamoured of the scientific method. During the eighteenth-century European Enlightenment, what had once been an integral part of philosophy—natural philosophy—evolved into the natural sciences: physics, chemistry, geology, biology, and so on. And the remaining part of the Western philosophic tradition—moral philosophy—had, by the end of the nineteenth century, begun its metamorphosis into the social sciences: economics, sociology, anthropology, and psychology. Science, in short, seemed poised to absorb into itself all areas of intellectual inquiry. Beleaguered but undaunted, a circle of philosophers outfitted themselves with a philosopher's variation on the scientific method, and succeeded in staking claim to a turf all their own. They emphasized the logical analysis of language. Anxious to establish an identity independent of and yet with the same legitimacy as the sciences, the protoanalytic philosophers approached the questions of their intellectual forebears—ultimate reality, the nature and limits of human knowledge, human virtue, duty, and so on—with a decided emphasis on methodology, and with relatively little interest in the more existential concerns of historical and cultural context. The complexity, which attended the big questions historically, was treated as a prescientific briar patch born either of unclear language or of uncritical emotion that could be cleared with positivism. Mainstream twentieth-century Western philosophy is their legacy.

ix

During the twentieth century, mainstream philosophy in the West, therefore, gradually shifted from its traditional cultural role. The irony is that just as philosophy, in response to science, was becoming more narrowly specialized and positivistic, science, in response to its own internal historical dialectic, was becoming more speculative and uncertain. The "external," "material" world of Newtonian physics, which philosophers had learned to love for its ostensiveness and definability, by the 1930s melted away into a pulsating, warped spatio-temporal continuum. This new and strange physical plenum, it was asserted, can become, in principle, fully actual only upon interaction with a sensible subject whose choice to know certain of its local properties precludes the knowledge of their complements. To say that relativity and quantum theory revolutionized the ontology and epistemology of modern physics is to understate the case. The twentieth-century scientific revolution at the foundations of physics invites—indeed, demands—a return to the kind of philosophical reflection, clarification, and generalization, in the grand manner of Plato, Descartes, and Kant, that had been the hallmark of Western philosophy for nearly two and a half millennia.

Developments in the life sciences during the twentieth century also invite more general philosophical exploration and extrapolation. The theory of organic evolution further sealed the fate of dualism, in both its mind/body and man/nature formulations; and ecology disclosed a living world more whole and internally related than classical normal science had figured.

These new developments in the physical and life sciences, moreover, bear profound practical portent, challenging the naturalistic fallacy that has worried twentieth-century philosophy, with its claim that *ought* does not follow from *is*, that value is divorced from fact, and that ethics and science are independent cognitive domains. Nevertheless, with some few and exciting exceptions, Western philosophers, content with the elegance and power of an ahistorical method, have been slow in embracing the challenge and opportunity presented by these novel and unexpected developments in science. Philosophers, by and large, are only gradually, and in fits and starts, distancing themselves from the prerevolutionary myth of monolithic, positive, empirical science; the world view of classical mechanics; and the refraction of the fact/value dichotomy. And many are still satisfied, although often cynical, to cultivate their own walled gardens. Consequently, as the century wanes, in the pluralistic movements of post-modernism, neo-pragmatism, neo-Marxism, and hermeneutics, Western philosophers evidence an emerging dissatisfaction with a discipline which has become self-absorbed and isolated from the larger intellectual community.

Concurrently, of course, the explosive development of twentieth-century technology is radically reducing the planet in effective size. Transportation and telecommunications technologies have created the European Economic

Community, multinational corporations, and a global supermarket. Western philosophy is now stirring from a methodologically imposed parochialism in which mainstream Anglo-American analysts have been unable (and often unwilling) to communicate with Continental phenomenologists, to say nothing of joining a dialogue with exponents of the non-Western traditions. Surely, the global cultural exchange, now become so familiar a fact of twentieth-century life in the social, economic, and political spheres, is properly served by an analogous cosmopolitanism in the sphere of ideas.

Contemporary comparative philosophy and environmental philosophy, each in its partial way, are factors in the current movement to restore to Western philosophy its erstwhile more comprehensive and integrative intellectual function. We hope that this book will represent a fruitful alliance in pursuit of that common vision.

Ames has been program chair of the Society for Asian and Comparative Philosophy since 1984. Callicott had piqued his interest in environmental philosophy; and so together we organized a series of Society panels on the topic of "the Asian traditions as a conceptual resource for environmental philosophy." To set the problematic, Callicott returned to the University of Hawaii in the spring of 1985 to present a paper outlining the principal conceptual issues of environmental philosophy—with special attention to its hitherto casual dalliance with Asian thought.

Two panels convened in December 1985 at the Eastern Division Meeting of the American Philosophical Association in Washington, D. C.; a third convened in March 1986, as part of the Association of Asian Studies Annual Conference in Chicago; and a fourth at the November 1986 American Academy of Religion meeting in Atlanta. Selected papers presented on these occasions were published in special issues of *Environmental Ethics* (8/4, Winter 1986) and *Philosophy East and West* (37/2, April 1987). They form the nucleus of this anthology.

To this nucleus we added other papers which addressed the same general topic, some written before and some after the occurrence of the panels and publication of the special journal issues. And we parsed the resulting collection into the geodoctrinal categories conventional in Asian and comparative philosophy. The book, accordingly, begins with a section developing the emerging Western ecological world view—with a weather eye on the Eastern horizon—as a basis for comparison. Subsequent sections provide discussions of various aspects of Chinese, Japanese, Buddhist, and Indian thought about the nature of nature, human nature, and their mutual relationship. We were careful to include in each section some papers that are readily accessible to the general reader and others that work at the frontiers of scholarly and philosophical research.

The purpose of the Institute for Comparative Philosophy, sponsored by the National Endowment for the Humanities, was to encourage the more thorough integration of Eastern thought into the philosophy curricula of American universities. This book directly advances that desideratum to the extent that part of its purpose is to serve as a text for courses in environmental and comparative philosophy.

But, as a tangible product of that first Institute for Comparative Philosophy, it represents much more. Environmental philosophers from the outset have supposed that an ecological wisdom was to be found in the East. This book sympathetically but critically explores that supposition for the first time in context and in detail. We are confident that it will stimulate further exploration, research, and critical discussion. On the other hand, through the process which culminated in this collection, specialists in Asian and comparative philosophy have become keenly aware of an intellectually engaging new direction in contemporary global philosophy to which their expertise can make a substantial contribution.

Our acknowledgements must begin with the assistance that we have enjoyed from the leadership in both environmental and comparative philosophy; in particular, the editor of *Environmental Ethics,* Eugene C. Hargrove, and the editor of *Philosophy East and West,* Eliot Deutsch. We also must thank all the other contributors to this volume for their cooperation during its assembly. To SUNY Press, we owe a debt to the director, William Eastman; the editor, Lois Patton; and the three anonymous reviewers for valuable advice and criticism. Thomas P. Kasulis made important suggestions that have been incorporated and are much appreciated, and Steve Goldberg was generous with his expertise in helping us with the cover art.

In addition, we would like to acknowledge the following permissions. "The Japanese Concept of 'Nature' " by Hubertus Tellenbach and Bin Kimura, first appeared in *International Philosophical Quarterly* XIX (June 1979) as "Some Meanings of 'Nature' in European Languages and their Correspondences in Japanese." "Pacific Shift," by William Irwin Thompson, is reprinted by permission of the State University of New York Press, which is presently preparing a conference volume edited by Stanislaw Grof in which it is also scheduled to appear. "Saigyō and the Buddhist Value of Nature," by William R. LaFleur, is condensed and revised from an article of the same title that appeared in *History of Religions* 13 (1974). "The Continuity of Being: Chinese Visions of Nature," by Tu Wei-ming, is reprinted from *On Nature,* edited by Leroy S. Rouner (Notre Dame, IN: University of Notre Dame Press, 1984). "The Jewel Net of Indra," by Francis H. Cook, is a marginally edited version of his first chapter in *Hua-yen Buddhism: The Jewel Net of Indra* (University Park: Pennsylvania State University Press, 1977).

Foreword

Eugene C. Hargrove

As a distinct scholarly activity, environmental philosophy is little more than a decade and a half old. Nevertheless, research in this new field has been intensive. Book-length treatments, as well as collections of articles, now appear on a regular basis. Although over the years, repeated allusions to Asian philosophy as a panacea for environmental ills have crept into popular literature on ecological issues, little sustained and professional attention has so far been given to the potential role of Eastern attitudes toward nature and the human-nature relationship in environmental philosophy. This book is consciously designed to make up for that neglect.

In retrospect, it is surprising that Eastern thought has not played a more fundamental and central role in environmental philosophy from its very inception in the early 1970s. Environmental philosophy is, after all, very much a product of the 1960s—which was not only a period of dawning environmental awareness but also one in which non-Western philosophies became very fashionable alternatives to conventional Euro-American attitudes and values. Interest in Zen Buddhism, in particular, was widespread. Made accessible through the writings of D.T. Suzuki, Alan Watts, Gary Snyder, and others, Zen significantly influenced Western popular culture. Formal comparative studies examining similarities between Zen and major Western philosophers, such as Wittgenstein and Heidegger, were common. Just a few years later, however, when the first serious work in environmental philosophy began to appear, little interest in Eastern thought was evident in it. Deep ecology as a popular movement within environmental philosophy did, of course, retain some Eastern elements, carried over by some thinkers, Gary Snyder, in particular, as they moved from Zen to deep ecology, but these references frequently appear out of place to environmentalists not familiar with the flavor of the 1960s, and anachronistic to many of those who are.

The scholarly inattention to Eastern thought in environmental philosophy might actually reflect only the whirlwind pace of change in the second half of the twentieth century. Indicatively, papers comparing Zen and the thought of famous Western philosophers soon stopped appearing. Thus, it could be that just when environmental philosophy commenced in earnest, Pop Zen (or West Coast Zen, as Callicott and Ames call it in their introductory essay to this volume) had gone—like Nehru jackets, miniskirts, and other trendy 1960s stuff—so far out of fashion that environmental philosophers (who were already working at the margins of academic propriety) steered clear of Eastern thought as a whole. A vigorous literature in comparative environmental philosophy may not have flowered, in other words, simply because an interest in Eastern thought went out of style just as environmental philosophy was getting started. But there must be more to it than that; and, indeed, there is. The Lynn White debate, as it turns out, is the principal reason that comparative environmental philosophy was nipped in the bud.

The debate started with the publication in 1967 of the controversial paper, "The Historical Roots of Our Ecological Crisis," by Lynn White, Jr., in *Science,* and it raged throughout most of the 1970s. On its surface—and so it was generally perceived—White's paper appeared to be a wholesale indictment of Christianity as the primary cause of Western environmental ills. In the concluding section, "An Alternative Christian View," however, White ends up by suggesting a way to *reform* Christianity, so that it can lead us *out* of the valley of the shadow of ecological death into which it had led us in the first place. He recommends that we declare Francis of Assisi the patron saint of ecology. Less idiosyncratically expressed, White may be taken to recommend that mainstream Christianity endorse a Franciscan theology and pan-psychism, as a basis upon which deliberately to construct a Christian (and, therefore, *a fortiori,* a Western) environmental ethic. But on the way to this recommendation, he raises—and rejects—an Eastern alternative.

> More science and more technology are not going to get us out of the present ecologic crisis until we find a new religion, or rethink our old one. The beatniks, who are the basic revolutionaries of our time, show a sound instinct in their affinity for Zen Buddhism, which conceives of the man-nature relationship as very nearly the mirror image of the Christian view. Zen, however, is as deeply conditioned by Asian history as Christianity is by the experience of the West, and I am dubious of its viability among us.

While these three sentences look harmless enough, in retrospect they appear to have made a powerful and unexpected impact on Western scholars concerned with the historical, philosophical, and religious underpinnings of the environmental crisis. White asserts that we must *either* "find a new religion" *or* "rethink our old one." Casually rejecting the former, he moves on, in the closing paragraphs of his seminal essay, to deal programmatically with the latter.

Most Western scholars followed White's lead and simply ignored the Eastern alternative. They had neither the interest nor the expertise to follow it up. Those few, however, who took it seriously appear to have been galvanized by White's disjunction. We must, they seem to have felt, find a way to fix Christianity from an environmental point of view, or run the risk that the momentum of the environmental crisis will cause the Western environmental movement to defect—lock, stock, and barrel—to the East. Christianity, after all, is an exclusive doctrine—an all or nothing affair. Apparently, to simply learn and borrow from the East did not appear to them to be a viable option. In any case, among them the perceptible effect of Lynn White's paper was like the perceptible effect of poking a stick into a hornet's nest. For them the pressing agenda set by Lynn White was to find a good way to reform Christianity, precisely in order to avoid a take-over of the nascent environmental philosophy by Eastern thought.

For example, the distinguished process theologian John B. Cobb, Jr. represents a moderate reaction to White's suggestion that one way to meet the ecologic crisis would be to adopt a new (to the West) Eastern religion. In *Is It Too Late?: A Theology of Ecology,* published in 1972, Cobb argues that the environmental crisis is ecological, that engineering and technology alone cannot be expected to solve its protean problems, and—citing Lynn White— that Christianity is largely responsible for the crisis as it has developed in the West. Cobb then examines the possibility—once again following White— that, as a remedy, non-Western views of nature be adopted by the West. He looks in particular at American Indian and Chinese world views. With regard to the American Indian world view, Cobb argues (1) that although respecting nature more than European Americans, Indians respected human life too little; (2) that they too engaged in destructive ecological practices—driving herds of buffalo over cliffs, etc.—and (3) that on practical grounds, it must be admitted that the Indian way of life cannot support the large human population living in North America today.

With regard to the Chinese world view (represented by Taoism), Cobb argues that it has many of the environmental assets of the American Indian world view without the liabilities. Nevertheless, he contends, Taoism and other Chinese views of nature were unable to prevent deforestation and other ecologically destructive practices in ancient China. Given the historically demonstrated ineffectiveness of these world views, he concludes that it is more prudent for us in the West to try to fix the Western tradition than to try to graft on to an alien one. Discounting Saint Francis as too radical to serve as a historical paradigm for a reformed Christian environmental philosophy, Cobb finally opts for a reverence-for-life ethic of the kind developed by Albert Schweitzer early in this century.

The distinguished Australian philosopher and historian of ideas John Passmore represents a more extreme and intemperate reaction to the prospect of Eastern thought exercising a decisive influence on environmental philosophy in the West. As Passmore puts it on the first page of *Man's Responsibility for Nature: Ecological Problems and Western Traditions* (published in 1974), although it is one thing to ask Western societies to be more prudent,

> it is quite another thing to suggest that they can solve their ecological problems only if they abandon the analytic, critical approach which has been their particular glory and go in search of a new ethics, a new metaphysics, a new religion.

On the second page, Passmore makes it clear that he is concerned primarily with the possible intrusion of "Hindu and Buddhist faiths . . . or the peasant cultures of Asia" into Western civilization. Such an Asian turn, Passmore points out, is entirely consistent with the way Lynn White framed the debate, even though White himself expresses doubt that "the West can simply take over [an Asian] form of thought. . . ."

Throughout his book Passmore characterizes Eastern thought as mystical, and warns that it will undermine Western science and technology— and thus endanger the future of Western civilization as a whole. To permit Eastern influence on Western environmental philosophy, Passmore claims in the final chapter, would expose Westerners once again to "one of the most dangerous illusions to which [Western civilization] has been subject, the mystical, totalistic illusion." According to Passmore, the German Idealism and American Transcendentalism of the nineteenth century were only a small step away from "the truth of Zoroastrianism." And in the twentieth century, the West is in equal peril from ecology, as exemplified by the views of Fraser Darling and Aldo Leopold—which, Passmore believes, can most properly be thought of "as being in essence mystical, as anti-scientific, or as entailing 'a philosophy of wholeness.' "

Like Cobb, Passmore argues that there is no point in turning to Eastern philosophies and religions because, even if they do putatively endorse ecologically congenial attitudes and values, they were ineffective in preventing environmental degradation in the East. Eastern reverence for nature, he notes, "has not prevented Japan from developing an industrial civilization second to none in its offensiveness to ear, eye, and nose." He goes beyond Cobb, however, in recommending that we not tamper at all with our inherited Western ethical and religious framework—doubting, on the one hand, that it is possible deliberately to change the direction of Western traditions in any significant way, but expressing concern, on the other, that a successful change in direction of any kind could mean the demise of Western civilization as we know it. With regard to the former, he writes that " 'needing a new ethic' is not in the least like 'needing a new coat.' A 'new ethic' will arise out of existing attitudes, or not at all." And with regard to the latter, he argues that taking environmentalists' concerns seriously will inevitably bring an end, among other things, to Western-style political freedoms; and he concludes, "better a polluted world than this!"

Eastern thought was not treated very favorably in the Lynn White debate even by some who were well informed about it and, presumably, generally sympathetic toward it. For example, the distinguished Chinese-American geographer Yi-Fu Tuan set out to soundly debunk any romantic illusions about ecologically congenial attitudes toward the environment among the Chinese in a very damaging paper, "Discrepancies Between Environmental Attitude and Behaviour: Examples from Europe and China," published in the *Canadian Geographer* in 1968. "As to China," according to Tuan, "Western humanists commonly show bias in favor of that country's Taoist and Buddhist traditions." The "official line" praising Eastern attitudes toward nature is approved by Tuan as far as it goes, but Taoism, he claims, may represent little more than a rarefied hermit's point of view. Meanwhile, the ordinary Chinese "through their long history [have] engage[d] in gigantic transformations of environment." And that ultimately renders them unsuitable for Westerners in search of an environmental role model. For the majority of Western environmental philosophers who were reluctant to take the trouble to explore Eastern ideas, Tuan's paper relieved them of any lingering doubts about the need to do so.

When the Lynn White debate was at its height in the 1970's, there was a general feeling that the controversy was helping us move toward the creation of a sound environmental philosophy. But the Judeo-Christian tradition was never fully cleared of Lynn White's charges, and no consensus for reforming it was reached. For comparative environmental philosophy, the whole phenomenon was a disaster. The twin arguments that Eastern thought was both insidious and environmentally ineffectual dissipated initial interest in the comparative study of environmental philosophy, and brought it almost completely to a halt. The latter argument preempted useful discussion and debate, and the former predisposed Western environmental scholars to greet references to Eastern philosophy and religion with cold silence or cultural chauvinism and unwarranted hysteria. The Lynn White controversy effectively turned off the lights and closed and bolted the door against the possible influence of Asian traditions of thought in the constructive project of environmental philosophy.

The appearance of this book might, in some quarters, again stir up strong opposition to the introduction of Eastern points of view into environmental philosophy. Indeed, if the paper by Holmes Rolston, III, "Can the East Help the West to Value Nature?" (published in the 1987 special issue of *Philosophy East and West* on environmental ethics), is any indicator, the preemptive strike response has already begun. Hence, I think that it is important to examine critically the confusions and misunderstandings that have precluded an Eastern contribution to environmental philosophy for nearly two decades, namely, (1) the belief that insidious Eastern ideas will destroy Western civilization, and (2) the belief that (a) Eastern environmental attitudes are too incompatible with Western traditions to be assimilable and (b) too ineffective in the East to be of any use in the West.

These beliefs have so frequently been expressed together that they seem to be parts of a single consistent position. A moment's reflection, however, should suffice to show that these two beliefs contradict one another. First, if it is true that Eastern traditions of thought are too incompatible with the Western tradition for most Westerners to be able to understand them and to take them to heart, then the fear that they will destroy Western civilization is obviously completely unfounded. People can hardly sell out to ideas that they cannot understand. Second, if, as its critics have long maintained, Eastern environmental attitudes and values have been ineffective in curbing environmental abuse in Asia, they would surely be equally ineffective in undermining Western civilization, one distinctive feature of which is environmental aggression and transformation.

Of course, if Eastern environmental ideas are in fact too incomprehensible, from a Western point of view, to be assimilable, then such a study would be fruitless; and if they were powerless to prevent environmental degradation in the East, and, therefore, presumably also in the West, then such a study would be pointless. Let's deal with each of these possibilities in turn.

First, is it reasonable to assume that comparative study will be fruitless? While it is very unlikely that the West will ever become radically "Easternized," the West has profitably borrowed from the East in bits and pieces, and the borrowed elements have been both benign and readily absorbed. Some of these borrowed bits and pieces have, in fact, contributed importantly to laudable and culturally widespread Western environmental attitudes. Consider the relatively recent (historically speaking) emergence of an aesthetic receptivity to nature in the West—a general topic, incidentally, upon which comparative environmental philosophy might shed considerable light. Significantly, the first informal gardens in Europe were called "Chinese gardens." Although it would be historically inaccurate to say that the West literally "borrowed" its late-blooming aesthetic receptivity to nature from the East, it is, nevertheless, true that Eastern natural aesthetic sensibilities played a significant historical role in the birth of Western natural aesthetic sensibilities. At the very least, we can say that the simple fact that seventeenth- and eighteenth-century Europeans knew that people in other parts of the world aesthetically enjoyed nature paved the way for similar values to emerge in Europe.

There has been considerable cross-cultural intercourse between the East and West for many centuries now. Throughout that time Westerners have been very much aware of Eastern traditions of thought. Has this long exposure to Eastern thought posed any real danger to Western civilization? It is difficult, I believe, to find any substantial evidence that those Eastern ideas that have made their way to the West have worked any mischief in their new home. To the contrary, what the historical record really suggests is that Western ideas have played havoc in the East. During a long period of armed Western colonial imperialism, Western philosophy, religion, and especially science and technology have made considerable cultural inroads in the East. Indeed, Western thought has made a significant impact on Eastern natural environments. If Japan is offensive to "ear, eye, and nose," it is largely because Japanese civilization has been infected by Western technology and industrial methods. As far as I am aware, the West has never been comparably damaged by anything that it has imported from the East.

Now, let us consider the more worrisome suspicion that a study of Eastern traditions of thought is pointless. From an environmental point of view, there is no conclusive evidence to show that Eastern environmental attitudes and values have been pragmatically ineffective. Granted, they may not have enabled Asian peoples to resist armed Western colonial imperialism and intellectual tyranny; and granted also, Asian environments were degraded prior to intrusive cultural disturbance from the West. Prior to Western influence, Easterners may, nevertheless, have been environmentally well intentioned, but unaware of the environmental consequences of their actions. After all, the fact that human actions could damage the environment on a large scale went unrecognized in the West until George Perkins Marsh pointed it out scarcely a century ago, and that information did not become common knowledge until very recently—the mid-1960s. Thus, it is possible that precolonial environmental degradation in the East, occurring gradually over centuries, was the result of empirical ignorance—a lack of scientific knowledge of ecological relationships—rather than the pragmatic inefficacy of Eastern environmental attitudes and values.

More deeply, however, the whole notion that attitudes and values are either "effective" or "ineffective" is something of a category mistake. It makes some sense to say that a law, enacted for a specific purpose, is either effective or ineffective. If, when people obey a law, and the result intended by the legislators does not obtain, then the law can be declared ineffective. But a world view is not created by legislation, nor is it intended to bring about specific social goals. A world view, including its associated ethics and ideals, is, rather, only generally, and often only indirectly, related to conduct. In some respectable interpretations of ethics, moral principles and precepts are not properly regarded as serving good consequences at all—but rather as promoting right action, which, in particular cases, may lead to evil consequences of tragic proportions. Morality, thus, certainly cannot be as readily (and may even not be as appropriately) assessed in terms of effectiveness as legislation can (and/or may) be.

But we still haven't gotten to the bottom of this business of the effectiveness or ineffectiveness of environmental attitudes and values. Setting aside the debate about the proper interpretation of ethics—as either oriented toward consequences or toward right action irrespective of consequences—by all accounts, moral principles and precepts are normative, not descriptive. They do not, in other words, describe how people actually behave; rather they prescribe how people—again often generally and obliquely—ought to behave. Thus, when a people's behavior falls short of the ideals that are either manifest or implied in their world view—and empirical ignorance of complex relations of cause and effect is not the culprit—it is not illuminating or even meaningful to say that their attitudes and values are ineffective. It is truer as well as simpler to say that people do not always live up to their standards or norms of conduct. But the pragmatic value of ideals and moral principles, even if routinely flouted, is, nevertheless, evident to all but the most inveterate cynic.

In assessing the relative worth of Eastern thought to contemporary *Western* environmental philosophy we must be careful not to overstate the case—any more than to understate it. It is most unlikely that Eastern thought will revolutionize Western environmental philosophy, despite its critics' fears and its proponents' hopes. More likely, ideas from Eastern traditions of thought will be selectively incorporated, gradually assimilated, and eventually lose their exotic flavor—while the main currents of contemporary Western environmental philosophy will flow on impelled by their own momentum. Although the direct contribution of Eastern thought to contemporary Western environmental philosophy will probably be, thus, incidental, the indirect contribution may be more pervasive. An open-minded comparative study of Eastern environmental attitudes and values will enable Western environmental philosophers better to recognize and criticize their most ingrained and otherwise unconscious assumptions inherited from the long and remarkably homogeneous history of Western thought.

While the value of the comparative study of Eastern environmental attitudes and values to Western environmental philosophy is likely to be either incidental or indirect (but significant nevertheless), it will be of the greatest value and, indisputably, of real importance to the development of a contemporary *Eastern* environmental philosophy. The contemporary environmental crisis is global in extent. Presumably, therefore, the East needs a new environmental philosophy as badly as does the West. Passmore is correct, I believe, when he asserts that needing a new ethic is not like needing a new coat. Ecologically sound attitudes and values to help the West through its environmental crisis will emerge, if at all, out of Western philosophy—however much comparative studies may be of assistance. But, by the same token, environmental philosophies that are meaningful and inspiring in nations of the Asian persuasion will have to emerge out of Asian traditions of thought.

One may hope that research in environmental philosophy will eventually produce a single set of universally valid environmental attitudes and values that will transcend all cultural frameworks. Experience seems to suggest, however, that research in environmental philosophy will produce, rather, a family of environmental attitudes and values growing out of a variety of intellectual traditions—Eastern and Western.

Looking back over two decades of work in environmental philosophy, two distinct phases of research are clearly discernible. The first focused primarily on Judeo-Christian responsibility—as both cause, and, properly reformed, cure of environmental ills. The second abandoned that debate and focused primarily on the theoretical foundations of environmental philosophy, but still almost exclusively from a Western point of view. We are now ready, I believe, for a third period of study; one that treats environmental philosophy globally, while at the same time respects cultural diversity; one that goes beyond the broad categories of East and West and takes full account of regional, national, and religious differences. It is to this project, happily, that this book is dedicated.

Introduction: The Asian Traditions as a Conceptual Resource for Environmental Philosophy

J. Baird Callicott and Roger T. Ames

Environmental philosophy first came on the scene during the early seventies in the form of relevancy offerings in progressive curricula primarily at teaching-oriented undergraduate institutions.[1] The first literature in environmental philosophy, correspondingly, took the form of hastily assembled multidisciplinary anthologies for classroom use.[2] Then, in the mid-seventies, environmental philosophy became more narrowly defined as a subdiscipline of philosophy proper, and there began to be produced a more specialized, technical literature, not directly designed for or related to pedagogy.[3] By the end of the decade, a journal, *Environmental Ethics,* had been established by Eugene C. Hargrove (the first volume was published in 1979) to provide both a forum and professional identification and recognition for environmental philosophy as a legitimate area of philosophical research.[4]

Superficially, environmental philosophy appears to be one among several new fields of "applied ethics," all originating almost simultaneously in the same context of curriculum reform in mid-century academic philosophy. Generally, applied ethics (epitomized by bio-medical and business and professional ethics) apply familiar, well-worked out (and worked over) ethical theories—utilitarianism in its multifarious forms, Kant, Aristotle, Hare, Rawls, or whatever—to novel problems emergent in modern technology: life support systems, genetic screening, genetic engineering, organ transplantation, and so forth in biology and medicine; and whistle blowing, mass media manipulation, electronic eavesdropping, global market control, and so forth in business and the professions.

"Environmental ethics," on the other hand, is actually a sort of *anti*-applied ethics. The real-world problems which taken together constitute the so-called "environmental crisis" appear to be of such ubiquity, magnitude, recalcitrance, and synergistic complexity, that they force on philosophy the task not of applying familiar *ethical* theories, long in place, but of rethinking the underlying moral and metaphysical assumptions that seem to have had a significant role in bringing on the crisis. Environmental philosophy, in other words, begins with the idea that traditional metaphysics and moral theory are more at the root of environmental problems than tools for their solution. Environmental philosophy, therefore, has been more

1

critically and conceptually oriented than the historically grounded and narrowly problem-centered species of applied ethics with which it is often confused. Environmental problems provide less the occasion for the exercise and application than for the criticism and recasting of Western moral and metaphysical presuppositions.

One of us (Callicott) attempted to articulate the difference between environmental philosophy and applied ethics in a recent, synoptic article in a mainstream philosophy journal:

> Over the last decade, environmental ethics has emerged as a new subdiscipline of moral philosophy. As with anything new in philosophy or the sciences, there has been some controversy, not only about its legitimacy, but about its very identity or definition. The question of legitimacy has been settled more or less by default: professional philosophical interest in environmental philosophy seems to be growing as, certainly, work in the field proliferates. The question of identity—just what is environmental ethics?—has not been so ingenuous.

> Environmental ethics may be understood to be but one among several new sorts of applied philosophies, the others of which also arose during the seventies. That is, it may be understood to be an *application* of well-established conventional philosophical categories to emergent practical environmental problems. On the other hand, it may be understood to be an *exploration* of alternative moral and even metaphysical principles, forced upon philosophy by the magnitude and recalcitrance of these problems. If defined in the former way, then the work of environmental ethics is that of a philosophical yeoman or underlaborer (to employ Locke's self appraisal); if defined in the latter way, it is that of a theoretician or philosophical architect (as in Descartes' self-image).[5]

A less than entirely sympathetic philosopher, Thomas E. Hill, agreed with this general assessment in a review of a recent collection of essays in environmental philosophy:

> The underlying project in almost all of the essays . . . is the search for fundamental theoretical grounds for an environmentalist stand on current issues. Unlike much recent work in medical ethics, the focus is not on deciding what should be done in "hard cases" posed by new technology. A wide area of agreement on what should be done seems to be taken for granted by the authors; their concern is rather how to articulate the philosophical grounding of environmentalist policies. Is a radical revolution in ethics required? Is traditional Western religion adequate to the task? Do alternative world views provide better models? Should ethical theory abandon the fact/value distinction—or return to belief in "intrinsic values"?[6]

In light of some of the essays included in this volume, however, even this description of the project of environmental philosophy might not go far enough. A deeper break with traditional Western philosophical commitments may be required: The problems implacably posed by the environmental crisis for environmental philosophy are so basic that the exploration of an alternative *metaphysics* or attendant ethical *theory* might not be a sufficiently radical solution.

II

The complex of problems constituting the "environmental crisis" (in chronological order of their popular notice) include environmental pollution, the aesthetic degradation of nature, human overpopulation, resource depletion, ecological destruction, and, now emerging as the most pressing and desperate of problems, abrupt massive species extinction. These problems are largely Western in provenance, albeit global in scope. They are big, tough, and interrelated. And they all appear to be symptoms of a fundamental misunderstanding of the nature of nature and of a tendency to exclude nature from moral concern or consideration.

Hence, to begin adequately to address environmental problems, philosophical presuppositions must be revised to jibe with an ecological description of nature and (since and ecological description of nature, most generally conceived, subverts the concept of ontologically independent *entities*) ethics must be enlarged so as to valorize and enfranchise nature *as a whole* as well as *individual* nonhuman natural entities. The project of environmental philosophy on each of these two heads—order and value—has two basic phases, the first critical, the second constructive.

Initial criticism (mostly by intellectual historians, not philosophers— who were slower to react) focused, simplistically, on the so-called Judeo-Christian tradition.[7] This criticism was primarily theological and cosmological, but has clear moral implications and overtones. These seem to be the main points which came under attack:[8]

1. God—the locus of the holy or sacred—transcends nature.
2. Nature is a profane artifact of a divine craftsman-like creator. The essence of the natural world is informed matter: God divided and ordered an inert, plastic material—the void/waters/dust or clay.
3. Man exclusively is created in the image of God and is, thus, segregated, essentially, from the rest of nature.

4. Man is given dominion by God over nature.
5. God commands man to subdue nature and multiply himself.
6. The whole cognitive organization of the Judeo-Christian world view is political and hierarchical: God over man, man over nature—which results in a moral peck order or power structure.
7. The image-of-God in man is the ground of man's *intrinsic* value. Since nonhuman natural entities lack the divine image, they are morally disenfranchised. They have, at best, instrumental value.
8. The theologically based instrumentality of nature is compounded in the later Judeo-Christian tradition by Aristotelian-Thomistic teleology—rational life is the telos of nature and hence all the rest of nature exists as a means, a support system, for rational man.

A particularly strident, but representative and widely influential example of this first, essentially nonprofessional phase of the criticism of Western cognitive and moral traditions from an environmental point of view was expressed by landscape architect Ian McHarg:

> The great Western religions born of monotheism have been the major source of our moral attitudes. It is from them that we have developed the preoccupation with the uniqueness of man, with justice and compassion. On the subject of man-nature, however, the Biblical creation story of the first chapter of Genesis, the source of the most generally accepted description of man's role and powers, not only fails to correspond to reality as we observe it, but in its insistence upon dominion and subjugation of nature, encourages the most exploitative and destructive instincts in man rather than those that are deferential and creative. Indeed, if one seeks license for those who would increase radioactivity, create canals and harbors with atomic bombs, employ poisons without constraint, or give consent to the bulldozer mentality, there could be no better injunction that this text. Here can be found the sanction and injunction to conquer nature—the enemy, the threat to Jehovah.
>
> The creation story in Judaism was absorbed unchanged into Christianity. It emphasized the exclusive divinity of man, his God-given dominion over all things and licensed him to subdue the earth.[9]

As Eugene C. Hargrove points out in the foreword to this volume, the attack on the Judeo-Christian tradition by McHarg, Lynn White, Jr., and others provoked a veritable flood of apologetic literature. In the ensuing debate about the causes and cures of the environmental malaise, critical attention remained riveted on only half of the story of the Western heritage of ideas. In the most general sense, modern Western intellectual culture is rooted in Greco-Roman as well as Judeo-Christian thought. And, in fact, it can be argued that the Greco-Roman legacy, which is less visible to lay persons than to philosophers, has more powerfully informed the prevailing assumptions and premises of modern Western thought than distinctly Judeo-Christian ideas.

But precisely because it is less manifest, the Greco-Roman legacy has not received anything like the thorough and systematic critical discussion that has been visited upon the Judeo-Christian tradition by environmentally oriented intellectual historians. Indeed, historian Lynn White, Jr., author of the landmark classic "The Historical Roots of Our Ecologic Crisis," who is followed by historian J. Donald Hughes and political scientist John Rodman, all look to Greek myth and philosophy—pagan naturalism (a sacred nature), Milesian hylozoism (a living Earth), Heraclitus (a process ontology) and Pythagoras (human-animal kinship) for ecologically fitting or environmentally useful ideas.[10]

The first Greek philosophy was natural philosophy, and although many ecologically adaptable or environmentally useful ideas were broached, the natural philosophy which was culturally selected by this dialectic of Western intellectual history, and thus survived to bequeath its characteristics to the modern period, is atomism.

Nature is represented in atomism as particulate, reductive, material, inert, quantitative, and mechanical. This concept of nature became institutionalized in early modern science and was pragmatically translated into an engineering agenda.[11] It is expressed in the ongoing Western Industrial Revolution by what is known as "modern technology." The environmental crisis may in large part be diagnosed as a symptom and a measure of the mismatch between the atomistic-mechanistic image of nature inherited from the Greeks, institutionalized in modern classical science, and expressed in modern technology, on the one hand, and the holistic-organic reality disclosed by contemporary ecology and quantum physics (and in a sense by the environmental crisis itself) on the other. Clearly, these two paradigms—the atomistic-mechanistic and the holistic-organic—sponsor widely divergent conceptions of entities and the nature of their relatedness.

Greek philosophical anthropology, meanwhile, which was revived and institutionalized in the West roughly contemporaneously with the revival and institutionalization of atomism, was paradigmatically expressed by Plato: Human nature is dualistic—composed of body and soul. The body (at least in Descartes' modern version) was, as any natural entity, exhaustively describable in atomistic-mechanistic terms. The soul, on the other hand, resides temporarily in the body—the ghost in the machine—and is of an otherworldly origin and destiny. Human beings, thus, are both essentially and morally segregated from nature. The natural environment, therefore, might be engineered to human specifications, no matter with what natural consequences, without either human moral responsibility or ultimate human penalty.

To these observations might be added those of David L. Hall and Roger T. Ames, who find in Greek philosophy, especially as paradigmatically and most influentially represented by Plato, the concept of transcendental principles of natural and moral order.[12] The Platonic forms are a metaphysical hypostatization of a logico-mathematical order assumed to be imposed upon a passive and chaotically inclined material to effect an ordered natural world. Modern ecology, on the other hand, represents the incredibly rich and complex order of the biosphere to be emergent and reciprocal, and for things to have become what they are through a process of mutual adjustment and evolutionary co-determination.

From the point of view of the dawning awareness of the environmental crisis of the late sixties and early seventies, modern Western civilization seemed erected on the worst possible mix of ideas inherited from both its Judeo-Christian and Greco-Roman roots (although the critique of the Greco-Roman heritage was only implicit). Given the metaphysical and axiological conceptual composite at the core of the predominant and prevailing Western world view, the environmental crisis is the predictable, the inevitable outcome, it was argued:

> Our failure is that of the Western World and lies in prevailing values. Show me a man-oriented society in which it is believed that reality exists only because man can perceive it [Berkeley], that the cosmos is a structure erected to support man on its pinnacle [Aristotle, Aquinas], that man exclusively is divine and given dominion over all things [Genesis], indeed that God is made in the image of man [Genesis inverted], and I will predict the nature of its cities and their landscapes. I need not look far for we have seen them—the hot-dog stands, the neon shill, the ticky-tacky houses, dysgenic city and mined landscapes. This is the image of the anthropomorphic, anthropocentric man; he seeks not unity with nature but conquest.[13]

So, it has been argued, in much of the literature to date, that to solve the environmental crisis, it is necessary to construct or to adopt a different world view and a different set of values and duties.

III

Since environmental problems were laid at the door of the *Western* world view and value premises, some thinkers naively leaped to the conclusion that, by contrast, *Eastern* traditions could provide, for these essentially Western ills, an alternative world view and set of values ready-made, as it were, to establish harmony between man and nature. Political scientist Hwa Yol Jung prescribed such an exotic intellectual elixir in an especially pure and innocent manner in 1972:

> I wish to challenge those Western writers who refuse to accept Zen (and indeed Eastern ideas in general) as an answer to the global problem of ecology . . . . And if . . . it needs "a Copernican revolution of the mind" to avert the impending ecological catastrophe, I suggest that Zen could be the fountainhead of that revolution.[14]

The way was paved for this journey to the East in search of a philosophical remedy for the environmental crisis, we conjecture, by a somewhat earlier (in the fifties) fascination with Eastern ideas in the then new prototype of a disaffected/alienated American subculture called the Beat Generation. The Beats read Alan Watts and Herman Hesse avidly, cut their hair close like Zen monks, and produced novels with titles like *Dharma Bums*. In the most widely read and quoted classic of the early literature in environmental ethics, Lynn White, Jr. makes the following revealing remark:

> What we do about ecology [i.e., the natural environment] depends on our ideas of the man-nature relationship. More science and more technology are not going to get us out of the present ecologic crisis until we find a new religion, or rethink our old one. The beatniks, who are the basic revolutionaries of our time, show a sound instinct in their affinity for Zen Buddhism, which conceives of the man-nature relationship as very nearly the mirror image of the Christian view.[15]

West Coast Zen Buddhism and the newly emergent environmental movement were further integrated in the popular imagination by Beat hero, California nature poet, and student of oriental thought, Gary Snyder, during the sixties. Among the most delightful as well as popular pieces by Snyder is his underground environmental poem, "Smokey the Bear Sutra," which parodies the format of Mahāyāna Buddhism's famous *Lotus Sutra* *(Saddharma-Puṇḍarīka)* but supplies it with an evolutionary-ecological world view and an environmental activist message:

> Once in the Jurassic, about 150 million years ago,/the Great Sun Buddha in this corner of the Infinite/Void gave a great discourse to all the assembled elements/and energies: to the standing beings, the walking beings,/the flying beings and the sitting beings—even grasses,/to the number of three billion,

each one born from a/seed, were assembled there: a Discourse concerning/enlightenment on the planet Earth.

"In some future time, there will be a continent called/America. It will have great centers of power called/such as Pyramid Lake, Walden Pond, Mount Ranier, Big Sur,/Everglades, and so forth; and powerful nerves and channels/such as Columbia River, Mississippi River, and Grand Canyon. /The human race in that era will get into troubles all over its head, and practically wreck everything in spite of/its own strong intelligent Buddha-nature . . . .

In that/future American Era I shall enter a new form: to cure/the world of loveless knowledge that seeks with blind hunger; /and mindless rage eating food that will not fill it."

And he showed himself in his true form of/SMOKEY THE BEAR . . . .

Wrathful but Calm, Austere but Comic, Smokey the Bear will/illuminate those who would help him; but for those who would/hinder or slander him,/HE WILL PUT THEM OUT.

Thus his great Mantra:/Namah Samanta vajranam chanda maharoshana/Sphataya hum traka ham man/"I DEDICATED MYSELF TO THE UNIVERSAL DIAMOND/BE THIS RAGING FURY DESTROYED"

And he will protect those who love woods and rivers,/Gods and animals, hobos and madmen, prisoners and sick/people, musicians, playful women, and hopeful children;

And if anyone is threatened by advertising, air pollution,/or the police, they should chant SMOKEY THE BEAR'S WAR/SPELL: DROWN THEIR BUTTS/CRUSH THEIR BUTTS/DROWN THEIR BUTTS/CRUSH THEIR BUTTS

And SMOKEY THE BEAR will surely appear to put the enemy out/with his vajra-shovel.[16]

Yale biophysicist Harold Morowitz, in a 1972 discussion (reprinted here in full), attempted to link the metaphysical implications of contemporary ecology with a specific ontological doctrine in Buddhism:

In a book entitled *Science and Buddhism,* P. Dahlke has elaborated the thesis that in theology everything stands, in science everything falls and in Buddhism everything burns. The notion of burning is a metaphysical expression of transience and impermanence . . . . Although the Buddhist syntax is entirely different from that of modern science, the notion is clearly present that everything is process—a process which only persists by virtue of some universal kind of energy flowing through the world. From this point of view, the reality of individuals is problematic because they do not exist per se but only as local perturbations in this universal energy flow. As originally presented this must have been a very mystical idea, but a similar kind of idea seems to emerge from modern science. Everything we know of is indeed process, which is mediated on the surface of our planet by the flow of solar energy through all organized structures.[17]

William R. LaFleur in a 1974 article (reprinted in condensed form in this volume) connected the Mahāyāna Buddhist valorization of nature to matters which were simultaneously emerging as issues in environmental ethics. LaFleur reviewed, in his scholarly discussion, the debate in East Asian Mahāyāna concerning the status and religious value of plants and trees. This protracted discussion in the tradition gradually elevated the valuation of plant life in Japan. It began with the fundamental question of the possibility of Buddhahood for plants and trees, and issued ultimately in the emblem of plant life as a model for human salvation. This extended class of religiously validated beings resulted, for many Japanese Buddhists, in an extension of the moral community.[18]

The first round of criticism of Western ideas and orientation to the Orient was largely descriptive, and even when sophisticated regarding the Asian cultures, as in the case of LaFleur's discussion, did not have systematic philosophical goals. In much of the earlier environmental literature, however, the very different traditions of Eastern philosophy, particularly those of the Indian subcontinent and those of the Far East, were conflated—so that it appeared that just as there was one fairly unified Eastern tradition, there was one fairly unified Western tradition. For example, in a celebrated classic of environmental history Roderick Nash wrote,

Ancient Eastern cultures were the sources of respect for and religious veneration of the natural world . . . . As early as the eighth century B.C., the Indian philosophy of Jainism proposed that man not kill or harm any living creature. While the Jains were largely intent on maintaining absolute detachment from the world, early Buddhists and Hindus professed a feeling of compassion and a code of ethical conduct for all that was alive. Likewise, China and Tibet produced philosophies which honored life other than man's and promulgated elaborate dietary rules in this interest.

In the Far East the man-nature relationship was marked by respect, bordering on love, absent in the West . . . . Man was understood to be a part of nature. And wilderness, in Eastern thought, did not have an unholy or evil connotation but was venerated as the symbol and even the very essence of the deity. As early as the fifth century B.C., Chinese Taoists postulated an infinite and benign force in the natural world . . . . Far from avoiding wild places, the ancient Chinese sought them out in the hope of sensing more clearly something of the unity and rhythm that they believed pervaded the universe . . . . In linking God and the wilderness, instead of contrasting them as did the Western faiths, Shinto and Taoism fostered love of wilderness rather than hatred.[19]

Huston Smith, whose academic post as Professor of Philosophy at MIT and whose books and articles on Eastern philosophy and religion provide him no excuse, has been guilty of a similar conflation, when speaking to environmentalists:

> Asia retained a deep, unquestioning confidence in nature, appreciative of it, receptive to it. Had the Chinese and Indians not risen above the natural plane at all, they would not have spawned civilizations. The way in which they did transcend it, however, was by confirming it. They dignified it by affirming it consciously. By contrast the West oppositioned [sic] herself to nature in a stance that was reserved and critical. Its civilization receded progressively from the natural and instinctive and set itself up against them . . . .

> China with her "Tao that can be spoken is not the true Tao" and India's Upanishadic truth that can be comprehended only through living in the presence of a life through which it actively shines . . . hold closer to tacit dimensions of knowing.[20]

In addition to the broad popular appeal of Gary Snyder's work, these remarks by Lynn White, Roderick Nash, and Huston Smith are typical of the early environmental literature and were also widely influential. (Those of Morowitz and LaFleur are less typical, albeit more interesting and insightful; and they were certainly less influential.) However, perhaps for the reasons Hargrove suggests in the foreword to this book, there has been very little subsequent work which carries through on these early mostly casual suggestions (and, until the recent conference forums which yielded many of the essays included in the present volume, there has been practically none by scholars whose expertise is primarily in Asian and comparative philosophy).[21]

Some recent work by specialists in Asian thought is relevant to environmental philosophy, even though no comparative reference either to environmental concerns or the description of nature in the environmental sciences (ecology first and foremost) is to be found in them. For example, with apologetic verge, Chung-ying Cheng has written:

> I think that we can derive the following three principles from the Confucian and Taoist metaphysics, which will lead to a characterization of causality in the Chinese perspective.

There is, in the first place, a *principle of holistic unity* . . . .

Second, there is the *principle of internal life-movements*. By this I mean that all things in the world have an intrinsic life-force which moves them in a way in which motion is not imposed from other things or a God but is derived from the inexhaustible source of energy of life, which is the Way. As the source is intrinsically related to an individual thing, the derivation of energy for movement is intrinsic as in an organism rather than extrinsic as in a machine. Similarly, as all things are interrelated to form a network of interchange of processes, the transmission of moving force is conceived of as an exhibition of life activity, in the absence of which the individual things will cease to be defined . . . .

Finally, there is the *principle of organic balance*. By this I mean that all things and processes in the world are related in processes which proceed toward a balance and a harmony . . . .

The model of causality in Chinese philosophy is exactly contrary and converse to the mechanical-atomistic model of scientific Europe in the eighteenth and nineteenth centuries. Whereas the Western scientific concept of causality is atomistic, externalistic, and mechanistic, the Chinese model of causality is antiatomistic and therefore holistic, antiexternalistic and therefore internalistic, antimechanistic and therefore organistic. The very radical differences between them is not difficult to explain: It is the difference between the Image of Life and the Image of Machine. Insofar as life is a concrete experience of man and a machine is built from an abstract design and quantitative draft, one may also say that the Chinese model of causality is basically reflective of the concrete experience of life, history, and time, whereas the Western scientific model of causality is basically a reflection of abstract thinking and quantitative calculation.[22]

The world view emerging from contemporary science (especially ecology and quantum theory) is remarkably similar to Cheng's characterization of Chinese philosophy.

IV

In the relatively new literature of environmental philosophy there has been an intense interest in finding new integrative and moral paradigms by means of which to establish a more harmonious and mutually fulfilling and beneficial relationship of man to nature. There has been a general assumption that Eastern traditions of thought could provide important conceptual resources for this project, and there has been lots of loose talk about how they might. But, with the exception of a handful of essays, no direct and extensive work by experts in Eastern thought has been undertaken on the environmental philosophy problematic.

The inspiration for the present volume, then, has been to redress this situation by bringing the Asian traditions to bear on the problems of environmental philosophy as they have been here generally defined—and on the very problematic itself.

The appropriation of "conceptual resources" for environmental philosophy from Asian cultural traditions, however, is an undertaking fraught with a variety of dangers, the most salient of which do not go unnoticed in several of the papers included here. As editors of this volume, therefore, we believe that it is important to state clearly, here at the outset, just what may— and may not—be expected of an extended exercise in comparative environmental philosophy.

Comparative *environmental* philosophy faces the same general problems that attend *any* comparative study in philosophy. Perhaps the most obvious general problem is that the ideas of Eastern cultures must be made intelligible to non-specialists in the West through the syntax and semantic discrimina- tions of Western languages (and vice versa). A full discussion of this problem would, of course, require a volume of its own.[23]

There are two radically opposed positions that generally limit such discussion. Some students of comparative culture are inclined to believe that, when all is said and done, representatives of other traditions are pretty much like us (in the West); others do not. Some believe that behind all the divergences, thinkers East and West inquire into universal problems that transcend cultural differences; others believe that beyond the more obvious gross physical and cultural similarities—ten fingers and toes, an upright gait, language, art, music, social and political institutions, and so on—there are profound and exotic differences that derive from culture-bound ways of thinking and living. Some believe that failing to regard the common characteristics as most important is to deny other peoples their humanity; others believe that to assert such an essential community is to deny other cultures the full value of their uniqueness. The difference between these two positions can be diagnosed, perhaps, as the difference between those who begin with the assumption that we are primarily and most significantly members of a single species, and those who begin with the assumption that we are, in the last analysis, particular and unique persons constituting and constituted by our peculiar social, cultural, and natural environments.

There is much at stake in this debate. On one extreme are theorists whose intellectual system-building and universalizing make them liable to hubris, condescension, and reduction as they force elements of one culture to fit a mold endemic to and derived from another. On the other extreme, are cultural apologists whose claims of incommensurability, and often superiority, can lead to arrogance, isolationism, and uncritical parochialism.

It is between these two extremes that we must confront the cultural specificity of philosophy itself. Philosophy proper may be an intellectual activity unique to Western civilization—as several of the papers in this volume imply. To seek conceptual resources of environmental *philosophy* in Asian traditions may thus be otiose—like trying to find, say, distinctly political institutions, for comparative or assimilative purposes, in tribal societies—because to do so rests on an ethnocentric "category mistake." If this is so, of course, all efforts at East-West comparative philosophy are just as ill-conceived—whether the focus be on ethics, metaphysics, aesthetics, epistemology, or any of the other well-established subareas of (Western) philosophy—because there is no Eastern philosophy.

Philosophy, of course, may be so narrowly defined that, by definition, nothing outside the Western tradition will count as a bona fide case. However, the very planetary and ecocentric perspective of environmental philosophy would suggest a more inclusive than exclusive understanding of the larger philosophical enterprise. In fact, as we have already suggested, if any set of issues is going to occasion the redefinition of philosophy as a broad engagement with and openness to the world, it is that concerning our shared human biocultural relationship with the environment.

One of our primary purposes in assembling this anthology is to challenge the aforementioned willingness among non-experts in the Asian traditions to combine what are, in fact, many (and often competing) philosophies into a generic "Eastern Wisdom." This presumption that there is some identifiable and, on some basis, unified "Eastern Wisdom" (if not philosophy)—a counterpart to the Western philosophic dialectic—is one signal of the absence of sophistication that has attended much of popular comparative environmental discussion.

There is a more persuasive argument for discovering this kind of unity in the development of Western philosophy, and it is perhaps by analogy with the Western tradition that this presupposition about Eastern philosophy is entertained. Though fed by a variety of tributaries and flowing into a similar variety of sloughs and backwaters, there has been, in the West, a main channel of thought. To shift metaphors, much of the edifice of the Western philosophic tradition has been constructed on the shared assumption that certainty is possible—the belief, bequeathed to us by Pythagoras, that on the model of mathematics, a unified and systematic structure underlying both the natural and moral order is in principle available to the human being in explanation of the surrounding world. And much of the contribution of Western philosophy has been the consequence of our confidence in this quest for certain knowledge. The successes in the natural sciences that followed upon the application of hypothetical reasoning occasioned the extension of similar methods in the pursuit of the same certainty in human philosophy: ethics, politics, economics, and so on.

The assumption that there might be some universal logical or causal principle that makes knowledge of both fact and value and its systematic explanation possible, has been broadly efficacious. On the back of a science of first principles, not only were the natural sciences possible, but, further, the social sciences could reach for respectability. It is the dominance of this rationalistic tendency in the development of Western philosophy that has established metaphysics and epistemology at its center, and that has encouraged the development of the theoretical sciences, both natural and social. And it is this emphasis on rational evidence over rhetorical that accounts in important measure for the seemingly universal features of the Western philosophic enterprise, establishing as it does the priority of methodology and demonstration over analogical thinking and praxis.

Of course, the Western philosophic tradition is rich and complex; and, particularly since the middle of the eighteenth century, the commitment to the underlying rationalist principle that has made systematic philosophy viable has become an increasingly serious complaint among those Western philosophers whom Isaiah Berlin has called the "counter-enlightenment" thinkers. From Vico to our own post-modernist thinkers, the orthodox assumption that there is discoverable some unchanging basis of order that is ultimately ahistorical and ahumanistic—be it Plato's realm of forms, the self-evidently clear and distinct ideas of Cartesian philosophy, Kant's categories of the understanding, or a fixed and universal human nature sought by a spectrum of philosophers from the natural law theorists to the structuralists—has come under intense scrutiny.

Now, the Eastern traditions are not devoid of systematic philosophies. On the contrary, analogous in role to the counter-current thinkers in the mainstream of our modern tradition is the existence of rationalistically oriented movements and personages within the domain of the alternative Asian cultures: the later Mohist logicians in classical China, the Nyāya logicians and grammarians in India, and so on. Audible within the Asian traditions, especially India, there are voices that resonate readily with the central rational enterprise of the Western philosophic tradition and that fit without force into the categories derived from the assumptions and presuppositions upon which that tradition rests. To the extent that these rationalistic elements are prominent, one may speak without error or equivocation of a unified tradition of "Eastern philosophy."

But the fact is that these rationalistic components do not occupy center stage in the Asian theater. On the contrary, the dominant prejudice in what we might perilously organize as "Eastern Wisdom" lies in the priority of the unique particular, a characteristic which in its nature, discourages systemic unity, promoting in its stead an aesthetic rather than a scientific sense of coherence. As Plato, at the fountainhead of Western rationalism, plainly recognized, particulars qua particulars cannot be grasped by a rational method. In the absence of a hypostatized rational system by means of which to organize experience, Eastern philosophy has typically sought analogical similarities—rather than identities—among particulars. By means of this approach one may at once preserve the uniqueness of particulars and at the same time achieve a coherency in one's intellectual grasp of nature and society. Since, for major components of the Eastern traditions, order is not reducible beyond a discernible harmony in the dispositioning of unique particulars, there is a significant resistance to abstract (*abstractus:* to move away) notions that are dependent upon the assumption of universalizing principle: system, unity, objectivity, transcendence, uniformity, conceptualization, and so on. And it is precisely these characteristics which unify the Western tradition. What makes things clear in the distinctly Eastern mode of thinking, on the other hand, is often an effectively focused image, not a theory; an inexpressible and inimitable experience, not an argument; an evocative metaphor, not a logically demonstrated truth. The aesthetic sense of coherence more typical of Eastern philosophical reflection fosters a pluralism in Eastern philosophies that is not present in the same degree in the Western tradition. While even the most strident cultural chauvinists would allow that other cultures can generally be explained by appeal to our established disciplines—history, sociology, economics, and so on—there has been at the same time a stubborn resistance among philosophers to acknowledge that other cultures have philosophies. We suggest that this resistance is attributable in large part to the disparity between the dominance of systematic philosophy in the West and its relative absence in Asia (and other parts of the world). And we also suggest that the relegation of Eastern reflection on fundamental natural and moral questions to something less than philosophy proper has been compounded by the way non-Western philosophies have been introduced to Western philosophical audiences— through categories and presuppositions which often do not belong to them, but rather to their Western counterparts. In consequence, Asian philosophies appear to be rather confused and inferior variations on Western themes. In other words, by Western paradigms, either there is no Eastern philosophy worthy of the name, or, if there is, it is of an inferior grade.

How then can Western philosophers critically and dialectically engage Eastern thought in the absence of shared goals and evaluative standards? Whatever the answer to this question may be, the first step is to appreciate the full degree of difference between Western and Eastern thought. A common understanding, East and West, of the philosophical enterprise may or may not be attainable; but to organize Eastern philosophy by means of Western philosophical categories and evaluate it by Western criteria of evidence, argument, and proof is as idle as it is parochial. Eastern philosophy lacks a unity similar to that so remarkably present in Western philosophy not only for the simple reason that Asia is larger, geographically more fragmented, and ethnically and culturally more diverse than Europe, but also because the unity characteristic of Western philosophy flows from its rational search for abstract structure and explanation. Hence the assumption that there is an analogous unity in Eastern philosophy can be pernicious.[24]

More directly and specifically to the present undertaking, Holmes Rolston, III, in a recent paper, critically poses the question, "Can the East help the West to value nature?"[25] To assume a posture of openness and receptivity to the difference in Eastern modes of understanding, and tentatively to answer this question affirmatively, immediately raises another question: "How exactly?" Even in the early enthusiastic and naive literature of environmental philosophy, the notion that an alien set of ideas could be mined from its cultural matrix, exported to the West, and intellectually consumed with therapeutic effect was skeptically greeted. For example, immediately after mentioning Zen Buddhism, Lynn White goes on to say, "Zen, however, is as deeply conditioned by Asian history as Christianity is by the experience of the West, and I am dubious of its viability among us."[26] White is certainly correct to think that Westerners cannot simply cut themselves loose from their cognitive roots and graft onto others.

To try to see the world through an alternative frame of mind, however, can be very revealing of one's own. One clear way that the East can help the West to understand and value nature is, therefore, by revealing certain premises and assumptions—concerning the nature of nature and who we human beings are in relation to it, as well as the kind of knowledge of it that we seek to obtain—which lie so deep within or which so pervade the Western world view that they may not come to light any other way. Western philosophy since Socrates has made self-examination a way of life. But the history of Western philosophy also shows how many of the intellectual biases that constitute the very ground of our philosophic inquiries elude even the most dedicated and sincere efforts to dig out and critically evaluate them. Comparative environmental philosophy may certainly contribute to the revelatory and critical phase of environmental philosophy.

The dissatisfaction with Western *traditions* of thought—that is, with *historical* Western philosophical paradigms—and the appeal of Eastern alternatives, often experienced by Western environmental thinkers, is not arbitrary or accidental. A dialectic internal to Western intellectual history has fostered the recent interest in Eastern ideas, an interest that goes well beyond merely a passing fascination with the exotic. The classical foundations of Western science have been steadily eroded during the twentieth century. Certainly, objectivity, dualism, and determinism have been abandoned. And the fundamental features of the natural world—albeit still, to be sure, theoretically and mathematically represented—are conceived very differently in contemporary Western science from the way they had been in the two thousand-year history of Western natural philosophy from Democritus to Newton. The emerging Western world view is nondualistic, nonreductive, integrative, systemic, holistic, and relational rather than substantive, and organic rather than mechanical. However, the conceptual foundations of contemporary science remain exceedingly abstract and remote from ordinary (cognitively conditioned Western) experience. Eastern traditions of thought, it has been suggested (perhaps most roundly by Fritjof Capra in the *Tao of Physics*), share certain untraditional insights into nature with contemporary Western science; but they express these insights, unlike contemporary Western science, in a rich vocabulary of imagery, symbol, and metaphor. If indeed there is a convergence of traditional Eastern philosophy and contemporary Western science toward a common understanding of the nature of nature, then the East may help the West express its own new natural philosophy (together with its new natural values) in a vocabulary more accessible to a lay public than the arid formulae typical of Western science. Eastern modes of thought, in short, may resonate with and thus complement and enrich the concepts of nature and values in nature recently emergent in the historical dialectic of Western ideas.

Accordingly, we begin this volume with several papers that attempt in very different ways and from very different points of view to characterize the recent developments in Western thought which bend its trajectory in an Eastern direction.

In "Pacific Shift," William Irwin Thompson provides a panoramic overview of the major episodes of Western geointellectual history from the Babylon-Memphis "Riverine" axis to the Tokyo-Los Angeles "Pacific-Aerospace" axis. We are presently experiencing, he suggests, the last of four major revolutions in Western cultural ecology. Thompson's popular discussion invokes Gregory Bateson's ecology of mind, Dōgen's Zen Buddhism, electronic technology, and Marshal McLuhan's theory of mass media to characterize the archetypal consciousness of the coming age of an integrated planetary culture.

Harold Morowitz's "Biology as a Cosmological Science" is included as a more focused and disciplined effort to explore the ecophilosophical ramifications of the contemporary ecological understanding of nature. Although Morowitz's central concern is with neither Asian traditions of thought nor environmental issues, his argument leads him to relate his primary theme to both.

J. Baird Callicott wrote "The Metaphysical Implications of Ecology" especially for this exchange of ideas among environmental philosophers and students of Asian thought. He attempts deliberately to articulate the new ecological paradigm in the context of the history of Western natural philosophy as a contemporary Western cognitive baseline to which the Asian intellectual traditions may be compared. From the point of view of ecology, the natural world is not, as represented in *classical* Western science, an aggregate of essentially independent entities. It is a relationally unified, differentiated, and integrated system. Human beings, moreover, are both emergent from and immersed in the ecosystem. To that extent, the world view of ecology is "holistic," and the man-world relationship "integrated" and "organic." Further, there is an immediately discernible complementarity between the scientific newcomer, ecology, and the fundamental metaphysical ideas of the most fundamental contemporary science, quantum physics. Both ecology and quantum theory gravitate toward the same holistic/integrated world view. A consolidated metaphysical consensus in the sciences, therefore, might be emerging that will occasion a broad revisioning of the human relationship with nature in Western thought.

Looking toward the Chinese tradition as a possible resource for compatible ideas and a more concrete vocabulary for expressing the nascent Western natural paradigm, Tu Wei-ming, in "The Continuity of Being: Chinese Visions of Nature," authoritatively outlines the organic model of nature characteristic of classical Chinese philosophy. More particularly, he explicates the central and ubiquitous but elusive concept of *ch'i* (both "vital force" and "basic stuff") in traditional Chinese thought.

Graham Parkes, in "Natural Man in Nietzsche and Taoism," develops a comparison between Nietzsche and the classical Taoists that, in addition to drawing upon novel definitions of nature from the Chinese world, alerts the reader to conceptual resources for environmental philosophy within the Western tradition itself that have not been fully excavated. Parkes, more than the other contributors to this volume, attempts to clarify Eastern thought— Taoism in this case—by comparing it with what he perceives to be a similar expression in the West, namely, certain aspects of Nietzsche's philosophy.

David L. Hall, in "On Seeking a Change of Environment," suggests that environmental *philosophy* is a specific case in point of the broader crisis in Western modes of thought. The environmental crisis challenges rationality and philosophy itself as a rational enterprise. It calls into question at a very fundamental level our most familiar understandings of the nature of order and relatedness. As a possible resource for an alternative understanding of order, Hall looks to classical Taoism and its elaboration of an alternative interpretation of order which, while adumbrated in the Western tradition, has not been fully developed. This interpretation of order, by appeal to several of the central ideas that structure philosophical Taoism—such as *wu-wei, wu-chih, wu-yü,* and *tzu-jan*—articulates a modality of relatedness that has application in understanding particular people in their environments.

In "Putting the *Te* Back into Taoism," Roger T. Ames argues that the problems of environmental philosophy are so basic that the exploration of an alternative metaphysics or attendant ethical theory is not a sufficiently radical solution. Like Gerald James Larson and David L. Hall, Ames suggests that the assumptions entailed in a definition of systematic philosophy that gives us a tradition of metaphysics might themselves be the source of the current crisis. We might need to revise the responsibilities of the philosopher and think in terms of the "artist" rather than the "scientist of first principles." Taoism proceeds from art rather than science, and produces an *ars contextualis:* generalizations drawn from human experience in the most basic processes of making a person, making a community, and making a world. He then develops this idea of an "aesthetic cosmology" as a basis for redefining the nature of relatedness *(wu-wei)* obtaining between particular and world— between *te* and *tao.*

"Units of Change—Units of Value" is a tour de force by Robert C. Neville which seeks to outline a moral metaphysics by appropriating and developing insights from the Taoist tradition. The problem as he sees it is to conceive of value as an achievement of enduring individuals who at once express their own integrity while remaining internally related to ecological processes. There is considerable agreement among Neville, Hall, and Ames about the Taoist understanding of order and relatedness.

In "The Japanese Concept of 'Nature,' " Hubertus Tellenbach and Bin Kimura introduce the Japanese world view by outlining the various ways in which "nature" is expressed in the Japanese language. Tellenbach and Kimura contrast the emergent Japanese concept of nature with the nexus of connotations evoked by the Latin *"natura"* and cognates in Western languages.

Complementing William R. LaFleur's ground-breaking essay discussed above, David Edward Shaner, in "The Japanese Experience of Nature," corroborates his insights and gives Japanese philosophy its due by highlighting those themes and presuppositions in the classical tradition that have led up to the peculiarly Japanese valorization of nature.

The penultimate section of this anthology is devoted to Buddhism, the first Eastern tradition to attract the interest of Western environmental thinkers. Francis H. Cook's "The Jewel Net of Indra" unfolds the Hua Yen Buddhist understanding of reality. In a style reminiscent of Alan Watts, Cook appeals throughout his discussion to analogies and contrasts available in a

Western vocabulary. There is much in the Hua Yen version of Buddhism that illumines the Taoist position on the nature of relatedness discussed in Part II, and registers the impact of indigenous Chinese ideas on the Indian import.

In "Environmental Problematics," Kenneth K. Inada focuses his discussion on Buddhist ontology as a basis for stimulating an alternative attitude to the world in which we live. He argues that what he would call the "parity principle of existence," originating with Buddha and elaborated by Nāgārjuna, grounds and permeates the central doctrines constituting the continuous core of Buddhism. Drawing an interesting parallel between the contemporary interface between Buddhism and Western culture on the one hand, and the introduction of Buddhism into East Asia on the other, Inada then posits this parity principle as a Buddhist resource for constructing an environmental ethics in the West. Perhaps most significantly, he is keen to underscore his conviction that the starting point for resolving environmental ills is the relationality of people and the natural environment.

In "Man and Nature: Toward a Middle Path of Survival," David J. Kalupahana analyzes the classical Buddhist conception of nature and human life that carefully avoids substantialist conceptions of opposites. On the basis of his interpretation of Buddhism as a radical empiricism, he argues that in the Buddha's articulation of "dependent arising" *pratītyasamutpāda)*, his concern was with the fruit—the effect or consequence that defines a thing or event. Given the obvious similarities between this interpretation of the early Buddhist tradition and American Pragmatism, Kalupahana suggests that the Westerner might be better off looking to his own Pragmatic tradition for answers to the ecological crisis than demanding more exotic solutions from the East.

Turning finally from South Asian Buddhism to other indigenous traditions of Indian thought, Eliot Deutsch's "A Metaphysical Grounding for Natural Reverence: East-West" is an argument against the adequacy of addressing the ecological crisis by relying entirely upon utilitarian moral values in combination with scientific understanding of the way in which natural systems function. Beginning with a critique of Kant's treatment of the sublime, Deutsch looks to Indian philosophy for inspiration in developing his notion of "natural reverence."—He posits this creative and spiritual "being together with nature" as an alternative to the rhetoric of superiority, dominance, and separation.

Gerald James Larson, in his essay " 'Conceptual Resources' in South Asia for 'Environmental Ethics,' " begins by rehearsing the several metaethical positions that are conventionally regarded as constitutive of South Asian philosophy, and shows how they might serve as conceptual resources for environmental philosophy. He then takes umbrage at the "economic" metaphor of exploiting alternative traditions as "resources" for profiting our own philosophical marketplace, and, further, at the appeal to a "conceptual" resource that signals our own theoretical presuppositions and consequent definition of philosophy. For Larson (as for David Hall), given what we define as "philosophy," there is *no* philosophical answer to our environmental crisis. On the contrary, philosophy itself (in the contemporary Western sense of the word, at any rate) is very much a part of the problem. Beyond his critique, Larson then outlines contributions that comparative philosophies might make toward a revision of the *problem* by positing alternative metaphors, by undertaking more broadly based cross-cultural and interdisciplinary inquiries into the crisis, and finally, by pointing out that in reenvisioning the environmental crisis from a comparative stance we are attempting nothing less than to reshape the power relations that structure our world, both economically and politically.

It is hoped that this exercise in bringing together scholars and philosophers from different areas of expertise to address a common and vitally important question will foster a continuing dialogue that will in some measure have an impact on environmental quality and ecological integrity. While it is indeed naive to expect immediate resolutions to our current crisis from exotic quarters, the perspective of alternative cultural traditions does at least provide us with a fresh and, it is hoped, a stimulating vantage point from which critically to clarify the assumptions in the Western legacy that have generated both the technological achievements and the environmental problems so emblematic of Western civilization. Moreover, this same project makes available alternative clusters of important ideas that have defined the way in which Asian peoples live in the worlds that they have created for themselves, and provides Westerners with the opportunity to draw inspiration from them in defining a new ecological world view.

I

The Ecological World View:
A Basis for Engagement

Pacific Shift

William Irwin Thompson

The transition from an industrial to an ecological world view is expressed in the shift from the materialistic modes of thought as expressed in the philosophies of Adam Smith and Karl Marx to the re-visionings of the relationship between Mind and Nature as expressed in such thinkers of the Pacific Rim as Gregory Bateson and Keiji Nishitani.[1] This philosophical and cultural movement is what I mean by the term Pacific Shift. Just as once before Reformation Protestantism was the transformation of Christianity in the shift from medievalism to modernism, so now is Reformation Buddhism part of the transformation from European to planetary culture. Precisely because Buddhism is not, strictly speaking, a religion, it is more relevant to the spiritualization of everyday life than the conservative modes of consciousness that are crystallized in Hinduism and the Abrahamic religions. This in no way means that these religions that are appropriate to the level of civilization will disappear, anymore than Catholicism disappeared in the Reformation, but it does mean that they will become the conserving and not the innovating force within the new global ecology of consciousness.

This new planetary culture, the *planetarische denken und planetarische bauen* that Heidegger called for in his *The Question of Being,* is not simply a meeting of East and West, it is beyond the old dichotomies of East and West. When you look at photographs of the earth, where is East and where is West? Where is up and where is down? And where is the ground when the space shuttle is so positioned that it looks as if you are under the earth rather than on top of it?

One cannot use the old frames, the old horizons, the old solidity of matter.[2] And so Buddhism, which seemed to us in the old days of empires, a heathen religion from the land of the rising sun, takes on a whole new relevance, much as Christianity took on a whole new relevance after the break-up of the Roman Empire. The great Irish mystic A.E. (George William Russell) said that in every passionate conflict there is an exchange of opposites. And so in the Pacific War that preceded the Pacific Shift, we fought. And now look at the United States and Japan. Japan took Henry Ford and now has Detroit, we took Dōgen and now have Zen monasteries. I think if you look at it from a thousand year point of view, we Yankee traders got the better deal. I'll take Dōgen Zenji over Henry Ford any day.

In the philosophy of mind of Gregory Bateson, information is not triggered by an impact, a materialistic chain of collisions, but by a recognition of difference. Information is an event of consciousness and not an impact of matter. The world view that follows from this is that the universe is not made out of stuff, but patterns; in this Bateson follows Heisenberg to see the universe as made out of music and not matter.

The philosophy of Gregory Bateson is a good example of the Pacific Shift, for Bateson in his own lifetime made the transition from Eurocentric thinking to the California world of cybernetics and Buddhism. In his recognition of the pattern that connects mind to nature, he realized that mind was not a substance or secretion locked inside the skull, but that the pathways of Mind extended outside the body. Nature is the unconscious, the process of information and not the products of sense perception that flash across the limited screen of consciousness to become the building blocks of our human world of culture and conscious purpose.[3] Another word for this kind of unconscious, this wildness of Mind, is Gaia.[4]

Bateson's work was to challenge the simple materialism that drove the engines of the industrial revolution. He challenged the basic assumptions that humans could dominate nature with agenda of conscious purposes. This project of challenging the very ground of industrial civilization has been continued in the work of Francisco Varela, for Varela's refutation of the notion of representation is more than a critique of neurophysiology, it is a dissolution of the ground of our materialistic world view. From the empiricism of Locke we in the West have inherited the idea that the mind is the brain and the brain is basically a template struck by the impacts of matter. Photons and molecules impact upon the skin and the retina, and suddenly we reassemble an image of an eagle on the little movie screen that is hidden in the back of our skulls.[5] Outside is wild and disordered matter; inside our skull are ordered perceptions and ideas about perceptions. In his *Two Treatises on Government,* John Locke developed his theory of mind into a theory of society, and thus showed us that all epistemologies have political implications. Locke said that it was the act of taking something out of the commons that began a piece of property. The social act of adding labor to the commons produced property. Looking back with 20-20 hindsight, we now can see that Locke is basically looking at nature through the lens of the Enclosure Acts which took land out of the medieval commons and turned it into private property, to the benefit of the lord and the dismay of peasant and cottager. Long before England leaped into its eighteenth-century industrial revolution, it prepared for the industrialization of nature by destroying the medieval sense of the agricultural community and elaborating the new economic sense of private property. Nature was the wild, the primitive commons, but the taking out of property created the new commonwealth. In the transformation of commons into commonwealth, the world view was transformed from patterns of relationship to objects of quantitative weight and measurement. The Enclosure Acts told the peasant and villager that he could no longer put his cow into the commons; he could no longer hunt or collect firewood, for the land was no longer a pattern of ecological and communal relationships; it had become property.

We have continued on with this notion of property all through the centuries of industrial "development." Eighteenth-century Jefferson continued seventeenth-century Locke's political challenging of the divine rights of kings in the elaboration of the rights of property by moving away from the commons of British oral Common Law to a written constitution. Rights are writs, and a constitution is a form of fencing in of custom into the definitions of written laws. In the *Declaration of Independence,* Jefferson assured his contemporaries that all men are endowed with certain inalienable rights, and he spelled them out. I can alienate my right to be free and become an indentured servant for a time, but I cannot alienate my right to breathe, for then I cannot even serve as a slave.

If we stop to consider the historical context of the Lockean idea of property, we can see that Bhopal in India is literally the last gasp of the concept of private property. The industrialist has looked upon the atmosphere as a commons, a wild that can be taken and through labor turned into property. Property then creates wealth, and in the commonwealth it is believed that these new riches will trickle down from top to bottom to create jobs for the unemployed. Nature is commons and can be turned into property, but people are also wild commons that can be turned into property through employment. And yet these distortions of conscious purpose, these representations of a fictional reality, are clearly false, for we can see in the fullest developments of industrialization the contradictions that were not so obvious at the beginning. The atmosphere is not a property, and the individual cannot alienate his right to breathe in exchange for the goods of the Commonwealth.

So good-bye Locke, Newton, and Jefferson, and hello Bateson, Nishitani, and Varela.[6] If the Earth is the unconscious, then it is the activity of consciousness and not labor that is productive of value. What we are all involved in is not a Commonwealth, but a Commonlife. In a materialistic world view, I may have objects in separating space; I may have mansions of Union Carbide's wealth in Connecticut and factories and poison in Bhopal; but in a world view of interpenetrating presences in the groundlessness of Buddhist Emptiness there is no space for these samsaric illusions. If we are all involved in the co-dependent origin of our Commonlife together, then we can no longer afford the luxurious illusions of the Lockean Commonwealth.

If consciousness is the activity that produces value, then even the industrially unproductive have value: the unemployable, the old, the young, the senile, and the dependent. Even a retarded human being or a senile person has the capacity to turn light into language and unconscious into conscious, and so he or she must be of value in our Commonlife. And, indeed, in traditional, preindustrial cultures, such people were valued.

So, by now, you can see "the pattern that connects" Bateson to Varela and Varela to Nishitani. It is not simply a question of a new epistemology, but of a new world view. It is an epistemology with political implications, a Gaia Politique. It is not the apologetics for reaction, for a return to the divine right of kings of feudalism; and it is not an apologetics for the industrial domination of nature in capitalism and Marxism. It is the political exploration for a truly meta-industrial, planetary culture.

The transition from the materialistic culture of the industrial nation-state to the planetary culture of a global ecology will take time, but given the speed of technological change and the implosive power of electronic forms of communication, the transition will be much faster than the shift from medievalism to industrialism. We will, of course, have the disruptions and catastrophes attendant upon any transition. When you move from one world view to another, you do have periods of denial, rigidity, crystallization, and violence. In the Renaissance there was an emergence of modernism in banking and art, and a shift from the Romans to the Greeks as the new favored ancestral culture, but this challenging of the power of the Roman Church also triggered the Inquisition. Now as the modern era comes to an end, its culture is being compressed and miniaturized in hysterical movements of fundamentalism. Essentially, personalities as different as Mishima, Reagan, and Khomeini are all expressive of the nativistic movements attendant upon a change in the deep structure of human culture. So you will have extremist right wing movements in Japan, just as we have them in the United States, but I doubt that Japan will become a samurai kingdom again, and I doubt that the United States will become "the Aryan Nation." Extremist groups are a form of paranoia, but paranoia means to know beyond and to the side, so there is often a poetry to the caricatures of the paranoid. It is indeed the period of the end of "the great White Race," and Los Angeles is now a world city of Hispanics and Asians, so the nativistic movement of "the Aryan Nation" should be looked upon as the Ghost Dance of the rednecks.

The Red Men were not able to stop the railroads, and the rednecks will not be able to stop the new aerospace and cybernetic technologies; they will not be able to lock the United States into the Protestant values and culture of the Reformation. They will, of course, be able to do a lot of damage, to create little eruptions of pus and hate in the American body politic, for there is always this release of heat in a phase change; but I do not believe they will be able to stop the emergence of the new planetary culture; nor will the Shi-ites of Islamic fundamentalism, nor will the monetarists of industrial fundamentalism. As Teilhard de Chardin pointed out so brilliantly and prophetically in his description of "the planetization of mankind," the very efforts of the nation-states to preserve their sovereignty in systems of global defense, only brings them closer together. With satellites and aerospace-cybernetic economies, an isomorphism of national structures begin to emerge. The unconscious begins to link the U.S. and U.S.S.R. together, for the enemy is the Batesonian "difference" that drives the system. The United States could lose Maine or North Dakota and still remain intact, but if it lost its enemy, the whole economic structure of its society would collapse. The danger of conflict comes not simply from destruction, but from the unconscious transformation in which we become what we hate; so, as the U.S.A. and the U.S.S.R. become intimate enemies, there is always the danger that the two empires will become identical structures camouflaged with the superficial contents of mere ideologies. We can see this all too clearly from the history of the conflict between Japan and the United States in World War II. Out of the Pacific War has now emerged the Pacific Shift of the world; had we the contemplative wisdom of Buddhism, we might have been able to move from mindless, passionate conflict to mindful, compassionate balancing, but Americans did not read Nishitani in the 1940s.

It is, therefore, small wonder that as we affirm traditions of the sacred we accept electronic technologies of communication. In many ways, the electronic technologies are, as McLuhan predicted, working to reverse some of the deleterious effects of industrial modernization. McLuhan called this "retribalization in the Global Village." My tribe is the Irish. We were the first Third World to feel the impact of imperial modernization. What the English did to the Irish, the Americans did to the Hawaiians. We came in and said, "Your *kahunas* are witch doctors. Your culture is inferior; let us modernize you with pesticides and automobiles. We will make Honolulu just like Los Angeles." For Americans, it is a "miracle of modern medicine" if you can create an artificial heart. Cleaning up the air would not seem technologically advanced to Americans, and, indeed, they would be happy living in artificial lungs if they could be designed to look like Cadillacs.

Very slowly, we are beginning now to understand that tribal consciousness like that of the "witch doctor," Dr. Mutwa of the Zulu, is not primitive, and that, in fact, the view of mind and body of such people is more advanced than that of the media hustlers. Looking back on the 1970s, we can now begin to see that what they were about in general, and what Transpersonal Psychology was about in particular, was the planetization of the archaic. Yoga, Zen, Tibetan Buddhism, Sufism, Kabbalah, Alchemy, Shamanism: all the ancient ways were made tributaries to the immensity of the sea. The project has now been accomplished. Now it's time for the "New Age" to become truly "new" and to move on.

What we are moving into is not simply a new outlook on the world, but a new mentality with which we look out and in. You can begin to appreciate the importance of this new mentality when you look back to consider those times when humanity passed out of one Mentality into another. Interestingly enough, these Mentalities are also associated with certain historical geographies. The relationship between a historical geography and a Mentality constitutes what I prefer to call a "Cultural-Ecology." The story of "Western Civilization" is basically a movement through four cultural-ecologies: 1. the Riverine, 2. the Mediterranean, 3. the Atlantic, and 4. the Pacific-Aerospace. The Riverine geography is the landscape of the first civilizations of the Euphrates, Tigris, and Nile. For "Eastern Civilization," the Riverine Civilizations would be those of the Indus and Yang-tze. The second historical geography of our Western Civilization was bound up with the Mediterranean. This is the Classical period. The emergence of the modern world involved a projection outward to the Atlantic, and such Western countries as Spain, Portugal, the Netherlands, and England became formative of this new oceanic cultural-ecology. After World War II, world power shifted, and the Pacific Rim became the focal point of the new cultural-ecology.

Now, each of these cultural-ecologies witnessed the emergence of a new polity: 1. city-state, 2. empire, 3. industrial nation-state, and 4. our contemporary enantiomorphic polity in which opposites are in unconscious political collusion. Each of these four cultural-ecologies witnessed the emergence of new economies, as Marx pointed out in his progress of 1. Asiatic economies, 2. feudalism, 3. capitalism, and 4. Socialism; and each of these witnessed the emergence of new forms of symbolic communication, as McLuhan pointed out in his progression of 1. script, 2. alphabetic, 3. print, and 4. electronic. If we review the literature characteristic of each of these periods, we can see that both the narratives of imaginative literature and mathematics are structurally organized within a dominant mode of integrating objects, persons, and events. This mode is what I mean by the term "Mentality." The Riverine Mentality is organized around enumeration, and the prevailing mode of narration is the list: the list of the names taken by the Goddess Inanna from Erech to Eridu, the catalog of the ships that came to the invasion of Troy, the lists of the genealogies of men and gods, and the lists of goods stored within the temple. In the shift from the Riverine Mentality into the Mediterranean one, there was a shift from the mode of enumeration to geometrizing. To appreciate the difference, one only has to contrast Hesiod to Pythagoras or Plato.[7]

To appreciate the next shift from the Mediterranean world to the modern one, contrast Galileo to Plato. Motion for Plato is sinful; motion is the locus of the fallen world. The eternal world of forms is a world of pure geometry and perfect circles. But for the modern world, motion itself—something that was inconceivable in Zeno's paradoxes—becomes the fascination, and Plato's perfect circles transform into Kepler's elipses of planetary motion. Galileo studies the motion of falling bodies, and Leibniz and Newton work out a calculus of infinitesimals. And for the painters the sky is no longer an iconic gold of sacred radiance, but a sky of dynamic movement. Think of the skies of Ruysdael and Rembrandt, and you will appreciate that for the modern world, the Mentality is one of dynamics.

In the nineteenth century, dynamics begins to modulate into transformations. From the thermodynamics of Carnot to the evolutionary changes of Darwin, "transformation" is the basic narrative idea in science, literature, and art. Evolution is a story of ape to man, and novels are stories of rags to riches.[8] In our century, this fascination with transformation has become so intense that we have moved from the simple narratives of dynamics to catastrophe theory. For us, Enumeration, Geometrizing, Dynamics are becoming cumulatively integrated into new forms of processual morphologies in a form of visual thinking that is being stimulated by computer animation and video synthesizers. If you stop to consider contemporary video art, in either its avant garde forms (with works like Jaap Drupsteen in *Hyster Pulsatu*) or in pop art forms (like The Cars' music video, "You Might Think I'm Crazy"), it is clear that art is not at all mimetic and that "reality" is clearly a fabrication. Video synthesizers are simply democratizing the contemplative insights of zazen, and the epistemology that seems elitist and esoteric in the work of Varela is rendered obvious in works of video art. As it is now for scientists and artists of the new mentality, so it was at the beginnings of science with Huyghens and Rembrandt, or later with Carnot and Turner.

Since Innis and McLuhan have shown us how the emergence of abstract thought was intimately bound up in the cultural history of the emergence of the alphabet for the Phoenicians and the Greeks, we should suspect that the emergence of electronics, computers, and video synthesizers are also intimately bound up with the emergence of new forms of right-brain, visual thinking. To monitor the emergence of this new mentality, simply watch the artists, and pay particular attention to new genres in which musical composition is wed to computer-assisted video. In these new art forms, mysticism and science come together. A good example of this kind of mythopoeic art would be the pioneering work of Walt Disney in *Fantasia,* especially in his blending of cosmogony with Stravinsky's *Rite of Spring*.

As you can see from my brief fly-over of the historical landscape of Western Civilization, the so-called opposition between art and science is spurious. Mountain and valley people may not get along, but when you look down on them with the eye of a pilot or an astronaut, you can see that they are both part of a common watershed. Lord Snow was wrong when he divided up the world of the mind into the sciences and the humanities. When I was teaching the humanities at M.I.T., I was told by the registrar that the engineers tended to take their elective courses in economics and political sciences, but that scientists tended to take their elective courses in the arts and the humanities. If there are two subcultures, they are not split between the sciences and the humanities, but between Archimedean and Pythagorean modes of imagination.

For the cultures of the West, there has always been a great gulf between the sacred and the profane, between God and matter, and this gulf has been carried on in the opposition between applied science and "pure" science. One is the realm of politics and atom bombs; the other is the empyrean of pure theory. But what electronics has done is to bring the opposites closer together by democratizing technology. Before, in the metallurgy of the artisan, the sword was only for the samurai; but now, with television, personal computers, and laser-disc *Sony Walkman's,* the technology is for Everyman. In the dislocations from "civilization" attendant upon these technologies, the old reifications of "matter" and the transcendent "God" are no longer appropriate, and it is for this reason that the epistemology of Buddhism has taken on a new meaning in the context of the groundlessness in the neurophysiology of Varela. We are witnessing not simply a sequence of "causes" in a cultural transformation, but a cybernetic system of emergence in which both recognizable patterns and non-cognizable "noise" are interacting with one another to stimulate the shift from one cultural ecology into another.

In the narratives of Western Civilization, phenomena are taken out of their total ecological context and turned into "causes." For Marx, the means of production causes a change in the superstructure of ideology; for McLuhan the alphabet causes a change in the nervous system.[9] This is too simplistic, and thanks to physics, cybernetics, and Bateson's pioneering work in *Naven,* we can now begin to think in terms of synchronous nets of causes and effects.

We live in an electronic world of planetary culture, but the fundamentalists of the American Moral Majority are still seeking to stop history and lock reality within the world view of the Protestant Reformation. But it would be a mistake to think that religion is always wrong and science and technology are always right, for the mode of our religious experience changes along with the transformation of our technologies.

In the ancient Riverine cultural-ecology, the mode of religious experience was Momentary Possession, either in shamanic trance or the *hieros gamos,* the sacred marriage of man and the Goddess, Dumuzi and

Inanna. In the imperial cultures of the Mediterranean cultural-ecology, the mode of religious experience became Surrender to Authority. And when civilization became too crystallized in the figure of the High Priest, surrender to authority was challenged by prophetic figures who celebrated pastoral pre-civilized ways of life. Moses would challenge Pharaoh, or Samuel would challenge Saul. What the prophet represents is a radical affirmation of the value of the individual. It is no longer the temple that holds value; the individual can be an epiphany of the Divine. This is a radical and revolutionary notion for a priesthood or a traditional culture, and this Old Testament tradition of prophecy and individuation is still difficult for a Japanese person to understand. But, as you can see, our traditions of individuality do not simply go back to Thomas Jefferson and the Declaration of Independence, they go back to the world of the Hebrew prophets.

With the Reformation and the expansion of Europe into the new Atlantic cultural-ecology, the mode of religious experience became Commitment to Belief. Religion was no longer simply a matter of ethnic identification, of the descent of the body, it was a matter of the mind and its forms of knowing expressed in doctrine. The structures of the modern world are based upon documents, on Luther's bible and Jefferson's constitution. They are based upon systems of belief in literate doctrines and laws in which Rights are Writs. This is the world McLuhan characterized as *The Gutenberg Galaxy*.

And now we have left that Atlantic world behind in the Pacific Shift. Now we enter a period of planetary implosion in which the individual is brought back into involvement with the ecology of the whole. Religion becomes holistic, and the mode of religious experience becomes a symbiosis of group consciousness. This is something that the Japanese can understand more readily than Westerners. In this new Pacific Shift of consciousness, the cybernetic net of synchronous events teaches us to recognize that the Truth cannot be expressed in an ideology, whether that ideology is capitalist, Marxist, or Islamic; that Truth is that which is above the conflict of opposed ideologies. If one thinks that the Truth can be expressed in an ideology, and that that ideology can become the personal possession of an ego, then that ideology gives me a license to murder. So the whole mode of religious experience in Commitment to Belief passes away in a transitional period of crystallization, rigidity, and violence. In the larger horizons of the new world view above these ancient fundamentalist hostilities opposites can coexist symbiotically, just as the organelles exist symbiotically within the cell. As we begin to realize that the Earth is a living cell, so we begin to see that the cell is a world of many different organisms, and we begin to understand through a new science of compassion to tolerate the "aliens" within us, and without us. Our medicine changes, and we no longer have John Wayne doctors trying to zap the aliens with powerful weapons. We begin to understand that our bodies are awash with thousands of interpenetrating beings, and that it is often the hysterical response of our own immunological systems that makes us sick.[10] We begin to see that from our bodies to our body politic, our systems of defense can kill us. As we grow into this new science of compassion, everything changes at once: the narratives of mathematics, of art, of medicine, of religion, and of politics. This is the world of change in which we all are living now.

As our mode of religious experience changes, so, of course, does our way of seeing Good and Evil. If for the Riverine cultural-ecology, Momentary Possession was Good, then pride and self-assertion was Evil. Dumuzi falls because of pride and self-assertion. But pride and self-assertion announce the next level of religious experience, the level at which the individual is able to challenge authority, the world in which Moses challenges Pharaoh. Moses gives us Mosaic law, and commitment to belief in the Torah makes us Good. If Commitment to Belief is Good, the ecstatic transcendence is Evil; it is an escape from the culture into dubious cults. But ecstatic transcendence means moving beyond limits and rediscovering the group consciousness. It is a noise that is a signal. In our culture now, collectivization is evil, and noise is evil. We see demonic polities in which people are brought together through terror and compression. And yet, in a strange way, these collectivizations, like rock festivals and fascist states of war, are temporary noetic polities. They are evil and signals of the emergence of the next level of historical order. What is good for Moses is evil for Pharaoh; what is good for Luther is evil for the Pope, and what is evil for us may be part of an emerging good that "civilized man" cannot begin to fathom.

Now you can begin to see why I choose to speak of cultural-ecologies instead of civilizations. I don't wish to operate within the doctrinal systems of any particular civilized ideology, for I observe as an artist and a historian that there is an isomorphic relationship between evil and pollution for any particular culture, and that this relationship is invisible to the people living within their own civilization. The shape that evil and pollution take for a culture is not simply random and accidental; rather, it is a systemic description of the culture, both in its conscious and its unconscious life. If you describe a civilization as a cultural historian, you often simply present a list of its heroes, its battles, its inventions, and its works of art. But the list is not the system. The cultural-ecologist must look under these lists to see the unconscious life of the civilization as presented in its characteristic forms of pollution and noise. For the Riverine cultural-ecology, the form of pollution is soil loss; but soil loss shows that the city cannot be defined by its walls, and that the true phenomenology is territorial. This territoriality is the sign of emergence to the next level of historical order in the shift from city-states within walls to empires bounded by geographical limits. The characteristic form of pollution for empires is deforestation, as the trees are turned into maritime vessels and conquering navies. But deforestation is not simply the movement of an object, as in soil loss; it is the alteration of the climate. This atmospheric change announces the next level of historical order in the shift from empire to world economy.[11] For our world economy, the characteristic form of pollution is atmospheric damage in such phenomena as acid rain and the Greenhouse Effect. But these forms of pollution express the shift from a world economy to a planetary culture. Now we have a global pollution that is our civilizational unconscious, and we have forms of collectivization that are beyond reason. The teenagers who go to rock concerts understand that noise is the new form of identification with the group. A recent rock concert by the group U2 was so loud that it registered as an earthquake on the seismographs of the University of Amsterdam. I have a young nephew who is a musician in a heavy metal group in Los Angeles; he is losing his hearing from playing in the group, but, as he says, "That's just the price you pay." If you are willing to lose the membrane of your biological integrity to play with a group, or join your body to the new body politic in a rock concert, then what you are demonically signaling is the emergence of the next level of historical order, the shift from literate civilizations to . . . what shall we call them? Noetic polities? Noetic plasmas?

As you look back and notice the isomorphic relationship between societal forms of pollution and cultural forms of evil, you will notice something that the mystics have often talked about, an esoteric observation that is unsettling for doctrinal moralists, namely, that evil seems to be part of the total ecology. Judas cannot betray Jesus until Jesus himself performs a shadow eucharist in which he gives Judas a sop of vinegar that enables the spirit of the devil to enter into him so that the apostle can betray him and the crucifixion can be consummated. Historically, I have described before this pattern as one in which the Roman engineers build the roads for conquest and the Christian missionaries use them for conversion. This is an ancient insight from alchemy and Taoism, the principle of reversal, the principle of *enantiodromia*. But it is not really an esoteric or occult phenomenon. When I lived in the Sangre de Cristo Mountains of southern Colorado, I would notice that in the morning when the sun came up the shadows would cover the entire San Luis Valley. Then the relationship between dawning light and extensive shadows was confusing; but as the sun came up higher, you could begin to see the true relationship between light and dark. The mountain would begin to take in its shadow until at high noon, the shadow would be entirely under it. And so it is with us an illumination: we no longer project our shadow outward on our neighbors, but we begin to draw it into ourselves. Some of the gurus of our age have cast very large shadows as they stood between their disciples and the light, but now in the period of democratization we have come to the end of the age of gurus and the light is high and available for everyone to see.

In the age of the illusions of matter, we sought to conquer and control, and we sent out missionaries and soldiers. But as Dōgen says: "To practice and confirm all things by conveying one's self to them, is illusion; for all things *(dharmas)* to advance forward and practice and confirm the self, is enlightenment."[12] What we see now happening in the world is not simply traditional, and not simply technological. Ultimately, the Pacific Shift to a new science of compassion is nothing less than this shift from illusion to enlightenment.

Biology of a Cosmological Science

Harold J. Morowitz

To set the tone for our inquiry I would like first to quote from the perceptive essay by the English biophysicist, J. D. Bernal.

> We may begin by asking the question, does biology exist? I believe there is a radical difference between biology and the so-called exact or inorganic sciences, particularly physics. In the latter, we postulate elementary particles which are necessary to the structure of the universe and the laws controlling their movements and transformations are intrinsically necessary, and in general, hold over the whole universe. Biology on the other hand deals with descriptions and ordering of very special parts of the universe, which we call life. Even more particularly in these days, terrestrial life. It is primarily a descriptive science more like geography, dealing with the structure and working of a number of peculiarly organized entities, at a particular moment in time, on a particular planet. Undoubtedly there should be a real and general biology but we can only just begin to glimpse it. A true biology in the full sense would be the study of the nature and activity of all organized objects wherever they were to be found on this planet and others in the solar system, in other galaxies and at all times future and past.[1]

This statement by Bernal, particularly the last sentence, lays down the credo of a cosmological biology: It is the study of the underlying principles behind the organization of matter, the evolution from less organized to more organized states. Stated in this way, our study takes us back to its intellectual roots in the nineteenth century. In 1862, Herbert Spencer[2] published his book *First Principles,* in which he argued that there is a fundamental law of matter which he called the law of persistence of force, from which it follows that nothing homogeneous can remain as such if it is acted on, because any external force must affect some part of the system differently from the way it affects other parts, and hence cause differences and varieties to arise. From this it follows that any force which continues to act on a homogeneous system must bring about increasing variety. Spencer believed that this law was the key to all cosmological development, as well as to all biological development. He was a universalist, who saw in the law of general evolution a transcendent principle for all philosophy. For him, evolution was an integration of matter and concomitant dissipation of motion, during which the matter passed from an indefinite incoherent homogeneity to a definite coherent homogeneity, and during which the retained motion underwent a parallel transformation. The original edition of Spencer's *First Principles* possessed a kind of buoyant optimism about the future of the universe as evolving toward better and better things. However, even as Spencer's *First Principles* were being formulated, two developments were occurring, one of which would bolster his theory and a second which would serve to drain much of the optimism from the philosopher's latter thoughts.

Charles Robert Darwin's world-view-shattering work on the origin of species was published in 1859. In retrospect, what Darwin did in a general sense was to force the intellectual community to look at man as being *in* nature, as being a part of nature. The biological uniqueness of man was obliterated, and hence his philosophical uniqueness was called into serious question. The *Origin of Species* was truly mankind's loss of innocence. From a scientific point of view, Darwin laid the empirical foundations for the theory of biological evolution, thus strengthening the arguments of general evolutionists, such as Spencer.

The second great scientific legacy of the nineteenth century was the development of the laws of thermodynamics. Their discovery was contemporaneous with the development of the evolutionary theory of biology, and they have had an equally profound effect on our world view. Thermodynamic theory had its beginnings in the industrial revolution and was therefore very closely related to the operation of the steam engine. Indeed, Professor Lawrence Henderson used to comment that the steam engine did much more for science than science ever did for the steam engine. Insofar as the second law of thermodynamics has affected our world outlook, we might likewise comment on the debt of philosophy to the steam engine.

In any case, beginning with Sadi Carnot's brilliant essay in 1824 there developed a purely physical theory which indicated that the universe as a whole is moving from orderly to more disorderly states. This theory was clearly stated in 1852 in a paper by William Thompson entitled "On the Universal Tendency in Nature to the Dissipation of Mechanical Energy." Thompson gloomily concluded that "Within a finite period of time to come, the earth must begin to be unfit for the habitation of man as at present constituted, unless operations have been or are to be performed which are impossible under the laws to which the known operations going on at present in the world are subject." This type of thermodynamic statement was completed when Rudolf Clausius introduced the concept of entropy in 1865 and enunciated the essentially cosmological view that the energy of the universe is constant and the entropy of the universe tends toward a maximum.

Entropy in this sense can roughly be equated with molecular disorder, so that in Clausius's view the universe was decaying to a maximally disordered state. Thus the biblical "end of days" eventually yielded to

> This is the way the world ends
> This is the way the world ends
> Not in a bang, but a whimper.[3]

When Herbert Spencer became aware of these developments in physics his thoughts took on a decidedly less optimistic hue. The first edition of *First Principles* read: "Evolution can only end in the establishment of the greatest perfection and most complete happiness." Alas, that cheerful sentence is completely missing from the sixth edition of his work.

We have spoken of Darwinian evolution as a loss of innocence. Indeed, it can be argued that the combined impact of evolution and the second law of thermodynamics represents the ultimate in nibbling on the forbidden apple. For not only is man himself a part of nature, a naked ape in the current idiom, but he is a naked ape in a universe that is decaying to a homogenized nothingness. Any philosophy of man or any theology which is not adjusted to this particular loss of innocence is simply ignoring the intellectual scientific milieu in which modern man must function.

It is extremely important to realize the full impact of the preceding ideas, because for Western man, at least, they represent a sharp break in the myth structure that has sustained him for many thousand years. Regardless of the mythological details, there was almost always an underlying assumption that man was something quite apart from the world in which he functioned, something special and unique from nature, and destined to rule forever. If he envisaged the end of the universe, it was in an eschatological sense which was itself centered on man and his eternal being.

These ideas of man and eternity were violently shattered by the scientific thought of the nineteenth century. We are only now beginning to realize what happened and to try to pick up the pieces that resulted from the impact of nineteenth-century biology and thermodynamics on the philosophical structure of Western thought. It is therefore extremely important to understand in a quite detailed and almost technical sense what is being said by these sciences, and what they do and do not allow us to admit with respect to a metaphysical world view. This is the philosophical thrust of C. P. Snow's message that the scientific and humanistic culture must learn in a rather detailed way to communicate with each other.[4]

One note of further interest is the claim by some environmentalists that the ecological crisis has arisen because of the failure of man to realize that he exists within nature. There is a cultural lag between the scientific realization and the social implementation.

Returning to a previous theme, we note that the two great scientific developments of the nineteenth century, one in biology and the second in physics, were apparently at odds with each other. Biologists noted an increasing development of complexity and evolution toward greater fitness. Physicists, on the other hand, spoke of energy running downhill and of cosmic processes taking place leading to universal molecular disordering. This apparent conflict between biology and physics began in the mid-1800s and still rages today among some who have failed to grasp the real nature of the problem. One of these is Julian Huxley, who as late as 1959 wrote that evolution is an antientropic process running counter to the second law of thermodynamics. This, however, just is not so. The solution to the dilemma which bothered Huxley in 1959 had in fact been glimpsed by Spencer in 1852 and was rather formally stated in 1866 when the very far-seeing Ludwig Boltzmann wrote:

> The general struggle of the living beings for existence is therefore not a struggle for materials nor for energy (that is present in every body and in large quantity as heat, unfortunately not interchangeable) but a struggle for the entropy that becomes available in the transition of the energy from the hot sun to the cold earth. To exploit this transition as much as possible the plants spread out the immeasurable areas of their leaves and force the solar energy in an as yet unexplored way to carry out chemical syntheses of which we have no idea in our laboratories.[5]

It is interesting to note that this statement by Boltzmann—which is many decades ahead of his time—contains, as we shall see, the essential solution of the apparent conflict between the second law of thermodynamics and biological evolution. An understanding of this point will allow us to project ourselves into cosmological biology.

First, we point out that the second law of thermodynamics in its simplest form states that it is impossible to construct a device which, operating in a cycle, will produce no effect other than the transfer of heat from a cooler to a hotter body. This simple notion that heat always flows from a hotter to a colder body can be generalized to predict the universal distribution of energy from its stored forms to heat, or more precisely to molecular motion. Second, we note that since its introduction over a century ago no evidence has come forth to challenge the second law of thermodynamics. There seems no reason to doubt that the universe, or at least that portion of the universe which is accessible to our observation, is running down in the sense that energy is being uniformly distributed by being drained from local sources such as the stars and gaseous nebulae and diffused into the radiation field of outer space. This view has two rather profound consequences: first, that the universe has an origin, or as some would rather term it, a creation; and second, that the known universe will retire into an equilibrium oblivion at some time in the very distant future.

Life as we know it, however, is not a property of the universe as a whole, but of planetary surfaces—in particular, the terrestrial surface. These surfaces are not at equilibrium and are not approaching equilibrium, at least not in the next few billion years, because they constantly receive radiant energy from their central star (which is the sun in our case) and re-radiate infra-red energy to outer space. A system which constantly receives radiation from a hot source such as the sun and constantly rejects energy to a cold sink such as outer space is not an isolated system, and need not be tending toward maximum disorder, that is, toward maximum entropy.

The requirement of the second law is that the entropy of the entire system is always increasing. This does not rule out the possibility of local ordering or entropy decreases which are offset by greater entropy increases elsewhere in the system. If we consider the whole system of sun, planet and outer space, the process of transfer of energy from the hot star to the cold of outer space is clearly a dissipation of cosmic energy, or an entropy increase. Therefore, there is no contradiction between local ordering on the surface or the earth (evolution) and the laws of thermodynamics.

Evolution of life cannot at the moment be predicted from the laws of thermodynamics. The physical principle merely states that the molecular organization of planetary surfaces which we know as evolution involves no violation of thermodynamics principles. That is to say, thermodynamically speaking, life can happen. Since we know that it has already happened, it is a comforting thought to realize that it is possible.

The reason that nineteenth-century physical chemists were unable to make any predictions about biological organization was because their elegant theoretical structures dealt almost entirely with equilibrium systems. In such systems, no processes are taking place, and a particular simplicity and uniformity results. These equilibrium states were used as conceptual devices to make limiting statements about what could and could not happen.

A few remarks on the structure of science might be helpful at this point. Scientific thought narrows down the whole universe of questions which can be asked and concentrates on the particular subset of those which are, in principle, amenable to answer. In picking that subset of questions in thermodynamics. Nineteenth-century physicists and physical chemists moved toward the abstractions and conceptualizations of equilibrium. An equilibrium state occurs in a system which has been in isolation and has aged for a very, very long time. This construct was a brilliant conceptual device which enabled the formulators to make all sorts of useful statements about what could and could not happen in particular systems. The approach is, however, very limited. It is confining because in day-to-day life we almost never encounter equilibrium systems. To be precise, we *never* encounter equilibrium systems. Everything is in a dynamic state in which energy is being moved from its sources to its sinks; there are great flows of energy, and the processes that we see around us, preeminent among them biology, geology and meteorology, are characterized by this nonequilibrium character.

It must be realized at this point that physics and physical chemistry have only made the first stumbling steps towards a nonequilibrium theory of thermodynamics. This is a discipline that is in its formative years. Lars Onsager's original papers on the subject were published in 1931. These papers are an introduction, and although there is an increasing effort in this area, there are still more questions than answers. At the moment, we lack either a theoretical or an experimental basis to talk very much about nonequilibrium processes in physics. It has not been a popular subject; actually one has the feeling that it has been pursued in recent years mainly in those countries that did not invest enormous resources in their own nuclear accelerators. Much of the work has come out of Belgium and the Netherlands. I am making these points about the sociology of modern physical sciences to stress the vast lacunae which exist in those areas of physics and physical chemistry which would be the most important for our understanding of biology, and our subsequent ability to use biology in a more general cultural sense. There is, however, an implied criticism of the extent to which physicists have pursued the popular and the faddish while ignoring some of the most important underlying areas of natural philosophy. I write this to alert physicists or physical chemists of the enormous potential of this area of inquiry.

Living organisms are preeminent examples of the kind of nonequilibrium system we have been discussing: indeed they are not only nonequilibrium systems but they are very far from equilibrium systems. A great part of the problem of general biology is that we do not know in detail how to deal with such systems. Some results which we have available to us today make it clear that both molecular and macroscopic organization inevitably occurs in nonequilibrium systems. That is, the molecular disordering which is characteristic of the second law of thermodynamics is reversed in nonequilibrium situations where there are local tendencies toward molecular ordering. There is a spatial ordering of components and selected tendencies towards certain chemical compositions.

A series of nonequilibrium experiments motivated by an interest in the origin of life has been carried out during the last twenty years. These studies began with the Urey-Miller syntheses in the early 1950s. In these first experiments, a gaseous mixture of methane, ammonia, and water was subjected to the continuous flow of energy from an electric spark, and the products of the reaction were trapped in liquid phase water. These reaction products were then chemically analyzed. The exciting result was the production of a wide variety of molecules which everyone had previously believed to be exclusively characteristic of biochemistry. This type of experiment has now been repeated many times, using different starting materials and different energy forms, such as heat, ultraviolet light, and ionizing radiation. These experiments have consistently produced chemical species which are characteristic of living systems. Thus this class of nonequilibrium experiments demonstrates a tendency toward that type of molecular order which we see in biology.

From the theoretical side, it has been possible to develop an interesting proof showing that cycles of matter must inevitably occur in a nonequilibrium system such as the one we have been discussing on the earth's surface.[6] Thus the major ecological cycles—such as the carbon or nitrogen cycles—are not biologically unique, are not something apart, but represent a general property of a certain class of nonequilibrium systems. A planet like the earth will therefore have something resembling ecological cycles whether or not it has a biology, in a conventional sense. Cycles of photosynthetic fixation followed by subsequent oxidation or reduction are not unique to biology, but may be theoretically predicted for a wide class of chemical situations. This means that planetary surfaces in general must be organized in virtue of being an intermediate in the flow of energy from the sun to outer space. As a consequence, whenever we get to examine the surface of another planet we should expect to find some kind of molecular organization on the surface. This is not to assert that the conditions will be right for the conventional forms of terrestrial biology, but that we should certainly expect to find some kinds of photosynthetically mediated molecular ordering. This should be true of any place in the universe, any portion of the system which represents an intermediate between the flow of energy from the stars to the almost absolute zero cold of outer space.

However, from our limited terrestrial scope this appears to be rather a bloodless description of life. It seems a long way from the molecular ordering of pre-biological chemistry to the exquisite set of ordered objects that we know as *Homo sapiens*. This brings us directly to the next question: Given the fact that ecological energies and molecular ordering in general follow from physical principles, what is the range of systems that will display the exquisitely high degree of atomic arrangement and broad developmental potential that we find in terrestrial living systems? At this stage, the essentially thermodynamic reasoning that we have been using appears to be too crude, and alternative approaches must be tried. How can we then explain the origin of self-replicating systems? How can we probe the philosophically most exciting questions that science has to offer? How can we ultimately know about the generality of biological process?

There are three rather divergent approaches that have been offered to this line of questioning. First, there has been a current restatement of the theological principle by Pierre Teilhard de Chardin, who has elevated the theory of evolution to a theo-cosmological status and endowed the whole universe with a spiritually driven evolutionary direction which surpasses in intensity even the evolutionary thrust of Herbert Spencer.[7] Second, there has been a point of view identified with Walter Elassaer, who maintains that the epistemological foundations of quantum mechanics are insufficient to deal with systems of biological complexity.[8] Hence physics, as we now know it, will always lack completeness in describing biology. Although no contradictions exist between biology and physics, physics is just insufficient to the task. Third, there is the point of view that there are principles of physics which guide the molecular organization of nonequilibrium systems.[9] For proponents of this point of view, the greatest challenge for modern students of biophysics is to develop an understanding of those principles.

If we are able to obtain this kind of theory of self-ordering, it should challenge us to apply the most profound insights we can muster to link biology to nonequilibrium physical chemistry. The job seems very formidable, indeed, but the rewards could be very great—the ability to seek our origins in terms of the laws of atomic interaction. This is truly a new frontier, and one that challenges the maximum intellectual effort of which we are capable.

The energy flow point of view of biology which we have just been discussing has some interesting philosophical spin-off which merits examination. Prior to the theory of evolution, Western biology was almost totally organism-centered, with an object-oriented view of reality. Linnaeus, the founder of modern taxonomy held a rather Platonic view of species and his taxonomy consisted of finding organisms and placing them in Platonic categories. Museums, zoos and herbariums housed individuals which constituted Platonic types in the Linnaen view. Given the theological presupposition that types were immutable products of divine creation, this approach fitted into the pre-Darwinian world view.

With the advent of Darwinian evolution and the subsequent development of genetics, the species itself became a diverse collection of variants.

Indeed the capacity for variation or mutation was a necessary part of the description of all species. The species in the new biology has properties that go beyond that of the individual. The gene pool, or the collection of genes, was the prime factor in the biological description of the species. The type and distribution of allelic genes within the genome is, however, a property of a group of organisms and can in no way be deduced from the study of a single individual or small collection of individuals. The important unit in biology shifted from the individual organism to the more distributed and abstract notion of the species.

The study of ecology goes even further, and indicates to us that the species itself exists only in relation to an ecological niche within a biome, which includes other living organisms as well as geological factors. The description of the species now includes a much broader phenomenological range. The energy-flow point of view of ecology expands this viewpoint because the biological description now begins with the sun's energy (photons of the solar spectrum), works its way through food webs, material cycles (such as the carbon, nitrogen, and sulphur cycles) and involves the global biosphere in a way that relates all life on the planet. Biology in the last century has thus moved from an object-centered view toward a continuum view of life.

In *The Meeting of East and West,*[10] F. S. C. Northrop has pointed out that Eastern thought is much more devoted to a directly given continuum view of reality, while Western thought is much more centered on theoretic constructs, such as objects. Western biology began with *Historia Animalium* and, in referring to this work of Aristotle, Northrop notes, "It led him to the thesis that it is the concrete individual embodying in itself both the prime matter and the abstract logical universal which is the real thing." Biology has developed within the Western object-centered atomistic view of reality which has come to fruition in modern molecular biology. More recently, much of biological thought has been moving from the Western orientation to a differentiated continuum view which is much closer to Eastern philosophy. The shift has not been easy to discern because the language of biology and its cultural setting identify the discipline with Western modes of thought.

Emphasis may, however, be shifting somewhat from objects such as atoms, molecules, and cells as the final explanation in biology toward viewing the entire planet as the focus of aliveness. Life in this emerging point of view is not so much a property of the individual as it is a property of the entire planetary surface. Individuals per se cannot exist, that is, an individual of one species can only *be* in so far as he is part of the food chain. Plants themselves cannot exist except by the process whereby they are eaten by animals, returning carbon dioxide to the small molecule reservoir in the atmosphere. Animals cannot exist apart from the food chain. The nitrogen supply that we use comes to us by courtesy of hundreds of other organisms which are chemically processing nitrogen in a wide variety of ways. This notion of life, which began in the purely object-centered view of Western culture, has been moving very steadily toward a continuum view. This represents what is perhaps one of the potentially most profound intellectual mergings of East and West, in the Northrop sense. It is therefore worthwhile to examine the presently emerging biology from this perspective.

Two paradoxical trends exist in contemporary life sciences. One which we have already mentioned is a tendency toward a global continuum view; the second, which emerges from genetics, stresses a kind of radical individuality. Each human is characterized by about one million genes, each of which can exist in any one of several forms called alleles. The number of possible genomes (individual genetic specifications) is a quantity given by one followed by a million zeros. It is one of those enormous numbers that we find difficult to state in a meaningful way. What is clear is that no two humans (with the possible exception of identical twins) have the tiniest probability of being genetically the same. Thus, at the genetic level there is a clear-cut distinction between all individuals. This kind of radical individuality is imposed on a continuum point of view which stresses that no individual human exists in any kind of biological isolation; every individual is really very much a part of the global system and his existence itself is related to the existence and the properties of the continuum.

Individuality entered the world, from a scientific point of view, somewhere along the path of pre-biological evolution. It is interesting to think back for a moment to the time when the earth was a kind of bubbling ocean of chemical reactions, and one of the groups of these reactions led to a class of oily types of molecules which formed a membrane or a surface. This membrane folded and sealed off a certain portion of the continuum from the rest of the continuum. This is the beginning of biological individuality in an atomic sense. This development of individuality is somehow at odds with the continuum point of view.

The philosophical distinction between continuum and individuality may relate to the problem we have previously mentioned, how order arises in homogeneous systems. As a prerequisite for the existence of individuality, the ordered continuum must be organized into identifiable entities. When we understand that ordering, we shall be better able to tackle the problem of individuality. It should be pointed out that individuality is not a necessary principle of physical theory. For example, in quantum mechanics electrons do not have individuality, and this profoundly affects the way in which particles can interact.

To further relate the Eastern and Western points of view, we want to state clearly the energy-flow concept of biology. Life exists because energy flows to the earth in the form of solar photons. These photons are incorporated into life processes by means of photosynthesis, and all subsequent life involves the dissipation of that original solar energy. Biological ordering is bought at the price of dissipating solar energy, which is then re-radiated as heat which flows to the limits of outer space. Curiously enough, when so stated, the scientific principle reflects a kind of view that has existed for a long time in Oriental thought. It did not exist as a precise scientific statement, but the general ideas can be clearly found in certain aspects of Buddhist thought.

In a book entitled *Science and Buddhism,*[11] P. Dahlke has elaborated the thesis that in theology everything stands, in science everything falls, and in Buddhism everything burns. The notion of burning is a metaphysical expression of transience and impermanence. As transmitted in the tradition, there is an accompanying mythology that we need not consider here. However, the metaphysics, in its purest form, is a very early statement of the energy flow point of view. Although the Buddhist syntax is entirely different from that of modern science, a notion is clearly present that everything is process — a process which only persists by virtue of some universal kind of energy flowing through the world. From this point of view, the reality of individuals is problematic because they do not exist per se but only as local perturbations in this universal energy flow. As originally presented, this must have been a very mystical idea, but a similar kind of idea seems to emerge from modern science. Everything we know of is indeed process, which is mediated on the surface of our planet by the flow of solar energy through all organized structures.

To make this concept more definite, let us try conceptually to shrink ourselves down to atomic dimensions and get a look at the world from the molecular point of view. At this level everything is in an incredible state of random thermal motion. There is just a violent whirling, swirling, and moving around in what looks like enormous atomic disorder. This atomic motion is in fact always breaking down existing molecular structures. Indeed, if we take a molecular approach to the second law of thermodynamics, we note that there is an inherent molecular tendency toward decay that is a part of all structures. This is not just a metaphor; for example, in every one of us about 7% of the protein molecules in our bodies breaks down every day and has to be rebuilt by processes within our systems. That stands as a quantitative statement of the Buddhist transience when applied to human beings: 7% per day is a numerical measure of our impermanence. There is a constant breakdown of molecular structures, and accompanying this breakdown there is a build-up that utilizes the solar energy entering the system through photosynthesis. Life is always a precarious balance between the organized build-up of atomic order and the decay brought about by random thermal motion at the atomic level. Classical physiology recognized this fact in its concepts of anabolism and catabolism, which together constitute the overall metabolic behavior of the organism.

Viewed from the point of view of modern thermodynamics, each living thing, including man, is a dissipative structure, that is, it does not endure in and of itself but only as a result of the continual flow of energy in the system. An example might be instructive. Consider a vortex in a stream of flowing water. The vortex is a structure made of an ever-changing group of water molecules. It does not exist as an entity in the classical Western sense, it exists only because of the flow of water through the stream. If the flow ceases, the vortex disappears. In the same sense, the structures out of which biological entities are made are transient, unstable entities with constantly changing molecules, dependent on a constant flow of energy from food in order to maintain form and structure. This description stands as a scientific statement of the Buddhist notion of the unreality of the individual. Among Western thinkers, one might identify this kind of description with Heraclitus.

This viewpoint gives us a "flow" or process conception of ourselves: rather than seeing ourselves as discrete individual entities, we become centers or foci for a build-up of order. The build-up and breakdown of molecular order are linked to the environment around us: the inflows of energy must come from outside ourselves, as we in turn must radiate energy to our surroundings. Unless there is balance in the surrounding world, the individual processes we have been describing cannot take place. This is a biological, thermodynamic statement of the real necessity for environmental balance. Environmental balance is not something which one must achieve for aesthetic reasons; it is the very key to transient existence in a flow-dominated nature. If we misdirect the flows to re-alter the system, the environment may undergo radical changes, and it may no longer be possible to maintain the kind of stability which we require.

We emerge from the foregoing considerations with some ideas that seem to be important ingredients of the viewpoint we want to take toward man and his relation to the world today.

It is clear that man is a part of nature. This is the underlying fact with which we must constantly confront ourselves. If we really took this notion seriously, we would not have ecological crises. The idea that man is part of nature is the ultimate Darwinian statement. The thermodynamic statement is that man is limited. Our surroundings are finite, and we are part of cosmological processes. In this sense, I think that we have not understood ourselves and our destiny; the challenge of the understanding still lies before us. The missing principles between physics and biology may be part of that challenge.

We do not yet understand ourselves or the world in which we live. Yet the development of biology, some clues to the universe from physics, and a few hints from the wisdom of the East suggest that the task of understanding may not be hopeless. With just a micromeasure of hope, the task of attempting understanding becomes a joyous endeavor. Cosmological biology tells us that there is more to the universe than we have yet dreamed of.

The Metaphysical Implications of Ecology

J. Baird Callicott

I

From an orthodox philosophical point of view, not only is value segregated from fact, but philosophy is substantively informed only by the universal and foundational sciences.[1] The idea, therefore, that ecology—a scientific newcomer and a science remote from the more fundamental natural sciences—might have *metaphysical implications* may appear, on the face of it, ridiculous. So, here at the beginning, let me enter a couple of apologetic caveats.

Although it is not a foundational science like physics or a universal science like astronomy, ecology has profoundly altered our understanding of the proximate terrestrial environment in which we live, move, and have our being. And by "implications" I do not mean to suggest that there exist logical relationships between ecological premises and metaphysical conclusions such that if the former are true and the latter must also be true. "Imply," "implicate," and "implication" have a wider meaning evolved from the Latin root *implicare*—to infold, involve, or engage—which I wish to evoke. Ecology has made plain to us the fact that we are enfolded, involved, and engaged within the living, terrestrial, environment—i.e., implicated in and implied by it. (This proposition is itself among the metaphysical implications of ecology.) Therefore, ecology also necessarily profoundly alters our understanding of ourselves, severally, and human nature, collectively. From this altered representation of environment, people (personally and collectively), and the relationships in it and between it and ourselves, we may *abstract* certain general conceptual notions. These abstractive distillates are the metaphysical implications of ecology to which I draw attention in this discussion.

Ecology and contemporary physics, interestingly, complement one another conceptually and converge toward the same metaphysical notions. Hence, the sciences at the apex of the hierarchy of the natural sciences and those at the base, the "New Ecology" and the "New Physics," respectively, draw mutually consistent and mutually supporting abstract pictures of nature in its most elementary and universal and in its most complex and local manifestations.[2] A consolidated metaphysical consensus thus appears to be presently emerging from twentieth-century science which may at last supplant the metaphysical consensus distilled from the scientific paradigm of the seventeenth century.

II

To bring dramatically to light the metaphysical implications of ecology, let me begin with a foil: the metaphysical ideas, just mentioned, implicated in modern classical science, including pre-ecological natural history. Modern classical science adopted and adapted an ontology first set out in Western thought by Leucippus and Democritus in the fifth century B.C. — atomic materialism.[3]

The classical atom is essentially a mathematical entity and its so-called primary qualities may be precisely and quantitatively expressed as aspects or "modes" of geometrical space. An atom's solid mass was thus understood, mathematically, as a positive or "full" portion of negative or "empty" Euclidean space, shape as its plane limits in a three-dimensional continuum, size as its cubic volume, and motion as its linear translation from one location (point) to another.[4]

The void and the simple bodies (or atoms) it contains were conceived by Democritus to be uncreated and indestructible. The theistic moderns, however, conceived space, time, and the atoms to have been uniquely created by God as the permanent theater and immutable constituents of the universe.[5]

Composite bodies, the macroscopic things composed of atoms, however, routinely come and go. The "generation" and "corruption" (or "coming into being" and "passing away") of composite bodies was understood as the temporary association and dissociation of the atoms in the course of their ceaseless jostling and shuffling.[6]

Thus, atomism is reductive. A composite body is ontologically reducible to its simple constituents. And the career of a composite body — its generation, growth, corruption, and disintegration — is reducible to the local motion of its constituents.

And atomism, thus, is mechanical. All causal relations are reducible to the motion or translation from point to point of simple bodies or the composite bodies made up of them. The mysterious causal efficacy of fire, disease, light, or anything else is explicable, in the last analysis, as the motion, bump, and grind of the implacable particles. Putative causal relations which could not be so conceived—those postulated in astrology, magic, witchcraft, priestcraft, Newton's gravitational theory, the Faraday-Maxwell representation of magnetism, etc.—were either dismissed as superstitions and their existence denied or regarded as physical problems awaiting a mechanical solution.[7] Only a mechanical solution could be satisfactory, since only a mechanical solution implicated exclusively the fundamental ontology of atomic materialism.[8]

This material, reductive, particulate, aggregative, mechanical, geometric, and quantitative paradigm in physics governed thought in other areas of interest, for example, in moral psychology and biology.

Although Democritus, Lucretius, and Hobbes, were thoroughgoing materialists and attempted to treat mind in exactly the same mechanical terms as, say, fire, light, and heat, dualism as espoused by Pythagoras, Plato, and Descartes became more characteristic of the dominant psychology of modern classical science.[9]

Mind, nevertheless, was derivatively and analogously conceived by the dualists in atomistic terms—as a psychic monad. Each mind, in other words, was a discrete psychic substance insulated within an alien (to its own nature) material cladding.[10] The mind was passively bedazzled and deluded by the bodily senses which were mechanically excited by the local "external" world. But minds were not otherwise informed by interaction with matter. That is, the rational structure of the human mind together with its passions and volitions was regarded as an independent given. By carefully sifting and sorting the raw, confused data afforded by sensation, disciplined rational minds could figure out the mechanical laws of the foreign material world and apply that knowledge to practical problem solving.

Given a monadic moral psychology, there are two fundamental options for ethics. As represented most clearly by Hobbes, ethics might consist in finding the most felicitous rules to harmonize the inertia-like appetites of individual egos (or social atoms).[11] Or, a conceptual talisman to overcome the appetitive egoism of the discrete psychic monads might be posited. The concept of Reason functions as such a transcendental principle in Kant's ethic.[12]

In biology, an even more subtle "conceptual atomism" prevailed. To explain the existence of natural kinds or species had been a major burden of Plato's theory of forms.[13] For each species or natural kind there was a corresponding eternal form or idea. Individuals acquired their "essences," their specific, discrete natures, by "participation" in the forms. Thus, lions were lions and differed from panthers because lions participated in the form Lion, and panthers in the form Panther. And so for horses, cows, and all other living specimens, each acquired the specific characteristics that it possessed to one degree or another through its association as token to type with a specific form.

Aristotle (whose relationship to subsequent Western biology is comparable to Pythagoras's relationship to subsequent Western mathematics), of course, rejected Plato's theory of independently existing forms. But he retained the more insidious Platonic doctrine of essences. According to Aristotle, a thing's essence was its definition, given in terms of a classificatory hierarchy.[14] The universals of this hierarchy (later modified and refined by Carl Linnaeus)—species, genus, family, order, class, phylum, and kingdom—were not real or actual; only individual organisms fully existed. Nevertheless, for Aristotle, a species acquires its peculiar characteristics not through interaction with other species but through the place it occupies in a logically determined classificatory schematism.

Aristotle's teleological conception of nature introduced into biology a hierarchy of another sort. Some species were "lower," others "higher" on the scale of ends. Lower organisms existed for the sake of higher ones.[15] This habit of identifying evolutionarily more venerable beings as "lower organisms" persists today as an Aristotelian residue in modern biology, much as the habit of referring to certain numbers as "square" or "cubic" persists as a Pythagorean residue in modern mathematics. The former, however, seems somehow more than a quaint and harmless terminological legacy of classical antiquity; it seems to impute a distinct peck-order to nature.

In sum, then, the endemic Western picture of living nature prior to its transformation by ecology might be characterized (or caricatured) somewhat as follows. The terrestrial natural environment consists of a collection of bodies composed of molecular aggregates of atoms. A living natural body is in principle a very elaborate machine. That is, its generation, gestation, development, decay, and death could be exhaustively explained reductively and mechanically. Some of these natural machines are mysteriously inhabited by a conscious monad, a "ghost-in-the-machine." Living natural bodies come in a wide variety of types or species, which are determined by a logico-conceptual order, and have, otherwise, no essential connection to one another. They are, as it were, loosed upon the landscape, each outfitted with its (literally God-given) Platonic-Aristotelian essence, to interact catch-as-catch-can.

Anthony Quinton has recently characterized (or caricatured) the modern classical world view similarly, but even more graphically.

> In that conception (the Newtonian) the world consists of an array of precisely demarcated individual things or substances, which preserve their identity through time, occupy definite positions in space, have their own essential natures independently of their relations to anything else, and fall

into clearly distinct natural kinds. Such a world resembles a warehouse of automobile parts. Each item is standard in character, independent of all other items, in its own place, and ordinarily unchanging in its intrinsic nature.[16]

III

Ecology was given its name in 1866 by Ernst Haeckel, but the concept of an "economy of nature" had been current in natural history since Linnaeus had devoted a treatise to it a century earlier.[17] Although the idea of an orderly economy of nature was an improvement over the Hobbesean picture of nature as a chaotic free-for-all, Linnaeus and his exponents explicitly represented it in mechanical terms. Living nature is, as it were, a mechanical Leviathan, a vast machine which is itself composed of machines. "Like a planet in its orbit or a gear in its box, each species exists to perform some function in the grand apparatus."[18] The grand apparatus and its functions, to which each species is fitted, were, like the component species, believed to be designed by God. So, all natural relations and interactions remain external, albeit orderly.

The subsequent Arcadian and Romantic intellectual countercurrents to eighteenth-century Rationalism and mechanism, however, gave the proto-ecological notion of a natural economy a more integrative and holistic cast. Ecology as it eventually emerged as a distinct subdiscipline of natural history was shaped by a complex of governing metaphors derived from these minority traditions. Natural relations among species were portrayed, for example, by Gilbert White in the late eighteenth century, as a "harmony" and as in a felicitous "balance"—balance both in the physical sense of a dynamic equilibrium and in the distinctly aesthetic sense of a tension and resolution of opposites, as in beautiful painting, poetry, and music.[19]

In contrast to the Linnaean designed and reductive mechanical Leviathan, in the late nineteenth century John Burroughs posited an evolving and animated organic Leviathan, an idea later given theoretical definition and articulation by the dean of early twentieth-century ecology, Frederick Clements.[20] Clements was a self-conscious philosophical holist with intellectual roots going back to Spencer, Goethe, Hegel, and Kant. He explicitly suggested that ecology was the study of the physiology of superorganisms.[21] From the point of view of the Clementsean ecological organicism at the turn of the century, the whole Earth's living mantle might similarly be represented as a vast "comprehensive" organic being. Furthermore, each higher level of organization—from single cell to multicelled organism, from organism to local superorganism (or "ecosystem," in a terminology not yet invented in Clements's day), from ecosystem to biome and biome to biosphere—is "emergent"; thus the whole cannot be reduced to the sum of the parts.

The original Linnaean notion of an economy of nature was itself a metaphor which Charles Elton in the 1920s and 1930s began to unpack in order to construct what probably has been ecology's most important theoretical model. Plant and animal associations might be studied as "biotic communities." Each species occupies a "trophic *niche*" in the biotic community which is, as it were, a "profession" in the economy of nature.[22] There are three great guilds—producers (the green plants), consumers, both first and second order (herbivorous and carnivorous animals, respectively), and decomposers (fungi and bacteria). In biotic communities the myriad specialists in each great group are linked in "food chains" which when considered together constitute tangled "food webs." Certain common structures characterized all biotic communities, however different their component species and peculiar professions. For example, the producers must be many times more numerous than the consumers, and the prey many times more numerous than the predators; and no two species could share precisely the same ecological niche.

The Oxford University ecologist Arthur Tansley coined the term "ecosystem" in 1935, deliberately to supplant the more metaphorical characterizations of biocenoses as "communities" of plants and animals or as "super-organismic" entities.[23] Tansley's ecosystem model of biotic processes was intended to bring ecology as a science out of a qualitative, descriptive stage, with anthropomorphic and mystic overtones, and transform it into a value-free, exact quantitative science. Hence, Tansley suggested that measurable "energy" contained in food coursed through the ecosystem and was at the foundation of its structure.

The scientific exemplar to which Tansley looked was physics. Of the so-called New Ecology, for which Tansley's ecosystem model was the critical ingredient, Donald Worster writes that

> it owed nothing to any of its forebears in the history of science. . . . It was born of entirely different parentage: that is modern, thermodynamic physics, not biology.[24]

Hence, it is no wonder that the New Physics and the New Ecology should be conceptually complementary and convergent. Tansley's exemplar for a new paradigm in ecology was, it turns out, the new paradigm emerging in physics. The ecosystem model was expressly designed to be the "field theory" of modern biology.

However, as Worster emphatically points out, the quantitative, thermodynamic, biophysical model of nature which is the hallmark of the New Ecology was immediately turned to economic advantage as a powerful new weapon in mankind's age-old campaign to conquer nature. With the quantitative precision of which Tansley's energy circuit model was capable, ecosystems could be made more "productive" and "efficient" so as to "yield" a higher caloric "crop." But just as the philosophical interpretation of the New Physics, the Copenhagen Interpretation and its variations and alternatives, is quite another thing from its economic and military applications—from T.V. to laser weaponry—so the philosophical interpretation of the new ecology is quite another thing from its agronomic and managerial applications—from Ducks Unlimited to the green revolution. As Worster prophetically remarks, "organicism has a way of gaining a foothold on even the most unpromising surface."[25]

IV

At mid-century, the ecologist and conservationist Aldo Leopold strove to erect a secular environmental ethic on evolutionary and ecological foundations.[26] In his land ethic one finds traces of Clements's organic image of nature, although Leopold himself earlier articulated the idea in terms borrowed from the Russian philosopher P. D. Ouspensky.[27] And certainly crucial to the conceptual foundations of the land ethic is Elton's community concept. However, when Leopold, in *A Sand County Almanac,* turns more deliberately to the construction of a "mental image" of the natural environment in relation to which he urged new ethical sensibilities, he sketches, in poetic terms, the physics-born ecosystem model. According to Leopold, "land," his shorthand term for the natural environment,

> is a fountain of energy flowing through a circuit of soils, plants, and animals. Food chains are the living channels conducting energy upward [sc., to the apex of the trophic pyramid]. . . . The velocity and character of the upward flow of energy depend on the complex structure of the plant and animal community. . . . Without this complexity normal circulation would presumably not occur.[28]

The ecologist Paul Shepard, a decade or so later, developed more consciously the metaphysical overtones of this field theory of living nature adumbrated by Leopold. According to Shepard, from the modern classical perspective, nature is epitomized by living objects rather than the complex flow patterns of which objects are temporary formations. . . . [T]he landscape [from the classical point of view] is a room-like collection of animated furniture. . . . [B]ut it should be noted that it is best describable in terms of events which constitute a field pattern.[29]

Thus, Shepard, more abstractively than Leopold, suggested that an object-ontology is inappropriate to an ecological description of the natural environment. Living natural objects should be regarded as ontologically subordinate to "events" and/or "flow patterns" and/or "field patterns." As reflectively represented at mid-century, from the point of view of a mature ecological science, the biological reality seems to be, at the very least, more fluid and integrally patterned and less substantive and discrete than it had been previously represented.

In the early 1970s, the Yale University biophysicist Harold Morowitz still more deliberately and emphatically set out the field-ontology suggested by Leopold and Shepard as a more ecologically informed portrayal of the natural environment.

Viewed from the point of view of modern [ecology], each living thing is a dissipative structure, that is, it does not endure in and of itself but only as a result of the continual flow of energy in the system. . . . From this point of view, the reality of individuals is problematic because they do not exist per se but only as local perturbations in this universal energy flow. . . . An example might be instructive. Consider a vortex in a stream of flowing water. The vortex is a structure made of an ever-changing group of water molecules. It does not exist as an entity in the classical Western sense; it exists only because of the flow of water through the stream. If the flow ceases the vortex disappears. In the same sense the structures out of which the biological entities are made are transient, unstable entities with constantly changing molecules dependent on a constant flow of energy to maintain form and structure.[30]

Later in the same decade, Norwegian philosopher Arne Naess attempted to persuade the community of academic philosophers that ecology might have important and sweeping metaphysical implications. Naess entered a caveat similar to the one registered at the outset of this discussion, namely, that metaphysical conclusions "are not derived from ecology by logic or induction."[31] Rather, according to Naess, ecology "suggests" or "inspires" a "relational total field image [in which] organisms [are] knots in the biospherical net of intrinsic relations."[32] Naess called this metaphysical dimension of ecology "deep ecology," and the nebula of normative and public policy tendencies associated with it, "the deep ecology movement."

Let me sum up and attempt to express more precisely the abstractive general concept of nature distilled from the New Ecology in the tradition of Leopold, Shepard, Morowitz, and Naess.

First, in the "organic" concept of nature implied by the New Ecology, as in that implied by the New Physics, energy seems to be a more fundamental and primitive reality than material objects or discrete entities—elementary particles and organisms, respectively.[33] An individual organism, like an elementary particle is, as it were, a momentary configuration, a local perturbation, in an energy flux or "field."

The metaphysical ecologists here quoted, however, if pressed, would seem hardly prepared to deny outright a primary reality to atomic and molecular matter per se in addition to energy and its "flow." Organisms, though conduits of and configured by energy, remain *composed* of molecules—solid material substances. Rather, ecological interactions, primarily and especially trophic relationships, constitute a macrocosmic network or pattern through which solar energy, fixed by photosynthesis, is transferred from organism to organism until it is dissipated. Organisms are moments in this network, knots in this web of life.

However, if we combine quantum theory with ecology, as well as compare them, and resolve the erstwhile solid and immutable atoms of matter which compose the molecules, which in turn compose the cells, of organic bodies into the ephemeral, energetic quanta, then we may say quite literally and unambiguously that organisms are, in their entire structure—from subatomic microcosm to ecosystemic macrocosm—patterns, perturbations, or configurations of energy.

The deep ecology poet and philosopher Gary Snyder captured this vertical integration of metaphysical ideas in a poem: "Eating the living germs of grasses / Eating the ova of large birds . . . / Drawing on life of living / clustered points of light spun / out of space / hidden in the grape."[34] In these lines, the "clustered points of light, spun out of space" apparently allude to the dynamic configurations of the microcosm, the patterns of energy in the subatomic world; and, obviously, eating grains, eggs, and fruit, unambiguously calls attention—especially by the persistent use of the progressive verb forms, "eating," "drawing")—to the dynamic, patterned energy flux at the core of ecological relationships as conceived on the ecosystem model.

Second, the concept of nature emergent from the New Ecology, as that emergent from the New Physics, is holistic. It is impossible to conceive of organisms—if they are, as it were, knots in the web of life, or temporary formations or perturbations in complex flow patterns—apart from the field, the matrix of which they are modes. Contrary to the object-ontology of classical physics and biology in which it was possible to conceive of an entity in isolation from its milieu—hanging alone in the void or catalogued in a specimen museum—the conception of one thing in the New Physics and New Ecology necessarily involves the conception of others and so on, until the entire system is, in principle, implicated.

Naess points out another sense in which ecology implies a holistic conception of the organic world, the import of which only an academic philosopher would be likely to notice. He claims, in effect, that ecology revives the metaphysical doctrine of internal relations.[35] This suggestion, remarkably, had been advanced even earlier by the comparative philosopher Eliot Deutsch, who also connected it with the Vedantic concept of *karma*.[36]

The doctrine of internal relations is, of course, associated with nineteenth- and early twentieth-century German and English Idealism—with the philosophies of Hegel, Fichte, Bradley, Royce, and Bosanquet. The basic idea is that a thing's essence is exhaustively determined by its relationships, that it cannot be conceived apart from its relationships with other things. Whatever the motives of the Idealists (coherency theories of truth, the omniscience and omnipresence of spirit, or whatever), and notwithstanding the inevitable entanglement of the doctrine of internal relations with other concurrently fashionable topics by mid-century neo-scholastic, academic philosophers (with "bare particulars," nominalism, the analytic-synthetic distinction, and so on), internal relations are straightforwardly implicated in ecology.

From the perspective of modern biology, species adapt to a *niche* in an ecosystem. Their actual relationships to other organisms (to predators, to prey, to parasites and disease organisms, etc.) and to physical and chemical conditions (to temperature, radiation, salinity, wind, soil and water PH, and so on) literally sculpt their outward forms, their metabolic, physiological, and reproductive processes, and even their psychological and mental capacities. A specimen is, in effect, a summation of its species' historical, adaptive relationship to the environment. This observation led Shepard to claim that "relationships of things are as real as the things."[37] Indeed, I would be inclined to go even further. To convey an anti-Aristotelian thought in an Aristotelian manner of speech, one might say that from an ecological perspective, relations are "prior" to the things related, and the systemic wholes woven from these relations are "prior" to their component parts. Ecosystemic wholes are "logically prior" to their component species because the nature of the part is determined by its relationship to the whole. That is, more simply and concretely expressed, a species has the particular characteristics that it has because those characteristics result from its adaptation to a *niche* in an eco*system*.

It is necessary to add immediately, however, that the holistic concept of nature implied, analogously, by the New Ecology and the New Physics at the macro and micro levels of organization is a holism of a different stripe from that associated with classical Hindu metaphysics. Eliot Deutsch and Fritjof Capra both have drawn this perhaps natural but unfortunate comparison in either domain. According to Capra, in the "Eastern world view" (which he seems to regard as a monolithic body of wisdom encompassing the independent indigenous traditions of thought from the Indian subcontinent to Japan) and in "modern [quantum] physics, all things are seen as interdependent and inseparable parts of this cosmic whole; as different manifestations of the same ultimate reality. The Eastern traditions constantly refer to this ultimate, indivisible reality which manifests itself in things. . . . It is called *Brahman* in Hinduism. . . ."[38] And according to Deutsch, "What does it mean to affirm continuity between man and the rest of life [as in ecology]? Vedanta would maintain that this means the recognition that fundamentally all life is one, that in essence everything is reality; . . . that *Brahman,* the oneness of reality, is the most fundamental ground of all existence."[39]

There is a crucial conceptual distinction, however, in the very different ways in which things are thought to be one in classical Indian thought, on the one hand, and in contemporary ecology and quantum theory, on the other. In classical Indian thought, all things are one because all things are phenomenal and ultimately illusory manifestations or expressions of *Brahman*. The unity of things is, thus, substantive and essential, and the experience of it is homogeneous and oceanic. In both contemporary ecology and quantum theory at their respective levels of phenomena, the oneness of nature is systemic and (internally) relational. No undifferentiated Being mysteriously "manifests" itself. Rather, nature is a *structured, differentiated* whole. The multiplicity of particles and living organisms, at either level of organization, retain, ultimately, their peculiar, if ephemeral, characters and identities. But they are systemically integrated and mutually defining. The wholes revealed by ecology and quantum theory are unified, not blankly unitary; they are one more in the manner in which organisms are one, than one in the manner that indivisible, homogeneous, quality-less substance is one.

V

Ecology has rather signal implications for moral psychology which we may treat here for convenience, as part of metaphysics. Since individual organisms, from an ecological point of view, are less discrete objects than modes of a continuous, albeit differentiated whole, the distinction between self and other is blurred. Hence the central problem of modern classical moral philosophy as elegantly exposed by Kenneth Goodpaster in a recent discussion—the problem of either managing or overcoming egoism—is not solved by the moral psychology implicated in ecology so much as it is outflanked.[40]

Paul Shepard remarked that

> in one aspect the self is an arrangement of organs, feelings, and thoughts—a "me"—surrounded by a hard body boundary: skin, clothes, and insular habits. . . . The alternative [aspect] is a self as a center of organization, constantly drawing on and influencing the surroundings. . . . Ecological thinking . . . requires a kind of vision across boundaries. The epidermis of the skin is ecologically like a pond surface or a forest soil, not a shell so much as a delicate interpenetration. It reveals the self ennobled and extended . . . as part of the landscape and the ecosystem.[41]

Shepard went on to endorse a notion earlier crystalized by Alan Watts (whose inspiration came from oriental philosophies)—that "the world is your body."[42]

Environmental philosopher Holmes Rolston alluded to and extended Shepard's notion of the "relational self" implied by ecology. Meditating by the shores of a Rocky Mountain wilderness lake, Rolston asked:

> Does not my skin resemble this lake surface? Neither lake nor self has independent being. . . . Inlet waters have crossed this interface and are now embodied within me. . . . The waters of North Inlet are part of my circulatory system; and the more literally we take this truth the more nearly we understand it. I incarnate the solar energies that flow through this lake. No one is free-living. . . . *Bios* is intrinsically symbiosis.[43]

As one moves, in imagination, outwardly from the core of one's organism, it is impossible to find a clear demarcation between oneself and one's environment. The environing gases and fluids flow continuously in and out. The organisms outside (and inside!) one's osmotic envelope continually, albeit selectively, are transubstantiated into and through oneself. In the time-lapse cinematography of imagination one can see oneself arising from the earth, as it were, a pulsating structure in a vast sea of other patterns large and small—some of them mysteriously translating through oneself—finally to be transmuted oneself into the others. The world is, indeed, one's extended body and one's body is the precipitation, the focus of the world in a particular space-time locale.

This idea is very old, even in the West, expressed abstractly and philosophically by Heraclitus in the Greek tradition, and concretely and poetically—with the phrase, "for dust thou art, and unto dust shalt thou return"—by the author(s) of Genesis-J. In the West, however, there still lingers the image of the substantive *nephesh, psyche,* soul, or conscious mind—the more diaphanous and insubstantial its organic cladding is perceived to be, the more vulnerable and self-pitying. Paul Shepard, however, has pointed out that the relational concept of self extends to consciousness as well as organism, to mind as well as matter.

> Internal complexity, as the mind of a primate, is an extension of natural complexity, measured by the variety of plants and animals and the variety of nerve cells—organic extensions of each other.
>
> The exuberance of kinds [is] the setting in which a good mind could evolve (to deal with a complex world). . . . The idea of natural complexity as a counterpart to human intricacy is essential to an ecology of man.[44]

In a subsequent discussion Shepard elaborated this insight.[45] The more primitive elements of animal consciousness—palpable hunger and thirst, fear and rage, pleasure and pain—are as clearly evolutionary adaptations to an ever more elaborate ecosystem as are fur and feathers, toes and digits, eye and ear. The distinctive mark of human consciousness and the *materiel* of human reason are the systems of concepts embodied by human languages. Shepard has suggested that conceptual thought evolved as the taxonomical array of animals and plants was mapped by the emergent consciousness of primate hunter-gatherers. In a very direct way, therefore, human consciousness, including abstract rational thought, is an extension of the environment, just as the "environment" becomes fully actual in the mind-body unity of the New Physics only as it interacts with consciousness.[46]

Shepard constructed on this basis an interesting argument for species conservation: If we simplify and impoverish the Earth's ecosystems, we shall risk rendering future generations of human beings mentally degenerate. Lacking a rich and complex natural environment to support—as correspondent, analogue, and stimulus—a rich and complex intelligence, human intelligence may atrophy.

The relational view of self—both self as bodily organism and self as conscious, thinking thing—transforms egoism into environmentalism, to borrow Kenneth Goodpaster's felicitous phrase. As I have elsewhere pointed out, egoism has been regarded as axiologically privileged.[47] The intrinsic value of oneself is taken as a given. How to account for the value of "others"—human others and now nonhuman natural others—has been the principal problematic of nonegoistic ethics.[48]

However, if the world is one's body, and one's consciousness not only images in its specific content the world around, but, indeed, the very structure of one's psyche and rational faculties are formed through adaptive interaction with the ecological organization of nature, then one's self, both physically and psychologically, gradiently merges from its central core outward to the environment. Thus, one cannot draw hard and fast boundaries between oneself, either physically or spiritually, and the environment.

For me, this realization took concrete form, as I stood two decades and an ecological education later, on the banks of the Mississippi River where I had roamed as a boy. As I gazed at the brown silt-choked waters absorbing a black plume of industrial and municipal sewage from Memphis, and followed bits of some unknown beige froth floating continually down from Cincinnati, Louisville, or St. Louis, I experienced a palpable pain. It was not distinctly locatable in any of my extremities, nor was it like a headache or nausea. Still, it was very real. I had no plans to swim in the river, no need to drink from it, no intention of buying real estate on its shores. My narrowly personal interests were not affected, and yet, somehow, I was personally injured. It occurred to me then, in a flash of self-discovery, that the river was a part of me. And I recalled a line from Leopold's *Sand County Almanac*—"One of the penalties of an ecological education is that one lives alone in a world of wounds."[49]

The Australian conservationist John Seed, musing on his efforts on behalf of rain forest preservation in Queensland, has come to a similar conclusion:

> [A]s the implications of evolution and ecology are internalized . . . there is an identification with all life. . . . Alienation subsides. . . . "I am protecting the rain forest" develops to "I am part of the rain forest protecting myself. I am that part of the rain forest recently emerged into thinking."[50]

Ecology, thus, gives a new meaning as well as new substance to the phrase, "enlightened self-interest."

II

The Chinese World View

The Continuity of Being:
Chinese Visions of Nature

Tu Wei-Ming

The Chinese belief in the continuity of being, a basic motif in Chinese ontology, has far-reaching implications in Chinese philosophy, religion, epistemology, aesthetics, and ethics. F. W. Mote comments that

> the basic point which outsiders have found so hard to detect is that the Chinese, among all peoples ancient and recent, primitive and modern, are apparently unique in having no creation myth; that is, they have regarded the world and man as uncreated, as constituting the central features of a spontaneously self-generating cosmos having no creator, god, ultimate cause, or will external to itself.[1]

This strong assertion has understandably generated controversy among Sinologists. Mote has identified a distinctive feature of the Chinese mode of thought. In his words, "the genuine Chinese cosmogony is that of organismic process, meaning that all of the parts of the entire cosmos belong to one organic whole and that they all interact as participants in one spontaneously self-generating life process."[2]

However, despite Mote's insightfulness in singling out this particular dimension of Chinese cosmogony for focused investigation, his characterization of its uniqueness is problematic. For one thing, the apparent lack of a creation myth in Chinese cultural history is predicated on a more fundamental assumption about reality; namely, that all modalities of being are organically connected. Ancient Chinese thinkers were intensely interested in the creation of the world. Some of them, notably the Taoists, even speculated on the creator (*tsao-wu che*) and the process by which the universe came into being.[3] Presumably, indigenous creation myths existed, although the written records transmitted by even the most culturally sophisticated historians do not contain enough information to reconstruct them.[4] The real issue is not the presence or absence of creation myths, but the underlying assumption of the cosmos: whether it is continuous or discontinuous with its creator. Suppose the cosmos as we know it was created by a Big Bang; the ancient Chinese thinkers would have no problem with this theory. What they would not have accepted was a further claim that there was an external intelligence, beyond

67

human comprehension, who willed that it be so. Of course, the Chinese are not unique in this regard. Many peoples, ancient and recent, primitive and modern, would feel uncomfortable with the idea of a willful God who created the world out of nothing. It was not a creation myth as such but the Judeo-Christian version of it that is absent in Chinese mythology. But the Chinese, like numerous peoples throughout human history, subscribe to the continuity of being as self-evidently true.[5]

An obvious consequence of this basic belief is the all-embracing nature of the so-called spontaneously self-generating life process. Strictly speaking, it is not because the Chinese have no idea of God external to the created cosmos that they have no choice but to accept the cosmogony as an organismic process. Rather, it is precisely because they perceive the cosmos as the unfolding of continuous creativity that it cannot entertain "conceptions of creation *ex nihilo* by the hand of God, or through the will of God, and all other such mechanistic, teleological, and theistic cosmologies."[6] The Chinese commitment to the continuity of being, rather than the absence of a creation myth, prompts them to see nature as "the all-enfolding harmony of impersonal cosmic functions."[7]

The Chinese model of the world, "a decidedly psychophysical structure" in the Jungian sense,[8] is characterized by Joseph Needham as "an ordered harmony of wills without an ordainer."[9] What Needham describes as the organismic Chinese cosmos consists of dynamic energy fields rather than static matter-like entities. Indeed, the dichotomy of spirit and matter is not at all applicable to this psychophysical structure. The most basic stuff that makes the cosmos is neither solely spiritual nor material but both. It is a vital force. This vital force must not be conceived of either as disembodied spirit or as pure matter.[10] Wing-tsit Chan, in his influential *Source Book of Chinese Philosophy,* notes that the distinction between energy and matter is not made in Chinese philosophy. He further notes that H. H. Dubs's rendering of the indigenous term for this basic stuff, *ch'i,* as "matter-energy" is "essentially sound but awkward and lacks an adjective form."[11] Although Chan translates *ch'i* as "material force," he cautions that since *ch'i,* before the advent of Neo-Confucianism in the eleventh century, originally "denotes the psychophysiological power associated with blood and breath," it should be rendered as "vital force" or "vital power."[12]

The unusual difficulty in making *ch'i* intelligible in modern Western philosophy suggests that the underlying Chinese metaphysical assumption is significantly different from the Cartesian dichotomy between spirit and matter. However, it would be misleading to categorize the Chinese mode of thinking as a sort of pre-Cartesian naïveté lacking differentiation between mind and body and, by implication, between subject and object. Analytically, Chinese thinkers have clearly distinguished spirit from matter.

They fully recognize that spirit is not reducible to matter, that spirit is of more enduring value than matter. There are, of course, notable exceptions. But these so-called materialist thinkers are not only rare but also few and far between to constitute a noticeable tradition in Chinese philosophy. Recent attempts to reconstruct the genealogy of materialist thinkers in China have been painful and, in some cases, far-fetched.[13] Indeed, to characterize the two great Confucian thinkers, Chang Tsai (1020–1077) and Wang Fu-chih (1619–1692), as paradigmatic examples of Chinese materialism is predicated on the false assumption that *ch'i* is materialistic. Both of them did subscribe to what may be called philosophy of *ch'i* as a critique of speculative thought, but, to them, *ch'i* was not simply matter but vital force endowed with all-pervasive spirituality.[14]

The continuous presence in Chinese philosophy of the idea of *ch'i* as a way of conceptualizing the basic structure and function of the cosmos, despite the availability of symbolic resources to make an analytical distinction between spirit and matter, signifies a conscious refusal to abandon a mode of thought that synthesizes spirit and matter as an undifferentiated whole. The loss of analytical clarity is compensated by the reward of imaginative richness. The fruitful ambiguity of *ch'i* allows philosophers to explore realms of being which are inconceivable to people constricted by a Cartesian dichotomy. To be sure, the theory of the different modalities of *ch'i* cannot engender ideas such as the naked object, raw data, or the value-free fact, and this cannot create a world out there, naked, raw, and value-free, for the disinterested scientist to study, analyze, manipulate, and control. *Ch'i,* in short, seems inadequate to provide a philosophical background for the development of empirical science as understood in the positivistic sense. What it does provide, however, is a metaphorical mode of knowing, an epistemological attempt to address the multidimensional nature of reality by comparison, allusion, and suggestion.

Whether it is the metaphorical mode of knowing that directs the Chinese to perceive the cosmos as an organismic process or it is the ontological vision of the continuity of being that informs Chinese epistemology is a highly intriguing question. Our main concern here, however, is to understand how the idea of the undifferentiated *ch'i* serves as a basis for a unified cosmological theory. We want to know in what sense the least intelligent being, such as a rock, and the highest manifestation of spirituality, such as heaven, both consist of *ch'i*. The way the Chinese perceive reality and the sense of reality which defines the Chinese way of seeing the world are equally important in our inquiry, even though we do not intend to specify any causal relationship between them.

The organismic process as a spontaneously self-generating life process exhibits three basic motifs: continuity, wholeness, and dynamism.[15] All modalities of being, from a rock to heaven, are integral parts of a continuum which is often referred to as the "great transformation" (ta-hua).[16] Since nothing is outside of this continuum, the chain of being is never broken. A linkage will always be found between any given pair of things in the universe. We may have to probe deeply to find some of the linkages, but they are there to be discovered. These are not figments of our imagination but solid foundations upon which the cosmos and our lived world therein are constructed. Ch'i, the psychophysiological stuff, is everywhere. It suffuses even the "great void" (t'ai-hsü) which is the source of all beings in Chang Tsai's philosophy.[17] The continuous presence of ch'i in all modalities of being makes everything flow together as the unfolding of a single process. Nothing, not even an almighty creator, is external to this process.

This motif of wholeness is directly derived from the idea of continuity as all-encompassing. If the world were created by an intelligence higher than and external to the great transformation, it would, by definition, fall short of a manifestation of holism. Similarly, if the world were merely a partial or distorted manifestation of the Platonic Idea, it would never achieve the perfection of the original reality. On the contrary, if genuine creativity is not the creation of something out of nothing, but a continuous transformation of that which is already there, the world as it now exists is the authentic manifestation of the cosmic process in its all-embracing fullness. Indeed, if the Idea for its own completion entails that it realize itself through the organismic process, the world is in every sense the concrete embodiment of the Idea. Traditional Chinese thinkers, of course, did not philosophize in those terms. They used different conceptual apparatuses to convey their thought. To them, the appropriate metaphor for understanding the universe was biology rather than physics. At issue was not the eternal, static structure but the dynamic process of growth and transformation. To say that the cosmos is a continuum and that all of its components are internally connected is also to say that it is an organismic unity, holistically integrated at each level of complexity.

It is important to note that continuity and wholeness in Chinese cosmological thinking must be accompanied in the third motif, dynamism, lest the idea of organismic unity imply a closed system. While Chinese thinkers are critically aware of the inertia in human culture which may eventually lead to stagnation, they perceive the "course of heaven" (t'ien-hsing) as "vigorous" (chien) and instruct people to model themselves on the ceaseless vitality of the cosmic process.[18] What they envision in the spontaneously self-generating life process is not only inner connectedness and interdependence but also infinite potential for development. Many historians have remarked that the traditional Chinese notion of cyclic change, like the recurrence of the seasonal pattern, is incompatible with the modern

Western idea of progress. To be sure, the traditional Chinese conception of history lacks the idea of unilinear development, such as Marxian modes of production depicting a form of historical inevitability. It is misleading, however, to describe Chinese history as chronicling a number of related events happening in a regularly repeated order.[19] Chinese historiography is not a reflection of a cyclic world view. The Chinese world view is neither cyclic nor spiral. It is transformational. The specific curve around which it transforms at a given period of time is indeterminate, however, for numerous human and nonhuman factors are involved in shaping its form and direction.

The organismic life process, which Mote contends is the genuine Chinese cosmogony, is an open system. As there is no temporal beginning to specify, no closure is ever contemplated. The cosmos is forever expanding; the great transformation is unceasing. The idea of unilinear development, in this perspective, is one-sided because it fails to account for the whole range of possibility in which progress constitutes but one of several dominant configurations. By analogy, neither cyclic nor spiral movements can fully depict the varieties of cosmic transformation. Since it is open rather than closed and dynamic rather than static, no geometric design can do justice to its complex morphology.

Earlier, I followed Mote in characterizing the Chinese vision of nature as the "all-enfolding harmony of impersonal cosmic function" and remarked that this particular vision was prompted by the Chinese commitment to the continuity of being. Having discussed the three basic motifs of Chinese cosmology—wholeness, dynamism, and continuity—I can elaborate on Mote's characterization by discussing some of its implications. The idea of all-enfolding harmony involves two interrelated meanings. It means that nature is all-inclusive, the spontaneously self-generating life process which excludes nothing. The Taoist idea of *tzu-jan* ("self-so"),[20] which is used in modern Chinese to translate the English word *nature,* aptly captures this spirit. To say that *self-so* is all-inclusive is to posit a nondiscriminatory and nonjudgmental position, to allow all modalities of being to display themselves as they are. This is possible, however, only if competitiveness, domination, and aggression are thoroughly transformed. Thus, all-enfolding harmony also means that internal resonance underlies the order of things in the universe. Despite conflict and tension, which are like waves of the ocean, the deep structure of nature is always tranquil. The great transformation of which nature is the concrete manifestation is the result of concord rather than discord and convergence rather than divergence.

This vision of nature may suggest an unbridled romantic assertion about peace and love, the opposite of what Charles Darwin realistically portrayed as the rules of nature. Chinese thinkers, however, did not take the all-enfolding harmony to be the original naïveté of the innocent. Nor did they take it to be an idealist utopia attainable in a distant future. They were acutely aware that the world we live in, far from being the "great unity" (ta-t'ung) recommended in the *Evolution of the Rites*,[21] is laden with disruptive forces including humanly caused calamities and natural catastrophes. They also knew well that history is littered with internecine warfare, oppression, injustice, and numerous other forms of cruelty. It was not naïve romanticism that prompted them to assert that harmony is a defining characteristic of the organismic process. They believed that it is an accurate description of what the cosmos really is and how it actually works.

One advantage of rendering *ch'i* as "vital force," bearing in mind its original association with blood and breath, is its emphasis on the life process. To Chinese thinkers, nature is vital force in display. It is continuous, holistic, and dynamic. Yet, in an attempt to understand the blood and breath of nature's vitality, Chinese thinkers discovered that its enduring pattern is union rather than disunion, integration rather than disintegration, and synthesis rather than separation. The eternal flow of nature is characterized by the concord and convergence of numerous streams of vital force. It is in this sense that the organismic process is considered harmonious.

Chang Tsai, in his celebrated metaphysical treatise, "Correcting Youthful Ignorance," defines the cosmos as the "Great Harmony."

> The Great Harmony is called the Tao. It embraces the nature which underlies all counter processes of floating and sinking, rising and falling, and motion and rest. It is the origin of the process of fusion and intermingling, of overcoming and being overcome, and of expansion and contraction. At the commencement, these processes are incipient, subtle, obscure, easy, and simple, but at the end they are extensive, great, strong and firm. It is *ch'ien* ("heaven") that begins with the knowledge of Change, and *k'un* ("earth") that models after simplicity. That which is dispersed, differentiated, and discernible in form becomes *ch'i*, and that which is pure, penetrating, and not discernible in form becomes spirit. Unless the whole universe is in the process of fusion and intermingling like fleeting forces moving in all directions, it may not be called "Great Harmony."[22]

In his vision, nature is the result of the fusion and intermingling of the vital forces that assume tangible forms. Mountains, rivers, rocks, trees, animals, and human beings are all modalities of energy-matter, symbolizing that the creative transformation of the Tao is forever present. Needham's idea of the Chinese cosmos as an ordered harmony of wills without an ordainer is, however, not entirely appropriate. Wills, no matter how broadly defined, do not feature prominently here. The idea that heaven and earth complete the transformation with no mind of their own clearly indicates that the harmonious state of the organismic process is not achieved by ordering divergent wills.[23] Harmony will be attained through spontaneity. In what sense is this what Mote calls "impersonal cosmic function"? Let us return to Chang Tsai's metaphysical treatise.

> *Ch'i* moves and flows in all directions and in all manners. Its two elements [yin and yang] unite and give rise to the concrete. Thus the multiplicity of things and human beings is produced. In their ceaseless successions of two elements of yin and yang constitute the great principles of the universe.[24]

This inner logic of *ch'i,* which is singularly responsible for the production of the myriad things, leads to a naturalistic description of the impersonal cosmic function. Wang Fu-chih, who developed Chang Tsai's metaphysics of *ch'i* with great persuasive power, continues with this line of thinking.

> The fact that the things of the world, whether rivers or mountains, plants or animals, those with or without intelligence, and those yielding blossoms or bearing fruits, provide beneficial support for all things is the result of the natural influence of the moving power of *ch'i.* It fills the universe. And as it completely provides for the flourish and transformation of all things, it is all the more spatially unrestricted. As it is not spatially restricted, it operates in time and proceeds with time. From morning to evening, from spring to summer, and from the present tracing back to the past, there is no time at which it does not operate, and there is no time at which it does not produce. Consequently, as one sprout bursts forth it becomes a tree with a thousand big branches, and as an egg evolves, it progressively becomes a fish capable of swallowing a ship. . . .[25]

The underlying message, however, is not the impersonality of the cosmic function, even though the idea of the moving power of *ch'i* indicates that no anthropomorphic god, animal, or object is really behind the great transformation. The naturalness of the cosmic function, despite human wishes and desires, is impersonal but not inhuman. It is impartial to all modalities of being and not merely anthropocentric. We humans, therefore, do not find the impersonal cosmic function cold, alien, or distant, although we know that it is, by and large, indifferent to and disinterested in our private thoughts and whims. Actually, we are an integral part of this function; we are ourselves the result of this moving power of *ch'i.* Like mountains and rivers, we are legitimate beings in this great transformation. The opening lines in Chang Tsai's *Western Inscription* are not only his article of faith but also his ontological view of the human.

> Heaven is my father and earth is my mother, and even such a small being as

I finds an intimate place in their midst. Therefore, that which fills the universe I regard as my body and that which directs the universe I regard as my nature. All people are my brothers and sisters, and all things are my companions.[26]

The sense of intimacy with which Chang Tsai, as a single person, relates himself to the universe as a whole reflects his profound awareness of moral ecology. Humanity is the respectful son or daughter of the cosmic process. This humanistic vision is distinctively Confucian in character. It contrasts sharply with the Taoist idea of noninterference on the one hand and the Buddhist concept of detachment on the other. Yet the notion of humanity as forming one body with the universe has been so widely accepted by the Chinese, in popular as well as elite culture, that it can very well be characterized as a general Chinese world view.

Forming one body with the universe can literally mean that since all modalities of being are made of *ch'i,* human life is part of a continuous flow of the blood and breath that constitutes the cosmic process. Human beings are thus organically connected with rocks, trees, and animals. Understandably, the interplay and interchange between discrete species feature prominently in Chinese literature, notably popular novels. The monkey in the *Journey to the West* came into being by metamorphosis from an agate;[27] the hero in the *Dream of the Red Chamber* or the *Story of the Stone,* Pao-yü, is said to have been transformed from a piece of precious jade;[28] and the heroine of the *Romance of the White Snake* has not completely succeeded in transfiguring herself into a beautiful woman.[29] These are well-known stories. They have evoked strong sympathetic responses from Chinese audiences young and old for centuries, not merely as fantasies but as great human drama. It is not at all difficult for the Chinese to imagine that an agate or a piece of jade can have enough potential spirituality to transform itself into a human being. Part of the pathos of the White Snake lies in her inability to fight against the spell cast by a ruthless monk so that she can retain her human form and be united with her lover. The fascinating element in this romance is that she manages to acquire the power to transfigure herself into a woman through several hundred years of self-cultivation.

Presumably, from the cosmic vantage point, nothing is totally fixed. It need not be forever the identity it now assumes. In the perceptive eye of the Chinese painter Tao Chi (1641–1717), mountains flow like rivers. The proper way of looking at mountains, for him, is to see them as ocean waves frozen in time.[30] By the same token, rocks are not static objects but dynamic processes with their particular configuration of the energy-matter. It may not be far-fetched to suggest that, with this vision of nature, we can actually talk about the different degrees of spirituality of rocks. Agate is certainly more spiritual than an ordinary hard stone and perhaps jade is more spiritual than agate. Jade is honored as the "finest essence of mountain and river" (*shan-ch'uan ching-ying*).[31] By analogy, we can also talk about degrees of spirituality in the entire chain of being. Rocks, trees, animals, humans, and gods represent different levels of spirituality based on the varying compositions of *ch'i*. However, despite the principle of differentiation, all modalities of being are organically connected. They are integral parts of a continuous process of cosmic transformation. It is in this metaphysical sense that "all things are my companions."

The uniqueness of being human cannot be explained in terms of a preconceived design by a creator. Human beings, like all other beings, are the results of the integration of the two basic vital forces of yin and yang. Chou Tun-i (1017–1073) says, "the interaction of these two *ch'i* engenders and transforms the myriad things. The myriad things produce and reproduce, resulting in an unending transformation."[32] In a strict sense, then, human beings are not the rulers of creation; if they intend to become guardians of the universe, they must earn this distinction through self-cultivation. There is no preordained reason for them to think otherwise. Nevertheless, the human being—in the Chinese sense of *jen* which is gender neutral—is unique. Chou Tun-i offers the following explanation:

> It is man alone who receives [the Five Agents] in their highest excellence, and therefore he is most intelligent. His physical form appears, and his spirit develops consciousness. The five moral principles of his nature (humanity, rightness, propriety, wisdom, and faithfulness) are aroused by, and react to, the external world and engage in activity; good and evil are distinguished; and human affairs take place.[33]

The theory of the Five Agents of the Five Phases (*wu-hsing*) need not concern us here. Since Chou makes it clear that "by the transformation of yang and its union with yin, the Five Agents of Water, Fire, Wood, Metal, and Earth arise" and that since "the Five Agents constitute a system of yin and yang,"[34] they can be conceived as specific forms of *ch'i*.

That humankind receives *ch'i* in its highest excellence is not only manifested in intelligence but also in sensitivity. The idea that humans are the most sentient beings in the universe features prominently in Chinese thought. A vivid description of human sensitivity is found in the "recorded sayings" (*yü-lu*) of Ch'eng Hao (1032–1085).

> A book on medicine describes paralysis of the four limbs as absence of humanity (*pu-jen*). This is an excellent description. The man of humanity regards heaven and earth and all things as one body. To him there is nothing

that is not himself. Since he has recognized all things as himself, can there be any limit to his humanity? If things are not part of the self, naturally they have nothing to do with it. As in the case of paralysis of the four limbs, the vital force (*ch'i*) no longer penetrates them, and therefore they are no longer parts of the self.[35]

This idea of forming one body with the universe is predicated on the assumption that since all modalities of being are made of *ch'i*, all things cosmologically share the same consanguinity with us and are thus our companions. This vision enabled an original thinker of the Ming Dynasty, Wang Ken (1483–1540), to remark that if we came into being through transformation (*hua-sheng*), then heaven and earth are our father and mother to us; if we came into being through reproduction (*hsing-sheng*), then our father and mother are heaven and earth to us.[36] The image of the human that emerges here, far from being the lord of creation, is the filial son and daughter of the universe. Filial piety connotes a profound feeling, an all-pervasive care for the world around us.

This literal meaning of forming one body with the universe must be augmented by a metaphorical reading of the same text. It is true that the body clearly conveys the sense *ch'i* as the blood and breath of the vital force that underlies all beings. The uniqueness of being human, however, is not simply that we are made of the same psychophysiological stuff that rocks, trees, and animals are also made of. It is our consciousness of being human that enables and impels us to probe the transcendental anchorage of our nature. Surely, the motif of the continuity of being prevents us from positing a creator totally external to the cosmic organismic process, but what is the relationship between human nature and heaven which serves as the source of all things? Indeed, how are we to understand the ontological assertion in the first chapter of the *Doctrine of the Mean* that our nature is decreed by heaven?[37] Is the Mandate of Heaven a one-time operation or a continuous presence? Wang Fu-chih's general response to these questions is suggestive.

> By nature is meant the principle of growth. As one daily grows, one daily achieves completion. Thus by the Mandate of Heaven is not meant that heaven gives the decree (*ming*, mandate) only at the moment of one's birth. . . . In the production of things by heaven, the process of transformation never ceases.[38]

In the metaphorical sense, then, forming one body with the universe requires continuous effort to grow and to refine oneself. We can embody the whole universe in our sensitivity because we have enlarged and deepened our feeling and care to the fullest extent. However, there is no guarantee at the symbolic nor the experiential level that the universe is automatically embodied in us. Unless we see to it that the Mandate of Heaven is fully realized in our nature, we may not live up to the expectation that "all things are complete is us."[39] Wang Fu-chih's refusal to follow a purely naturalistic line of thinking on this is evident in the following observation: "The profound person acts naturally as if nothing happens, but . . . he acts so as to make the best choices and remain firm in holding to the Mean."[40] To act naturally without letting things take their own course means, in Neo-Confucian terminology, to follow the "heavenly principle" (*t'ien-li*) without being overcome by "selfish desires" (*ssu-yü*).[41] Selfish desires are forms of self-centeredness that belittle the authentic human capacity to take part in the transformative process of heaven and earth. In commenting on the *Book of Change,* Ch'eng Hao observes:

> The most impressive aspect of things is their spirit of life. This is what is meant by origination being the chief quality of goodness. Man and heaven and earth are one thing. Why should man purposely belittle himself?[42]

Forming a trinity with heaven and earth, which is tantamount to forming one body with the myriad things, enjoins us from applying the subject-object dichotomy to nature. To see nature as an external object out there is to create an artificial barrier which obstructs our true vision and undermines our human capacity to experience nature from within. The internal resonance of the vital forces is such that the mind, as the most refined and subtle *ch'i* of the human body, is constantly in sympathetic accord with the myriad things in nature. The function of "affect and response" (*kan-ying*) characterizes nature as a great harmony and so informs the mind.[43] The mind forms a union with nature by extending itself metonymically. Its aesthetic appreciation of nature is neither an appropriation of the object by the subject nor an imposition of the subject on the object, but the merging of the self into an expanded reality through transformation and participation. This creative process, in Jakobson's terminology, is "contiguous," because rupture between us and nature never occurs.[44]

Chuang Tzu recommends that we listen with our minds rather than with our ears; with *ch'i* rather than with our minds.[45] If listening with our minds involves consciousness unaffected by sensory perceptions, what does listening to *ch'i* entail? Could it mean that we are so much a part of the internal resonance of the vital forces themselves that we can listen to the sound of nature or, in Chuang Tzu's expression, the "music of heaven" (*t'ien-lai*)[46] as our inner voice? Or could it mean that the all-embracing *ch'i* enables the total transposition of humankind and nature? As a result, the aesthetic delight that one experiences is no longer the private sensation of the individual but the "harmonious blending of inner feelings and outer scenes"[47] as the traditional Chinese artist would have it. It seems that in either case we do not detach ourselves from nature and study it in a disinterested manner. What we do is to suspend not only our sensory perceptions but also our conceptual apparatus so that we can embody nature in our sensitivity and allow nature to embrace us in its affinity.

I must caution, however, that the aesthetic experience of mutuality and immediacy with nature is often the result of strenuous and continual effort at self-cultivation. Despite our superior intelligence, we do not have privileged access to the great harmony. As social and cultural beings, we can never get outside ourselves to study nature from neutral ground. The process of returning to nature involves unlearning and forgetting as well as remembering. The precondition for us to participate in the internal resonance of the vital forces in nature is our own inner transformation. Unless we can first harmonize our own feelings and thoughts, we are not prepared for nature, let alone for an "interflow with the spirit of Heaven and Earth."[48] It is true that we are consanguineous with nature. But as humans, we must make ourselves worthy of such a relationship.

Human/Nature in Nietzsche and Taoism

Graham Parkes

> To translate the human being back into nature; to master
> the many vain and fanatical interpretations and connota-
> tions that have hitherto been scrawled and painted over the
> eternal basic text of *homo natura* . . . that would be a
> strange and wonderful task.

Beyond Good and Evil

Before we can react to and act upon our natural environment aright, we must learn the text of nature properly. Many of the proposed solutions to the current ecological crisis are taken in by traditional interpretations, ignore questions of hermeneutics, and so overlook the underlying fantasies and prejudices that condition (for the most part, quite unconsciously) our perception of the natural world—and thereby also our interactions with the environment. It has been noted frequently that the Chinese Taoist tradition embodies an understanding of nature which may help us reorient ourselves, here in the West, toward the natural world. This is so not only because the Taoist attitude toward nature is in itself more sane, less obviously exploitative, and embodies a minimally self-serving interpretation of the phenomena, but also because—as a perspective on nature that has disparate social-historical roots and is based on philosophical assumptions very different from our own—it allows us to gain a fresh perspective on what may be characteristically Eurocentric interpretations of the natural environment. It is customary, in comparative essays on environmental issues, to seek enlightenment by moving from Western ideas to the wisdom of the East; but on the present topic it may be helpful heuristically to try moving counter to the general flow of the present collection.

The Taoist understanding of nature and the natural is itself complex, and it is not immediately clear—beyond their criticisms of what they saw as a degenerate way of understanding nature—just how the Taoists think we should understand ourselves and behave in relation to the natural realm. In order to bring into relief this aspect of the Taoist world view, it will be instructive to make a comparison with the ideas of a Western thinker whose perspective is remarkably similar, namely, Nietzsche. Since there is no

79

evidence that Nietzsche knew anything about Taoism, the number of his ideas about nature which correspond to Taoist views suggests that there may be further, hitherto unexplored philosophical (re)sources in the Western tradition which may prove helpful to consider in our current predicament.

Taking our cue from Nietzsche's characterization of the human as "the sickest animal," as being the one farthest removed from its instincts, we may frame the invitation for dialogue in terms of a medical metaphor. Beginning from the premise that there has been something sick about the predominant Western attitude towards nature over the past century, and that the Chinese attitude during the fourth to the second centuries B.C.E. was at least ailing, we can look at the relevant ideas under the headings of diagnosis, etiology, and prescription. Both Nietzsche and the Taoists share the view that the major problem is anthropocentrism—as a cause and also a symptom of a relationship with nature that is out of joint. The Taoists bemoan the lack of natural spontaneity in our actions, while Nietzsche emphasizes a want of creativity. Both posit comparable causes for this sickness, namely, a misunderstanding of the human/nature relation through its being conditioned by ego-centered fantasy projections and anthropocentric readings of the book of nature. For the Taoists, the major pernicious force here is a certain kind of discriminative consciousness, while Nietzsche in addition blames herd mentality (as imaged especially in the domesticated animals that populate *Thus Spoke Zarathustra*).[1] The prescription on both sides is to see through and withdraw the ego-generated anthropomorphic projections that vitiate our relations with natural phenomena, allowing us to live in what Chuang-tzu calls "a full view of heaven [*t'ien*]," and to engage in what Nietzsche would style a "dance" through the myriad perspectives on ourselves and the world that are open to us.[2]

The disrelation to nature manifests on two levels, corresponding to the two senses of the English word: as applied to the natural world, and also to a particular creature (as when we talk, for instance, of human nature"). On the level of the individual there is the natural spontaneity of the newborn child, in whom no hiatus has opened up between impulse and action. Then, with the advent of culture, the harmony is disrupted as drives begin to conflict with each other and with the drives of others, and the person becomes alienated from the natural instincts of the body. A reintegration would involve an incorporation of the acknowledgement of one's difference from the rest of nature into the undistorted unfolding of the individual's nature. On the collective level, the first phase consists in a social group's living in a harmoniously utopian unity with the natural environment—though Nietzsche would say: *literally* utopian, since he doubts whether such a condition ever actually obtained—and to judge from the way in which the Taoists project the fantasy, they probably doubt it too. This gives way to a separation of the social from the natural world—a more radical split in the West, thanks to the greater depth of the subject-object dichotomy—which again would be resolved by some kind of integration of identity and difference.

I

The question of how to understand nature is not, for the early Taoist thinkers, a merely abstract philosophical question, but rather an existential one that bears directly on the problem of how to live one's life in the most fulfilling way. The prescriptive force of early Taoist philosophy, simply conceived, is something like "Act in harmony with *tao*." But since for most mortals the true *tao*–being nameless, empty, deep, dark, insubstantial—is difficult if not impossible to discern, the Taoist injunction comes down to "follow the natural way," or "behave in harmony with nature." This simple-sounding prescription is difficult to follow, because the human being is alienated from nature and from his or her own nature by an inherent (one is tempted to say "natural") drive to conceptualize and thereby falsify his experience of the world.

The problem of the natural in Taoism is compounded by the lack of a single term in Taoist vocabulary that corresponds exactly to our word "nature." There is rather a complex of related terms, of which the most important in the present context is *t'ien*, or "heaven/sky," which often—especially in the compound *t'ien-ti*, "heaven-and-earth"—comes closest to what we mean by the natural world.[3] The notion of *t'ien* was traditionally that of a divine power responsible for the ongoing creation of the universe, and by the time of Confucius it had come to be seen as responsible for the destiny of human beings and as a pattern for their proper conduct. With Taoism, the sense of *t'ien* as a personal presence seems to have diminished, thereby bringing the idea closer to that of "nature." In the *Lao-tzu* it is said to be impartial (Nietzsche constantly emphasizes the amoral character of the natural world—see, for example, *GS* 109, 301, 344), and to work by not-contending, through "inaction" (*wu wei*). Its operations, often referred to as the "way of heaven," are to be emulated by human beings, and themselves ultimately depend on the spontaneous "self-so-ing" (*tzu-jan*) of all things.

> Man models himself on earth, earth on heaven,
> heaven on the way, and the way on what is naturally so.
>
> (*Lao-tzu* 25)

Heaven and earth thus provide mediating patterns in the realm of the sensible for the movements of *tao*. The great majority of similes for *tao* are drawn from nature: in order to emulate the way, human beings are encouraged to be like water, thawing ice, uncarved wood, a valley, grass and trees, and so on (8, 15, 76). The way of heaven can be discerned not only by observing external natural phenomena but also by "internal" reflection: "Without looking out of the window / One can see the way of heaven" (47). The notion of *t'ien* occupies a more prominent position in the *Chuang-tzu* than in *Lao-tzu*, being in some respects emphasized more than *tao* itself—an issue we shall take up later.

The comparison with Nietzsche can be initiated by looking at the idea in the *Lao-tzu* of a movement away from the "natural state." Several chapters imagine an original, innocent oneness with nature through the image of the infant or the child (10, 20, 28, 55), which is disrupted by the advent of calculative thinking. The text posits a parallel shift on the collective as well as the individual level—from a primordial utopian society in which "small is beautiful" and the necessities of life are met simply and fully (cf. 80), to the larger-scale society of the Warring States period with its relatively sophisticated tools and weaponry.

We find an account of a corresponding condition in a passage from a public lecture delivered by Nietzsche the year his first book was published (1872), which is worth quoting at some length since it is not well known and because it points up the Romantic character of Nietzsche's early views. In the course of offering his audience some advice on education, he distinguishes between two different ways relating to nature:

> If you want to lead a young person on to the right path of education, be careful not to disturb his naively trustful and personally immediate relationship with nature: forest and cliff, storm and vulture, the single flower, the butterfly, the meadow and the mountainside must speak to him in their own tongues; at the same time he must recognize himself in them as in countless dispersed reflexes and reflections and in a multi-colored whirl of changing appearances; in this way he will unconsciously sympathize with the metaphysical oneness of all things in the great metaphor of nature, and at the same time calm himself with their eternal perseverance and necessity. But how many young people are permitted to grow up disposed so closely and almost personally toward nature! The others must early on learn another truth: how one subjugates nature toward one's own ends. This is the end of that naive metaphysics, and the physiology of plants and animals, geology, and inorganic chemistry force their pupils to a quite different view. What has been lost in this newly imposed view is not merely some poetic phantasmagoria but the instinctive, true and unique understanding of nature: and in its place we now have clever calculation and a cunning overcoming of

nature. Thus someone who is educated properly is afforded the invaluable gift of being able to remain faithful without any breach to the contemplative instincts of his childhood, and thereby to achieve a condition of peaceful oneness and harmonious integration . . .[4]

The beginning of an unpublished essay from the following year conveys Nietzsche's sense of the overweening anthropocentrism that characterizes the modern attitude towards the natural world in remarkably Taoist terms, and also suggests a comparably modest view of the status of human knowledge.

> In some out-of-the-way corner of the universe which flows out into innumerable solar systems, there once was a star on which some clever animals invented knowing.
>
> . . . how shadowy and ephemeral, how aimless and arbitrary an exception the human intellect makes of itself within nature . . . only its possessor and begetter takes it so pathetically seriously, as if the axis of the world turned within it. But if we could communicate with the gnat, we would realize that it flies through the air with a similar seriousness, and feels within itself the flying center of the world.[5]

Nietzsche's critiques of anthropocentrism remain vigorous through to his last works, where he speaks of the vanity of behaving "as if humankind were the grand intention behind animal evolution. The human being is in no way the crown of creation; every creature is, beside him, at a similar stage of perfection" (*AC* 14).

Whereas the early Taoist thinkers were arguing in the context of the Confucian tradition, which had more or less ignored the natural world in its concentration on the sociopolitical sphere, Nietzsche had a longer history and greater weight of anthropocentrism to work against. It will be helpful to sketch this history by adducing briefly some of his remarks about the various epochs of misunderstanding in the West.

In a section of *Human, All-too-Human* on the "Origins of religious cult," Nietzsche suggests that we transpose ourselves imaginatively back into primitive society in order to appreciate the human being's very different relation to nature then. "The whole of nature is for [those] religious people a sum of activities of conscious and volitional [*wollend*] beings, an enormous complex of *willed acts*" (*HA* I, 111). The superstitious belief in magic then arises in an attempt to exert some measure of control over these powers: "to determine nature toward human advantage, and so to *impress upon it a lawfulness which it does not have from the start.*" This is the beginning of a move, on the collective level, away from what Nietzsche earlier called the "personally immediate relationship with nature" toward a more detached attitude; and the greater the distance, the less the identification, and the easier it becomes to assert control over the environment.

The ancient Greeks came to terms with the forces of nature, according to the account in *The Birth of Tragedy,* through the means of a powerful artifice. The move toward a more "depersonalized" view of nature was effected by a process of projection—and so at the expense of a concealment and falsification of the world. While the Dionysiac experience consisted in "an overwhelming feeling of unity leading back to the heart of nature" (sec. 7), this merging was experienced as both blissful and terrifying in its "lethargy" (the *lêthê* here being a forgetting of the individual self). Since the forces of nature were too terrible and cruel to be faced directly, the Greeks had to interpose the Apollinian "veil of beautiful seeming" in order to be able to live. The link with nature was still maintained through the powers of Dionysus and the satyr-chorus of Greek tragedy, but the projection of the illusory dreamworld of Apollo, the major element of which was the realm of the Olympian gods, veiled the terrible nature—meaningless—of the natural world sufficiently to make life bearable.

Nietzsche later ridicules the Stoics (and their philosophical epigoni of subsequent epochs) for their claiming to live "according to nature": "While you rapturously pretend to be reading the canon of your law from nature, you actually want the opposite. . . . Your pride wants to prescribe to nature, even to nature, your own morality and ideals . . ." (*BGE* 9). This kind of falsification is further developed by Christianity, which widens the gulf between nature and the human. Nietzsche reproaches the Christian tradition for elaborating "an imaginary science of *nature* (anthropocentric; completely lacking the concept of natural causes)," and shows how "after the concept 'nature' had been made the counter-enemy to 'God,' 'natural' had then to mean the same as 'reprehensible' " (*AC* 15). Christianity's mistrust of and contempt for the body, as expressed in the attempt to extirpate or deny the majority of the human beings' natural drives and passions, divorced from its animal past and made it "the sickest animal"—though at the same time also "the most interesting" (*AC* 14).

While the Christian tradition falsified our view of nature by imposing moralistic judgements on it, Kant continued and refined the practice of imposing laws—but now in the form of conceptual structures: "When Kant says that 'the understanding does not draw its laws from nature but prescribes them to it,' this is completely true with respect to the *concept of nature* which we are obliged to connect with it (nature = the world as representation, that is, as error), but which is the summation of hosts of errors on the part of the understanding" (*HA* I, 19). While Nietzsche may be grudgingly grateful to Kant for bringing these operations of the human intellect out into the open, he nevertheless sees this kind of thinking as the root of the modern attitude towards nature, which he later describes (quite prophetically—the year is 1887) as *"hubris,* our raping of nature by means of machines and the inconsiderately employed inventions of technology."[6]

It is possible to distinguish in this account several layers of anthropocentric projections on to the natural world which need to be lifted off before we can read what Nietzsche calls "the basic text of nature." The first consists of moral evaluations, primarily from the Christian—but also from the Socratic/Platonic—tradition: "Human beings have ascribed to all that exists a connection with morality, and have laid an ethical significance on the world's shoulders" (*Dawn* 3). Nietzsche has a basic mistrust of what the title of an early aphorism calls "the habit of opposites," especially in relation to nature, and all the more so when the values in question are ethical: "Our generally imprecise observation sees opposites everywhere in nature ('warm and cold,' for example), where there are no opposites but only differences of degree" (*HA* II/2, 67).

While this mistrust is surely inherited from Heraclitus, its denial of the existence of fixed and independent opposites is perfectly congruent with the basic tenets of Taoism. Nietzsche would heartily endorse this passage from the *Lao-tzu,* so reminiscent of the obscure Ephesian:

> The whole world understands that which makes beauty beautiful,
>   yet this is simply the ugly;
> The whole world understands that which makes goodness good,
>   yet this is simply the bad;
> Thus Something and Nothing give birth to one another;
> The difficult and the easy complement one another . . .

(Chap. 2; see also Chap. 20)

Given that the Taoists were writing in an atmosphere dominated by a moral dogmatism preached by the followers of Confucius, they are particularly forceful in arguing against such hardened ethical concepts from that tradition as goodwill/benevolence (*jen*) and duty/rectitude (*yi*) which they regard as damaging or running counter to the way of heaven.[7]

Moving to the next level, we discover that Nietzsche's penchant for "unmasking" supposedly moral judgements and actions and showing the various kinds of utility-based motivations behind them is matched by his fondness for exposing considerations of utility as being crass in comparison with the aesthetic standpoint. To liberate all things from their "bondage under purpose," as Zarathustra puts it,[8] to free natural phenomena from utilitarian judgements of the form "this thing is good/useful for doing such-and-such," is a goal pursued by Nietzsche throughout his career. His tactics have their counterpart in some of Chuang-tzu's best known and most effective strategies for pointing up the anthropocentrism inherent in our everyday judgements, that is, his anecdotes concerning "the usefulness of being useless," in which natural things are seen to be able to last out their allotted span precisely by *not* being useful for any human purposes.[9]

Chuang-tzu wants us to see that all value judgements are relative insofar as they are made from a particular perspective, and that particular perspectives are by their nature narrow and limited in comparison with the openness of heaven or the way. Thus, in contrast to discriminative consciousness, which "picks out a stalk from a pillar, a hag from beautiful Hsi Shih, things however peculiar or incongruous, the Way interchanges them and deems them one" (Chap. 2; *IC* 53). In just the same way, Nietzsche follows Heraclitus in advocating a flexibility with respect to perspectives, an "interchanging" of them, which lets one always entertain— literally: "hold [oneself] between"—the opposite of any current viewpoint. As Chuang-tzu asks (through the persona of Wang Ni): "How do I know that what I call knowing is not ignorance? How do I know that what I call ignorance is not knowing?"; of loaches, apes and humans—"which knows the right place to live?"; of humans, deer, centipedes, owls, and crows— "which has a proper sense of taste?"; of monkeys, birds, fish and men— "which knows what is truly beautiful in the world?" (Chap. 2; *IC* 58).

At the next level, one encounters views that see things as true/genuine or false, correct or incorrect, appropriately or inappropriately ordered. One of Chuang-tzu's most far- and deep-reaching questions is this:

> By what is the Way hidden that there should be a genuine or a false? By what is saying darkened that sometimes "That's it" and sometimes "That's not"? . . . No thing is not "other," no thing is not "it." If you treat yourself too as "other" they do not appear, if you know of yourself you know of them. . . . Are there really It and Other? Or really no It and Other? Where neither It nor Other finds its opposite is called the axis of the Way (Chap. 2; *IC* 52–53).

The ground level involves the most basic conceptualizing into opposites—distinctions between self and other, inner and outer, cause and effect—and even taking natural phenomena as "things" at all, as unities of any kind. The notion that the concept of a thing is merely a fiction, made up for the sake of convenience in coping with and controlling the world, is one that Nietzsche elaborates with increasing frequency and sophistication in his later works. But the idea appears early, in "On Truth and Lie in the Extra-Moral Sense," and in a context that is directly relevant to our present concerns. With respect to the formation of concepts, Nietzsche writes:

"Every concept arises from the positing as equal of what is not equal. . . . We obtain the concept, and also the form, by overlooking what is individual and actual, whereas nature in contrast knows no forms or concepts . . ."

The Taoist position is nicely summed up in a passage from *Chuang-tzu* which describes a progressive degeneration, beginning from a mythical past, of human beings' relation to the world—and which, if we were to imagine it reversed, would be strikingly congruent with the process we have seen Nietzsche sketch with respect to the Western tradition.

> The men of old, their knowledge had arrived at something: at what had it arrived? There were some who thought that there had not yet begun to be things—the utmost, the exhaustive, there is no more to add. The next thought that there were things but there had not yet begun to be borders. The next thought there were borders to them but there had not yet begun to be "That's it, that's not." The lighting up of "That's it, that's not" is the reason why the Way is flawed (Chap. 2; *IC* 54).

II

Let us examine more closely the process by which the anthropocentric standpoint is dissolved through an identification of the human being with natural phenomena. Since this transformation is vividly exemplified in so many passages in Taoist writings, the major focus will be on the text of Nietzsche's in which it predominates—*Thus Spoke Zarathustra*. Almost as remarkable as the plethora of images of natural phenomena in this work, in both literal and metaphorical presentation, is the paucity of imagery drawn from culture or city. And the few manifestations of civilization that do appear—the machinery of the state, newspapers and other publications, the trappings of religious institutions—are roundly excoriated.

The force of Zarathustra's often repeated dictum, "The human being is something that shall be overcome," is in part that the condition of the "overman" (*Übermensch*) is attained by transcending the egocentric and anthropocentric standpoints. In the Prologue, Zarathustra proclaims his love for "him who works and invents to build a house for the overman and prepare for him earth, animal and plant: for in this way he wills his own going under," and also for "him whose soul squanders itself, who does not want thanks and does not give back: for he gives always and does not want to preserve himself" (sec. 4). Somewhat paradoxically, Zarathustra also loves "him whose soul is overfull so that he forgets himself, and all things are in him: thus all things become his going under."

This double movement (worthy of Kierkegaard) of the soul's self-emptying and self-filling corresponds to Chuang-tzu's idea that one enters the realm of heaven by forgetting about all things—including heaven. The first of the Inner Chapters speaks of "the man who rides a true course between heaven and earth, with the changes of the Six Energies for his chariot" (*IC* 44). The "Energies" referred to here are forms of *ch'i,* the vital principle that animates the entire universe, and are traditionally the forces of *yin* and *yang,* wind and rain, dark and light. The text often speaks of a kind of person who is "daemonic" (*shen*) insofar as he "yokes the clouds to his chariot, rides the sun and moon and roams beyond the four seas."[10] This represents for Chuang-tzu the ultimate relationship with natural forces: one is able to empty the "heart" (*hsin*—for the ancient Chinese, the organ of thought) of conceptual ratiocination and discriminative evaluation, in order to respond spontaneously to the forces of nature in the light of heaven—that is, in full awareness of the global context.[11] This process involves a forgetting of one's self which is characterized in an enigmatic remark by Lao-tzu to Confucius in a dialogue from the Outer Chapters: "To forget all about things, forget all about Heaven, the name for that is 'forgetfulness of self,' and it is the man forgetful of self who may be said to enter the realm of Heaven" (Chap. 12, *IC* 132).

A corresponding relationship to natural forces—the totality of which Nietzsche sometimes calls "will to power"—is to be found somewhere between the protagonist of *Zarathustra* and the overman, as an existential potentiality of which Zarathustra is the herald. Zarathustra concludes the speech just quoted from with one of several elemental exemplifications: "See, I am a herald of the lightning and a heavy drop from the cloud: but this lightning is called overman" (sec. 4). From the book's first page to its last, both Zarathustra and the overman are closely related to the sun, that major representative of the element of fire, and again in the Prologue the overman is proclaimed to be "the sense of the earth," and also "a sea" (sec. 3). In the chapter "Before Sunrise," Zarathustra addresses a lyrical eulogy to the heavens, speaking to the sky as a close relative, in intimate terms; and by the time of the later section "At Midday," the relation is made even closer through the pristine image of his soul as a drop of condensation from the sky.

> When will you drink this drop of dew, which fell upon all earthly things—when will you drink this wonderful soul—
>
> —when, you well of eternity! you serene and ghastly midday-abyss! when will you drink my soul back into you (IV, 10)?

Other meteorological phenomena with which Zarathustra is identified are clouds and storms—"Too great was the tension of my cloud: from laughing lightning I want to hurl showers of hail into the depths" (II, 1); winds from both directions—"I am a north wind to ripe figs" (II, 2), and "They hear only my winter-storms whistling: and *not* that I also travel over warm seas, like yearning, heavy, hot south winds" (III, 6); as well as seasons, and light itself (II, 6, 8).

One of the primary images for psychological mutability in the early Taoist texts is water, an element that forms a major stream of imagery in *Zarathustra* for the transformation of the ego-centered person into the overman.[12] Zarathustra's love for his fellow humans has filled his soul to overflowing during his prolonged period of solitude on the mountaintop.

> Mouth have I become through and through, and the roaring of a stream out of high rocks: I want to plunge my speech down into the valleys. . . .

> There is indeed a lake within me, hermit-like and self-sufficient; but the river of my love carries it away with it—down to the sea (II, 1)!

Moving up the scale of organic complexity we come to vegetation, a realm from which much Taoist imagery is drawn—presumably, because the growth of plants unfolds spontaneously from within, they are nurtured through the roots from the cool, damp, *yin* forces of the earth, and the careful cultivation of them is a paradigm example of that central, non-interfering *modus operandi* of Taoism: *wu-wei*. The practice of agriculture is a particularly good exemplification of being a "helper of Heaven" (*Chuang-tzu* 19; *IC* 182), insofar as the good farmer responds to the progression of the seasons by the appropriate activities so as to help his plants attain their full fruition. "Returning to the root" is a central image in the *Lao-tzu*, and it figures prominently in the Outer Chapters of the *Chuang-tzu* as well.

While vegetal imagery runs through all Nietzsche's works, it is particularly luxuriant in *Zarathustra*. The seeds for this branch of metaphors are sown in the Prologue (sec. 5), when Zarathustra says:

> It is time for the human being to plant the seed of his highest hope.

> His soil is still rich enough for it. But his soil will become poor and tame and no high tree will be able to grow from it.

Roots figure in one of the book's most telling psychological images, which has distinctly Taoist overtones. Zarathustra says to the youth by the tree on the mountainside:

> . . . it is the same with the human being as with the tree.

> The more he aspires to the height and light, the more strongly his roots strive earthwards, downwards, into the dark, the depths—into evil (I, 8).

To ignore this law of psychospiritual development would be to try, in the words of *Chuang-tzu,* "to take Heaven as your authority and do without earth" (Chap. 17; *IC* 147), and to run the risk of having the tree of life and soul topple over owing to an overly shallow root structure.

Just as all the talk about the advantageous uselessness of gnarled and knotty trees in *Chuang-tzu* is to be applied to the analogous uselessness of the sage and of Chuang-tzu's own words, so Zarathustra is himself closely identified with the arboreal. "I am indeed a forest and a night of dark trees," he says, "but whoever is not afraid of my darkness will find rose-bushes beneath my cypresses"; and later one of the retired kings likens him to a magnificent pine.[13] "Among all that owe their destiny to the earth, only the pine and the cypress are due on course," Chuang-tzu has Confucius say (Chap. 5; *IC* 77). A major reason for Zarathustra's taking so long to proclaim the book's central idea, the thought of eternal recurrence, is that he himself has to go through a lengthy process of ripening. Although he says to his followers fairly early, "like [ripe] figs these teachings fall to you, my friends" (II, 2), it is not until the beginning of Part IV that he is able to say to his animals: "What is happening to me is what happens to all fruits that become ripe. There is *honey* in my veins, which makes by blood thicker and also my soul stiller" (IV, 1). After all the agricultural imagery, it is not surprising that Zarathustra's offspring, his "children," turn out to be—as the "living plantation of [his] thoughts"—trees.

> My children are still verdant in their first spring, standing close together and shaken by the same winds, the trees of my garden and my best soil. . . .

> But some day I want to dig them up and plant each one on his own, so that he may learn solitude and defiance and foresight.

> Gnarled and crooked and with pliant hardness he shall then stand by the sea, a living lighthouse of invincible life (III, 3).

The Taoists would appreciate that the ithyphallic nature of Zarathustra's tree has to do only with its being a manifestation of light, a *Leuchtturm* or "light-tower"; the primary image is of Zarathustra's thought-children as "gnarled and crooked" rather than singularly upright—and with a "pliant hardness" to match the most striking of Taoists oxymorons.

Figs and honey are associated particularly with Dionysus, a God of vegetation in general, and it is he who informs the most lyrical development of the vegetal imagery in *Zarathustra*. Just as we speak of the Chinese tradition of "self-cultivation," and the Taoists talk in particular of nourishing and cultivating *te,* that potentiality in an animate being which comes from heaven, so Zarathustra tends and cultivates his soul, now imagined as a vine.

> Oh my soul, I gave your soil all my wisdom to drink, all new wines and also all unthinkably old and strong wines of wisdom.

> Oh my soul, I poured every sun upon you and every night and every silence and every yearning:—then you grew up for me like a vine.

> Oh my soul, overrich and heavy you stand there now, a vine with swelling udders and crowded brown gold-grapes:—
> . . . you would rather, oh my soul, smile than pour out your suffering.

> —to pour out in torrential tears all your suffering over your fullness and over all the vine's urge for the vintager and his vine-knife (III, 14)!

This magnificently bizarre imagery furthers the parallel but also marks a point at which Nietzsche begins to diverge from the Taoist way: while Chuang-tzu counts as unfortunate the trees that because of their usefulness as lumber are felled before their prime, Nietzsche—in a trope of quite unabashed anthropomorphism—imagines the vine in its ripeness as *lusting* after the vintager's knife, likening its pain at its overfullness to that of a cow's needing to be milked. It is difficult to imagine Chuang-tzu's speaking of a tree's "urge" to be made into a bell-stand by a master woodworker (Chap. 19; *IC* 135)—though he would surely have allowed that the vine and wine are special cases. But this excess on the part of Nietzsche may be what brings him into a more vital participation in the natural world than that of his Taoist counterparts.

Zarathustra's grafting of the mammalian metaphor of the cow's udders on to the vegetal imagery of the vine leads us to the next level of biological complexity: the animal realm. Having discussed several aspects of the animal imagery in *Zarathustra* and *Chuang-tzu* elsewhere,[14] I shall make the treatment here correspondingly short. The primary function of the numerous animal anecdotes in *Chuang-tzu* is to help shift the reader from the anthropocentric standpoint, through invitations to adopt the perspectives of a variety of animals. The best known examples of this are the story of Chuang-tzu's dreaming he was a butterfly (or vice versa), and his exchange with Hui Shih about the joy of the minnows in the stream.[15] Images of animals are also used in describing the ways in which an accomplished Taoist understands death as simply the next in the endless series of transformations that make up the way. When Master Yü succumbs to a disfiguring illness that is clearly about to become fatal, he and his friends wonder what the maker of things is going to transform him into next—a cock, a horse, a rat's liver, or a fly's leg (Chap. 6; *IC* 88).

At a somewhat more figurative level, Zarathustra in his first speech imagines the "Three Transformations of the Spirit" as a camel, a lion, and a child—this final transformation (a reappropriation of the natural) being characterized as "innocence and forgetting, a new beginning, a play" (I, 1). The text of *Zarathustra* contains more animals—over seventy different species are mentioned by name—than any work of Western philosophy since Aristotle's magnificent zoological treatises. Most of these fauna figure in tropes of metaphor or simile, but a significant feature of the narrative content is that Zarathustra's closest companions are his eagle and serpent. For Nietzsche, the basic human drives (*Triebe*) are thought of as perspectives and also imagined as animals (snakes, beasts of prey, etc.). But the importance of being able to adopt the perspective of animals pertains to the "higher" faculties as well: in addition to the chthonic wisdom of the serpent, Zarathustra's "wild wisdom" takes the form of a lioness (II, 1); and he wants his words to tear open the ground of his listeners' souls "like the boar's snout" (II, 5). He speaks of himself as having the legs of a horse and the stomach of an eagle (III, 11); and the more he practices the art of flying—a favorite sport of the Taoist adept—the more he comes to rely on "bird-wisdom" (III, 16).

As a verse from the Outer Chapters of *Chuang-tzu* puts it:

Without praises, without curses,
Now a dragon, now a snake,
You transform together with the times,
And never consent to be one thing alone.

(Chap. 20; *IC* 121)

III

Having seen the extent to which Nietzsche and the Taoists advocate a regaining of our participation in the continuum of natural phenomena extending from the basic elements through the vegetal to the animal realm, let us conclude by delineating in greater detail the nature of this recommended relationship. Both parties have been misunderstood to be calling for a simple return to a primordial and unreflective participation in the natural world, a regression to the primitive innocence of childhood, in which one is merely carried along by the flux of change and driven only by raw impulse and desire. But if we are not simply being advised to "go with the flow," to grow like plants or behave like animals, then what *is* the force of the injunctions to participate in natural phenomena? Let us approach this question indirectly, by way of remarking on a phase in Nietzsche's thought during which his denigration of participation makes him appear to veer away from the path that runs parallel to the Taoist way.

In *The Birth of Tragedy,* a Dionysiac union of the self with nature and the primordial ground of all things is understood as an experience that embodies the most profound truth of which human beings are capable—and a deeper wisdom than that afforded by cool and clear Apollinian detachment from the world according to the *principium individuationis.* Poetic imagination is said to allow empathetic identification with beings of all kinds and to afford deep insight into their nature. "On Truth and Lie" (from the following year) fills out this idea through speaking of the formation of images and metaphors as "the fundamental human drive," asserting the importance of "the mass of images that streams forth originally from the primal faculty of human phantasy like a fiery liquid," and affirming the human being as "an *artistically creating* subject." The imagination is here (as it was for the German Idealists) the realm that mediates between inner and outer, subject and object, human and nature; not merely one faculty among others but "a freely creating and freely inventing intermediate-sphere and mediating force." Thanks to the work and play of such primordial imagination, "trees can speak as nymphs," as they did to the ancient Greeks, and so "at every moment anything is—as in a dream—possible, and the whole of nature swarms around human beings as if it were a masquerade of gods." So far, we are not far removed from the panpsychism of *Chuang-tzu* and associated notions; but during the following few years, Nietzsche's "positivist" leanings draw him away from that kind of world view.

Beginning with *Human, All-too-human,* he tends to denigrate original participation in nature as primitive "animism," and to see it not as an interfusion of subject and object through the medium of primordial imagination, but rather as a projection of human psychology on to the inanimate world.[16] This tendency persists until *Dawn,* where an aphorism entitled "Good and evil nature" begins: "First human beings projected themselves imaginatively into nature: everywhere they saw themselves and things like them, their bad and capricious dispositions, hidden in clouds, thunderstorms, beasts of prey, trees and plants: at that time they invented 'evil nature' " (*Dawn* 17). Before and after this phase in his thinking Nietzsche emphasized the primacy of the *between* (what Heidegger would later explicitly call *das Zwischen*), the field in which the interplay of nature and human nature is played out.

By the time of *The Gay Science*, however, Nietzsche again acknowledges the operations of an all-pervasive phantasy-activity that is archaic and impersonal, and which conditions all experience. He challenges the "realists": "That mountain there! That cloud! What is 'real' about that? Withdraw from it the phantasm and the whole human contribution, you sober ones! Yes, if only you could! The withdrawal is hard because the projection is voluntary, not willed, and has behind it the pressure of many generations. If only you could forget your heritage, your past, your previous education— your entire humanity and animality!"[17] The point—to which Chuang-tzu also subscribes—is that not only does the external environment exert an effect on the natural world within, on the moon and trees and butterflies and fishes of dreams and the imagination, but this inner nature just as much—and more primordially—conditions our apprehension of the external environment. We are here back on the middle ground of Nietzsche's early works, and the paradoxical idea that we live in the midst of the imagination—as an *oikos* with its own peculiar ecology—as much as the imagination is a vital power within us.

"Unutterably vast, the Heaven within him," writes Chuang-tzu (Chap. 5; *IC* 82). This is also nature as imagined in the Neoplatonic tradition, as a realm of the last reaches of emanation from the world soul, which rises up both within and outside the individual. It is the nature-imbued soul of *Zarathustra*:

> the most comprehensive soul, which can run and roam and wander astray the farthest within itself . . .

> the one that loves itself the most, in which all things have their flowing and counterflow, and ebb and flood . . . (III, 12).

But to realize oneself as this kind of non-encapsulated soul requires not only a breaking away from an unconscious immersion in the flux of phenomena and a seeing through of the anthropomorphic and religious projections that have vitiated our apprehension of the natural world, but also an all-embracing reintegration with it. "When shall we have completely de-deified nature!" asks Nietzsche; "When shall we be able to start to naturalize ourselves with pure, new-found, newly redeemed nature!" (*GS* 109). The task is to naturalize ourselves—but only after we have seen nature in "the light of heaven" (as Chuang-tzu would say) rather than illumined by our own projections. Because this clarified nature is terrifying in its amorality, to engage it demands courage. As Nietzsche writes in one of his last remarks on the issue, in *Twilight of the Idols,* "I too speak of a 'return to nature' though it is not actually a going back but rather a *coming up*—up into a high, free, even terrible nature and naturalness" (IX, 48).

Here is another difference between Nietzsche and Lao-Chuang, in whom the element of terror is absent and whose equanimity is undisturbed by the consideration that "Heaven and earth are ruthless/amoral" (*Lao-tzu* 5), and that "Heaven is impartial to everything it covers" (*Chuang-tzu* 6; *IC* 93). The disparity presumably stems from differences in the historical contexts: Nietzsche is more extreme than the Taoists because he has the pressure of a longer historical tradition behind him, or—as he likes to put it—because "the tension of the bow" has become much greater in his culture. The peculiarity of our modern historical situation is felt and voiced by Nietzsche in biological terms: In contrast to the relatively homogeneous societies the early Taoists were addressing, Nietzsche's readers—as end-of-the-century Europeans—bore (and bear) "the inheritance of a multifaceted descent in their bodies . . . contradictory and often not only contradictory drives and value-standards which fight among each other and seldom give each other peace . . ." (*BGE* 200). And just as nature, for the Taoists, lapses from its impartiality and "punishes" by shackling a person with the fetters of morality (*Chuang-tzu* 5; *IC* 79), for Nietzsche it is "the 'nature' in [every morality] which . . . implants the necessity of limited horizons . . . which *teaches the narrowing of perspectives* . . . as a condition of life and growth" (*BGE* 188).

The Taoists inherited from the Confucian tradition the idea of the "three spheres" of heaven, earth, and the human, which are intimately interfused with each other. A consideration of the relationship between heaven and the human in *Chuang-tzu* reveals that there is a movement of reintegration parallel to the one we saw in Nietzsche, though the terms in which it is described are different. A typical dictum from the *Chuang-tzu* is: "Don't let man extinguish heaven, / Don't let deliberation extinguish destiny" (Chap. 17; *IC* 149). Here is the central Taoist distinction between two aspects of our being: destiny—that portion of our activities and abilities that lies outside the will, our spontaneous nature; and deliberation—our voluntarily developed and guided powers of conscious reasoning. It is significant that we have to acknowledge the contemporary Japanese philosopher Keiji Nishitani, who has looked at Nietzsche from the perspective of Zen, for pointing up the presence of two comparable ideas in Nietzsche's thought by emphasizing the importance of his idea of *amor fati* and the enterprise of integrating *ego* with *fatum*.[18] To be able to distinguish between the two, and keep the former from encroaching upon the latter, is to be well on the way. "To know what is Heaven's doing and what is man's is the utmost in knowledge. Whoever knows what Heaven does lives the life generated by Heaven" (*Chuang-tzu* 6; *IC* 84).

We encountered earlier in *Chuang-tzu* the notion of forgetting even heaven (which has a significant parallel in the Mahayana Buddhist injunction not to hold fast to the experience of *śūnyatā*). The more surprising remark that "the perfect man hates Heaven" (Chap. 23; *IC* 106), points up the paradoxical nature of the relationship between heaven and the human. An essay at the beginning of one of the Outer Chapters, which explains the often repeated phrase "the essentials of our nature and destiny," describes the process by which one detaches oneself from the world and then, by "renewing life," becomes "one with Heaven" and "returns to become the helper of Heaven" (*Chuang-tzu* 19; *IC* 182). This idea, which succinctly sums up the Taoist project of a separation from the primal oneness with nature together with a reintegration informed by the broader perspective achieved thereby, is also found in the *Lao-tzu* where the sage is said to "Learn to be without learning . . . in order to help the myriad creatures to be natural . . ." (64). The human being's "natural" inclination to diverge from its true nature can, if informed by a more comprehensive understanding of the ways of the natural world, be turned to the advantage of all beings.

Again, however, there is a difference in emphasis between Nietzsche and Lao-Chuang. It is true that some of Nietzsche's ideas are impressively serene: there is a distinctly Taoist tone to Zarathustra's saying, for instance, that "All things are baptised in the well of eternity and are beyond good and evil," and to his blessing them by "standing over each individual thing as its own heaven, its round roof, its azure bell and eternal security" (III, 4). Nevertheless, the way to such serenity appears more difficult in Nietzsche, and full of passion and suffering. In the realm of self-cultivation the discrepancy is brought out by Nietzsche's fondness for the word *Zucht* in this context. The word refers both to the cultivation of plants and to the breeding, or rearing, of animals, and when applied to humans it has the connotation of discipline, or training. In agriculture of the soul, one has to be not only the plants which grow but also the farmer who tends them. "Woe to the thinker who is not the gardener but only the ground of what grows in him" (*Dawn* 382)! And in rearing the inner animals, one must be wary of confusing the discipline of breeding (*Züchtung*) with taming (*Zähmung*): the beasts of burden and prey can be trained and their forces harmonized with the others in such a way that their power is not lost but is retained.[19]

However, along with the creatures comes the creator—and it is at this point that the metaphor of the artist supervenes upon that of the cultivator/breeder. In speaking of "the discipline of *great* suffering," Nietzsche distinguishes between the "material, fragments, superfluity, dirt, nonsense, chaos" that we are and the "creator [and] hammer-hardness" within, and suggests that the former must be "formed, broken, forged, torn, burned, annealed, refined" by the latter (*BGE* 225). If this seems a far cry from the *Lao-tzu*'s exhortations to "return to being the uncarved block," we must remember that this image for the reductive and subtractive aspects of the Taoist project is deceptively simple. The paring away of the accretions of conceptual thinking is a long and arduous process, and the natural ease of

Taoist spontaneity strangely difficult to attain. "Wherever desires and cravings are deep," says Chuang-tzu, "the impulse which is from Heaven is shallow" (Chap. 6; *IC* 84). The detachment from and reduction of egocentric desires which afford an openness to the profounder impulses from nature, appear to lead to this goal by way of a certain *apatheia*. Nietzsche diverges here, insofar as he wants to exploit the tyrannical tendency of the natural drives by strengthening them and turning them against each other, and to push the strictures of morality (and all other "anti-natural" regimens) to the farthest extreme—at which limit a conversion comes about through which they overcome themselves.[20] Given harder material to work on than the Taoists, Nietzsche's task is more intense and his imagery for it wilder and often alchemically tinged, suggesting more of an *opus contra naturam* in order to effect the transformation and translation of our selves into renatured nature.

In the end, however, both sides are trying to understand that enigmatic relation, human/nature, and to bridge—without closing it—the chasm that joins the moments.

On Seeking a Change of Environment

David L. Hall

I

Philosophers, those individuals most likely to be credited with (or blamed for) upholding the importance of thinking for its own sake, are often accused of succumbing too readily to a crisis mentality. Something significant is always coming to an end or collapsing, or is in need of renewal; philosophers are often urging us to move beyond this or that limited vision or are goading us into taking part in the latest in a series of conceptual revolutions. Carried to the extremes of a continual celebration of global or cosmological disaster, philosophers are justifiably mocked for overly zealous reportage, but, upon reflection, what sensible human being would not realize that "of course" philosophers are crisis-thinkers. For thought itself is born of crisis. And important thinking presupposes important crises.

History tells of the emergence of ideas from actions which serve not only to interpret these activities, but to elicit novel practices as well. In the beginning, these are blind practices initiated by the compulsive character of brute circumstance. Subsequently, they can be the informed practices of reasoning individuals. In the Anglo-European tradition, the dialectical movement from the particularity of human actions to the theoretical sphere which serves to interpret these actions and back again to the world of concrete praxis abetted by tools of theoretical interpretation provides the dynamic context in which thinking may be said to take place.

The separation of *theoria* and *praxis* lies at the root of both the greatness and the weakness of our tradition. For not only may alternative practices lead to conflict, but theoretical interpretations divorced from their experiential ground may war with one another as well. And most debilitating is the manner in which individuals and societies exploit theoretical norms to mask practices which in no wise are justified by these norms.

There is a crisis with respect to some philosophic subject matter when the sense of theoretical and practical disjunction is raised to the level of consciousness. This disjunction may receive threefold expression: as the disjunction of alternative practices in relative independence of ideological justifications of such practices; as the disjunction of theory and the practices which that theory is meant to interpret; and as the conflicts of theory with theory in relative detachment from the sphere of public praxis to which they are putatively relevant.

In the face of such crises, the philosopher, as thinker, seeks to bring a renewal of harmonious and productive interactions among alternative practices, between theory and practice, and among alternative theoretical interpretations. This kind of thinking cannot be identified with the implementation or elaboration of ideas or principles, but with the discovery of novel principles or exceptions to established principles. Such discoveries are born out of the "on the contrary" or "on the other hand" mode of thought.

Thinking, then, entails the search for novel evidences. At the level of philosophic thinking, there are three, perhaps four, principal sources of such evidences. First, there is the private psychological field of the thinker highlighted by the contrast between his own reflective life and the weightiest norms of the sphere of public theoria and praxis. If, as surely must be so, every individual is more complex than the society to which he or she belongs, then the private reflective sphere is an important source for novel evidence. Second, there is *original* culture—the origins of one's tradition. Here one discovers the seeds and scraps of one's cultural milieu—that is, the unsown seeds and discarded scraps of one's tradition. Third, there are the cultural traditions alternative to one's own, traditions in which what one has uncovered as seeds or scraps in one's indigenous culture may be encountered as fully articulated ideas and practices.

The fourth source of evidence is rather odd: it is the future entertained with respect to the plausibility of realizing one's novel reflections. A crisis is a turning point which invites a novel future. But the future is not passive to just any set of possibilities; by turning to the future one hopes to assess the sort of matrix of possibilities it might be seen to constitute with respect to one's novel proposals.

The future may be the relatively immediate future of this or that particular social grouping, or the long-range future of the entire human species on the surface of this planet, or, as in the case of the ecological sciences in their most general forms, the future of the entire cosmological context.

The purpose of these introductory remarks may now be made clear. The attempt to demonstrate the importance of Oriental resources for the articulation of questions, issues, and proposals in environmental ethics involves the philosopher in demonstrating that (1) the subject of environmental ethics and the sphere of its applicability are characterized by significant crises and thus can be made the subject matter of philosophic thinking; and (2) the resort to alternative cultures is an important element in the attempt to resolve certain of these crises.

I believe that I have indicated the means whereby I would hold comparative philosophy of culture to be such a responsible exercise, since, as I have conceived the meaning of thinking, such recourse is always at least implicit in any exercise of responsible thought. Characterizing the specific nature of the crises which qualify the discipline of ecological ethics will require further discussion.

My strategy in this essay will be as follows: I shall attempt to characterize one important element in the contemporary crisis of ethics and moral theory. I will suggest that this crisis is in fact but a specific expression of the crisis in philosophy itself; then I will claim that the healthiest response to the crisis in philosophy is to look at alternative meanings of order, with respect to which one might characterize the world that philosophers investigate and the means that they possess to investigate it. Such a response will in fact permit an interpretation of the notion of "environment" that can serve to stimulate responsibly novel reflections upon questions of environmental ethics. Finally, I will have recourse to the Taoism of classical China as a means of elaborating the novel sense of order and of indicating that these relatively novel reflections are not simply ad hoc elaborations of justly ignored concepts from our own tradition, but have in fact possessed a fully articulated presence in at least one other cultural matrix.

The arguments and proposals of this essay derive from the employment of the culturalogical method outlined above, but I will not rehearse the auto-biographical elements that led to these reflections, nor will I in the context of these pages attempt to assess the viability of these proposals by recourse to a characterization of the effective future of Anglo-European culture.[1]

II

Reason and rationality are, in both their positive and negative senses, crucial to the vast majority of ethical projects carried out within contemporary culture. Presently, the notion of rationality is under attack both within and outside the philosophic community. So the viability of ethical reflection is called into question. But if reason is under attack, then the very notion of philosophy as a rational enterprise is likewise assaulted. This attack may, therefore, be characterized with respect both to ethics and to the general activity of philosophy itself.

One way of highlighting the crisis character of ethical reflection is to recall the significance for contemporary ethics of Kant's attempt to construct a rational moral theory. Kant's project was to make ethics self-referentially secure by eschewing a foundation in concepts of human nature and attempting to ground ethical deliberations and actions upon the nature of rationality itself. He sought thus to discipline ethics in accordance with the demands of rational thought by deriving ethical principles from the very meaning of what one might be able to recognize as a universalizable statement concerning human conduct. Thus, if one is to be rational, one must be ethical in the manner dictated by the categorical imperative and the presuppositions of God, Freedom, and Immortality.

Alternatives to the rationalist approach have sorted themselves out into two types of view: one which would ground ethical action in the passions, and the other in the will's ability to decide. Hume's project, against which Kant took his stand, was the former; Kierkegaard's philosophy, developed in response to the excessively rational vision of Hegel, exemplifies the latter. The discovery of the foundation and context of ethical activity in either the reason, the passions, or the will harks back to the original Platonic and Aristotelian articulations of the psyche in terms of its tripartite structure and functioning.

The other salient contrast among modern ethical theories is that of theories explicitly based upon concepts of human nature and those grounded in the analyses of reason, passion, or willful choice, which claim to be dissociated from concepts of the meaning of being human. Hume and Kierkegaard, less so than Kant, may be viewed as dealing with notions of human nature in their reflections, but the subsequent history of ethics well illustrates that ethical theories can easily give rise to an analysis of, for example, "the logic of belief" or of "the conditions of choice"—analyses which make the pretense of divorcing emotivist and volitional theories from the meaning of being human.

Such theories cannot altogether succeed in separating the modalities of passion and volition from rationality, however, for attempts to provide a logic of belief or the conditions of choice require rational argument, if only in the negative sense. One has but to take a look at Kierkegaard's *Either/Or* to see how important is the status of rational argument in the analysis of ethical and aesthetic lives, the choice between which is not itself rational. C. L. Stevenson's *Ethics and Language* is a paradigm of rational argument employed to establish a negative conclusion with respect to reason-based ethics, namely, that ethical propositions are not rational but are expressions of idiosyncratic preference.

Even Hume, who asserted that "reason is and always shall be a slave of the passions," held the strongest passion to be that of "belief." And the belief in the canons of reasonableness serves as a principal ground of consensual understandings for Hume. Thus, Hume allows "reasonable" discourse at the level of consensual understanding to proceed in accordance with rules and principles.

The situation with regard to ethics is complicated by the fact that one can, of course, deny the Kantian project of grounding ethics in rational principles and still affirm the effectiveness of rationality in other spheres. Unlike the extremes of Hume and Kierkegaard, therefore, some emotivists, and even certain volitional ethicists, maintain a sphere of effective rationality which permits reason to be employed in other than simply a negative sense. In such cases, the status of reason and rationality is maintained, and ethics is made into an arbitrary, often inconsequential, aspect of intellectual culture.

Thus, in contemporary culture, those who assault reason per se level serious criticisms not only at rational ethics but at the reasonable articulation and contextualization of ethical theories grounded in the passions or the will. The Freudo-Marxian thinkers associated with the Frankfort school, for example, find that reason has from the beginning served only as a technique of domination and control. The post-structuralists and deconstructionists hold the project of rational thinking to be a self-referentially inconsistent attempt to create a language of presence where no such language is possible.

Ethicists and social philosophers of the more constructive variety have been forced continually to reduce the sphere of presumed applicability of their principles and theories to increasingly more exclusive contexts. Claims have been made on behalf of certain minorities that intelligence and reasoning ability are class- and status-based concepts that effectively exclude non-mainstream individuals from adequate assessment and evaluation. Feminists have made the claim that ethical and political norms—along with the norms of science, literature, and literary criticism—have been derived in fact from a seriously truncated understanding of the meaning of human nature, one defined solely in terms of the white, male Anglo-European.

The significant challenge of the critiques of reason is that they identify the character of rationality with means-oriented, exploitative thinking. Such thinking, of course, is associated with and receives its fullest elaboration with respect to technological rationalization, the precise phenomenon that is presumed to be the major factor in the degeneration of the environment.

The critiques of rationality are ultimately challenges to the very notion of philosophy, since neither the emotivist nor the volitional approaches to ethics and to philosophy per se have been able to operate in detachment from the criteria of rational discourse in either its positive or its negative senses. Criticisms of rational ethics are, *a fortiori,* criticisms of the philosophical thinking that provides either the logical or the rhetorical ground for such theories.

To characterize our situation in a quasi-Kantian vocabulary: The crisis which serves as the principal stimulus for contemporary ethical reflection is not one which requires that we begin with the construction of yet another metaphysics of morals; rather, in an ironic twist on the Copernican revolution, we must first concern ourselves with the question of the morality of metaphysics as the most general rational science.

The chaos of ethical theories that pattern contemporary intellectual culture is characterized by a dramatic rift between the rhetoric and the reality of ethical reflections. Presumably, modern ethicists have developed theories with respect to two questions: First, should ethics be grounded in a theory of what it means to be human, or rather, in a capacity of the human creature in detachment from any considerations of the norms for realizing such a nature? Second, is it some form of reason, the passions, or the will that should serve as the primary focus of ethical understandings?

It is certainly arguable that all prominent ethical theories which initially emphasize volition or the passions in their conceptualization are nonetheless subject to so-called rational criteria in the elaboration and contextualization of their ethical perspective. It is further defensible to claim that all ethical theories, insofar as they focus upon the psychic elements of reason, passion, or volition, ultimately depend upon conceptions of human nature.

I myself do not find the second conclusion disconcerting. I believe that a viable ethics may well be grounded in an understanding of human nature— that is, in a sense of what it means to be truly human. On the other hand, I do believe that the contemporary crisis with regard to ethical theory requires that we investigate grounds for the characterization of human nature other than those which depend upon the presumed tripartite structure of the psyche.

In what follows I shall attempt to highlight alternative sources for speculations concerning human nature. And though, out of deference to the place from which my thinking perforce must begin, I will attempt to employ rational argumentation to establish my general conclusions, one implication of my remarks will be that a gradual freeing of ourselves from dependency upon such a style of argumentation will follow from the use of these relatively novel resources.

III

If economics is to be known as "the dismal science," perhaps we should dub the discipline of environmental ethics "the sentimental science." For so much of what one reads in that field is rife with romantic excess: there are cloying resorts to the pathetic fallacy, or to a "white man's burden" style of thinking, maudlin rejoinders of the "noblesse oblige" variety, soft-headed invocations of "enlightened self-interest"—all of which are directed against the sort of "my species right or wrong" principle which these sentimental thinkers (rightly, I believe) suspect is at the heart of practically every major theoretical justification for human interactions with the natural world.

And recourse to strict principles of rationality in order to overcome the anthropocentrism that is structured into the vast majority of speculations concerning the relationships of human beings to nature is rare, precisely because most recognize that anthropocentrism is an implication of reason itself and that the attempt to be reasonable is ipso facto an attempt to establish the dominance of the human over the natural order.

Is there, in fact, a way of freeing our manner of articulating and communicating with our environs from its dependence upon rationality? Is it possible to provide a sense of what it means to be human which does not involve anthropocentric claims with respect to the relation of human beings to nature?

My assumption is that a novel conception of human nature would involve a reconstitution of the meaning of philosophic thinking such as is not determined by the demands of abstract rationality or, for that matter, those of the passions or volitional activity. Such a task involves a critique of philosophic thinking at its most general level, which is to say at the level of metaphysics as, presumably, the most general science of order.

Western philosophic speculation emerged from a cultural context that included at its very beginnings two problematics with respect to the question of cosmological order.[2] The first problematic was that which allowed for the possibility of many world orders. This problematic is associable with the thought of Leucippus and Democritus, among others. Its primary contemporary spokesman is A. N. Whitehead, whose doctrines of the immanence of law and of "cosmic epochs" (contexts within which general laws of nature may be presumed relatively stable but between and among which there may obtain vastly different types of order) promote the notion of a plurality of world orders. The second problematic is that which dominates and has dominated the history of philosophic and scientific cosmology. It is the view that there is only one world order whose laws are relatively stable from the "beginning" to the "end" of the order. On this view, if there is to be a renewal of the world, it will be more or less a repetition of the original ordering of things.

The contrast between first and second problematic thinking is in fact a contrast between distinctive concepts of order, which I have elsewhere discussed as a contrast between "aesthetic" and "rational" order.[3] Rational order is that sort of ordering which instantiates or realizes a presupposed structure or pattern. This sort of order is broadly quantitative and mathematical in the sense that the elements signaling the order are replaceable, substitutable. Aesthetic order is composed of irreplaceable elements. The elements of a given order are thus more than mere place holders, as, for example, are the physical elements, which may configure geometrical lines, planes, and solids. Aesthetic ordering, at its extreme, is a consequence of certain specific particulars and no others. Rational ordering is such as to be realizable by recourse to an indefinite number of elements.

Reason and rationality are notions which presuppose both the second problematic—that is, a single-world vision—and the indefinite substitutability of the elements composing such a world. It is a simple enough feat to demonstrate that rational ordering is an anthropocentric notion, for the physiological, linguistic, and conceptual uniformities defining the human species determine in advance the sorts of ordering that will be anticipated with respect to one's understanding of the natural world. The sorts of beings we presume ourselves to be define the sorts of orders we may recognize and deem important. Alternative orders are considered unknowable, since to know an order would be to be able to anticipate its patterned regularities, to recognize its realized uniformities, and to establish plausible grounds for causal sequences among the elements serving to instantiate those uniformities.

Aesthetic ordering, on the other hand, presupposes an alternative method of knowing—one which has as yet received little elaboration in our tradition. An order in which the ordering elements are insistently unique particulars cannot be discussed in terms of pattern concepts defining regularities or uniformities. Even the normal form of metaphors which serve to extend the meaning of a literal term are of little use in characterizing such orders. In fact, one of the main burdens of contemporary speculative philosophy has been to search for a new language for philosophy which can accommodate aesthetic understandings.[4]

The requirements for philosophic thinking grounded upon notions of aesthetic order are the following:

1. A cosmological theory which entails the denial of any privileged perspective—divine, human, material, or ideal. Such a theory would constitute a form of cosmological perspectivism.
2. A method of characterizing actions which neither give rise to nor are grounded upon principles of the sort that are associable with reason and reasonings.
3. A theory of language as "nonreferential" in the sense that denotative reference is avoided. Such a theory would permit a consistent denial of any inventory of objects which could be claimed to exist apart from some construing perspective.

In this essay I shall treat only the first two of these criteria.[5]

Questions of ecological ethics from an aesthetic perspective would revolve about a sense of the natural environment which would be passive to any number of alternative construals. Those things which would survive, the sorts of pattern regularities that would be promoted by one's decisions and actions, would be functions of the recognition that every element constituting the totality of things lays a claim upon that totality since it constitutes a focus of construal.

It would appear that ecological ethics as a general science of the manner in which organisms and environment(s) interact would be well-nigh impossible without some ordering principle which established hierarchies in terms of the presumed value of one being or set or species of beings vis-à-vis others. It might simply be that we ought to own up to the fact that ethics is a rationalization of the means or rules promoting survival of the human species or some economically or politically privileged portion of that species, and that such an anthropocentric science, apart from a whole series of argumentative supports which are seldom forthcoming, is wholly arbitrary.

Apart from an anthropocentric perspective, or the disguised anthropocentrism of a theologically grounded ethics, where shall we look for a normative standard for ethical theory? The heritage of Second Problematic Thinking urges us to think in terms of a single-ordered world, and such a world requires a single ordering principle. In the world of the philosopher F. P. Ramsey, "The foreground is occupied by human beings and the stars are all as small as threepenny bits." Such a vision hardly gives the stars their due. On the other hand, proponents of a single-ordered world are forced to believe that a perspective upon the world that would treat the stars equitably would be no improvement, since it would relegate the human being to a position of relative insignificance.

The question arises how one might go about exploiting the understanding of the World as a complex of orders construed from the perspective of each being in the totality of beings. In itself, the notion of such a many-ordered totality sounds silly and unproductively bizarre. Apart from any other evidence, we can only believe that such a suggestion is a mere ad hoc resolution of a presumed conceptual problem. Certainly the history of philosophy illustrates quite a number of such ad hoc resolutions.[6]

It is at this point that the resort to comparative philosophic speculations is helpful, for it is possible to discover in the thought of the classical Chinese, particularly in philosophical Taoism, a tradition of reflection which permits the articulation of certain of the stranger implications of the first problematic thinking. As I indicated above, there will be no assessment in this context of the practical viability of these Taoist proposals within our own culture.[7] Let it suffice to say here that, as Unamuno has insisted, "the fact that the consequences of a proposition are catastrophic cannot be said to count against its truthfulness."

IV

The Taoist concepts most pertinent to the development of an altered sense of human nature and of nature per se are the following: *tao, te, tzu-jan, wu-chih, wu-wei,* and *wu-yü.*

In the *Tao Te Ching,* there is a characterization of *tao* as both nameless and namable. I have construed this notion in the following way: *Tao* per se is the total process of becoming, Becoming-Itself. Nameless and namable *tao* are the *That Which.* That which *is* and that which *is not* are the polar elements of Becoming-Itself. The fundamental truth of the *tao* is contained in the proposition: Only becoming (coming into being which illustrates some mixture of being and nonbeing) is; not-becoming (either being or nonbeing abstracted from its polar relationship with its opposite) is not.

This interpretation of *tao* makes of it a totality not in the sense of a single-ordered cosmos, but rather in the sense of the sum of all possible orders. Any given order is an existing world that is construed from the perspective of a particular element of the totality. But as a single world it is an abstraction from the totality of possible orders.

Each particular element in the totality has its own *te.* The notion of *te* may be understood as the particular focus or intrinsic excellence of a thing. The *te* of an element serves as the means in accordance with which it construes the totality of things from its perspective and thus "names" and creates a world.

The concepts of *tao* and *te* form a single notion, *tao-te,* which is best understood in terms of the relationship of field (*tao*) and focus (*te*). By recourse to the model of a holograph, one may get some notion of the relationship of *tao* and *te.* In a holographic display, each element contains the whole in an adumbrated form; so each thing in accordance with its *te* contains the totality; the particular focus of an item establishes its world, its environment. In addition, the totality as sum of all possible orders is adumbrated by each item.

Given the *tao-te* structure as so conceived, it is possible to understand the manner in which the concepts of *wu-chih, we-wei, and wu-yü* function. *Wu-chih* means "no-knowledge"; it is best understood, I believe, as "unprincipled knowing," the sort of knowing that does not have recourse to principles as external, determining sources of order. *Wu-chih* involves knowing the *te* of a thing rather than knowing that thing in relation to some classifactory concept—as an instance of a universal, or a member of a class. Ultimately *wu-chih* permits a grasp of the *tao-te* relationship of each encountered item and permits, therefore, an understanding of the world construed from the particular focus (*te*) of that item.

Wu-wei, or "nonassertive action," is action in accordance with unprincipled knowing, acting in such a way as to take up, or at least to appreciate, the particular perspective of a thing. Such actions must be spontaneous (*tzu-jan*), which is to say that they must not be mediated by rules or principles. This simply means that one cannot understand *wu-chih* and *wu-wei* as distinguishable in the same manner as are knowledge and action in the Western senses of those terms.

Wu-yü means something like "the absence of material desires." I would characterize that term as meaning "objectless desire." This seemingly odd locution is justified, I believe, by the fact that neither unprincipled knowing nor nonassertive action can in the strict sense objectify a world or any element in it. The sort of desiring associated with the Taoist sensibility, therefore, must be understood as in the strictest sense "objectless." The claim here is that enjoyments are possible without the demand that one define, possess, or control the occasion of one's enjoyment.

The Taoist "no-soul" doctrine that we have just rehearsed, a doctrine that would apparently negate the knowing, acting, and feeling characteristics of the person, is best conceived on its own terms and not as a dialectical negation of the tripartite psyche of Western philosophical anthropology. The *wu* forms do not simply amount to knowing, doing, and feeling *nothing;* they are modalities of articulating the relationship between an item and its environs which possess rather distinctive meanings.

The understanding of "environment" entailed by the quasi-Taoist vision just adumbrated is one that is radically perspectival. As yet, however, I have suggested no method of deriving ethical considerations from the view. The Taoist totality is "horizontal"—there are no hierarchies built into its ontology. No "great chain of being" or "hierarchy of perfections" exists in the Taoist cosmology. For the development of a viable ethical theory, some "normative" criterion is required.

In the Anglo-European classical tradition, it is the possession of a rational soul that has permitted one to make the greatest normative claims upon one's environment. But what we would understand as rationality the Taoist would see as in conflict with the naturalness and spontaneity that permit a creature to remain congruent with its *te.* In Taoism the norm-bearing quality is, one must believe, *tzu-jan*—self-creativity, spontaneity.

The ethical import of the Taoist sensibility can most likely be discovered in the notion of *tzu-jan.* Were one, contrary to Taoist predilections, to construe a "categorical imperative" from out of the notions just outlined, granting the central role that *tzu-jan* would play in the development of a Taoist ethics, it would likely be something like "Always act with *tzu-jan*"— that is, "Act always in accordance with your *te.*"

One must, however, add something to the preceding, if ethical implications are to be drawn. There must be some sense as to how one would act with respect to others. I would argue that the *tao-te* relationship, understood in terms of a focus-field or holographic model, would require that one's *te,* as the particular focus of the totality, always contain within it adumbrations of the alternative *te* a well. Thus, an implication of the Taoist imperative "Act always in accordance with your *te*" is that one would always in some way take into account the *te* of those one encounters. Another formulation of the imperative, therefore, might be, "Act always in appreciation of the *te* you encounter."

Since this imperative could consistently be formulated as "Act always so as to treat those whom you encounter as ends in themselves and never merely as means," it might be presumed that we have simply reconstructed the Kantian vision from Taoist elements. But, of course, this is not so. The Taoist does not treat merely of the *te* of rational beings, but of all beings — both "animate" and "inanimate." By extending the sense of "environment" such that it is now a nonexclusive context, anthropocentrism is well-nigh eradicated from the vision. But the very comprehensiveness of the vision has also rendered it well-nigh incomprehensible. How does one decide and act when there are no normative measures in accordance with which one can choose this act over that or prefer the welfare of this being over that?

It is certainly true, at least as I read the Taoist philosophy, that the ethical vision is a peculiar one. It does not have as its *sine qua non* the promoting of the continued existence and welfare of the human species on the surface of the planet. Is this, then, truly ethics? Surely it must be. For if a vision that does not place the human species above other sorts of beings is for that reason held not to be an ethical vision at all, then it seems clear to me that ethics per se is nothing more than a case of cosmological special pleading. After all, we can seek truth "though the heavens fall," and we are capable of appreciating the beauty in natural disasters and in the agencies of such disasters. Thus, the values of truth and beauty are not narrowly anthropocentric concepts. At the level of ethical action, must we see "right" and "good" in specifically human terms?

Taoist ethics is in fact a sort of aesthetics in which we are "enjoined" to be spontaneous (*tzu-jan*) — that is, to act (*wu-wei*) in harmony with things by deferring (*wu-chih, wu-wei, wu-yü*) to the intrinsic excellences (*te*) of items encountered and by enjoying acts of deference directed toward us by virtue of the appreciation of our *te.* Such an aesthetic ethics eschews antecedent principles or norms in the same manner that a creative individual would refuse to depend upon past norms for the determination of present actions. Creativity is the spontaneous (*tzu-jan*) production of novelty. There can be no rules for it.

There can, however, be models. We may find in the lives of individuals who are especially sensitive to environment as the nonexclusive, "horizontal" totality of perspectives some sense as to how one might by oneself develop such sensitivities. Such an intuition (*wu-chih*) of relatedness with the environs does not, as is too often the case, have to evoke a sense of cosmic pathos or *noblesse oblige*.

The so-called *philosophia perennis* seems to be a constant of both the Oriental and Western traditions. Taoism is one of its more fascinating expressions. The appeal of this vision is that it compels human beings to stretch themselves beyond their present understanding of themselves and, in place of philosophizing for the sole convenience of the sorts of beings that they conceive themselves to be, to realize that they are not primarily *sorts* of being at all but insistently unique particulars dwelling amidst other insistent beings whose claim upon the environs calls for the appreciation of differential excellences and the initiation and enjoyment of acts of deference that such excellences evoke.

It is unlikely that this sketch of a Taoist perspective upon environmental ethics could seem at all compelling to anyone attached to traditional modes of ethical reflection. Indeed, it is doubtful that traditional ethicists would even grant that this vision qualifies as ethics. There are, nonetheless, two considerations which may recommend this view to some.

Even if the human species does not do itself in by recourse to its rational technologies, it is plausible to assume, given the complexity and variegated inventory of the total environment, that some cosmic or viral incident will extinguish us sooner or later. Those who are concerned with exceedingly long-run considerations (as philosophers well must be) may find the nonanthropocentrism of Taoist ethics appealing and suggestive of some novel strategies for handling their encounters with their ambience.

And if we neither undo ourselves nor are undone, we shall eventually outrun ourselves by virtue of some kind of evolutionary transmogrification. A narrow form of anthropocentrism even here could not serve us well. The fish that, ages past, refused to leave the ocean missed an interesting opportunity. (Doubtless theirs was an ethical decision, aimed at the protection of the species.)

Whatever the perceived value of such considerations, they should at least qualify the appreciation we might feel for the all-too-oft-quoted words from Faulkner's Nobel Prize acceptance speech to the effect that man ought not merely endure, but prevail. For it is from out of this sort of desperate arrogation of privilege that most of what is tawdry about traditional approaches to ethics arises.

Putting the *Te* Back into Taoism

Roger T. Ames

I. Introduction

In this essay, my intention is to interpret and articulate certain insights of Taoist *ars contextualis* as an alternative set of categories for rethinking some of the issues of environmental ethics. Let me begin by trying to make clear why I choose this pretentious neologism rather than the more familiar term, *metaphysics*.

J. Baird Callicott, in a recent article in the *American Philosophical Quarterly,* seeks to distinguish the concerns of environmental ethics from the new and popular field of applied ethics with which it is often confused.

> Environmental ethics may be understood to be but one among several new sorts of applied philosophies, the others of which also arose during the seventies. That is, it may be understood to be an *application* of well-established conventional philosophical categories to emergent practical environmental problems. On the other hand, it may be understood to be an *exploration* of alternative moral and even metaphysical principles, forced upon philosophy by the magnitude and recalcitrance of these problems. If defined in the former way, then the work of environmental ethics is that of a philosophical yeoman or underlaborer (to employ Locke's self appraisal); if defined in the latter way, it is that of a theoretician or philosophical architect (as in Descartes' self-image). If interpreted as an essentially theoretical, not applied discipline, the most important philosophical task for environmental ethics is the development of a non-anthropocentric value theory.[1]

Callicott, in service to what he perceives as the bedrock nature of his task, prefers the "theoretician-architect" persona of Descartes to the "yeoman-underlaborer" image of Locke. But his position here reflects the "pulling-oneself-up-by-one's-own-bootstraps" quandary that environmental ethics might face if it attempts to resolve its issues by appeal to alternative theories sponsored out of the very same philosophical presuppositions that have given rise to these problems.

I argue that our problem in environmental ethics is so basic that it is possible that the approaches of neither a "yeoman" Locke nor even a "theoretician" Descartes will do. We might need to assume a more radical and creative posture such as that of Nietzsche — "*actual philosophers . . . are commanders and law-givers:* they say 'thus it *shall* be!' "[2] — or perhaps even that of the poet Chuang Tzu, beating his drum and interpreting his world one moment as a butterfly flitting about and the next as a turtle dragging his tail in the mud. That is, rather than the *exploration* of an alternative metaphysics or attendant ethical theory, we might need to revision the responsibilities of the philosopher and think in terms other than those of metaphysics. The assumptions entailed in a definition of systematic philosophy that gives us a tradition of metaphysics might demand that the philosopher be a theoretician when the most fruitful approach to the issues of environmental ethics might require that he be the artist.[3]

Taoism does not provide us with metaphysics — a "universal science of first principles." Lao Tzu and Chuang Tzu are both described in the early literature as "finding enjoyment in the ancient 'art' of *tao* (*tao shu*[a])."[4] Proceeding then from art rather than science, it produces an *ars contextualis:* generalizations drawn from human experience in the most basic processes of making a person, making a community, and making a world. This neologism, *ars contextualis,* is an attempt to express the classical Chinese notion of an "aesthetic" cosmology. In contrast to the investigation of the general character of the being of things (*ontologia generalis*) or the articulation of the principles of a universal science (*scientia universalis*), the classical Chinese sensibility presupposes the activity of contextualization in which any particular in its environment is assessed by recourse to its construal of the environment and, alternatively, the contribution made by the environment to the constitution of that specific particular.[5]

Because the complaint we must address is such a fundamental one, let me restate it by citing an alternative formulation of the project of environmental ethics in which these same presuppositions of systematic philosophy are apparent. Po-Keung Ip states:

> I take it that the major task of environmental ethics is the construction of a system of normative guidelines governing man's attitudes, behavior, and action toward his natural environment. The central question to be asked is: how *ought* man, either as an individual or as a group, to behave, to act, toward nature? By *nature* I mean the nonhuman environment man finds himself in. . . . Any viable environmental ethics, it seems to me, should provide adequate answers to three questions: (1) what is the nature of nature? (2) What is man's relationship to nature? (3) How should man relate himself to nature?[6]

It is the basic presuppositions that provoke Ip to define nature as the "nonhuman environment," to assume a subject/object relationship in addressing nature, and to reduce the cultivation of an *ethos* to compliance with a system of "normative guidelines" that reveals the extent to which our problem is embedded in our fundamental philosophic categories. Callicott observes in framing the problematic of environmental ethics that

> historian Lynn White Jr., author of the landmark classic, "The Historical Roots of Our Ecological Crisis," who is followed by historian J. Donald Hughes and political scientist John Rodman, all look to Greek myth and philosophy—pagan naturalism, Milesian hylozoism, Heraclitus (a process ontology) and Pythagoras (human-animal kinship) for ecologically fitting or environmentally useful ideas.[7]

In fact, Callicott himself, in looking back to Heraclitus and ahead in the direction of contemporary physics, makes the same point.[8] These scholars are trying, as did Nietzsche and Heidegger, to escape the presuppositions that have given rise to the predicament, one way or another, by sidestepping the tradition that has been built upon them. To return to cultural beginnings is one method of attempting to identify and avoid these often unannounced presuppositions; to question the assumptions of our foundational sciences in an Einsteinian or Whiteheadian manner is another. Perhaps a third alternative is the hermeneutical sensibility that can be gained by positioning oneself outside of the Western philosophic tradition and viewing it from relatively neutral ground. It is to this end that I employ a comparative methodology and appeal to the Taoist tradition, hoping that this tradition will serve, first, as an alternative perspective that illuminates our own assumptions and, second, as a conceptual resource for addressing some of the more fundamental issues of environmental ethics.

II. Aesthetic Versus Logical Order

Preliminary to reconstructing the specific Taoist concepts that will illuminate its "aesthetic" cosmology, *tao* and *te,* I want to borrow from collaborative work that David L. Hall and I have done in making some general observations on classical Chinese philosophy.[9] Many of the presuppositions shared by not only the earliest Confucians and Taoists, but even the proto-Chinese in the preliterate period,[10] can be recovered by invoking the distinction between a logical and an aesthetic order.[11]

At a popular level, a common observation on classical Chinese thought is that the Chinese were inclined to see life more as an art than as a science. They expressed a "this-worldly" concern for the concrete details of immediate existence as a basis for exercising their minds in the direction of generalities and ideals. They began from an acknowledgement of the uniqueness and importance of the particular person and the particular historical event to the world, while at the same time, stressing the interrelatedness of this person or event with the immediate context. These observations lead us to a useful distinction that has been posited as a device for organizing and understanding human experience. The abstractness of this elaborated logical/aesthetic distinction might seem to distinguish it from the appeal that a Chinese philosopher would make in explanation of his own tradition; but again, for the Chinese philosopher as well as for us, the perspective of an alternative philosophical tradition can be illuminating.

The essential difference between two fundamentally antithetical extremes of order—the logical and the aesthetic—consists in the primacy of the abstract in the logical construction as opposed to the primacy of the concrete particular in the aesthetic composition. We can highlight the notion of "logical construction" as having the following features:

(1) It begins with a preassigned pattern of relatedness, a "blueprint" wherein unity is prior to plurality as determinative of the construction.

(2) It registers concrete particularity only to the extent and in those respects necessary to satisfy this preassigned pattern, and will permit of substitution by any particular that can satisfy these same conditions.

(3) Given that it reduces the particular to only those aspects needed to illustrate the given pattern, it necessarily entails a process of formal abstraction, moving away from the concrete particular toward the universal.

(4) It constitutes an act of "closure"—the satisfaction of predetermined specifications—and is hence describable in a quantitative terminology of completeness.

(5) Being characterized by necessity, it limits creativity to conformity, and renders novelty defect.

(6) "Rightness" in this context refers to the degree of conformity to the preassigned pattern.

A ready example of this logical model is what Stephen Pepper calls "transcendent formism."[12] Plato's realm of Ideas constitutes a preassigned pattern that registers particular phenomena as "real" or "good" only to the extent that they conform to the preexistent Ideas. In Plato, realization is movement away from the concrete particular to the abstract universal, and novelty is defect to the extent that it deviates from preestablished perfection, the "real" Ideas.

To the extent that metaphysics has been a science of order from which we can articulate those uniformities of existence and experience, it functions as a basis for "logical construction." In a social or political context, to whatever degree we conform to obligatory rules or ideals or principles—objective forms of relatedness—we constitute ourselves as a "logical order."

The other side of this distinction, the "aesthetic composition," by contrast, has the following features:

(1) It begins with the uniqueness of the one particular[13] as it collaborates with other particulars in an emergent complex pattern of relatedness, and as such, will permit of no substitutions: plurality is prior to unity and disjunction to conjunction.

(2) It takes as its focus the unique perspective of a concrete, specific detail revealing itself as productive of a harmony or an order that is expressed by a complex of such details in their relationship to one another.

(3) Given that it is concerned with the fullest disclosure of particularity for the emergent harmony, it necessarily entails movement away from any universal characteristic to the concrete detail.

(4) It is an act of "disclosure"—the achieved coordination of concrete details in novel patterns that reflect their uniqueness—and hence is describable in the qualitative language of richness, intensity, etc.

(5) In that it is not determined by preassigned principles, it is fundamentally anarchic and contingent, and as such, is the ground for optimum creativity, where creativity is to be understood in contradistinction to determination.

(6) "Rightness" in this context refers to the degree to which the insistent particularity of the detail in tension with the consequent unity of these specific details is self-evidently expressive of an aesthetically pleasing order.

This aesthetic model is immediately distinguishable from transcendent formism in that there is no preassigned pattern. The organization and order of existence emerges out of the spontaneous arrangement of the participants. The work of art, where its "rightness" lies in large measure with the comprehension of just those particular details constituting the work, is an example of the aesthetic composition. Given the uniqueness of each aesthetic composition, this conception of order is more complex than that of the logical construction.

Perhaps an appropriate and certainly a very Chinese example of this aesthetic composition is the Chinese "stew pot," the possible etymological source of the character, "harmony (*ho*[b])." According to archaeological data, the proto-Chinese staple was *keng*[c], a millet broth or stew similar to the popular *chou*[d] (Cantonese, *jok*).[14]

The *Lü-shih ch'un-ch'iu*[e] (ca. 250 B.C.) describes the culinary art of the stewing pot.

> In the business of proper flavoring and seasoning, there must be sweet, sour, bitter, acrid and salty, and there must be an order in the mixing and proper proportion. Blending these together is extremely subtle, and they all must be self-expressive. The variations within the cooking pot are so delicate and subtle that they defy words and conceptualization.[15]

In the pursuit of this kind of harmony, there is the "chopping up and cooking (*ko-p'eng*[f])" of locally and temporally available ingredients. The combination and blending of these particular ingredients—*this* cabbage and *this* piece of pork—is undertaken in such a manner as to integrate them in mutual benefit and enhancement without allowing them to lose their unique and particular identities. There is, in this sense of order, the priority of the particular ingredients and the emergence of a uniquely available aesthetic composition.

The distinction between the logical and aesthetic models of order is apparent in the etymology of *cosmos*. It can mean a set of independent ordering principles that discipline chaos, as in a *cosmogonic* theory, or alternatively, it can mean the "cosmetic" order that reveals an interpretation and a consequent ornamentation of the harmonious interrelatedness constituted by the insistent particularity of preexisting details.

We can illustrate this distinction by contrasting ways of organizing ourselves as a group of people. To the extent that, in our interaction, our conduct is limited by appeal to a preassigned pattern of relatedness, be it political or religious or cultural, and to the extent that we conform to and express this pattern faithfully and precisely as rules determinative of our conduct, we constitute ourselves as a logical construction. On the other hand, to the extent that we interact freely and without prejudice, without obligatory recourse to rule or ideal or principle, and to the extent that the organization which describes and unites us emerges out of a collaboration of our own uniqueness as particulars, we are the authors of an aesthetic composition.

It must be underscored here that because the aesthetic composition is concrete rather than abstract, the perspective from which it is entertained is itself particular. While perspective is irrelevant to logical construction, an aesthetic event is always engaged from *a* particular perspective that itself constitutes a defining condition.

I would suggest, then, that the philosophy of the early Taoists tends toward the aesthetic rather than the logical paradigm.

III. Polarity Versus Dualism:
An Uncommon Assumption

It is a widely proclaimed feature of classical Chinese philosophy that, in contrast to that of the early Greeks, it all but lacks a developed cosmogony.[16] There have been many reasons suggested in explanation of this phenomenon, from sexual inhibitions in the culture to disparate notions of creativity.[17] More fundamental than many of these alternative explanations, we might take this apparent difference as a signal of the priority of the aesthetic over the logical order in the classical Chinese tradition. The epistemological counterpart to the interpretation of the cosmos as an aesthetic composition both constituting and constituted by the elements which compose it, is conceptual polarity. Such polarity requires that concepts which are significantly related are correlatively related, each requiring the other for adequate articulation. This characteristic is much reported about the nature of Chinese thinking, and is most often illustrated by invoking the polar concepts of *yin*[g] and *yang*[h]. *Yin* does not transcend *yang,* nor vice versa; rather, *yin* entails *yang,* and *yang* entails *yin.* I would like to borrow and elaborate the distinction between *dualism* and *polarity* that David L. Hall develops to clarify the nature of "opposites" in the Chinese tradition and to ultimately explain the noncosmogonic nature of early Chinese thought. This distinction, I believe, can be an important instrument in disclosing underlying premises as a starting point for our discussion of environmental ethics.

A *dualism* exists in *ex nihilo* doctrines because a fundamentally indeterminate, unconditioned power is posited as determining the essential meaning and order of the world. It is a "dualism" because of the radical separation between the transcendent and nondependent creative source, and the determinate and dependent object of its creation. The creative source does not require reference to its creature for explanation. This dualism, in various forms, has been a prevailing force in the development of many of our early cosmogonies, and has been fundamental in the elaborated pattern of dualisms that have framed our metaphysical speculations: supernatural/natural, reality/appearance, being/becoming, knowledge/opinion, reason/experience, theory/praxis, self/other, fact/value, subject/object, substance/attribute, mind/matter, form/matter, agent/act, animate/inanimate, birth/death, *creatio ex nihilo/destructio in nihilum,* and so on.

Polarity, on the other hand, has been a major principle of explanation in the initial formulation and evolution of classical Chinese *ars contextualis.* By polarity I wish to indicate the nature of the relationship that obtains between two or more events where each requires the other as a necessary condition for being what it is. The contention is that in contrast to being the creature of and hence deriving its meaning and order from some transcendent source, each participant in existence is "self-evidencing (*tzu-jan*[i])." There might seem to be some inconsistency in asserting that each particular is self-creative yet can only be accounted for by its symbiotic relationship with every other particular. Yet, as Hall observes:

> [T]he great difficulty for the radical view of creativity is to account for the apparent interconnectedness of things given the fact that each process is self-creative. It is the polar character of each process that establishes the ground for such an explanation.[18]

In other words, the notion of "self" in the locution "self-evidencing" has a polar relationship with "other." Each particular is a consequence of every other, such that there is no contradiction in saying that each particular is both self-determinate and determined by every other particular. That is, the "other" particulars which make up existence are intrinsically related to and thus constitutive of "self." The principle distinguishing feature of conceptual polarity is that each "pole" can be explained by reference to the other. *Left* requires *right, up* requires *down, yin* requires *yang,* and *self* requires *other.*

The separateness implicit in dualistic explanations of relationships conduces to an essentialistic interpretation of the world, a world of "things" characterized by discreteness, finality, closedness, determinateness, independence, a world in which one thing is related to the "other" extrinsically. By contrast, a polar explanation of relationships give rise to a holographic interpretation of the world, a world of "foci" characterized by interconnectedness, interdependence, openness, mutuality, indeterminateness, complementarity, correlativity, coextensiveness, a world in which continuous foci are intrinsically related to each other.

Not only are the dualistic categories mentioned above inappropriate to the orientation of *ars contextualis,* they are a source of serious distortion. As we discover immediately on opening the *Tao-te-ching,* conceptual polarity has its correlative sets of terminologies which are applied in explanation of the dynamic cycles and processes of existence: *wu*[j] (not-having)/*yu*[k] (having), *nan*[l] (difficult)/*yi*[m] (easy), *ch'ang*[n] (long)/*tuan*[o] (short), *kao*[p] (high)/*hsia*[q] (low), *ch'ien*[r] (before)/*hou*[s] (after), *kang*[t] (hard)/*jou*[u] (soft), *ch'eng*[v] (completeness)/*ch'üeh*[w] (deficiency), *ying*[x] (fullness)/*ch'ung*[y] (vacuity), *hsi*[z] (gathering up)/*chang*[aa] (spreading out), *jo*[ab] (weakening)/

ch'iang[ac] (strengthening), *hsing*[ad] (rising)/*fei*[ae] (falling), *yü*[af] (giving)/*ch'ü*[ag] (taking), and so on. Further, since all existents fall on a shared continuum differing in degree rather than in kind, the distinctions which obtain among them are only qualitative: *ch'ing*[ah] (clear)/*cho*[ai] (turbid), *cheng*[aj] (correct)/ *p'ien*[ak] (one-sided), *hou*[al] (thick)/*po*[am] (thin), *wen*[an] (genial)/*pao*[ao] (over-bearing). And, since these existents constitute one order of being, the changes which they undergo cannot be fairly described in essentialistic terms such as *substantial* or *accidental*. Rather, we require a notion of "reality as transformation (*chen*[ap])."[19]

The conceptual polarity which characterizes early Chinese thought discouraged the interpretation of reality in terms of *creatio ex nihilo* and *destructio in nihilum*.[20] The process of change, generating its own motion by the interaction of forces, is fundamentally transformational. There is no final beginning or end in this process; rather, there is the identifiable rhythm, order, and cadence of transformation. Given that reality in the early Chinese tradition is thus conceived of as a process, the absence of cosmogony is compensated for by an elaborate cosmological tradition which purports to describe and interpret the currents and cadence of *ch'i*[aq], the hylozoistic vapors that constitute the process of existence. Witness the several schools and commentarial traditions centered on *I Ching* (*Book of Change*), the concepts of *yin-yang*[ar] and *wu-hsing*[as] (five dynamic phases), and of course, the Taoists.

Relative to this commitment to cosmology rather than cosmogony, it is significant that the notion of "birth" and the process of "growth" (or "life") are not clearly differentiated in Chinese; both are denoted by the character, *sheng*[at]. Further, this same character is used to denote the "nature," or better "disposition" of all things, both animate and inanimate.[21] The notion of particular and its "nature" in this tradition should be broadly understood not in terms of essential differences, but as specific perturbations and transforming configurations in *ch'i*.

IV. Taoism Misnamed

In looking to the Taoist tradition, I reconstruct four concepts: *te*[au] (conventionally translated "virtue" or "power"), *tao*[av] ("the Way" from whence "Taoism" takes its name), *wu-wei*[aw] ("nonaction") and *yu-wei*[ax] (variously rendered "willful, intentional or unnatural activity"). This, of course, is a major undertaking, but the sheer necessity of dealing with all four of these concepts itself determines the course of my argument. That is, given their correlative nature, we can only attempt to explain them by mutual reference: we almost need to say all in order to say anything. My sources are primarily the *Tao-te-ching*[ay] (also known as the *Lao Tzu*[az]), with corroboration sought from the *Chuang Tzu*[ba] and the *Huai Nan Tzu*[bb].

I begin this discussion with a historical observation by suggesting that this school of classical Chinese philosophy, Taoism, has been done a profound disservice by being misnamed in the tradition. In December 1973, at an archaeological site called Ma-wang-tui[bc], two silk editions of the *Lao Tzu* dating back to approximately 200 B.C. were unearthed. One important contribution of this find is that it sheds new light on the structure of the *Lao Tzu* text[22]. In the tradition, the *Lao Tzu* has also been known as the *Tao-te-ching*, "the classic of *tao* and *te*." This alternative title reflects its division into two parts. D. C. Lau, in his earlier translation of the *Lao Tzu* from 1963 describes this division of the text in the following terms:

> The text of the *Lao tzu* is divided into two books. This was done probably simply to conform to the statement in the biography of Lao Tzu that he wrote a work *in two books* at the request of the Keeper of the Pass. At any rate, the division into two books goes at least as far back as the first century A.D. . . . . By the end of the second century A.D., the work was also known by the alternative title of the *Tao te ching*. More specifically, Book I was known as the *Tao ching*, and Book II the *Te ching*.[23]

Lau's opinion at this writing was that the division into two parts was really of little significance. Interpreting the designation of this text according to one convention of titling in the classical Chinese tradition, he continues:

> This practice seems to have no more foundation than the mere fact that the first word in Book I is *tao* while in Book II the first word (discounting the adjective *shang* which has no special significance) is *te*.[24]

Lau's position here is important for our analysis because it reflects his interpretation of the relative weight of the concepts, *tao* and *te*, in the philosophic content of the text. He regards *tao* as paramount in importance.

> From the fact that the school of thought supposed to have been founded by *Lao Tzu* is known as Taoism (*tao chia*, the school of the way), it can be seen that *tao* was considered the central concept in the thought contained in the *Lao Tzu*.[25]

On the other hand, Lau feels that *te* has a very minor role in the text.

> There are certain ideas which we have, so far, not touched on in our account

and to these we must turn our attention. As the work is known as the *Tao te ching*, it must seem strange that we have not said anything about the term "*te*". . . . But in the *Lao Tzu* the term is not a particularly important one and is often used in its more conventional senses.[26]

The two silk manuscripts of the *Tao-te-ching* recovered at Ma-wang-tui are both divided into two books with the *Te ching* preceding the *Tao ching*. Although the two books are not specifically titled "*Te ching*" and "*Tao ching*," the "B" manuscript[bd] has the character *te* at the end of the first book and *tao* at the end of the second. Given classical Chinese titling conventions clarified in other recent archaeological finds (notably the *Sun Pin ping-fa*[be] and *Huang-ti ssu-ching*[bf] texts), it is not overstatement to suggest that these two characters do in fact constitute a title.

The point here is that very early in the tradition, the *Tao-te-ching*, as the title would suggest, was in fact divided into two parts: *te* and *tao*. Contrary to Lau's contention that *te* and *tao* are used as titles for these two parts of the *Tao-te-ching* only because they are the first characters in the text, I suggest that the fundamental importance of both of these concepts is a more persuasive explanation. *Tao* occurs seventy-four times in the *Tao-te-ching* and *te* occurs thirty-six times; in the "authentic" *Chuang Tzu,* the "Inner Chapters," *tao* occurs thirty-nine times to *te*'s thirty-four.[27]

In what follows, I argue that the concept *te* as found in the Taoist corpus has been severely undervalued in later commentary and in our present understanding of this tradition. *Te* and *tao* are both central concepts in the Taoist literature that must be understood as correlatives on the model of *yin* and *yang*. W. T. Chan in his discussion of the historical development of Taoism observes:

Of course the name "Taoist School" was not used until the first century B.C., but the teachings of Lao Tzu and Chuang Tzu about Tao were so impressive and influential before that time that the name was inevitable.[28]

Not only was this name not inevitable, but it was, furthermore, most unfortunate. I suggest that the interdependence of *tao* and *te* is of such importance that the historian, Ssu-ma T'an (died ca. 110 B.C.), should have been deferred to when, in his Preface of the Grand Historian, in listing the six schools he referred to Taoism not as *tao chia*,[bg] "the school of *tao*," but as *tao-te chia*[bh], "the school of *tao* and *te*."[29]

This, then, leads us to a brief synopsis of the Taoist conception of particularity, *te*. In what follows, I suggest that in order to define the relationship that obtains between *te* and *tao,* and to appreciate the nature of order that emerges out of this relationship, we must invoke our notion of conceptual complementarity and aesthetic composition.

V. *TE:* The Integrity and Integration of
Particular Foci

The prominence and the ambiguity of *te* in the corpus of pre-Ch'in literature is adequately illustrated in Mote's translation of Hsiao Kung-chuan's *A History of Chinese Political Thought* in which he renders *te* in the following ways: "ethical nature," "spiritual powers," "Power," "moral excellence," "power imparted from the *Tao*," "*virtus*" (in the sense of a thing's intrinsic and distinctive character), "moral force" (citing Waley), "the powers native to beings and things," and frequently, perhaps in despair, simply as "*te*." Beyond the meaning of "virtue" or "power" that is cultivated and increased in the thing itself, *te* also has the sense of "favor" or "bounty" extended outwards, and further the gratitude that it evokes. For the Confucian and Mohists, it is generally translated "virtue," while for the Taoists it is usually some order of "power."

I would certainly not fault Mote for the latitude in his renderings; it is common if not characteristic of the early Chinese thinkers to rework a shared set of locutions that come to have very different values in each of their respective philosophies. On the other hand, I would suggest that the various extensions of meaning taken on by a given concept are related, being grounded in some more primitive level of meaning.

Scholars have made much of the disparate meaning of *te* for the Confucians and Taoists to the point of separating them entirely.[30] While a different emphasis is apparent, I suggest that the radical nature of the distinction which they draw reflects different *levels* of meaning rather than different conceptual content. The focus of the Taoists' discussions is predominantly a cosmological account of the transformational process of existence where *te* is regarded as categorical: the presencing of a particular. In the Confucian *Analects,* on the other hand, *te* is specifically ethical in its applications: the extent to which, through patterns of deference, the influence of the particular takes on normative force. When we lay bare the cosmological presuppositions underlying Confucian ethical theory, however, and when we draw out the social and political implications of *te* in the Taoist texts, we find that the distance between their respective interpretations of *te* closes significantly.

Before dealing with *te* at a conceptual level, I want to explore it philologically in order to uncover the "core idea." In the *Shuo-wen*[bi] lexicon, *te* is importantly defined as an event, "arising" or "presencing" (*sheng*[bj]). Although traditional commentators flex some philological muscle in their struggle to discipline this explanation into something more conventional—the cognate of *te* meaning "to get" (*te*[bk])—their arguments are decidedly unconvincing.[31] Again, given the process cosmology to which philosophical reflection of this period is committed, it is curious that they would want to argue against "arising" as an explanation for *te*.

The character *te* is comprised of three elements: *ch'ih*[bl] "to move ahead"; a second element[bm] which most etymologists take as a representation of the human eye; and *hsin*[bn], the "heart-and-mind." The eye and heart-and-mind elements suggest that the unfolding process of *te* is disposed in a particular direction. *Te* then is the transforming content and disposition of an existent: an autogenerative, self-construed "arising."[32]

There is another twist in the philological analysis. It is general scholarly opinion that the character *te* is a later variant of the character, *te*[bo] (at times found as *chih*[bp]). This earlier alternative form of *te* is constituted of this *chih*, commonly used in its derived sense as "straight," but perhaps better understood in its more fundamental meaning of "to grow straight without deviation" in the context of organic issuance.[33] The organic dimension of *chih* is underscored by its cognates, *chih*[bq], "to sow," and *chih*[br], "to plant." The heart-and-mind element in this variant character again contributes a sense of disposition to the basic meaning of organic germination and growth. The *Shuo-wen* has a separate entry for the variant *te*, taking advantage of the homophonous cognate *te*, "to get," in defining it as "to get from oneself within and from others without."[34] Finally, there is some philological significance in the fact that Karlgren classifies both *te* and the earlier variant *te* in a phonetic category deriving from *chih*, "to grow straight without deviation."

Knitting the several strands of these philological data together, I suggest that *te*, at a fundamental cosmological level, denotes the arising of the particular in a process vision of existence. The particular is the unfolding of a *sui generis* focus of potency that embraces and determines conditions within the range and parameters of its particularity. As I observed above in my discussion of the presuppositions characteristic of this tradition, for the classical Chinese philosopher, the world of particulars is alive in the sense that they are aware of and hence "feel" or "prehend" other particulars in their environment. The expression "self-evidencing (*tzu-jan*)" is a physical and a psychical characterization which means that reality is self-causing and self-aware. And to be aware is to invest interest and thus value other things. The range of its particularity is variable, and is contingent upon the way in which it interprets itself and is interpreted. It is a focus because its context, in whatever direction and degree, can alternatively be construed as "self" or "other." The presencing of particulars is not random and chaotic. Rather, it is characterized by an inherent dynamism which, through its own disposition and self-direction, interprets the world. It has the possibility of making a direction appropriate by expressing itself in compromise between its own disposition and the context which it makes its own. Just as any one ingredient in the stewpot must be blended with all of the others in order to express most fully its own flavor, so harmonization with other environing particulars is a necessary precondition for the fullest self-discourse of any given particular. It is thus a calculus of the appropriate directions of the particulars that constitutes the unifying harmony and regularity observable in the world. The potency of the arising event as innovative interpreter is dependent upon the range and quality of its self-construal. There is an openness of the particular such that it can through harmonization and patterns of deference diffuse to become coextensive with other particulars, and absorb an increasingly broader field of "arising" within the sphere of its own particularity. This then is the "getting" or "appropriating" aspect of *te*.[35] As a particular extends itself to encompass a wider range of "presencing" or "rising," the possibilities of its conditions and its potency for self-construal are proportionately increased.

The *Chuang Tzu* can help us to sort out this terminology.

> *Tao* is the opening out and arraying of *te:* the process of living and growing (*sheng*) is the radiating of *te*. The natural disposition (*hsing*[bs]) is the raw resources for living and growing. The activity of the natural disposition is called "making/becoming" (*wei*[bt]); "making/becoming" that is contrived is called "losing" (*shih*[bu]). Being aware (*chih*[bv]) is being in touch; being erudite is being the schemer. And the limitations on the awareness of one who is aware are a consequence of staring in one direction. Activity that issues from what is inevitable is called *te;* activity that is entirely self-expressive is called appropriate order (*chih*[bw]).

This passage characterizes the "making/becoming" of the particular as both "inevitable (*pu te yi*[bx])" and "entirely self-expressive (*wu fei wo*[by])." This seeming contradiction is the consequence of having two different ways of conceptualizing particularity. The shifting context and conditions in which the particular "becomes" determines its range of possibilities. In this sense, the activity of the particular is inevitable. But in that these conditions can be seen as being embraced within the particular's own autogenerative identity and as being in no sense determined by something "other," the particular is self-expressive. Since there is no conflict between inevitability and self-expression when the particular is understood in this way, the *Chuang Tzu* passage continues by collapsing this distinction:

> By definition, inevitable activity and self-expressive activity seem to be contraries, but in fact, they are mutually consistent.[36]

Across the corpus of pre-Ch'in literature, this concept *te* seems to have a primitive significance from which its other connotations are derived. In the Taoist literature, it is explicitly described as a variable focus of potency in the process of existence. This dynamic process viewed *in toto* and integrated from a particular *te* perspective is called *tao,* but when viewed in terms of the integrity of individuated existents, is a collocation of particular *te.* The *Tao-te-ching,* for example, states:

> The Great *tao* is so expansive. It reaches in all directions. All of the myriad things arise because of it. . . .[37]

And the myriad things are described in terms of their *te:*

> *Tao* engenders them
> And *te* nourishes and rears them.
> Things give them shape
> And conditions bring them to completion.
> Thus, all of the myriad things revere *tao* and honor *te.*
> Why *tao* is revered and *te* honored
> Is because they are constantly "self-so-ing (*tzu-jan*)"
> And not because of anyone's mandate.[38]

All existence is a continuum on which every aspect is undergoing a constant process of transformation determined by its own disposition and the matrix of conditions which sponsor it. The particular is not understood in terms of discrete and essentialistic self-nature; rather, it is an open focus in the process of existence which shrinks and swells, depending upon how it is interpreted and construed. When disclosing its uniqueness and difference, it is apprehended as a particular *te;* when considered in terms of the full complement and consequence of its determining conditions, it constitutes its own whole.

In discriminating one aspect and constituting one perspective on *tao, te* can be understood as a *principium individuationis.* But while *te* as a particular has its integrity, it is also a principle of integration. *Te* is most often used to denote a particular aspect of the *tao,* but as a particular, it is elastic, and can be extended even to the extent of embracing the whole. In the *Tao-te-ching,* for example, locutions such as "constant *te*" (*ch'ang te*[bz]), "perpetual *te*" (*heng te*[ca]), "dark *te*" (*hsüan te*[cb]), and "superlative *te*" (*sheng te*[cc]) all denote the coincidence of *tao* and *te* where the entire field is entertained from a particular perspective. The *Tao-te-ching* states:

> If you are a ravine to the empire,
> The constant *te* will not desert you.

When the constant *te* does not desert you.
You will again return to being a babe. . . .

If you are a model to the empire,
The constant *te* will not deviate.
When the constant *te* does not deviate,
You will again return to the boundless. . . .

If you are a valley to the empire,
The constant *te* will be sufficient.
When the constant *te* is sufficient,
You will again return to being the uncarved block.[39]

When *te* is cultivated and accumulated such that the particular is fully expressive of the whole, the distinction between *tao* and *te* collapses and *te* becomes both an individuating concept and an integrating concept. It is because the distinction between *tao* and *te* is one of degree rather than kind that most of the language used to describe *te* in the early literature is quantitative: thick (*hou*[cd]), broad (*kuang*[ce]), great (*k'ung*[cf]), accumulated (*chi*[cg]), replete (*sheng*[ch]), pervasive (*p'u*[ci]), abundant (*feng*[cj]), deep (*shen*[ck]), and so on.

As in the passage cited above, the "babe" metaphor recurs in the *Tao-te-ching*. For example, it states: "One who possesses *te* in abundance is comparable to a new born babe."[40] The point here is that an infant with his "oceanic feeling" does not distinguish himself from his environment. There is no circumscription or separation from his whole. Such being the case, because the infant is a matrix through which the full consequence of undiscriminated existence can be experienced, it can be used as a metaphor for the *te* which is *tao*. Other metaphors frequently seen in the Taoist literature which allude to this extension and coincidence of *te* with *tao* are the uncarved black (*p'u*[cl]), darkness (*hsüan*[cm]), and water in its various forms. These metaphors underscore the notion that any particular *te* when viewed in terms of its intrinsic relatedness entails the full process of existence, and as such, is a perspective on *tao*. Throughout the early literature, this collapse of *te* into *tao* is often expressed as a paradox:

Where one is *te* he is without *te*.

The person of superior *te* is not *te*
And that is why he has *te*.
The person of inferior *te* does not lose his *te*
And that is why he has no *te* . . .
Hence, *te* arises after the *tao* is lost;
Jen arises after *te* is lost. . . .[41]

The *Chuang Tzu* also describes *te* as a unifying principle.

> This man and this kind of *te* will extend things in all directions to make one.
>
> If you look at things in terms of how they differ, the gap between liver and gall is as great as the distance from Ch'u to Yüeh; if you look at them in terms of their sameness, everything is one. A person who is like this, totally oblivious to what is appropriate to each sense, sends his heart-and-mind rambling in the harmony of *te*. As for things, he sees wherein they are one and fails to see what they lose.[42]

There is a harmonious order, a regularity, a pattern achieved in the process of existence that is empirically evident and which brings unity to diversity, oneness to plurality, similarity to difference. *Te,* when seen as a particular focus or event in the *tao,* is a principle of individuation; when seen as a holograph of this underlying harmony, diffusing in all directions in coloration of the whole, it is a principle of integration.

The *Chuang Tzu,* in defining *te,* uses water as a metaphor for suggesting both the determinateness and indeterminateness of *te*.

> Placidity is the highest state of water at rest, and can be used as a gauge or measure. Within it retains this condition, and is undisturbed from without. *Te* is the completion of the cultivation of harmony. That *te* does not assume a shape is because things are inseparable from it.[43]

The water metaphor is illuminating. On the one hand, water at rest is so plane that it can be used for measurement; on the other, it is utterly fluid and indeterminate. *Te* is similar. It functions to constitute a determinate and identifiable harmony—a regularity and rhythm. But then, given that it cannot be abstracted from context, it is fluid with no fixed determinateness.

In the Taoist tradition, which challenged the anthropocentrism of classical Confucian philosophy by going beyond the human world to extend its sphere of concern to all of existence, the activity which integrates the particular *te* with the *tao* is described as *wu-wei,* conventionally rendered "nonaction," or *tzu-jan,* "spontaneity." The Taoist texts, like their Confucian counterparts, see the dissolution of discriminating ego-self as a precondition for integrative natural action and the concomitant extension of *te*.

> Yen Hui said, "I have sat and forgotten."
> Confucius, noticeably flustered, inquired: "What do you mean by 'sitting and forgetting?' "
> "I have demolished my appendages and body, expurgated my perceptiveness

and perspicacity, abandoned my physical form and repudiated wisdom to identify with the Great All," said Yen Hui. "This I call 'sitting and forgetting.' "[44]

As one overcomes ego-self and dissolves the boundary between self and "other," his *te* swells to become coincident with the *te* of what had been construed as "other." The early texts speak of "accumulating" *te*, "cultivating" it, "piling it up" and "extending" it.[45] Perhaps the most helpful metaphor is that of the tally in the Taoist texts. The *Tao-te-ching* states:

> The person of *te* takes charge of the tally;
> The person without it looks after collection.[46]

The meaning of this rather obscure passage is illuminated in the fifth chapter of the *Chuang Tzu,* the title of which is "*Te* Satisfies the Tally." This chapter is a series of anecdotes about mutilated cripples, who, under normal circumstances and under the sway of conventional values, would be ostracized from their communities. Their mutilated physical forms, often the result of amputatory punishment, would be certain grounds for societal rejection. Having overcome ego-self and extended their *te* to integrate themselves in the spontaneous unfolding of their social environs, however, they "satisfy the tally" and not only blend harmoniously with their respective societies, but further come to exercise considerable influence in their world making. The extent and quality of their *te* is such that they are important factors in the ongoing process of defining values and establishing an *ethos*. This new order is determined by and reflective of the natural dispositions of its constituent *te*.

In the Taoist tradition, the swelling of one's *te* is described in diffusive terms. There are innumerable anecdotes in which a person's *te* extends to embrace the *te* of other members of his human society. As in the Confucian tradition, at times he becomes the embodiment and protector of the human order, a styler of new culture and a source of new meaning. But the Taoists take it beyond this into the natural world. The *chen jen*[cn] — the Taoist version of the consummate person — embraces the *te* of his natural as well as his human environment. By becoming coextensive with the *te* of the ox, for example, the person of pervasive *te* is able to express and interpret the natural disposition of the ox to become an efficacious butcher,[47] by becoming coextensive with the *te* of the clay, he is able to express and interpret the natural disposition of the clay to become an efficacious craftsman.[48] The absence of a "dis-integrating" ego-self makes him open to the *te* of his whole natural environment so that the environment contributes to him, making him potent and productive, and he contributes to his environment, strengthening, enhancing, and interpreting its natural direction. His presencing in the world is colored by the *te* of his whole environment extending out to embrace ultimately all of existence.

The person of pervasive *te* in the Taoist tradition is called *chen jen.* The character, *chen*[co], meaning "true" or "real," is classified under the radical *hua*[cp] meaning "to transform." In the *Chuang Tzu,* the process of existence is frequently referred to as the "transformation of things" (*wu hua*[cq]). As the Taoist *chen jen* extends himself to become coextensive with the natural direction of his context, he becomes an increasingly influential "transformer" of things. Viewed from the perspective of discriminated particularity, he is transforming something other than himself; from the perspective of his diffusion within his context, he has become a larger focus of what it is that is self-transforming. To the extent that his broad presencing has possibilities for creativity and novelty, so too does he. To the extent that he embraces the *te* of the whole within his particularity, he is integrated and efficacious at whatever he does. What might be perceived as his interface with "other" is in fact coincident *te* such that he facilitates and interprets the natural expression of whatever he encounters. His hands express the clay, and the clay expresses his hands.

VI. *Tao*: Environment as *Ethos*

Tao, in the conceptual complements, *tao-te,* is not as obscure as *te,* perhaps, but still requires some considerable clarification. Again, as with *te,* let us begin from some summary philological observations.

The character *tao* is comprised of two elements, *ch'o*[cr], "to pass over, to go over," and *shou*[cs], "head, foremost," both of which contribute meaning to this "combined-meaning" character (*hui-yi tzu*[ct]). The structure of the character indicates that it, like almost all of the characters constructed with *ch'o,* is fundamentally verbal.[49] This observation is reinforced by the *Book of Documents* (*Shu-ching*), where *tao* is used repeatedly in the context of cutting a channel and "leading" a river to prevent the overflowing of its banks.[50] If we take the verbal *tao* as primary and allow that the *shou* component contributes the suggestion of "to lead" or "to give a heading," the several derived meanings of this concept emerge rather effortlessly: heading—to lead through—road, path, Way—way, method, art, teachings— to explain, to tell. It is important for this analysis to stress that *tao* at a fundamental level seems to denote an active "making" or "doing." If we consider *tao* in its derived meaning of "road," for example, it is first the "road making" and then by extension, "the road."

In this section, I appeal to two distinctions outlined above—logical construction/aesthetic composition and dualism/polarity—in order to further illuminate the concept, *tao*. I have suggested that coherence requires that *tao* and *te*, field and focus, be understood as polar rather than dualistic categories. Given this interdependence of *tao* and *te*, the order of nature is better understood as an emergent regularity rather than an abstract, preexistent principle.

In the Taoist corpus, *tao* in its broadest meaning is the "spontaneous (*tzu-jan*)," or perhaps a better translation, "self-evidencing," process of all that is as it presences for a given particular. It would be a contradiction to suggest that the all-embracing *tao* is entertained from some objective perspective beyond it: rather it is always engaged from some particular perspective within it. This, then, is the basis of the polar relationship between *tao* as field and *te* as particular focus. *Tao* is the defining conditions—the context or environment—for the particular *te*.

That *tao* at a cosmological level is the process of becoming apprehended from a particular perspective is not problematic. In this sense, we might call *tao* "the natural environment of any particular," and mean by it whatever is becoming. But *tao* is not only the *what*, it is also the *how*. That is, *tao* is the order of the particular's natural environment. It is here that clarification is required. Given the two senses of order that have been outlined above, the order of *tao* can have two rather distinct meanings.

The first of these senses of order is captured in the typical description of the *laws of nature* as a given to which the aggregate of all physical, chemical and biological processes conform.[51] All things follow nature in an absolute sense. This means the absolute laws of nature "transcend" the environment in the strict classical sense of transcend in that they determine nature while themselves remaining undetermined by it. This interpretation of the laws of nature as transcendent principles establishes an ontological disparity that gives rise to and justifies dualistic categories such as God and the natural world, man and nature.

This familiar understanding of order is not only common in our Judeo-Christian tradition; it is not unknown in existing interpretations of Taoism. In fact, many if not most commentators on Taoism have, intentionally or otherwise, invoked this conception of order in their explanations of *tao*. W. T. Chan is very clear in construing *tao* as a preassigned pattern to which nature must conform.

> It is not an exaggeration to say that Tao operated according to certain laws which are constant and regular. One may even say there is an element of

necessity in these laws, for Tao by its very nature behaves in this way and all things in order to achieve their full realization, have to obey them. Tao, after all, is *the* Way. . . . When things obey its laws, all parts of the universe will form a harmonious whole and the universe will become an integrated organism.[52]

Izutsu, for example, says of *tao*—"the Absolute or the Way"—that "in its personal aspect it is God, the creator of Heaven and Earth, and Lord of All things and events."[53] Yü Ying-shih, in a recent paper, describes *tao* in Platonic categories, suggesting that *tao* is not only "the law of Nature" and the "creator," it is "clearly comparable to Plato's idea of the Good." Citing Arthur O. Lovejoy on "otherworldliness," he states:

> Moreover, both the "real" and the good are believed to exist only "in a higher realm of being differing in its essential nature, and not merely in degree and detail, from the lower." Indeed, if we accept, as I do, this general characterization of Lovejoy's, then not only early Taoists (especially Chuang-tzu) clearly belong to the otherworldly camp but even some of the early Confucianists (especially Confucius and Yen Hui) were not without their otherworldly moments.[54]

Needham, in ascribing a scientific mentality to the Taoists, begins from the interpretation of *tao* as the order of nature.

> For the Taoists the Tao or Way was not the right way of life within human society, but the way in which the universe worked; in other words the *Order of Nature*. . . . The Tao as the Order of Nature, which brought all things into existence and governs their every action, not so much by force as by a kind of natural curvature in space and time, reminds us of the *logos* of Heraclitus of Ephesus, controlling the orderly processes of change. . . . the Tao was thought of not only as vaguely informing all things, but as being the naturalness, the very structure, of particular and individual types of things. . . . If there was one idea which the Taoist philosophers stressed more than any other, it was the unity of Nature, and the eternity and uncreatedness of the Tao.[55]

The argument that *tao* is an unconditioned absolute constituting a primordial reality beyond the world of particulars is frequently supported by appeal to sections of the *Tao-te-ching*.

> *Tao* engenders one,
> One engenders two,
> Two engenders three,
> And three engenders the myriad things.
> The myriad things shoulder the *yin* and embrace the *yang,*
> And in coalescing their hylozoistic vapors they achieve harmony.[56]

A careful reading of this passage certainly suggests that the *tao* gives birth to and nurtures the myriad things. But the idea does not end here. The myriad things as perturbations of "living" vapors coordinate themselves to constitute the harmonious regularity (*ho*) which is *tao*. *Tao* produces the myriad things, and the myriad things constitute *tao*.

This same point is made in another chapter of the *Tao-te-ching* where the metaphor of the infant is used to suggest the integrity and the integrativeness of *te*.

The ingesting of an abundance of *te* can be likened to the newly born baby.[57]

The baby here is described as having the highest degree of particular potency and as being entirely integrated in his environment such that "poisonous insects will not sting him" and "ferocious beasts will not maul him." Making his own contribution, the baby is productive of harmony.

Realizing harmony is called constancy.[58]

And it is this constancy that is the *tao* order. Again, we have the mutual determination of *tao* and *te*.

This mutuality of *tao* and *te* is further elaborated in the *Chuang Tzu*.

Now were you, in charioting *tao* and *te,* to go drifting and wandering, it would not be so.
Without praises or curses,
Now a dragon, now a snake,
You transform together with the times.
And not willing to act unilaterally,
Now above, now below,
You take harmony as your measure.[59]

This passage sheds light on the *tao-te* relationship. There is the notion of fluidity among perspectives that are always particular—"now a dragon, now a snake"—suggesting that particular integrity itself is always being renegotiated in the process of transformation. There is a rejection of unilateral activity (*chuan wei*[cu]) as inimical to harmony. And it is the achievement of this harmony that is a measure of the aesthetic composition that is *tao*.

An alternative to interpreting the *tao* as preexistent laws of nature that govern and determine the course of nature, then, is to understand it as the regularity and cadence achieved by nature—an aesthetic rather than a scientific order. In this case, *tao* is not some preassigned pattern that disciplines a sometimes recalcitrant natural world, but the harmony consequent upon the collaboration of intrinsically related particulars as it is perceived from some particular perspective. Under these conditions, the order of nature cannot be understood by appeal to first principles, but must be seen like *tao* itself as fundamentally "self-evidencing *(tzu-jan)*." Particular *te* are described, like *tao,* as *tzu-jan,* "self-evidencing." This means that they are self-disclosing within the conditions of their unique contexts, and cannot be explained fully by appeal to principles independent of them. Importantly, given the intrinsic relatedness and interdependence of particulars, the "self-evidencing" of any one particular requires the "self-evidencing" of its environing conditions. And the particular *te* will perceive nature to be ordered to the extent that it provides it with the opportunity to disclose itself fully.

We can look specifically at the case of the human being. Were we to interpret *tao* as laws of nature such that the laws of nature determine human conduct without human conduct determining the laws, the existence of these laws themselves would entail an ontological disparity between nature and the human being. Because nature "by nature" would be independent of the human being, he would be required to devise some principles on which to deal with nature. A science of morals could be derived from these laws that would enable the human being to act in concert with nature. This then would be the justification for an environmental ethic.

The alternative understanding of *tao* as the aesthetic order of nature would not provide us with an ethic, but an *"ethos"*: the expression of the character or disposition of an integrated natural environment that conduces most fully to the expression of the integrity of its constituent particulars. The particular and its environment (i.e., a *te* and its *tao*) in this paradigm as polarities are not separable. Further, the perceived order is not a given but an achievement. It is an order that cannot be valued on the basis of conformity to principle; it must be assessed as we would a symphony or painting in terms of creative expression—ultimately, its "rightness" for what it is. It does not disclose a necessary order, but only one of many possible orders available under prevailing conditions. In this paradigm, the particular achieves its own self-expression through patternings of deference: deferring to its environing conditions to establish an efficacious and fruitful integration while at the same time fully disclosing its own integrity as a particular. The achievement of this quality of activity is referred to in Taoism as *wu-wei* ("nonaction"), *tzu-jan* ("spontaneity" or "self-evidencing") and *hsiao-yao-yu*^{cv} ("free and easy wandering"). In this paradigm, meaningfulness is a function of the coordination of participating diverse elements into relationships which allow the particular to disclose its own significance.

VII. *Wu-Wei* and *Yu-Wei*[cw] Activity

Above we have defined *te* and *tao* as polar categories, precluding any interpretation of *tao* that would reduce it to preexisting laws that govern nature. Instead, we suggest that *tao* be understood as an emerging pattern of relatedness perceived from the perspective of an irreducibly participatory *te*. With this interpretation of *tao-te* in hand, we move closer to our specific problem of environmental ethics. Let us now try to address the question of the most appropriate relationship between *te* and *tao*—between a particular and its environing conditions. In Taoist literature, this most appropriate action is perhaps most often described as "*wu-wei*," formularistically rendered as "nonaction." Those translators who seek to avoid the passive and quietistic implications of this translation generally render it with something like "not acting willfully" or "acting naturally." Of course, any attempt to thus define *wu-wei* as "natural action" and distinguish it from "unnatural action" (*yu-wei*) will give rise to the perennial question that haunts most interpretations of Taoism: if all is *tao,* and *tao* is natural, what is the source, the nature, and the ontological status of unnatural activity? Robert C. Neville, for example, has articulated this as a "dialectical" problem: "If the *tao* is an ultimate reality such that nothing can depart from it and such that every movement illustrates it, how is it possible for there to be unspontaneous actions?"[60]

Before attempting to address this problem, I want to try to shed some light on the concept, *wu-wei,* by pursuing a more appropriate translation. I want to suggest *anarchic* as a possible translation for the adverbial *wu-wei*. There is an immediate philological sympathy between *wu-wei* activity and *anarchism*. Anarchism, understood in its root sense, is: "*an + archos > archē:* not/without + ruler > something that was in the beginning/a first principle." *Wu-wei* can be analyzed as: "*wu + wei:* not/without + to make, to act, to do." Philologically significant here is the fact in the classical language, there are two words frequently used for "to make, to act, to do": *wei* and *tso*[cx].[61] Both of these terms have cognates which bear comparison.

1. **gwia/jwie/wei*   make, do, act, to be
   **gwia/jwie-/wei*[cy]   for, because
   **ngwia/ngjwie-/wei*[cz]   false, spurious, cheat
   **ngwâ/nguâ/o*[da]   deceive, false, act, work

2. **tsâk/tsâk/tso*   act, do, make, work
   **tsăg/tsa-/tso*[db]   treacherous, deceive
   **dz'âg/dz'uo-/tsu*[dc]   to reward, to confer a fief on, to give prosperity, a matching libation[62]

Both terms have *ch'ü sheng*^{dd} (Mandarin fourth tone) cognates that mean "false" or "deceive." When *wei* is read in this tone, it means "for the sake of, on behalf of, because of"—that is, "to act on behalf of something other." When *tso* is read in this tone as *tsu*^{de}, it also means to respond to something other with some kind of sacrifice, a giving over.[63]

Taking these philological data into account, we can make the following observations. First, neither *anarchic* nor *wu-wei* can be used to describe *individual* action inasmuch as these terms properly refer to a relationship obtaining between things. Secondly, *anarchic* is the negation of the authoritarian determination of one thing by another. On the political level, it is the negation of coercive authority, but this is more primitively derived from the metaphysical: the negation of first principle as "beginning": teleological purpose, divine design, or Providence. With respect to *wei*, the etymologies of this character with *hands* as a prominent element would suggest that it fundamentally denotes "making" in the broad sense of "authoring." *Wu-wei*, then, is a negation of that kind of "making" or "doing" which requires that a particular sacrifice its own integrity in acting on behalf of something "other," a negation of one particular serving as a "means" for something else's "end." *Wu-wei* is the negation of that kind of engagement that makes something false to itself. The sympathy between *anarchic* and *wu-wei* that lies in their common reference to activity performed in the absence of coercively determinative constraints would recommend *anarchic* as a translation for *wu-wei*.

But there is also an important difference. Anarchy fundamentally describes the relationship between a particular and a determinative principle: an *archē*. Because the *archē* is a "beginning"—that which determines without itself being determined—there is an ontological disparity between the *archē* and the particular. Principle and particular stand in a dualistic, not a polar relationship. David L. Hall makes this point:

> A polar relationship has no beginning: to claim otherwise would be to provide some concept of initiation and, thus, to give priority to one of the elements in the creative relationship.[64]

Wu-wei, then, differs from *anarchic* in that it does not describe the relationship between principle and particular, negating principle as a precondition for the self-actualization of the particular. Rather, *wu-wei* negates that kind of relatedness that obtains between two particulars that will compromise their opportunity for "self-evidencing" (*tzu-jan*). Significantly, *wu-wei* as a disposition is generally couched in positive rather than negative terms in the context of "making" or "doing" something: it is a relationship negotiated between two particulars. A typical example is the *Tao-te-ching* 3:

He (the sage) causes the "erudite" not to dare to make/do/act.
In making/doing/acting with a *wu-wei* disposition
There is nothing that is not properly (i.e. "according to oneself") ordered.[65]

Wu-wei as the disposing of particulars is bidirectionally deferential in that it entails both the *integrity* of the particular and its *integration* in context. The *Tao-te-ching* repeatedly describes this posture as "making/doing/acting without claims of dependence (*wei erh pu shih*[df])."[66] The intrinsic relatedness of particulars means that self-disclosure can only be pursued within an environing context. This integrative dimension of the *wu-wei* attitude is generally overstated, prompting even the most prominent commentators to read Taoism as a passive and quietistic philosophy: "a Yin thought-system" in which the particular capitulates to the demands of its environment and "flows with the *tao*."[67] Against such an interpretation, I would argue that *wu-wei* as "making" is the particular authoring itself, on the one hand, deferring to the integrity of its environment, and at the same time demanding that the environing conditions defer to its integrity. *Wu-wei* as "making" is irrepressibly participatory and creative. In human terms, the integrity that must be sustained in the project of self-disclosure requires an awareness that uncoordinated action between oneself and one's environment not only deprives environing particulars of the possibilities of "self-evidencing," but further, impoverishes one's own possibilities. The inseparability of integrity and integration collapses the "means/end" distinction, rendering everything both an end in itself, and also a necessary condition or "means" for everything else to be what it is. This, restated in the language of the *Chuang Tzu*, is his doctrine of "the parity of things and events (*ch'i wu*[dg])."

David L. Hall illuminates this *wu-wei* relationship and takes us one step further in establishing a criterion for distinguishing *wu-wei* activity by making a useful distinction between *power* and *creativity*.

> Whereas "power" often suggests the correlative concepts of domination and control, "creativity" is a notion that can be characterized only in terms of self-actualization. Unlike power relationships that require that tensions among component elements be resolved in favor of one of the components, in relations defined by creativity there is no otherness, no separation or distancing, nothing to overcome. . . . Creativity . . . requires that each element of a relationship be continually in the state of creating the other.[68]

We are now ready to address the following question: if all is *tao* and *tao* is natural, what can it mean to be unnatural? Stated in Taoist terminology, the question becomes: if all is *tao* and *tao* is *wu-wei*, what can it mean to be *yu-wei?*

We can define *wu-wei* activity in a positive way as the extent to which the disposing of specific particulars conduces to the self-realization of those same participants. *Wu-wei* describes a productively creative relatedness. *Wu-wei* activity "characterizes"—i.e., produces the character or *ethos* of— an aesthetic composition. There is no ideal, no closed perfectedness. Ongoing creative achievement itself provides novel possibilities for a richer creativity. If we take a cultural tradition as an example, cultural attainments themselves provide a ground for an ascending culture. In this context, then, *wu-wei* activity is fundamentally qualitative: an aesthetic category rather than an ethical one. The distinction between *wu-wei* and *yu-wei* activity is not to be made by appeal to some fixed standard or principle. There is no invariable structure to provide a science of "correct" relatedness. *Wu-wei* is to be measured in the qualitative categories of an aesthetic achievement. Just as in an aesthetic composition, alternative possibilities preclude the perfect painting or the perfect piano concerto, so they preclude the perfect *wu-wei* "making." Events are always more or less *wu-wei;* they are never purely *wu-wei*.

In the *wu-wei/yu-wei* distinction, *wu* and *yu* retain their polarity. That *wu-wei* is always an active "doing" of *wu-wei*—a "*wei*" *wu-wei*[dh]—makes this point. There is an intendedness or insistence of the particular that makes it particular, and that is served in the creative process. Stated in another way, there is no "pure creativity" that is not in fact an abstraction from a concrete and unique set of circumstances. There is not creativity without context: no *wu* without *yu*. If we allow that *tzu-jan,* "self-evidencing," is a positive statement of *wei wu-wei*, the *tzu*[di], "self/selves" are the *te,* the particular "selves" that constitute the loci and produce the possibilities for creative expression.

But just as there is no *wu*—no "pure creativity"—without a specific context, so there is nothing that is not subject to creative transformation. There is no *yu* without *wu*.

The interpreter's problem with Taoist *unnaturalness*—*yu-wei* activity— is resolved by regarding *naturalness* or *wu-wei* as an aesthetic rather than a logical category—a description of the quality of a given event. If we accept this, any particular event is always, in some discernible measure, *wu-wei*. It is just that some events are more *wu-wei* than others; some events disclose a higher quality of the self-expressiveness of their constituent elements than others. We distinguish *wu-wei* from *yu-wei* activity by the quality of the creative event—the same way that we distinguish a good piece of music from a bad one, or a good painting from one that is not so good.

Among contemporary interpreters of Taoism, the philosopher with the keenest appreciation of this aesthetic core in Taoism seems to be Angus Graham. He repeatedly underscores the critically important observation that the message of the *Chuang Tzu* is in large measure conveyed by artisans of one kind or another, and suggests that "grasping the Way is a matter of 'knowing how,' not 'knowing that.' "[69] In fact, it will help to clarify my interpretation of *wu-wei* activity by citing a passage from Graham's discussion of *spontaneity* and registering the contrast.

> People who really know what they are doing, such as crooks, carpenters, swimmers, boatmen, cicada-catchers, whose instruction is always available to any philosopher or emperor who has the sense to listen to them, do not go in much for analyzing, posing alternatives, and reasoning from first principles. They no longer even bear in mind any rules they were taught as apprentices. They attend to the total situation and respond, trusting to a knack which they cannot explain in words, the hand moving of itself as the eye gazes with unflagging concentration. . . . The Taoist ideal is a spontaneity disciplined by an awareness of the objective. Let us say then that "Follow the Way" is translatable as "Respond with awareness (of what is objectively so)." The awareness will be, not only of the mirrored situation, but of how as a matter of objective fact things can be done (not of what on prudential or moral grounds ought to be done), knowing how, knack, skill, art.[70]

The presuppositions that have been outlined above—aesthetic composition and polarity—would not allow Graham's assertion that the Taoist functions on the single imperative of "responding with awareness to what is objectively so." The intrinsic relatedness of particulars precludes any notion of "objective fact." In spite of this, there is much in Graham's interpretation that can be taken as corroborative. His interpretation of "following the Way" as "responding" parallels the notion of integration that has been developed above. His use of expressions such as "awareness" and "respect for things as they objectively are" is reminiscent of my description of intrinsic relatedness as patterns of deference. Graham's emphasis on "what is objectively so," although arguably flawed with the assertion of "objectivity," is consistent with my stress on the importance given the integrity of the particular—the notion of insistent particularity. Graham is appreciative of the ultimate appeal in Taoism to aesthetic criteria, although his tendency to trivialize aesthetic sensibility by reducing it to a term such as "knack" is a source of some consternation. The kinds of choices made by Graham's Taoist are clearly not those of the scientist working off of a hypothesis; they are those of the artist addressing his canvas.

A revisioning of Graham's imperative to take account of these differences might suggest an interpretation of *wu-wei* as "responding with an awareness that enables one to maximize the creative possibilities of himself in his environment."

VII. Taoism as a Conceptual Resource for an
Environmental *Ethos*

In "The Historical Roots of our Ecological Crisis," Lynn White, Jr. identifies several cultural presuppositions in our tradition that have resulted in our present ecological condition. In summary, he suggests, first, that the radical anthropomorphism of the Judeo-Christian tradition has construed the human being as the steward of a transcendent God. This intimate relationship with God justifies an arrogant, exploitative attitude toward nature. Second, this sanctioned exploitation of the environment has encouraged an insensitive and often brutal science and technology. And finally, the cosmogonic and teleological dimensions of our religious heritage, defining history in a linear way, have established a largely unquestioned belief in perpetual progress.

In this same benchmark paper, White dismisses as a nonviable alternative the possibility of addressing the environmental concerns generated by these presuppositions by looking to non-Western cultural traditions.

> More science and more technology are not going to get us out of the present ecological crisis until we find a new religion, or rethink our old one. The beatniks, who are the basic revolutionaries of our times, show a sound instinct in their affinity for Zen Buddhism, which conceives of the man-nature relationship as very nearly the mirror image of the Christian view. Zen, however, is as deeply conditioned by Asian history as Christianity is by the experience of the West, and I am dubious of its viability among us.[71]

White is undoubtedly right in questioning the possibility of wholesale mass conversion to a non-Western religion, even though stranger things have befallen cultural traditions. But if he is also right in identifying our ecological crisis as the consequence of presuppositions deeply sedimented in every corner of our culture, one wonders where else we can turn in order to clarify our own assumptions and to seek alternatives. In these days of mass communication and cultural flux, we do have access to the insights of other traditions. Certainly, we cannot escape the problems of having to understand these insights through the medium of our own culture, but if they are to transform us in any way at all, they must be meaningful to us. From what has been said above in the attempt to interpret the central vocabularies of Taoist philosophy, the need to transform these ideas to make them appropriate to our own circumstances is entirely consistent with this Taoist tradition.

In the Taoist *ars contextualis* we can discern attitudes which make this world different from our own. First, the underlying commitment to the interdependence of polar categories precludes the man/nature dualism that ultimately warrants the is/ought, fact/value, moral/amoral distinctions. Polarity requires that the human being is irreducibly "person-in-environment." Under this conceptual framework, personal cultivation and the cultivation of one's environment are coextensive. To reduce nature to a "means" is not only to compromise the creative possibilities of nature, but also to impoverish one's own.

The notion of personal responsibility is altered since we cultivate the environment not as an "other" but as an immediate dimension of ourselves. In fact, the immediacy entailed by the Taoist notion of polarity requires that we further refine the definition of the human being as "person-in-environment" by making it "personal." That is, given the Taoist concern for the priority of the concrete particular, "person" is an unjustifiable abstraction that distances the specific person from immediate responsibility. Taoism's concreteness returns us to our own particularity as the beginning point of natural order. We cannot play the theoretician and derive an environmental ethic by appeal to universal principles, but must apply ourselves to the aesthetic task of cultivating an environmental *ethos* in our own place and time, and recommending this project to others by our participation in their environments. This commitment to aesthetic composition is encouraged both by the sense of personal responsibility and the enjoyment possible in the expression of personal creativity.

Another dimension of Taoism that might stimulate reflection is the consequence of taking the notion of intrinsic relatedness seriously. Beyond the profound responsibility entailed by the recognition that any personal disposition affects all things, there is the reverence for the environment as a determining condition of one's own actualization. The doctrine of "the parity of things" requires that one respect the integrity of these environing conditions as ends in themselves as well as means to one's own ends. The acknowledgement that everything must be what it is in order for me to be what I am challenges our anthropocentrism and its attendant pathetic fallacy.

The other side of this deference for one's environment, and the humility that it entails, is self-respect: "Only when one can govern the empire with the same attitude as he loves his own person can he be commissioned with the empire."[72] If one considers that all of nature conduces to one's personal fulfillment and the pleasure that it brings, and that all of nature is affected by one's own unique disposition and is enriched by the quality of one's contribution, it makes the integrity of each person of staggering consequence.

Another point of reflection is the consequence of accepting the Taoist conception of transformation. That is, all of the manifold particulars in existence are ongoing participants in the process of change. Continuity and diversity are valued, but any notion of permanence is rejected as a misconception of the nature of reality. For better or worse, the principles of conservation, to the extent that they are antagonistic to change, require rethinking. If the quality of the environment can justify it, massive transformation is not necessarily unacceptable.

Taoism, furthermore, does not concentrate divinity in one transcendent God. In fact, far from separating *spirituality* and *divinity* as irreconcilables, these two concepts are represented by the same term, *shen*[dj]. This term, *shen,* is etymologically derived from the more primitive notion of *extension,* suggesting that one becomes increasingly spiritual and ultimately divine by virtue of the quality of one's contribution to significance to the world. This contribution is made both by the realization of one's own particular integrity and by the quality of integration that it entails. The aesthetic experience of fully disclosing one's specific particularity for the harmony of one's environment opens into a broader religious sensibility as the perimeter of the environment is extended. Again, given the hylozoistic nature of the cosmos, there is no reason to conclude that spirituality and divinity are the exclusive concerns of humanity. More likely they are cultivated ubiquitously in nature.

That the Taoist presuppositions, in large part characteristic of the evolution of Chinese culture generally, put specific constraints on the appropriateness of scientific and technological development is a historical fact. Although the Taoists expressed reservations about the notion of cumulative culture, it is also the case that the sensibilities of this tradition have supported the pursuit of aesthetic and religious experience among the Chinese. Given that the quality of this experience is always a function of the imagination and a spiritual effort of the specific participants, there is no teleology that would underwrite the concept of perpetual progress.

In conclusion, the aesthetic rather than the metaphysical starting point of Taoist philosophy means that the disposing of the environment is always a negotiated achievement that seeks to maximize the possibilities of the participating details, and as such, reflects an attractive spirit of tolerance and compromise.

CHARACTER GLOSSARY

a 道術	aa 張	ba 莊子	ca 恒德	da 翦
b 和	ab 弱	bb 淮南子	cb 玄德	db 詐
c 羹	ac 強	bc 馬王堆	cc 上德	dc 祚
d 粥	ad 興	bd 乙本	cd 厚	dd 去聲
e 呂氏春秋	ae 廢	be 孫臏兵法	ce 廣	de 祚
f 割烹	af 與	bf 黃帝四經	cf 孔	df 爲而不恃
g 陰	ag 取	bg 道家	cg 積	dg 齊物
h 陽	ah 清	bh 道德家	ch 盛	dh 爲無爲
i 自然	ai 濁	bi 說文	ci 普	di 自
j 無	aj 正	bj 升	cj 豐	dj 神
k 有	ak 偏	bk 得	ck 深	dk 呂氏春秋本味遍
l 難	al 厚	bl 彳	cl 樸	dl 登
m 易	am 薄	bm 亜	cm 玄	dm 木
n 長	an 溫	bn 心	cn 眞人	dn 外得於人內得於己也
o 短	ao 暴	bo 悳	co 眞	do 知
p 高	ap 眞	bp 直	cp 匕（化）	dp 被
q 下	aq 氣	bq 種	cq 物化	dq 誠
r 前	ar 陰陽	br 植	cr 㠯	dr 彼
s 後	as 五行	bs 性	cs 首	ds 知者
t 剛	at 生	bt 爲	ct 會意字	
u 柔	au 德	bu 失	cu 專爲	
v 成	av 道	bv 知	cv 逍遙遊	
w 缺	aw 無爲	bw 治	cw 有爲	
x 盈	ax 有爲	bx 不得已	cx 作	
y 沖	ay 道德經	by 無非我	cy 爲	
z 敝	az 老子	bz 常德	cz 僞	

Units of Change—Units of Value

Robert C. Neville

At least the following three projects suggest themselves as requisite for an adequate understanding of environmental ethics.

1. A conception of understanding, including natural and social science, must be developed which facilitates showing the carry-over of value from one thing to another. Ecology is ethically interesting to the extent that changes carry value over from one thing to another, modifying it in various ways. The ethical question for ecology is how value is altered by changes.

2. An axiological conception of value must be developed which shows both that value is an achievement in actual things and that it is constituted in part by the relations in which things stand. A conception of this sort is presupposed in the first project.

3. A cosmological conception must be developed that displays how there can be enduring individuals with their own integrity which at the same time are internally related to some ecological systems. The theory must comprehend how both individuals and systems have value, and how value is transformed as it passes through a system to individuals and from the individuals to the system. In particular, the theory must show how an individual can belong to several systems at once, is determined in part by the roles played there, and at the same time mediates the effects of one system on another and might contribute some free effects in its own to the systems, thereby modifying them.

While these three projects by no means provide a complete philosophic position for discussing environmental ethics, they are at least necessary conditions. I want now to ask how Chinese philosophy might contribute some resources for them.

I. The Carry-over of Value in Change

The Chinese tradition in its most ancient roots conceives of the elementary units of reality as changes from *yin* to *yang* or vice versa. More particularly, an identifiable unit of reality is a harmony of *yin-yang* transformations. A harmony is stable when all of its transformations repeat themselves; this can be called inertial change. A harmony is moving when some of its transformations are replaced by other transformations. Stability is thus a species of harmonic change. A harmony is always a harmony of harmonies. Though ancient, this idea was explicitly articulated by Chou Tun-i in his "Explanations of the Diagram of the Great Ultimate."

That *yin-yang* transformations can repeat themselves means that there are measures or patterns ingredient in harmonies—so much *yin* here relative to so much *yang* there, again and again. Differences between transformations consist in different measures of *yin* and *yang* being exhibited. Thus there are patterns that can be ingredient in a harmony, and over time those patterns can be repeated or exchanged for other patterns. Furthermore, there are relations between patterns so that some patterns can be ingredient in a harmony because they are sustained or tolerated by the ingredience of other patterns. Despite all the activities of my body, the repeated general functional interdependence of my organ systems is tolerated by all body movements; to move in ways that prohibit that functional interdependence entails death of the body. Because patterns ingredient in the same harmony mutually influence one another, changes in some alter the conditions for the possibility of changes in others. It may be safe to say that all harmonies are constantly changing patterns, but according to different rates of exchange. The stability in our environment consists in the repetition of patterns. The greatest stability consists in repeated patterns that are tolerant of very great changes elsewhere. Perhaps the Neo-Confucian notion of *li,* principle, is a resource for developing the notion of pattern and pattern exchange.

The Taoist sensibility articulates a cultural aesthetic expressive of this conception of change. All things are in movement, and the movements relate to one another so as to constitute a great flow. Harmonic processes show patterns coming together in harmonies so as to allow for more complex harmonies, such as in the story of Chuang-tzu's wife, and then change so as no longer to tolerate the complex harmony, returning the situation to more basic elements. The Taoists properly called attention within process to those elements making up the general tolerance of change, the feminine, motherly, womblike patterns that both survive the special changes and provide the matrix out of which the special changing harmonies can arise. For instance, *t'ai chi ch'uan,* the Taoist exercise, cultivates those fundamental movements which, when practiced and perfected, pull all the other physical and emotional movements into a reinforcing harmony and support them, allowing for extraordinary, because fundamentally well-grounded, special movements.

Suppose value consists—as I shall argue shortly—in achieving the ingredience of a pattern within process. If the pattern is reiterated, the value is carried over to the new stage of the harmony. But since many elements in the harmony are moving, the pattern may be exchanged for a somewhat different pattern, achieving a somewhat different value. Ecological ethics presupposes a science which can explain how values are altered by the changes in their environment. Of course, the elements in the environment are altered as well, which means that they alter in value.

Some harmonies are environmental systems, which means that they exhibit diachronic patterns that essentially relate the earlier and later elements of the enduring harmony. There are also many other kinds of harmonies between these two poles. Environmental science should be able to trace how patterns are altered by changes moving around a system, from the system to enduring individuals, from earlier to later stages of the enduring individuals, from the individual back to the system, and from one system through an individual to another system in which the individual functions. This science is properly formulated for ethics when it can explain how patterns as achieved values are transformed as they move through these change points. Ethics is interested in the ways that changes affect the worth of things, and it needs structural analyses that display changes in worth.

II. Value as Achievement

This is not the place to introduce a formal axiology. Let us suppose, however, that value consists in achieving an existential integration of things; the specific value is the sum of the values of the things integrated plus the extra value achieved by integrating them this way rather than that (if there are alternatives). Now there are two components of the integration. There are the "other things" which enter into the process as the conditions which have to be integrated, and there is the existential process itself of fitting them together. A patterned harmony can be analyzed into its component parts, and is related to all the other harmonies around through those parts; its pattern is what it is because all those things can fit together. Because of this a harmony is defined in terms of its relations, not in terms of any isolated nature. On the other hand, the patterned harmony has its own existential process of integrating things together, and this is its own essential individuality. Without the essential features of the process of integration, the harmony would reduce to its components and their relations. Without the relational components there would be nothing to integrate, hence no definiteness of integration. Therefore, a harmony is a harmony of two different kinds of features, the conditional ones and the essential ones; neither is more important than the other. This conception differs both from atomisms that give too much autonomy to isolated individuals, externally related by somewhat unreal laws, and from idealisms or monisms which swallow up all existential differences in super-unities.

The Taoists again have created a cultural aesthetic for a theory of things in relation such as this. On the one hand, they emphasize the inner spontaneity and individuality of things, and on the other hand, the relatedness of things, the deference each thing's existence pays to other things. Perhaps the Confucianists have extended this analysis of inner existential integration and environmental relatedness to the social sphere.

III. Enduring Individuals and Systems

The central practical problem for environmental ethics has to do with those values which consist in the achievement of systematic environments, filled with valuable individuals, and those values that have to do with the special claims, if any, made by human individuals and societies. That problem can never be addressed adequately until we understand just what kinds of values are involved in both cases, in commensurable terms, and understand also what their relations are. More than that, we need to understand the specific environmental—physical and social—systems involved, with their specific values.

I would like to call attention here to the special kinds of values to be found in human life, values that are likely to be neglected when employing ecological models that treat people as species members and niche occupiers. These are the values focused on by Confucianists.

The temporal endurance of a human being is not just the maintenance of typical patterns through a long stretch of time, nor the growth of a maturing organism embodying a diachronic career pattern. It is also the case that at any time within a person's life, the existential process of integrating life's elements includes both part and future states of the person as essential, not merely conditional elements. That is to say, a contemporary pattern does not merely integrate past and future states with present conditions, but does so essentially. Who the person is now depends in essential ways on that person's identity in the past and future. There are thus special patterns, such as moral identity, rationality, ego identity, and family and social role identity, which a person develops over time, building one upon the others, which must be embodied in each moment for the person to be himself or herself. Most of the structures of the social environment are designed to foster these epitomes of human achievement that must be integrated across time into personal identity. These are the virtues which, although socially defined, must be individually developed and must take a somewhat self-conscious position vis-à-vis the normative demands of life's situations.

Ecological ethics needs to pay special attention to the ways by which the physical and social environments bear upon the development, maintenance, and articulate recognition of the epitomizing achievements of value normative for human life. In Western discussions, the biological language of ecology is incommensurate with the ethical language about people. In Chinese thought, the Confucian ethical language might not be wholly discontinuous with the more biologically oriented language of the Taoists. At least it is to be hoped that the attention China has given to reconciling both Taoist and Confucian worlds can provide clues to a common, nontechnical language for environmental ethics.

III

The Japanese World View

The Japanese Concept of "Nature"

Hubertus Tellenbach and Bin Kimura

Origin of "*Shi-Zen*" (*Ji-Nen*) and Nature

The Japanese "*Shi-zen*" or "*Ji-nen*" corresponds to the European term *nature*.[1] Inquiry into the derivation of these terms begins with the meaning attributed to them in the past.

Nature stems from the Latin *natura* which has been taken over directly into all European languages—the exception being Slavic, which did, however, translate the term according to its original signification. The term stems from *gnascor*, which means *to be born, grow, emerge, originate*. *Gnascor* is related to the synonymous Greek term *gignomai*. Thus *nature* is really the translation of *genesis*. The Romans, however, employed *natura* to translate the Greek term *physis*. Just as the Japanese adopted and retained the Chinese term for *nature*, the Romans held on to the Greek meaning of *physis*, without however taking the term itself over into the Latin language.

Shi-zen is originally a Chinese term which the Japanese took over about 1,500 years ago together with all other characters. In ancient Chinese culture the term had already gained fundamental significance. In Lao-Tse for example, we read, "Man is based on earth, earth is based on heaven, heaven is based on the Way (*Tao*) and the Way is based on nature (*Tsu-jun*, Japanese: *Shi-zen*)."

Physis and *Onozukara/Mizukara*

It is interesting to set the tone permitting a comparison between the ancient Japanese and Greek comprehensions of nature. This is only possible if one reverts to Heidegger's uncovering of the original (Greek) understanding of *physis*. In contrast to the ancient Japanese, the Greeks gave *physis* a temporal connotation encompassing all of nature; furthermore with the onset of Greek philosophy the term *physis* meant "being as such in its entirety."[2] It was worthwhile paying attention to the full spectrum of meanings (in Heidegger's interpretation) of *physis* and to the adverbial and adjectival expressions in ancient Japanese. *Physis* is "that which comes forth of itself (e.g. the sprouting of a rose), that which in opening itself up unfolds, and in unfolding makes its appearance, maintains itself and abides—in short, that which in coming forth and abiding, governs."[3] Heidegger emphasizes, however, that *physis* in this sense is not simply synonymous with such processes as are observed in nature, in beings. On the contrary, according to Heidegger, because the Greeks had a fundamental poetic-philosophical experience of being, "that which they felt compelled to name *physis* opened itself up to them," nature in the sense of the world of beings, that which becomes and that which endures. In this sense *physis* is "being itself, by virtue of which beings are first observable and durable."[4] Originally *physis* meant "both heaven and earth, stone and plant, animal and man, history of man as work of man and gods, finally and foremost the gods themselves under fate . . . *physis* is that *coming into being,*" which brings itself forth out of concealment into appearance. Later on, the essence of *physis,* as that which governs in coming forth and abiding, is experienced above all in that which manifests this character most emphatically—*Ta physei onta, ta physika*—nature-like being which then becomes *physis* in the narrow sense of the term. (If from this subsequent restricted aspect one questions being as such, then the questioning proceeds beyond this: *meta.* Philosophical questioning of beings as such is then metaphysical.)

Before the term *Shi-zen/Ji-nen* was taken over from China, the Japanese had no single concept to uniformly express the totality of mountains, rivers, plants, and so on. In their own language the Japanese lacked the concept corresponding to the European *nature.* Although in ancient Japanese there was no substantive for *nature,* it did have adjectival and adverbial expressions for *Shi-zen/Ji-nen* such as *Onozukara.* In the oldest Japanese collection of poetry, *Manyōshū* (fifth to eighth century), one finds the term *Onozukara* written with the same character as *Shi-zen. Onozukara* corresponds in meaning to the German *von selbst* or *von sich aus,* the English *of itself.* In an English translation of Lao-Tse (A. Waley), *Tsu-jan* (= *Shi-zen*) means *what-is-so-of-itself.* Generally *Onozukara* is written with the first of the two characters for *Shi-zen.* The same character, however, also stands for two other original Japanese terms: *Mizukara* (self, oneself/itself) and *Yori* (of/from . . .). Analyzing the first two, *Onozukara* and *Mizukara,* they apparently tend in opposite directions. As *of itself Onozukara* expresses an objective state which begins of itself without any external mediation. *Mizukara* as *self* expresses, on the other hand, a subjective state in which someone himself spontaneously carries something through to completion. That the Japanese believe they can express these seemingly autonomous terms by means of a single character points towards a deeper insight by which they apprehend *Onozukara* and *Mizukara, nature* and *self,* as originating from the same common ground.

That which essentially binds the spontaneous processes in nature with the self-fulfilling events and activities in the course of my own self-development is the third meaning attributed to the same character: *Yori* (*of/from* . . .). This is also expressed as the suffix *-kara* in *Onozukara* and *Mizukara.* In this case *-kara* also signifies *of/from.* . . . Whereas *Ono* in *Onozukara* signifies *on its own, self,* the *Mi* in *Mizukara* means *flesh* or *body. Onozukara* signifies accordingly *of/from oneself/itself* and *Mizukara of/from the body.* The common root of *Onozukara* and *Mizukara,* which led the ancient Japanese to express both meanings by a single character, lies not in the *self* but rather in the *of/from.* . . . In expressing the common ground of *Onozukara* and *Mizukara,* nature and self, the Japanese thus point to something like a spontaneous becoming, a force flowing forth from an original source.

Referring prudently to a comparable range of meanings, certain similarities seem to become apparent. The *of/from oneself/itself* expressed in *Onozukara* appears to us to be essentially related to the coming forth of itself, to the becoming, a force flowing forth from an original source.

Referring prudently to a comparable range of meanings, certain similarities seem to become apparent. The *of/from oneself/itself* expressed on *Onozukara* appears to us to be essentially related to the coming forth of itself, to the becoming and enduring of *physis*—related therefore in the phenomenal structure of the of/from. . . . A further essential relationship seems to exist, namely between *Onozukara* and *Mizukara,* nonhuman and (bodily) human. As aspects of the one, the whole, they stem from the same origin characterized in the of/from . . . structure of *coming into being.*

Nature and *Shi-Zen/Ji-Nen*

With the translation into the Roman *natura* the original meaning of *physis* was lost.[5] As mentioned above *natura* was taken over into all Occidental languages. One sees already in Latin how many different kinds of meanings had been assigned to *nature.* A glance at the different ways the term 'nature' is employed in Western vernacular languages shows the wide range of meanings it has assumed. Normally 'nature' signifies what is *outside,* in the sense of what is opposite us—e.g., the tree over there, the flower here in the garden, the animals over there at pasture. 'Outside' can also mean what "begins" beyond the city limits: plants, the greens, the abode of both game and domestic animals; but also stones, water, the *elements*. The meaning of *being outside* recedes into the background, however, in cases where we employ the term 'nature' to denote certain constant traits in man and animals. When we speak, for example, of animals having shy or aggressive *natures*, or of irritable or indolent *natures* in people, we mean different types of habitual disposition which have developed of themselves without our doing.

In a related sphere the term *nature* is used to imply modes of behavior designating membership in a species characterized by certain qualities. Thus when a member of a particular race or blood relationship is said to be especially daring or particularly cool or determined, we are again being addressed by the *voice of nature*. There is also a manner of *seeing* nature which does not primarily have the character of standing opposite. What is meant is nature as prototype or model for the arts. Thus, for example, an artist paints *according to nature*. Similarly one says that painting has become *second nature* to an artist.

Of/from itself can also be found in a further context with the term *nature*, where man is still said to be in the state of nature. This is said of a man on a desert island, a state he forfeits in becoming civilized. The opposition seems fully removed where nature is presented as the correlate of man and climate. Kimura has pointed out that the Japanese thinker, Watsuji, borrowing on ideas from Herder and A. von Humboldt, has developed a "Philosophy of Climate" (Fuhdo).[6] Corresponding to the climate of the desert, meadowlands, and monsoon are different types of temperaments or reactibility such as an inclination to nearness to or distance from fellow human beings, the development of the gifts of intuition or of cool sobriety, even a readiness to trust or distrust. In all countries in which plains and mountains converge this can be experienced in the vivid differences between people from the mountains, the valleys, or the broad plains.

The position adopted at the other end of the spectrum, that which observes nature as something standing opposite or an object, reduces nature to the status of being the object of the natural sciences. This interpretation of nature concentrates upon the elementary components of material things and their kinetic processes. This became possible when the meaning of *physis* was narrowed in the establishment of metaphysics—and especially in the dethronement by Aristotle and encroaching Christianity of the gods bound up with the Greek *physis*. Thus in the late Hellenistic period the Greeks named the Christians, among other things, the *Atheoi* (those without gods).

With an eye to the problem complex of inside and outside as it is presented in Japanese art forms, there is perhaps no intuition or thinking in Europe which so approximates that of the Japanese as Goethe's. In his writing on the philosophy of nature there is the famous text: "Everything which is in the subject is also in the object, and even something more. Everything which is in the object is in the subject, and even something more. In a twofold manner we are both secure and lost."

In modern Japanese one normally employs *Shi-zen* to signify *nature*. For some time now the European *natura* has been translated by *Shi-zen*. In this manner it is also used as a substantive. So used, its meaning coincides completely with the European understanding of nature as *outside,* as that *opposite* me, withdrawn from the sphere of human arbitrariness. Such a translation of nature by *Shi-zen* is correct etymologically inasmuch as an *original* meaning of Shi-zen names "something like mountain, river, ocean, plant, animal, rain, wind, etc.," signifying therefore a way of being which exists without human intervention. This use of *Shi-zen* developed from the adverbial or adjectival applications of this term in which the typical Japanese, Far-Eastern way of viewing and thinking manifests itself most originally. Apparently under the influence of the Buddhist tradition, *Shi-zen* so used was pronounced like *Ji-nen*. This was particularly the case with the Japanese before and during the Meiji period. In Buddhist texts *Ji-nen* has two meanings: (1) without human intervention; (2) of/from oneself/itself so, truly so.

Even outside Buddhist circles *Ji-nen,* with suffixes (*Ji-nen-ni, Ji-nen-to*), is mainly used as an adverb: "as something is so of itself, as it becomes thus of itself." The pronunciation of the character as *Shi-zen* must however have existed along with that of *Ji-nen* from the beginning and have meant essentially the same: that which without human intervention is self-evident and natural, something eventful which befalls man (e.g., sudden death). However, despite all such correspondences in meaning between nature and *Shi-zen* or *Ji-nen,* still the subtle though decisive differences cannot be overlooked. Contrary to the object-oriented meaning of nature, *Shi-zen/Ji-nen* has no such meaning. It never signifies the object as such, but presents only its respective manner of being and becoming. Even if *Shi-zen/Ji-nen* is used as a substantive, one signifies by this less the objects of nature as such than their way of being "which exist without human action." *Shi-zen* in no way stands opposite the subject, rather it always indicates a certain state or mood in the subject. When one encounters something as it is of itself, sometimes one instinctively feels familiar and at home, sometimes anxious and wary. *This state of familiarity or anxiety constitutes the essential meaning of Shi-zen/Ji-nen.* Certainly the realm of feeling is also affected in the European's encounter with nature. But even then the European remains "opposite nature." It is not so that this *feeling* as such is considered to be *nature* as is the case with the Japanese. This can perhaps best be made clear by taking *Shi-zen* in the sense of an *unforeseen event.* "Were a case of *Shi-zen* to arise" means "were something unexpected to occur, a case of necessity, or should I meet with an accident." From a European perspective such an event must appear unnatural or contrary to nature. Consider in this regard the difference between the European and Japanese garden. In the English garden, for example, one seeks nature free of all "artificiality." In the Japanese garden, on the contrary, one attempts to express within a confined space the total of mountains and rivers. This is a highly artistic act representing the highest meaning of *Shi-zen*. The English garden is available to everyone, that is, it has the character of a public garden. The Japanese garden, on the other hand, is of a private nature created solely for the few who are artistically gifted. Nature in the English garden relates itself equally towards everybody. The *Shi-zen* of a Japanese garden requires one who is able to experience *Shi-zen* as such. This implies that *Shi-zen* is never outside, but rather within this or that person. The same holds true for the *Shi-zen* of the tea-ceremony, Ikebana art or the typical Japanese pastoral art. One senses this radical distinction in the attitude of man to nature, which prevented the Japanese from arriving at a conception of nature from which natural science could have evolved.

Nature and *Mu-Joh*

We also call *nature* that which primarily and immediately envelops us: light and darkness, warmth and coldness, humidity and dryness (the climates), and the omnipresent air. Like migratory birds on the wing and fish on their journey to spawning places, we too are affected by the times of day and seasons. Just as in the case of race, sex, bodily constitution, and talents, we inherit determined possibilities, so too we are *cast* (Heidegger) into these periodic rhythms. Here nature is that which casts man into a position of involuntariness and indisposability. This in turn manifests how much in European thinking the will is linked to freedom. Nature's indisposability or nature's command over man—especially in being ill—poses a fundamental problem to our understanding of freedom. Freedom, particularly as health, means the equilibrium of the fundamental conditions of human existence. Through knowledge, of course, we can once again gain a certain degree of control over this indisposable aspect of nature. A broader knowledge of the details of life's natural flow enables the farmer or forester, for example, to make prognoses concerning nature's course. Skilled laymen are acquainted with the healing effects of plants: the effects of the red foxglove (digitalis) on the heart, or that of *Pagal-kadawa* (Reserpin) employed in India to treat psychoses. *This application of nature to human being-ill presents a splendid example of the complimentarity between (nature) casting and (man) cast.* In European vernacular languages the term nature is also used to denote the limits of what is possible. We say of a man who oversteps the bounds of his abilities that he is "doing violence to his nature." If this becomes habitual the individual must "pay nature its dues"—i.e., he will become ill or must die.

The Japanese expression for nature in the sense of the indisposable or that which is in no way disposable to life-oriented care, is *Mu-joh,* which means literally *nothing permanent. Mu-joh* comes most directly to mind in connection with the deep melancholy experienced by man in not being able to ward off the transitoriness of life. *Mu-joh* manifests itself as an ascendent or descendent life as in being ill or dying. Nevertheless the fleetingness of nature expressed in *Mu-joh* cannot be understood in only a pessimistic or even "nihilistic" way. In a manner comparable only to Heidegger, Dōgen, the thirteenth-century Japanese Zen Master and thinker, developed from a profound *Mu-joh* intuition his radical concept of the relationship between time and being. Dōgen conceives truth in both its transitory and permanent character as the event of being in time.

> Being-time means that time as such is being and that every being is time. . . .
> Thus the pine tree is time, the bamboo is time. Time is understood not only
> as flying. . . . Should time arise only in flying, then gaps must occur. The
> entire universe follows one after the other, time, time, time. Since being is
> time, I too am being-time.[7]

Thus for Dōgen the essence of *being-time* is the *eventual character* of truth as a *coming to pass of that which discloses itself.* Every being, cast in its *Mu-joh* way of being, reveals of itself the lasting truth. Insofar as truth is always freedom, the indisposable in nature experiences its determination primarily through the medium of freedom: as its dimension.

In Heidegger's terms, the (nature)-*casting* (man)-*cast* character of nature manifests itself to the Japanese not as a (relative) disposability over the indisposability of its inherent laws, but in its essential character as the sublime freedom and spontaneity of that which, though indisposable to man, is *of itself* (= *Ji-nen* = *Onozukara*). Instead of ascertaining its inherent laws "objectivity," the Japanese lives this great spontaneity of nature "subjectively" as the source of his own self (*Ji-ko* = *Mizukara*).

We have seen that where (each person's) self and the (great) nature disclose themselves as originating from the same source, the latter reveals itself as the spontaneity of freedom. To be free, however, means that something truly is of itself. Thus the Japanese word *Shi-zen/Ji-nen* can in a similar fashion to the German term 'Natur' signify specific ways of being proper to things. When man, animals, or things manifest their own particular manner of being themselves, then they are in their *Ji-nen* and thus are wholly free.

The basic presupposition of Morita therapy, a Japanese psychotherapy influenced by Zen Buddhism, is founded on this conception of nature and freedom. The neurotic patient endeavors to escape his agonizing *symptoms*. The result is a desperate conflict with himself. The sick person cannot bear to be as he is; he wants instead to be just what he is not. This, however, is the very opposite of being free. The Morita therapy aims at a complete acceptance of being disturbed, rendering oneself fully to the disturbances. Interaction with nature in the form of occupational therapy in the garden plays a major role here. Its purpose is to allow the sick person to be absorbed directly in the great spontaneity of nature, in Onozukara's *of itself*. Only when he, thanks to the spontaneity of nature opening itself up, is prepared to tolerate himself calmly in his disturbances, will he be in the position to truly and freely come to himself. He shall then be no longer disturbed by his *symptoms*.

Nature as Great *Ji-Ko*

In European vernacular languages the term *nature* is also employed to denote specific ways of being by which something is experienced. Thus we speak, for example, of the nature of birds, the nature of fishes. In doing so we refer the animals to their *element,* to air and water. We even speak of a divine nature, the *Nature of God*.

We also speak of human nature in the sense of man's specific way of being. *The term nature, then, characterizes human existence in the full range of man's possibilities*. In his existence determined by the category of the possible, man has passionately grasped freedom as the freedom of choice. Along with it, however, came anxiety into the world. To the European mind, since Kierkegaard, herein lies the absolute origin of neurosis and the starting point of its anthropological-existential treatment.

From poetry came the first misgivings about the inextricability of all our possibilities from nature at large. Stefan George, for example, writes:

> You, free as fish or as a bird,
> Wherein you hang you're not aware.

In Japanese thought the interdependence of *self* and *nature* in an original unity manifests itself as constitutive. The concept of nature as the great self was the starting point of Kitaro Nishida's thinking, one of Japan's leading twentieth-century philosophers (1870–1945). A key concept of the young Nishida is the *pure experience* in which the *subject,* without any reflection or separation from its *object,* merges with it in pure oneness of being. It is not that there is first individual self and hence experience, but rather first experience as such and hence self.[8] In a later formulation he states, "When the world becomes aware of itself, so too the self; when the self becomes aware of itself, so too the world."[9] *In this becoming aware of itself, Ji-nen (nature) and Ji-ko (self) can be revealed as an original unity.* In the spontaneity of *from itself,* Ji-nen as Onozukara signifies at the same time *Ji-ko* as Mizukara in its spontaneity of *from oneself.* The common structure of *Ji-nen* and *Ji-ko* corresponds to the common origin (in this spontaneity). This can be expressed as follows: *of itself to itself.* Thus the pure experience of nature—or better, nature as pure experience—reveals itself *as absolute freedom.* Freedom, *Ji-yuh,* means literally, originating from itself. Being free is thus the mode of being characterizing the interwovenness of nature and self. Insofar as my self is nature itself, it is also free.

Nature and *Sho/Sei*

The term *nature* is applied in still another way in European vernacular languages to denote the specific manner of being which is experienced over and beyond the sphere of living beings. Thus in the realm of values we speak, for example, of the *nature of good or the nature of evil.* This usage of the term extends itself to the realm of artefacts. One says, for example, it lies in the *nature of things* (even if it concerns, for example, plastics); or we complain that the *nature of the circumstances* (i.e., conditions historically evolved) is stronger than we are.

In the case where the European speaks of nature in the sense of the nature of things, the Japanese does not employ the term *Shi-zen/Ji-nen,* but *Sho* or *Sei,* which means quality, character, species. The Japanese also applies this term in cases where the European speaks of the constant states of living beings, for example, of mild or aggressive, balanced or passionate, gentle or hot-tempered, irascible or indolent *natures.*

Nature a Bearer of the Divine—*Ji-Nen* as Divine

The meaning attributed in the Occident to *nature* reaches its fullest significance in the case where it (nature) is sanctified in bread and wine and fills man with divine life in communion: in "bread, the fruit of the earth and human toil" and in "wine, the fruit of the vine and human toil." Such a division into man, God, and nature is incommensurable with the Japanese understanding of self and world. In *Ji-nen* it is the spontaneous, the boundless which manifests itself in nature. Similar to the concept *natura naturans,* nature is itself the creative, and, as that which brings itself forth, the divine.

We have seen how in European vernacular languages a variety of different meanings have been attached to the term *nature,* and by contrast how Japanese colloquial language expresses the same meanings in a different way. Every attempt to bring the cultures with the fullness of their meaningful forms together in a dialogue begins with the careful and tentative weighing and comparing of the terms determining human existence. This is essential to any possible understanding. The difficulties involved in adopting this starting point are hidden by present-day temporal and spatial conditions facilitating such "contacts," even if the adoption of technical possibilities can hardly be more effectively motivated than through the possibility they offer for true intercultural encounter.

The Japanese Experience of Nature

David Edward Shaner

Examining the Japanese experience of nature may supplement contemporary studies in environmental philosophy. Two relevant themes will be developed herein. First, the Japanese philosophical and religious tradition represents a resource for environmental philosophy in its long-standing theoretical and practical commitment to an ecocentric, as opposed to homocentric or egocentric, world view. Second, exploring the Japanese emphasis upon cultivation (Jp. *shugyō*[a])[1] [of one's personhood or Being[2]] will help us to make a distinction between injunctive rights-based moral theories and ethics [referring to Aristotle's notion of character (Gk. *ethos*) development]. In the Japanese tradition, ecocentricism and cultivation represent two threads that weave a seamless ethical fabric characterized by developing one's sensitivity to others and nature. By describing presuppositions at the heart of the Japanese ecocentric world view and its relation to personal development, it will be possible to lay the groundwork for responsible participation in nature.

When considering Japanese cultural history, it is often helpful to remember that Japan is an island nation. This natural boundary creates a colorful and varied history characterized by successive waves of isolation and assimilation of foreign ideas. Philosophically, Japan is heir to three distinct traditions: (1) Buddhist philosophy originating in India and coming to Japan by way of a variety of Korean and Chinese schools, many of which were profoundly influenced along the way by indigenous Chinese philosophies; (2) Confucian philosophy originating in China and coming to Japan in the form of multiple neo-Confucian schools; and, of course, (3) the indigenous Shintō mythology.

Early Buddhist philosophy was characterized by radical empiricism; metaphysical speculation was considered outside the domain of legitimate epistemological processes whereby that which one could know was restricted to meaningful sense data. Accordingly, "natural experiences" were given value and significance in the sense that ideas issuing from metaphysical stances—for example, ideas concerning the status of the self, life after death, the status of unseen worlds—were denounced as serving only to create conceptual dust on an otherwise "naturally" (primordially/originally) clear epistemic window.

163

In the archetypical ideas of pre-Confucian philosophy, there existed, in agrarian China, a sentiment of consanguinity between persons and nature. In later Taoist philosophy "natural experiences" were also given value and significance insofar as they were characterized as achieved experiences enhancing an awareness of active participation with the Tao, that is, the well-balanced and harmonious processes that are the cosmos itself. When Buddhist schools with the empirical tendencies described above filtered through China, the indigenous philosophies, particularly Taoism, served to enhance, in many diverse ways, their common presuppositions. The neo-Confucian emphasis upon relations and community, though not always extended to nature, also served to enhance a general holistic orientation that was received later in Japan.

Finally, the themes espoused above found a basically receptive culture in Japan insofar as the Shintō mythology describes a pantheistic/animistic world view. Let us now take stock, resisting the sweeping generalizations above, and consider in greater detail, albeit briefly and necessarily selectively, specific concepts that form the backbone of ecocentric attitudes towards nature in the Japanese philosophical tradition.

The Japanese culture is for the most part monolinguistic and monoracial. At various intervals in Japanese cultural history, people have assumed an isolationist posture and have thus been unreceptive to foreign ideas. During less frequent and usually politically motivated periods, the Japanese have assimilated new ideas—such as writing, religious texts, art forms, and instruments enhancing productivity. Assimilation in Japan, however, requires going through an informal, but ever-present, rite of passage. Indeed, appreciating that which is adopted and that which is not is one of the best ways to discover a more authentic understanding of the Japanese world view. Rarely is new information assimilated if it cannot be reinterpreted in such a way that it can be made ideologically relevant to indigenous belief systems. Accordingly, the place to begin an overview of Japanese attitudes toward nature is with pre-Buddhist Shintō mythology.

Apart from a few notable exceptions,[3] a systematic study of early Japan (that is, Japan prior to the introduction of writing occasioned by the importation of Buddhist texts) has been neglected until recently. Heretofore, the Japanese intelligentsia turned their attention toward the study of the cultural history of more ancient civilizations, namely, China and India, whose rich literary and artistic history offered much in comparison with their own limited oral traditions and few cultural artifacts.[4] In recent decades, however, this omission has been addressed with some rigor. Scholars such as Yuasa Yasuo are creating a new interdisciplinary field, sometimes referred to as *Nihongaku*[b] [the equivalent of Gk. *logos* (Jp. *gaku*) plus Japan (*Nihon*); hence "Japanology"] that crosses traditional academic boundaries incorporating philosophy, history, religion, psychology, anthropology, and archaeology. In his work, *Kamigami no Tanjō*[c] [*Birth of Kami*],[5] Yuasa suggests that ritual practices and ceremony were commonplace in pre-Buddhist Japan. In fact, Kōbō Daishi Kūkai (774–835), the founder of the Shingon school of Esoteric Buddhism in Japan, was first attracted to Buddhism as a result of his predilection for religious practice, not theology.[6] Yuasa writes:

> This convergence between Heian Buddhism and Shintō mountain worship probably took place because of the common tradition of cultivation in the mountains. According to the world view of the Japanese mountain religions, the mountains were where the gods (*kami*)[d] were in attendance; a beautiful mountain was called a *kan'nabi*[e] (god's mountain). Usually a stone sacred area was constructed on it and called *iwasaki*[f] (divine throne); the appropriate gods attended the rites.[7]

During this period the philosophical orientation was pantheistic or animistic, wherein all things were believed to participate equally in a "seamless"[8] web of divine presence. Since the million of *kami* were seen as ordinary empirical phenomena instead of being considered symbols of reality itself, one might argue that cultivating a sensitive understanding of nature required a "non-symbolic interpretation of symbols."[9] Early Japanese mythology did not sharply distinguish orders of existence; both feet were planted firmly on the ground. In one of the most famous early Japanese literary collections, the *Man'yōshū*[g] (ca. 759), this love of nature (*biophilia*) was celebrated throughout.[10] The experience of intimacy with nature requires the cultivation of a non-symbolic attitude wherein one does not search for any hidden symbolic meanings or evidence of realities "beyond" or "after" (Gk. *meta*) the physically apparent. It is "natural" in the sense of its purity, sincerity, and simplicity. The natural world was thus considered to be intrinsically valuable. To adulterate the primordial condition of nature was to interfere with the dynamic processes that sustain the nature of nature.

It can be noted that this orientation reflects a philosophical commitment to radical empiricism consistent with early Buddhism. To "see" nature in an undistorted fashion is reminiscent of a Buddhist metaphor concerning one's original mind. One's original mind, sometimes referred to as one's original face, is said to be like a polished mirror reflecting all things clearly. To be truly aware of nature is to prepare oneself to be a good listener, as it were. Buddhist and Shintō ritual practices can therefore be appreciated from the perspective of cleansing and polishing oneself in preparation for an encounter with oneself, others, and nature. The Japanese philosophical tradition is thus filled with terminology that connotes this basic ecocentric orientation. For example, wa^h (harmony), $shugy\bar{o}$ (cultivation), $jinen^i$ (naturalness), $mitsu^j$ (intimacy), and ma^k (interval) each refer to preparing oneself for a relation with others and/or nature. Even specific objects can become the focus of one's cultivated harmony. In calligraphy, dramatic theater, flower arrangement, or the martial arts, one might be instructed to act "naturally" (Jp. $shizen\ ni)^l$ in order to learn to become intimate with the paper, brush, audience, flowers, or opponent, respectively.

It can be noted in this context that the large, standing, outdoor Shintō gates $(t\bar{o}rii)^m$ are considered the entrances to temples without walls. A deep affinity with nature is thus occasioned by a lack of separations between man-made architectural artifacts (places of worship) and that which is being honored. When entering the gate, one is thus reminded of the possibility of acquiring more than just a deep appreciation of nature in its pristine form; one enters nature fully engaging an experience of mutual interpenetration. Similarly, the paper walls $(sh\bar{o}ji^n$ screen) typical of Japanese architecture, are constructed to include nature's participation; one can be sensitive to, for example, changes in light, wind, and temperature. To this day, one can visit the urban centers of Japan and notice a conspicuous absence of buildings on surrounding hilltops. The land that would be considered optimal scenic real estate in most cities world-wide is preserved in a natural setting despite overcrowding and housing shortages. The needs of Japan's industrial complex have thus faced a head-on collision with the more ancient religio-aesthetic ideal centered in ecocentrism and personal "natural" cultivation.

The Sino-Korean Buddhist theories and practices that eventually did find roots in Japan did so because the respective Japanese patriarchs cultivated an ideological affinity with the indigenous "seamless" cosmological perspective—Kūkai is particularly illustrative because of his emphasis upon the intrinsic value and unity of all things participating equally in a dynamic cosmos. Kūkai was born in Sanuki province on the island of Shikoku. A precocious child and a member of a scholar-aristocratic family, he received instruction in poetry and Confucian classics. After formal studies at Nagaoka, he went to the mountains to devote himself to the practice of meditation. It is believed that he spent some time with the $Jinenchish\bar{u}^o$ (School of Natural Wisdom) and was influenced by $Shugend\bar{o}^p$ (The Way of Mountain Asceticism). Each of these mountain religious activities appealed to what Yuasa refers to as the "archaic"[11] aspect of Kūkai's personality.[12] While in the mountains as a youth, Kūkai internalized the notion that *kami* were embodied within the forests, streams, rocks, wind, and mountains. According to this Shintō tradition, these natural phenomena were said to be the offspring of $Izana$-gi^q and $Izana$-mi^r—the mythical creators of the universe. Of specific interest to us is his attitude to the child *Amaterasu* (Sun

Goddess) who gives light to the entire universe. This point is worth noting for the following reason. It is said that in a dream Kūkai was told to consult the *Mahāvairocana Sutra* (*Daibirushana jōbutsu jimben kajikyō*ˢ, popularly known as *Dainichikyō*ᵗ).¹³ It has been suggested that the "ultimate Buddha" (Sk. *Tathāgata Mahāvairocana*, Jp. *Dainichi Nyorai*ᵘ lit., 'great' + 'sun' + 'Thus-come[gone]-one') was understood by the Japanese as "Buddha-nature that shines like a great light within all things."¹⁴ In other words, the pervasive infinite character of *Mahāvairocana* (*Dharmakāya*) was likened to the *Dainichi* (Great Sun) which not only shined over the entire universe, but also, in the sense of *Amaterasu*, shared the same heritage with all other natural phenomena, that is, as the offspring of *Izana-gi* and *Izana-mi*. Just as *Amaterasu* participates in and shares the same reality as that upon which she shines, *Dainichi Nyorai*, as the anthropomorphization of the *Dharmakāya*, permeates all things. However, possessing only this parallel from which to work, Kūkai would not understand fully the esoteric doctrines and many symbolic explanations describing interrelationships within the *Dainichikyō* without instruction.

Convinced that an understanding of this sutra would enable him to grasp the highest truths of Buddhism, Kūkai went to China (804)¹⁵ in search of a Tantric master to guide him. Kūkai met the esoteric master, Hui-kuoᵛ (746–805), and was received by him as his long-awaited successor. In thirty months' time, Kūkai studied Sanskrit, poetry, calligraphy, and other minor arts and became the eighth patriarch of Esoteric Buddhism. He returned to Japan in 806, carrying with him valuable sutras and the paraphernalia necessary for esoteric practice. Kūkai was thus able to return to Japan thoroughly instructed in Esoteric Buddhist theory and practice. His early understanding of the *Dainichikyō*, dependent as it was upon parallels to the Shintō tradition and a limited knowledge of Esoteric Buddhism, gave way to a more thorough knowledge occasioned by the oral instructions passed on to him as the *dharma* successor to Hui-kuo.

While in China, Kūkai would have been exposed to a view of nature that similarly expressed a "continuity of being."¹⁶ His esoteric practices (*mikkyō*)ʷ were not designed to elevate the consciousness of practitioners toward transcendental spheres of reality. Rather, the cultivation of these "natural experiences" reflects a thetically neutral or intentionless perspective whereby the practitioner can enter fully into the very process of being that is nature itself.¹⁷ The complex system of esoteric rituals was, in principle, not entirely different from the aforementioned Shintō rites and ceremonies. In fact Yuasa suggests that

> both Saichōˣ [the founder of the Japanese Tendai School (767–822) and Kūkai had the experience of cultivating themselves in the mountains and they

always paid due respect to the gods [*kami*] of ancient Japan. The idea of receiving the precepts by invoking the presence of the Buddhas at the initiation platform, making one's vows in front of them, arises out of the convergence with this Shintō tradition. At any rate, the attitude of understanding *kairitsu*[y] [ceremonial rites] in this manner, placing the cultivation method of *samadhi* or meditation ["natural experiences"] at its center, is a uniquely Japanese Buddhist idea that shaped the later tradition.[18]

Although the details of esoteric[19] practices and Shintō ritual are far apart, the important point for our purposes is to appreciate that in both traditions any dichotomy between the theory and practice is very thin. Later, Dōgen Kigen[z] (1200–1253), the founder of the Sōtō school of Japanese Esoteric Buddhism, articulated the doctrine that since theories have no import apart from the practices that enable practitioners to authenticate (empirically verify) their meaning, theory and practice should be considered the same—*shushō ichinyo*[aa] [the oneness of cultivation and authentication]. A characteristic, therefore, that typifies Heian, Kamakura, and later Japanese Buddhism is the notion that the meeting ground of religious experience and the experience of nature are identical.

The concept of enlightenment may be the most frequently misunderstood concept in Japanese Buddhism. A brief historical overview may help clarify a number of points concerning enlightenment as it is related to the concept of nature. In many schools of Japanese Buddhism, the close relation between theory and practice can be understood, philosophically, as a close relation between ontology and epistemology. Since humans are not considered to be ontologically privileged or set apart in any other way from the processes of nature, the Way (Jp. *dō;*[ab] Ch. *Tao*)[ac] of coming to know (epistemology) is not considered to be separate from the Way of reality (ontology). The epistemic mode of experience to be cultivated is therefore a dynamic process; it is primarily an attitude, a becoming that occasions an intimacy with the whole of dynamic nature.[20]

In India, Esoteric Buddhism reached its peak around the ninth century A.D. Two main sutras came to China—the *Mahāvairocana Sūtra* (Jp. *Dainichikyō*) and the *Vajrasekhara Sūtra* (Jp. *Kongōchokyō*).[ad] In the former, the Sanskrit concept of *garbha* (womb) underscores the notion that all things share the same *Ur*-ground without discrimination. *Garbha,* as it is used in earlier Hindu schools, also connotes activity, transformation, appropriation, or birth into an enriched state of being. In short, it suggests development via becoming. In the latter sutra, *vajra* connotes being, that is, that which is unchangeable and thus transcends procreation and phenomenal states of existence.

At this point in our study we are prepared to appreciate that the emphasis upon becoming was more appealing to Japanese thinkers. In addition, the ontological presupposition characteristic of Buddhism was the concept of impermanence (Sk. *anicca,* Jp. *mujō*).[ae] There is little ideological consistency between abstract essentialist concepts such as *vajra* and the greater web of Buddhist doctrines that took hold in Japan. The emphasis upon this changing world, the phenomenal world of "things and events" (Ch. *shih,*[af] Jp. *ji*),[ag] was truly consistent with the pre-Buddhist Japanese conceptual framework. Frequently abstract concepts that had been symbolized by various Buddhist deities (*bodhisattvas*) were assimilated and concretized into the Japanese tradition by equating them with *kami.*[21] The *kami* were depicted as *Gohōshin*[ah] [gods guarding the truth (*dharma*)] and became included, albeit at the periphery, in the Japanese pantheon of deities.[22]

It is in this important sense that Japanese Buddhism is *not* world-denying. Unfortunately many works on Buddhism in the West emphasize, without sufficient clarification, the doctrine of suffering or unsatisfactoriness (Sk. *dukkha*). Leading an unsatisfactory existence is merely a ramification of one's own covetousness, craving, and excessive ("unnatural") desire. By seeking to *have* a certain type of knowledge or *have* certain material things, one sets oneself up for later suffering. That is, people often seek to manipulate nature or people or information into static positions in order to control them. The problem, according to Buddhist cosmology, is that all these things, being grounded in a state of nature, are in flux and are therefore unobtainable. Since these desired things or qualities are constantly in a state of becoming, the preferred orientation is to acknowledge the state of their becoming and one's own becoming as well.

As an illustration of the degree to which this aspect of Buddhism has been misrepresented in the West, consider the following example. J. Baird Callicott has expressed some of these misconceptions regarding the place of, and attitudes toward, nature in Buddhism. In a recent article, Callicott lumps early Buddhism with Hinduism and Jainism and states that it is "world-denying or even world-loathing." Citing A. L. Herman, Callicott continues to argue that Buddhism has "a profound disaffection for life as it is given in the phenomenal world (dynamic life, which is throughout motivated and driven by striving and desire) which often seems to be identified with— as if that were its most salient characteristic—suffering, sorrow, or misery."[23] I hope that my brief arguments will demonstrate that this position is in error.

The phenomenal world and dynamic life are given the greatest value and significance in Buddhism because they interpenetrate *becoming* reality itself. The point of meditative practice is not, therefore, world-denying; it is a form of cultivation that neutralizes excessive desires and false conceptions (the cause of our own suffering) so that the practitioner can become intimate with the process of becoming depicted by the phenomenal world. If Buddhists were indifferent to the world, there would be no emphasis upon cultivation. "Suffering" in the Buddhist sense is not a metaphysical or ontological declaration concerning a pessimistic human condition; it is rather an epistemologically relevant term that defines the perspective of those whose perception of nature is clouded by desires, false self-images, and the like.

Similarly, consider the Japanese Buddhist themes of emptiness $(k\bar{u})^{ai}$ and nothingness $(m\bar{u})$.[aj] Neither concept is world-denying. Rather, each concept connotes potentiality and opportunity. Each term could as easily be referred to as "fullness" and "everythingness," respectively, since their meaning issues from a nondiscriminating mode of consciousness. A discriminating mind might consider the relative merits, for example, of thinking and not thinking, good and bad, or plus and minus. But now consider the fact that each has discernable meaning only insofar as one understands the meaning of its opposite. If, for example, our entire universe were a single constant temperature, the concept of temperature may have as little meaning as discussions of dimensions other than those of space and time. In this sense, nothingness and emptiness are not to be understood as relative terms to be juxtaposed with some more affirmative sounding complement. Their import rests solely upon our consideration of them as the absolute ground, or arena, or stage, upon which all possible relative meanings can acquire significance. When Callicott refers to the "apparent negativity of *nirvāṇa* in traditional Indian Buddhism," he incorrectly interprets *nirvāṇa* as a relative term (depicting relative nothingness), and overlooks the affirmation of being-in-the-world characteristic of *nirvāṇa* in both Early and Mahayana Buddhism.[24]

Pursuing this analysis one step further, we can appreciate that the doctrine of no-self (Sk. *anātman*, Jp. *muga*)[ak] is also *not* world- or self-denying. The doctrine of *muga* issues from the more axiomatic consideration that nothing in this cosmos has been empirically verified as existing in a theory that may cause unsatisfactoriness by unrealistically portraying the condition of things and persons in this world. According to the Buddhist tradition, all things in this world are impermanent (Sk. *annica;* Jp. *mujō*).[al] The self is therefore subject to constant change. Time, as conceived by Dōgen, is thus interpreted as a function of our own changing attitudes. Dōgen's concept of *uji*[am] or "being-time" refers to an understanding of time that is informed by our intentional interaction with persons and events. When we say "time flies (*tempus fugit*) when we are having fun," or "time stands still," we refer to time as a function of our own engagement with our surroundings. In his fascicle entitled *Uji*, Dōgen articulates numerous modes of awareness in which we experience time differently. The fundamental point is that awareness of time's passing in a variety of ways is indicative of having cultivated a sensitivity and intersubjective relation with things "in time." That is, sensitivity toward temporality itself enhances our experience of life. Being aware of our existence in time, our timeliness as it were, makes life more intense and precious precisely because of our passing experiences.

Implicit in the notion of *uji* is the notion of seasonal change. Time's passing is detected through our involvement in nature. To be aware of time's passing necessarily requires our being in a dynamic and changing cosmos. Our awareness of the passage of seasons cannot, therefore, be separated from our being in any particular season. There does not seem to be an experiential correlate for a view of time that refers to an ontologically independent force in the universe. Time is passage and passage is not separate from concrete experiences of such phenomena as light, fragrance, texture, and sound. To be aware of nature's passage is to be intimately aware of one's passing in nature.

Considerations of the self that are not sensitive to such phenomena tend to elevate the status of persons above other creatures and the environment. Such attitudes are world-denying because they devalue an otherwise intimate relation with nature. The feeling of potentiality and opportunity occasioned by intersubjective experiences can thus be interpreted as issuing from a nondiscriminating mode of consciousness. The experiences of compassion, empathy, sympathy, and love arise from this intersubjective experience. If one understands (experientially, not merely intellectually) the golden rule, then intersubjectivity must be presenced in order to "do unto others as you would have them do unto you" or "love they neighbor as thyself." The I-It or I-Thou relation must be one of mutual interpenetration. Similarly, the nondiscriminating mind can engage an intersubjective experience with nature. The love of nature depicted here is not merely directed from knowing subject to inanimate object. Rather, one loves nature more fully by participating in an intimate experience with the phenomenal world itself. In general, when Japanese Buddhists speak of detachment, it must be interpreted not in the context of denying the phenomenal world of nature, but in the context of detaching oneself from either one's own striving for permanence in a changing world, or the fruits of one's labor. When one is freed from the quest for permanence, one enters fully into the process of becoming within nature's context.

Since both Kūkai and Dōgen develop these themes in detail, let us turn our attention to a few illustrative theories and practices for further clarification. If by an authentic experience of nature we mean a mode of awareness untainted by the habits of conceptualization, then it would be helpful to cite a few reasons why Buddhists believe that such habits are both common and destructive. According to early Buddhist epistemology our contact with nature begins when our sensory organs come into contact (Sk.

phassa) with the phenomenal world. Immediately a causally dependent (Sk. *pratītyasammutpāda*) chain of events occurs. If persons become attached to that which they perceive, occasioned by a false sense of ego (Sk. *ātman*), then dispositions (Sk. *saṅkhāra*) arise and distort their awareness of the changing world. When attachments are reinforced, more and more dispositions begin to cloud their understanding of themselves, others, and nature.

In order to instruct persons to realize the original mirror-like clarity of experiencing the world untainted by dispositions, the historical Buddha and later patriarchs developed theories and practices that might be employed as catalysts for learning. Both Kūkai and Dōgen, for example, taught the theory of (Jp. *hosshin seppō*),[an] meaning "the *Dharmakāya* expounds the *dharma*." This term refers to an experience wherein "each and every thing we experience (*hosshin*)[ao] is teaching, expounding or explaining (*setsu*)[ap] the *dharma* (*hō*)[aq]."[25] Hence, the third Buddha-body (*Dharmakāya*) expounds the truth (*dharma*) by manifesting itself immanently within each and every thing. For Kūkai, this term has far-reaching implications and occupies a central position in his system. In his *Benkenmitsu nikyō ron,*[ar] Kūkai used *hosshin seppō* "as a criterion by which to distinguish Esoteric and Exoteric Buddhism."[26] Kūkai insisted that the esoteric truth (*dharma*) was preached by the *Dharmakāya* by manifesting itself within each and every thing. Tamaki Koshirō has suggested that "the main line of Japanese Buddhism itself can be seen from the fact that one of the fundamental characteristics of Esoteric Buddhism which Kūkai has further developed on the ground of the Kegon[as] Sect in this sermon by the *Dharmakāya* (*hosshin seppō*)."[27]

In the *Dainichikyō* it is said that the realization of the presence of the *Dharmakāya* in all things is immediate. Since Kūkai believed that *Dainichi Nyorai* was "the cosmos itself, limitless, without beginning or end," there was no place for mediate interrelationships with respect to *Dainichi Nyorai,* that is, distinctions could be made with respect to some other criterion but all things were endowed equally with the presence of *Dainichi Nyorai.*[28] In this way, earth, water, fire, air, space, mind, and matter were all considered inseparable and equal. Accordingly, Kūkai believed that there could be no mediate or indirect awareness of *Dainichi Nyorai.* The *Nyorai* was considered to be directly knowable as it manifested itself in all things.

The explanation given for *Dainichi Nyorai's* participation in the world is that his grace (*kaji*)[at] works to aid the practitioner to participate here and now in *Dainichi Nyorai* himself.[29] Using "expressive symbols" (*monji*),[au] *Dainichi Nyorai* can make its presence felt in the objects of sight, hearing, smell, touch, taste, and thought.[30] Included in the implications of *kaji* are the notions of "communication" and "penetration." That is, since *Dainichi Nyorai* permeates all reality without exception, its presence is "communicated" to all individuals by "penetrating" the very existence of all things. These aspects of *kaji* have been characterized by the expressions *Nyūga Ganyū*[av] "[the Buddha] entering into me and I entering into [the Buddha]" and *ga soku Butsu*[aw] ("I am the Buddha and the Buddha is myself ").[31] Kūkai also often describes this character of *Dainichi Nyorai* by the term *hōben*[ax] (Sk. *upāya*). *Hōben* literally means "expedient," "means," or "instrument," and originally meant "the way of evangelization to lead people, or the means of saving them."[32] Yuasa calls it "sacred expedient" and refers to it as that which leads the practitioner to the common universal truth—*Dainichi Nyorai*. Together, *kaji* and *hōben* represent the all-pervasive, penetrating, and benevolent character of the personified *Dharmakāya* included in the meaning of *hosshin seppō*.

Given this doctrinal basis, it is possible for us to anticipate the meaning of *satori*[ay] (enlightenment) for Kūkai. *Satori* is immediate, and describes the condition of seeing the *dharma* nature of all things (*hosshin seppō*). *Satori* is made possible through the grace (*kaji*) and permeation of *Dainichi Nyorai* in all things.

As with Kūkai, Dōgen believes the *dharma* permeates all sentient and nonsentient beings.[33] When Dōgen describes metaphorically the pervasive character of the *Dharmakāya* and says "the entire universe [*jippō*][az] is the Buddha-land,"[34] he refers to the mode of experience (cultivation) wherein things are experienced as they are (authentication), independent of intentional thesis positing. Insofar as one can experience this way anytime and anywhere, the entire universe, as it is primordially given to consciousness, may be experienced microcosmically.[35] That is, although the *Dharmakāya* pervades *all* things equally, it is authenticated in microcosm by finite sentient beings who experience things as they are independent of the distortions that accompany discursive modes of experience. For Dōgen, knowledge of the *Dharmakāya* does not require omniscient or omnipresent knowledge. Dōgen would argue that just as we cannot experience the entire universe [land of the Buddha (*jippō*)] at once, we cannot experience the totality of the *dharma* (the *Dharmakāya*) at once. Yet, when we consider the finite periphery of our individual experience, the meaning of *dharma* (individual things experiences as they are) may be experienced microcosmically. The full force of the meaning of the *Dharmakāya,* for Dōgen, may be interpreted without positing an inconsistent speculative metaphysical theory of mystic vision upon an otherwise radically empirical Buddhist system.

In defense of this interpretation of *dharma,* the following statements by Dōgen are suggested for consideration: "The ocean speaks and mountains have tongues—that is the everyday speech of Buddha. . . . If you can speak and hear such words you will be one who truly comprehends the entire universe."[36] When the ocean, mountain or anything is experienced as it is, its primordial untainted *dharma* nature "speaks" to the viewer. From this perspective, communication and communion sustain one another.[37] When one is united equally with everything within one's experiential periphery, one "hears" or presences the *dharma* nature shared by all the constituents. In this way, the primordial qualitative nature of the "entire universe" (a quantitative expression) can also be presenced as is.

Both Kūkai and Dōgen argue that we are originally enlightened (*hongaku*)[ba] insofar as our interdependent relationship with others and nature can, at any time, be authenticated by perceiving the world from a nondiscriminating mode of awareness. Both agree that this understanding can be achieved by cultivating the body (*sokushin jōbutsu*[bb] — "this very body is Buddha") and mind (*sokushin zebutsu*[bc] — "this very mind is Buddha"). For Kūkai, the theory of the "three intimacies" (*sanmitsu*[bd] — "speech, mind, and body") and corresponding practices employing mantras, mandalas, and mudras, respectively, instructed practitioners concerning the varied paths they may wish to follow. For Dōgen, theories such as *shinjin datsuraku*[be] ("casting off one's body and mind"),[38] and the corresponding practice of *zazen*[bf] ("seated meditation") were similarly instructive.

We have observed that in two schools of Japanese Buddhism one's most intimate[39] and immediate understanding of oneself, others, and nature is stimulated by various forms of Buddhist cultivation (*shugyō*). Therefore, the discipline of training "mind and body [bodymind][40] oneness" (*shinshin ichinyo*),[bg] wherein the nondiscriminating mode of awareness occasions an intersubjective relation with all things, is elevated as a key element for leading a virtuous existence. In his fascicle *Shōakumakusa*[bh] "the non-production of evil"), Dōgen underscores the importance of participating authentically in the diversity of situations or occasions (*jisetsu*)[bi] that call for ethical decisions. For an ethical decision to be made sensitively and appropriately, one must enter fully into the situation and presence (*genjōkōan*)[bj] its unique setting.[41] Dōgen argues against simply following a set of prescriptive normative injunctions or commandments—for instance, the proclamation "do no evil"—because the truly enlightened person has no evil intentions. To lead a virtuous life one must concentrate upon cultivating oneself thoroughly (bodymind). Merely to memorize a list of injunctions is not conducive to developing oneself in Dōgen's deeper sense. If one is engaged in an intersubjective relationship with others and the natural environment, then the treatment of all things as brothers and sisters emanates naturally (*shizen ni*). The experience of personal harmony (bodymind) and corresponding interpenetration with others occasions the realization that injuring others or nature also injures oneself. Injury is not a product of evil in any ontological sense; it is rather a product of one's false ideas and dispositions as they contribute to an epistemological disorientation. When one has cultivated oneself by sedimenting the clear orientation of bodymind awareness (*shinjingakudō*),[bk] the non-*production* of evil follows "naturally."

The problem for our purposes, in consideration of alternative conceptual resources that might ground a sound and viable environmental ethic, is that the aforementioned ethic is viable only if all people who interact with nature cultivate the "natural experience." The ethic has compelling meaning only from a perspective within the tradition. Since the intrinsic value of nature issues from the intersubjective relation with nature, the justification of an action stems almost exclusively from cultivation. The emphasis upon clarifying one's intentions is thus not entirely separate from modern Western philosophical ethicists since Hume who focus upon the importance of intention when considering the possibility of genuine freedom, choice, and altruistic action.[42] Compassion, empathy, and sympathy for others and nature ultimately reside in one's ability (or lack thereof) to participate fully *with* them. In short, there can be no ethical injunctions here; caring and compassion emanate from individuals who are capable of entering into intimate relations.[43]

I have stressed the role of cultivation in order to make the case that responsible action in and with nature emanates from a particular type of person. Stated simply, character development in the Japanese tradition depends upon an emotional engagement with nature and others. At this point in the discussion we are prepared to respond to the question: *What area of our own recent reflections provides the most appropriate avenue for considering Japanese commitments to nature?* Two avenues may provide an exciting research agenda. First, the classical Aristotelean and modern communitarian ethical traditions underscore the theme of character development and the axiomatic role of relationality. Second, the ecocentric orientation of noted American naturalists, for example, Louis Agassiz and Edward O. Wilson, shares with the Japanese tradition a commitment to cultivating an intimate and emotionally charged relationship with the natural world. Let us consider, albeit briefly, each position respectively.

Since Aristotle's concept of *ethos* (character) includes the sense of personal development, it is in concert with the Japanese emphasis upon cultivation (*shugyō*). Accordingly, the classical and modern Aristotelean tradition provides a more fruitful source of comparison than, say, the bulk of rights-based moral theories in the West. Whereas rights-based theories begin with the individual agent as one with guaranteed entitlements, the aforementioned developmental approach focuses upon a person as a participant in a more axiomatic relation. Persons are fulfilled by entitlements only because they are in relationships first. "Rights" have meaning only in ethical contexts; rights implicitly refer to others.

In his celebrated book entitled *After Virtue,* Alasdair MacIntyre develops his own version of a communitarian approach to ethics. MacIntyre shares the Japanese philosophical perspective that our communal lifestyle is indicative of the fact that we are social creatures first and foremost. Our solitary rights prove to be empty when we are forced to live in isolation from others and nature. This axiomatic sense of relatedness, however, is not easy to analyze rationally. Like the Japanese intellectuals we have already considered, and leading environmentalists to be discussed below, MacIntyre believes that our emotions serve as the source of our sense of intimacy. Referring to Aristotle he writes:

> Virtues are dispositions not only to act in particular ways, but also to feel in particular ways. To act virtuously is not, as Kant was later to think, to act against inclination; it is to act from inclination formed by the cultivation of the virtues. Moral education is an 'education sentimentale.'[44]

The pressing question at this point in our discussion concerns how we might be able to develop greater sensitivity such that we too might experience nature more intimately. If it is not enough to be *told* how to interact harmoniously with nature, then we must ask how we might *be* enlightened regarding our existence in nature? Clearly, there are many ways of fostering this care for the natural world. Although the naturalist and the artist, for example, "see" the world according to a different agenda, their "seeing" is nevertheless made more clear by allowing themselves to participate in nature fully. Whereas the sensitivity of a field biologist may issue from his or her knowledge and appreciation of the elaborate mechanisms sustaining the biosphere, the sensitivity of the Zen priest may issue from cultivating a more primordial "natural" experience. Both encounters with nature may be referred to as *biophilia*.

On January 14, 1979, in the *New York Times Book Review* (p. 43), the sociobiologist, entomologist, and (coincidentally) island biogeographer Edward O. Wilson first used the term *biophilia* in referring to the cultivated sense of a "love of nature." His 1984 book *Biophilia: The Human Bond with Other Species* begins as follows:

> On March 21, 1961, I stood in the Arawak village of Bernardsdorp and looked across the white-sand coastal forest of Surinam. For reasons that were to take me twenty years to understand, that moment was fixed with uncommon urgency in my memory. The emotions I felt were to grow more poignant at each remembrance, and in the end they changed into rational conjectures about matters that had only a distant bearing on the original event.
>
> The object of reflection can be summarized by a single word, biophilia,

which I will be so bold as to define as the innate tendency to focus on life and lifelike processes.[45]

We do not yet know if this tendency is innate or the product of cultural development or both.[46] It can be argued however that biologists like Louis Agassiz (1807–1873), Wilson, and leading Japanese intellectuals—like Kūkai (774–835), Kaibara Ekken (1630–1714), and Motoori Norinaga (1730–1801)—developed a keen emotional sensitivity to and empathy with the natural environment. Agassiz, Wilson, Kūkai, and the others cultivated an intimacy with nature early in life and renounced other career plans in favor of time spent in relative natural isolation.

Agassiz provides us with an interesting example because he also happened to teach natural history to the then young William James. In a few decades James became one of the most celebrated American philosophers (whose influence reached all the way to Japan).[47] Agassiz was James's teacher both at Harvard University and in Brazil during the 1865–66 Thayer expedition up the Amazon. James absolutely idolized Agassiz, as evidenced in particular by his letters to his parents.[48] Agassiz was a radical empiricist *par excellence* and was famous for his impatience with metaphysical rhetoric. When the young James asked him probing philosophical questions, Agassiz would quip, "read nature to understand God's mind and works, not books!"

In a letter dated "Christmas day" (1861–63?), James describes Agassiz's method of instruction as one that taught his students to become naturalists by developing a *feel* for their subject matter in the same way artists learn to feel their way into a new medium. For this reason Agassiz preferred new students who were wholly uninstructed. He wanted his students to come to him as if they were blank tablets. James writes that Agassiz would then mold the students' skills by not letting them "look into a book for a long while," forcing them to "learn for themselves, and be *masters* of it all." James goes on to say, "he makes naturalists of them [the students], he does not merely cram them. . . . He must be a great teacher."[49]

Agassiz was one who was truly intimate with nature. He passed on to James a feeling that an experience of intimacy with the empirical world has religious significance. However, this religious sensitivity required cultivating an inner feeling for one's subject matter.

Ernst Mayr, the present-day nestor of evolutionary biology, similarly emphasizes (personal communication) that mastering the techniques of a skilled cladistic systematist requires developing a feeling for one's subject matter. This feeling reflects the skill of a master professional. Like the guild system of training, true professionalism in the discipline of phyletic classification requires a long time in order to nurture the sensitivity required to collect and properly classify flora and fauna. It is this sort of developed awareness between self and world, personified by Agassiz's example, that James tried to capture through the phrase "pure experience." The immediate, intimate, and prereflective character of pure experience is what the famous modern Japanese philosopher Nishida Kitarō[bl] (1870–1945) found complementary[50] with central themes in the Japanese philosophical and religious tradition. *The central theme among Agassiz, James, and Nishida revolves around their shared commitment to cultivating a feeling of sensitive interaction between persons and their natural environment.*

Agassiz believed that genuinely appreciating the fact that we are actively involved as actors in a dynamic ecosystem required a quasi rite of passage. To truly understand this point its meaning must touch our lives empirically, and Agassiz believed this could only come about through a form of cultivation occasioned by direct experience and field work, not speculative theories. The emphasis upon direct or immediate experience in nature, as described by scholars of the early Japanese tradition, has been characterized as a product of a primitive and archaic world view. In Japan, this emotional and aesthetic attitude provides the basis for becoming sensitive to the *detail* of nature's presence as evidenced by subtle changes of light, shadows, wind, seasonal change, and so on.[51] This so-called primitive quality, however, was what Agassiz purposively sought in his students. Without preconceptions to clutter the mirror-like "feel" of a working field naturalist, the detailed and subtle differences in nature could be detected and recorded.[52]

The illustrations discussed thus far suggest that cultivating an intimacy between persons and nature requires a clarity and purity of experience in the East as well as the West. James's pure experience, which I suggest is (in part) an extension of Agassiz's lasting influence, parallels Nishida's own radical empiricism. Both D. T. Suzuki and Nishida had empiricist predilections in concert with Dōgen's philosophy discussed herein. Indeed it was Suzuki who suggested to Nishida that he read James. The radical empiricist orientation of Dōgen/Nishida and Agassiz/James suggests an interesting potential connection linking the ecocentric orientation of noted American environmentalists and the Japanese philosophical tradition. The common denominator I forge among the Japanese tradition, Aristotle, and people like William James, Louis Agassiz, Edward O. Wilson, Ernst Mayr, Alasdair MacIntyre, hinges upon the cultivation of an emotional and aesthetic "feel" for nature that provides the necessary and sufficient condition for an intimate ecocentric interaction (*biophilia*) with our natural surroundings.

Agassiz's coincidental Japanese predilections are revealed in his *Contributions to the Natural History of the United States* (1857). His view was that all species are creations of God's mind. For him, science and religion were brought together beautifully by learning to sensitively understand nature's book as a reflection of God's mind and character. By teaching his students (James included) how to "see" the world from his cultivated perspective, he believed that he was actually teaching courses in theology, environmental ethics, and personal development.[53] The view that nature is endowed with divine presence that can be appreciated by cultivating one's way of being-in-the-world potentially serves as an interesting ideological bridge linking Japanese commitments to nature and the ecocentricism prevalent in ecology and biology.

It would seem that when it comes to some issues relevant to environmental philosophy, the apparent cultural obstacles of the East and West can be overcome by cultivating or acknowledging an emotional attachment to nature. Once one's intimacy with and dependence upon nature are understood and internalized, such cultivating seems to engage a holistic ecocentric view characterized by a feeling of an aesthetic and material oneness with all things. For Wilson, it is this feeling that serves as the ground of and anchor for environmental philosophy. Accordingly, the goal of environmental philosophy "is to join emotion with the rational analysis of emotion in order to create a deeper and more enduring conservation ethic."[54] Since the classical texts of ancient Japan (*Man'yōshū, Tale of Genji,* and *Kojiki*)[bm] similarly depict the prominence of a deep emotional affinity between persons and nature, perhaps studying the Japanese rationale that describes these feelings can shed light upon our own reflections for, as Wilson says, "a more enduring conservation ethic."

The expression of this Japanese emotional and aesthetic attitude is frequently summarized by scholars, especially Motoori, employing the famous dictum "*mono no aware*"[bn] ("sensitivity to things"). From the beginning of recorded history, the Japanese world view seems to be one characterized by an intimate, prereflective, and emotional encounter with the natural world. Emotion thus served as the basis for a type of interspecies awareness. By cultivating one's sensitivity to one's surroundings, one could more effectively intuit feelings of identity with the environment as a whole. For the leading conservationist Edward O. Wilson and most of the Japanese intellectual tradition, reasoned reflection serves only to document and organize more basic feelings that issue from deep within us. The emotions speak to us directly and are unencumbered. When these intimate feelings occur, they are free from moralistic reflection; yet, they serve as a ground for later remembrances and assertive action.

Perhaps the most important link between ecologists, biologists, and the Japanese tradition is the concept of community wherein there is no vestige of a Platonic ontological hierarchy of existence. The theme of community has been important in modern Japanese philosophy and in Neo-Darwinian thinking as well. While Darwin considered the target of natural selective processes to be the individual, the neo-Darwinian concept of inclusive fitness allows for competition to be considered a shared phenomenon among relatives, thus providing the axiomatic basis for competing hypotheses regarding altruistic behavior, namely, kin selection, group selection, reciprocal altruism, and so on.[55] Accordingly, an entire species' adaptive fitness can be considered in terms of a more holistic frame of reference.[56] A species' survival as a whole may thus be considered in accordance with the ability of individual members to participate effectively in a community. Since much of the Japanese tradition is in concert with the aforementioned ecocentric and communitarian[57] perspective, it would be worth our while to consider aspects of the Japanese experience of nature as a possible conceptual resource for environmental philosophy. Perhaps we will be able to piece together attitudes toward nature and communities that the Japanese tradition and modern ecological theory have in common.

There is a famous relevant Buddhist maxim that has various forms. To imitate the "child-like mind" and show one's "original face" refer to a mode of experience that is uncluttered by discursive reflection. When we create elaborate rationalizations to justify meeting our needs and desires, we effectively remove ourselves from our natural setting. The child-like mind is originally intimate with its world, for the child has not yet learned to compartmentalize his or her experiences into socially accepted places. The emotional ties between the child and the environment are powerful and often uncontrolled. As the child develops, however, it is easy for the original intimacy to be lost. The mystery and splendor that accompanies an emotional attachment to nature can become covered, forcing us, in adult stages, to recultivate our child-like minds. In the ontogeny of *Homo sapiens,* the innocence and naïveté of childhood may be lost forever, but I am optimistic that we can learn to cultivate a renewed and enlightened intimacy with the environment that sustains us. I am optimistic because, of all the species on the planet, biologically speaking, we are the most capable of actually fulfilling this admittedly romantic fantasy. As a neotenic species, we have the longest childhood of all.

"Neoteny" literally means holding on to youth. In evolutionary theory it refers to the retention of the juvenile characteristics of one's ancestors (as opposed to "recapitulation"—a nineteenth-century term referring to the terminal addition of developmental traits occasioned by an acceleration of the rate of embryonic development). While "recapitulation" stood at the foundation of dated "ontogeny recapitulates phylogeny" rhetoric (which was thought to explain, for example, the formation of gill slits in the early stages of human embryological development), neoteny stands today as a cornerstone for more accurately understanding human evolution. Human evolution has proceeded by a *slowing down* of the developmental rates of primates (human adults more closely resemble juvenile chimps than adult chimps).

The point, in this context, is an epistemological one. The rate of human development is slowed down so much that we are born as living embryos, and require an abnormally long dependence upon our parent guardian/teachers. This long childhood, as it has sometimes been called, suggests the importance of cultural evolution in human development. As a neotenous species, *Homo sapiens* are characterized by epistemic plasticity. Part of our evolutionary success as a species capable of shaping landscapes, as opposed to being occupiers of more limited niches, can be explained in part by our behavioral plasticity and accelerated learning (assimilating languages, role models, and so on), evidenced especially prior to sexual maturity. The sedimented habits of cultural imprinting in the earlier years of development suggest a close relationship between different patterns of cultural evolution (nurture) and the prior biological developmental processes (nature) that culminate in the birth of a healthy fetus that is characterized most importantly by its tremendous epistemic plasticity. The physiological/epistemological apparatus giving us the potential for learning is seized upon (metaphorically) by the teachers who instruct us during the crucial developmental years. The rate of "acquired" knowledge, versus instinctual knowledge, is accelerated because this later type of development (cultural evolution) is essentially Lamarkian in its structure.

The plasticity of human behavior patterns that has made possible cultural diversity and cultural evolution[58] is also capable of facilitating swift changes concerning our collective attitudes about nature. As our knowledge of biological systems increases, it becomes ever more apparent how limited our natural resources are and how dependent we are upon them. By combining informed views concerning our planetary systems and a renewed emotional sensitivity that (as Wilson says) probably issues from our evolutionary ties to the planet, we may begin to make progress searching for "a more enduring conservation ethic."[59]

In the words of Johann Wolfgang von Goethe:

He who knows himself and others,
will also recognize that East and
West cannot be set apart.

CHARACTER GLOSSARY

a 修行	aa 修證一如	ba 本覺	ca 慧能
b 日本學	ab 道	bb 即身成佛	cb 善の研究
c 神々誕生	ac 道	bc 即心是佛	cc 純粹經驗
d 神	ad 金剛頂經	bd 三密	
e 神奈備	ae 無常	be 身心脱落	
f 磐境	af 事	bf 坐禪	
g 萬葉集	ag 事	bg 身心一如	
h 和	ah 護法神	bh 諸惡莫作	
i 自然	ai 空	bi 時節	
j 密	aj 無	bj 現成公案	
k 間	ak 無我	bk 身心學道	
l 自然江	al 無常	bl 西田幾多郎	
m 鳥居	am 有時	bm 古事記	
n 生死	an 法身說法	bn もの の あわれ	
o 自然智宗	ao 法身	bo 稽古	
p 修驗道	ap 節	bp 倫理學	
q イザナギ	aq 法	bq 日本記	
r イザナミ	ar 辯密二敎論	br 高野勝	
s 大毗盧遮那成佛神變加持經		bs 本地垂迹	
t 大日經	as 華嚴	bt 草本國土悉界成佛	
u 大日如來	at 加持	bu 如淨	
v 惠果	au 文字	bv 塵	
w 密敎	av 入我我入	bw 塵	
x 最澄	aw 我即佛	bx 身	
y 戒律	ax 方便	by 身	
z 道元	ay 悟	bz 慧能	
	az 十方		

Saigyō and the Buddhist Value of Nature

William R. LaFleur

Within the history of Buddhism in East Asia the world of nature gained and retained an exalted position—something seen as having an exalted inherent religious value. This essay reviews aspects of the history of this upward valuation of nature in Chinese and Japanese Buddhism, and analyzes the interpretative shifts and changes made necessary by this impulse toward the attribution of increasingly great religious significance to nature. The development is carried as far as the twelfth century in Japan and the poetry of the Buddhist monk Saigyō[a] (1118–1190), poetry which not only itself moved the valorization of nature beyond the point where earlier writers had brought it, but also, since as poetry it gained a position in the public mind and a place in the popular imagination of the Japanese people, historically "fixed" a lasting nexus between Buddhism and nature in the popular consciousness of the Japanese people.

Saigyō, whose name before he became a monk was Satō Norikiyo, saw his Buddhist vocation as something to be carried out in the mountains rather than in temples and monasteries. Before becoming a monk he had been a military guard in the service of Emperor Toba, and a member of an elite corps of palace guards known as the *Hokumen no Bushi* or "North-facing warriors." But at age twenty-three he relinquished his career in court and became a Buddhist monk. He was at first loosely attached to Shingon and Tendai temples in the vicinity of Heian-kyō (now Kyoto) and seems to have retained a lifelong attachment to the memory of Kūkai[b] (774–835), the Japanese founder of the Shingon school. But Saigyō's forte lay in his composition of *waka,* or thirty-one-syllable verse, and it is in the context of his writing of these that we gain an understanding of his visions of nature, Buddhism, and the correlation of these two. For Saigyō, the world of nature was the primary world of Buddhist values.

Buddhahood and the Plant World

A potentially instructive and intriguing but, unfortunately, neglected episode in the history of Buddhism in East Asia lies hidden in something which—at first sight, at least—appears to be a rather sterile series of discussions by Chinese and Japanese Buddhists about the limits of salvation.

Their discussions were concerned explicitly with the problem of whether or not "plants and trees" *(sōmoku)*[c] could "attain Buddhahood" *(jōbutsu)*[d]. Implicitly, the problem was not limited to a question concerning vegetation alone but included all of the natural world in distinction from that which is human. Because the history of this discussion and the poetry of Saigyō are mutually illuminating and, as I shall try to show, historically related, the course and direction of these discussions deserve explication. I will begin, therefore, with the history of the question in China, move on to developments in Japan, and, from that point, to the analysis of Saigyō's verse.[1]

There is irony in the manner in which the problem historically came into existence. It was occasioned by the fact that, when Buddhism had been well established in China, what in the Indian sutras had been intended as a Mahayana extension of the umbrella of salvation, namely, the stress upon the eventual enlightenment and Buddhahood of "all sentient beings," was viewed as a limitation rather than as an expansion. To certain Chinese, it seemed that although the promise of Buddhahood was extended to all sentient beings, it was at the same time denied to beings that were not sentient. Sensitivity to this problem seems to have led at least two Chinese Buddhist thinkers, Chi-tsang[e] (549–623) and Chan-jan[f] (711–782) to give it consideration. With them begins the process whereby intellectual devices were fashioned to overcome the implicit limitation upon the range of potential Buddhahood. First these two Chinese thinkers bent the teaching derived from India to the contours of the Chinese ethos; after them, Japanese Buddhists refashioned the tradition to meet their own requirements.

The first of the two important Chinese Buddhists concerned with this problem was Chi-tsang of the San-Lun school. Chi-tsang, a native of Turkestan and a master of Madhyamika dialectic in China, was the first to use the key phrase "Attainment of Buddhahood by Plants and Trees." He made the first, although highly qualified, step in the direction of seeing Buddhahood in the nonsentient. In his *Ta-ch'eng-hsüan-lun*[g] he stated that in theory plants and trees, since they are essentially like sentient beings, can achieve Buddhahood, but he allowed this as a possibility only within the realm of theory. Outside of theory, they seemed to him not to attain this. Beyond this point he seemed unwilling to go.[2]

The real development comes, however, in the thought of Chan-jan, the first of many important T'ien-t'ai (Japanese, Tendai) thinkers to give their attention to this problem and promote the development of the doctrine. The T'ien-t'ai concern for this may be due to the fact that this particular school, both in China and Japan, seems to have been eager to explore the meaning of Mahayana universalism and to push it to logical conclusions. There seems to be a significance, therefore, in the fact that Chan-jan was the ninth patriarch of T'ien-t'ai Buddhism in China.[3]

When we review his position, we see that he was the first to have moved the problem to the conclusion that "even nonsentient beings possess the Buddha-nature" *(wu ch'ing yu hsing)*[h]. In his *Chin-kang Pi,* Chan-jan argued as follows:

> Therefore we may know that the single mind of a single particle of dust comprises the mind-nature of all sentient beings and Buddhas. . . . Therefore, when we speak of all things, why should exception be made in the case of a tiny particle of dust? Why should the substance of the *Bhutatathata* [= *tathata;* or "Suchness," "Thusness"] pertain exclusively to "us" rather than to "others"? Thus there is no water without waves; there are no waves without wetness. This wetness does not distinguish between the muddy and the limpid, yet the waves are of themselves either clear or turbid. Irrespective of their clarity or turbidness, there is for them only the one undifferentiated nature.[4]

And in another place, Chan-jan writes:

> The man who is of all-round perfection, knows from beginning to end that Truth is not dual and that no objects exist apart from mind. Who, then, is "animate," and who "inanimate"? Within the Assembly of the Lotus, all are present without division. In the case of grass, trees, and the soil (from which they grow), what difference is there between their four kinds of atoms? Whether they (merely) lift their feet or (energetically) traverse the (long) path, they will all reach the Precious Island [a poetic term for Nirvana]. By snapping their fingers and joining their palms, they will all achieve the causation for Buddhahood. Whether they agree with the One or the Three (Vehicles), they will none of them run counter to the original concept (of Buddhism). How can it still be said unto today that inanimate things are devoid (of the Buddha-nature)?[5]

Fung Yu-lan's comment upon this is very instructive. He writes: "Logical premises existed for this universalistic theory. Hence Chan-jan's extension of Tao-sheng's thesis that the Buddha-nature is possessed even by the *icchantikas* or non-believers in Buddhism is no mere accident. There is no doubt, however, that in the history of Chinese Buddhism, Chan-jan represents the culmination of this particular trend of thought."[6]

Chan-jan holds to the Buddha-nature of the natural world not primarily because he is interested in the natural world and its religious meaning, but because the logic of Mahayana universalism is that to which he is especially sensitive. Fung Yu-lan, in my opinion, is correct in seeing him in the tradition of Tao-sheng (360–434) who had, on the basis of the Mahayana principle, proposed that even nonbelievers *(icchantikas)* would attain Buddhahood, and he was later vindicated in his hypothesis when the full text of the *Parinirvāṇa Sūtra* was brought into China and verified his claim textually.

When in what follows we shift the venue of the discussion from China to Japan, there seems to occur also a gradual but inevitable shift in the motivation for carrying on the discussion. Whereas the Chinese mentioned above were superb logicians and interested in pressing their Buddhist universalism to the phenomenal and mundane world as a whole, the Japanese after Kūkai seem to restrict their area of concern to the natural world—in distinction to that which is civilization—rather than the whole of mundane reality. The stress is not so much on the value of the concrete and mundane per se as it is upon the special value, from a Buddhist perspective, that the natural world might have for man.

In Japan, terminology derived from the discussion appears before the discussion itself does, and it appears, significantly, in the writings of Saichō[i] or Dengyō Daishi[j] (766–822). Saichō had studied in China and had, in fact, become the person responsible for the transmission of the T'ien-t'ai school to Japan; he became, therefore, the founder of Japan's Tendai school. No doubt because he had heard the term in China and because he felt its appropriateness within the universalism of Tendai, he was the first Japanese to use the phrase "the Buddha-nature of Trees and Rocks" *(mokuseki bosshō)*[k] in his *Futsuwaku Shūchū Saku,*[l] where it merely appears without explanation.[7]

A much more substantial contribution to the discussion was made by Kūkai or Kōbō Daishi[m] (774–835), the founder of Japan's Shingon school of Buddhism. We find him simply assuming the presence and acceptance of the doctrine in his *Unji Gi* or "The Meanings of the Word Hūṃ," where the following line appears:

> If trees and plants are to attain enlightenment,
> Why not those who are endowed with feelings?[8]

Kūkai's explicit rationale for attributing Buddhahood to plants occurs, however, in his *Mitszō Ki* or "Record of Secret Treasury." I translate the key section as follows:

> The explanation of the Buddhahood of insentient trees and plants is as follows: the Dharmakaya consists of the Five Great Elements within which space and plants-and-trees [*sōmoku*] are included. Both this space and these plants-and-trees are the dharmakaya. Even though with the physical eye one

might see the coarse form of plants-and-trees, it is with the Buddha-eye that the subtle color can be seen. Therefore, without any alteration in what is in itself, trees-and-plants may, unobjectionably, be referred to as [having] Buddha [-nature].[9]

Kūkai's argument differs from those discussed above inasmuch as he is less interested in pursuing the logical consequences of a universalistic trend in Buddhism and more interested in the positing of an identity of the Buddhist Absolute, the dharmakaya or "body of the dharma," with all forms and things in the phenomenal, mundane world. The whole of Kūkai's thought seems to be directed toward the forging of such an ontological union of the absolute with the mundane. Therefore, in his view, plants and trees are capable of having Buddha-nature simply because they, along with everything else in the phenomenal world, are ontologically one with the Absolute, the dharmakāya. The only real problem, then, is epistemological, and Kūkai in the section translated above suggests that there are two ways of viewing plants-and-trees. The ordinary physical eye sees the coarse form of things, but the person in possession of "the Buddha eye" sees the subtle form.

Because of his identification of the phenomenal world with the dharmakaya, Kūkai dissolves the older distinction between sentient *(yūjō)*[n] and insentient *(mujō)*[o] beings. In his *Sokushin Jōbutsu Gi* or "Attaining Enlightenment in this Very Body and Lifetime," a work which, characteristically and logically, deals with the question of why it happens that Buddhahood for human beings can occur while they live temporal and bodily lives, he writes the following: "In Exoteric Buddhist teachings, the four great elements [earth, water, fire, and wind] are considered to be non-sentient beings, but in Esoteric Buddhist teaching they are regarded as the *samaya*-body of the Tathagata. The four great elements are not independent of the mind. Differences exist between matter and mind, but in their essential nature they remain the same. Matter is no other than mind; mind no other than matter. Without any obstruction, they are interrelated."[10]

What is significant in this, aside from the ease with which Kūkai can remove the distinction between sentient and insentient beings through his placing of himself in the esoteric tradition and, therefore, derived from the Mahāvairocana Buddha rather than Śākyamuni Buddha, is his reference to earth, water, fire, and wind as the *samaya*-body of the Tathāgata. This term for Kūkai has great importance, for it means "symbolic body," but is conceived of as being somehow really participant in the thing symbolized. That is, it is a "symbol" which is ontologically and in some peculiar way even substantially united with what is symbolized. This means that in the above-quoted paragraph, Kūkai sees phenomena in the natural world (earth, water, fire, and wind as the Great Elements, and plant-and-trees as one of the combinations of these) as both symbols of the Absolute, the Tathāgata, and as themselves the reality of the Tathāgata. Both are involved and implied in the designation of these as *samaya*.[11]

Kūkai in this way opens up many new possibilities for the discussion. First, by subscribing to the esoteric tradition, which he regards as final and superior to the one derived from Śākyamuni, he places himself beyond the need for concern about the "orthodoxy" of seeing Buddhahood potential in plants, trees, and anything else within the natural world. Second, he implies that the Buddhahood of the natural world is not so much a matter of potentiality as it is of actuality. The question is not "How will these things become Buddha?" but rather "How will we come to realize that they already are Buddha?" Third, with his conception of *samaya* he has opened up the possibility of a particularly Buddhist conception of symbolization, one which relates the natural world to the absolute in a special way and one which, as we shall see below, seems implicit in Saigyō's religious valorization of nature.

However, Kūkai's position seems to have moved too far and too quickly. Or, at least, even though he had produced a position from which all phenomenal things could be identified with the absolute, the Tathāgata, some of his contemporaries, as well as thinkers of subsequent generations, remained concerned about the specific question of the Buddhahood potential of the plant world. Miyamoto Shōson correctly observes: "[Kūkai] still does not explain things in terms of plants and trees (of themselves) resolving to attain Buddhahood, then undergoing (ascetic) disciplines, and then attaining such (Buddhahood). The lucid explanation of the doctrine in terms such as this was the work of later theorists."[12] In any case what for Kūkai was a *fait accompli* was something that others still felt the necessity of debating and discussing.

Again we find scholars of the Tendai school arguing the case for the Buddha-nature of plants. One of the most important figures in this was a Tendai priest who eventually became the head abbot of the monastery complex on Mount Hiei. He was Ryōgen[p] (912–985), also referred to as Jiei Daishi.[q] Ryōgen is of special importance in the history of the problem because he participated in an important public debate on it. The debate is known as the Intersectarian Debate of the Ōwa Era (in the third year Ōwa or 963) and was, in fact, a series of forensic matches held under imperial auspices and involving ten representatives of the Hossō school and ten of the Tendai school in verbal contest on matters of Buddhist doctrine. The question considered during this particular series in 963 was the one traced here, namely, the possibility of seeing all things as having a potential Buddha-nature. This debate, known and remembered for its scale and intensity,[13] is historically important also because it demonstrates that the question debated had a *public* interest, one at least of interest to court circles.

The principal debaters on each side were Ryōgen for the Tendai school and Chūzan (935–976) for the Hossō. Throughout the disputations, the arguments advanced by the Tendai participants were based on the principle that "All Things Have [Buddha] Nature" *(issai-kaijō butsu)*[r], whereas the Hossō position was based upon the "Distinctions between the Five Groups of Beings" principle *(goshō-kakubetsu)*[s],[14] a principle according to which the Hossō school had traditionally divided sentient beings into five groups ranging from *śrāvaka* or "hearer" of Śākyamuni's teachings to *icchantika* or those actively hostile to Buddhism.

To substantiate his position Ryōgen cited a phrase from the Chinese text of the *Saddharma-Puṇḍarīka* or *Lotus Sutra* which he interpreted as "[There is] no one [which] does not attain Buddhahood." Chūzan[t], however, interpreted the first two characters ("no one" or "not one") as meaning "one without [i.e., not having] [Buddha-nature]. Thus, for him the phrase meant: "[Whatever has] no [Buddha nature] does not attain Buddhahood." At another time the debate focused on the interpretation of a passage selected by Ryōgen from the *Sutra on Perfect Enlightenment* or *Yüan-Chüeh-ching* (Japanese *Engaku-kyō*), one which Ryōgen read as meaning, "Both hell and the Heavenly Palace become the Western Paradise; both sentient and insentient beings are equally put on the Buddha path"; whereas Chūzan interpreted it as meaning, "If one [hypothetically] makes both hell and the Heavenly Palace as deserving of the Western Paradise, then sentient beings and insentient beings in the same way would not be on the Buddha path."[15] In this manner the debate went on. The crucial points of divergence centered on the interpretation of sentences in Chinese texts and upon what was and what was not implied in those sentences. The debate was inconclusive. Many said that "there had never before been a debate such as this one in terms of its scale and intensity" in Japan.

But the real importance of Ryōgen lay in what he wrote in his *Sōmoku Hosshin Shugyō Jōbutsu Ki* or "Account of (How) Plants and Trees Desire Enlightenment, Discipline Themselves and Attain Buddhahood." In this work he further elaborated his case for the Buddhahood potentialities of botanical life. Ryōgen admitted that prior to that time when Śākyamuni revealed the teachings found in the *Lotus Sutra,* the teaching on this matter was not yet in the world. But according to him the provision of this sutra to the world made all the difference. In this sutra he saw implicit the understanding that the life cycle of plants moves though four stages, stages which correspond to the process of human enlightenment.

The orthodox meaning of the "Original Buddha" is an argument for the enlightenment and the Buddhahood [of plants]. Grasses and trees already have four phases, namely, that of sprouting out, that of residing [and growing], that of changing [and reproducing,] and that of dying. That is to say, this is the way in which plants first aspire for the goal [*hosshin*] undergo disciplines [*shugyō*], reach enlightenment [*bodai*], and enter into extinction [*nehan*]. We must, therefore, regard these [plants] as belonging to the classification of sentient beings. Therefore when plants aspire and discipline themselves, sentient beings are doing so. When sentient beings aspire and undergo austerities, plants are aspiring and disciplining themselves.[16]

Obviously, Ryōgen; has pushed the argument to a new degree of explicitness in this, and it is of importance here to analyze more exactly what he has done.

In the first place, he has tied the doctrine to the *Lotus Sutra* very definitely. That is, he has "solved" the problem of the doctrine's "orthodoxy" by appeal to the hermeneutics employed by the T'ien-t'ai school in China, according to which the principle of *p'an-ch'iao* or "dividing the teachings" gave preeminence to this particular sutra. As worked out for example by Buddhists such as Chih-i (538–597) in China, the teachings of the Buddha were arranged into chronological periods during the Buddha's life so that the *Lotus Sutra* or *Saddharma-Puṇḍarīka* would be not only temporarily final but also final as an authority. "Therefore the *Saddharma* is considered to be the epitome of the Buddha's teachings."[17] This sutra, it should be noted, was one which was famous for the universality of salvation taught within it; so it precisely fit the T'ien-t'ai desire for universalism. But even more important, the *Lotus Sutra* could serve as a *locus classicus* for the "Buddhahood of Plants" doctrine because of the presence in it of a chapter "On Plants," one which employs rich vegetation imagery to portray the beneficence and salvation of Tathāgata.[18] The presentation there of the grace of the Tathāgata coming down upon all things as rain does on various forms of botanical life suggested, apparently, to these thinkers of the Tendai school that this was more than imagery and analogy; to them it suggested the participation of vegetation in the process of enlightenment and salvation.

But Ryōgen's most significant contribution to the discussion lay in his creation of a nexus between the biological life cycle of a plant and the process of enlightenment as experienced by human beings. In the passage translated above, he interprets the natural process as being, in fact, a religious one. The sprouting forth of a plant is really the mode by which it bursts forth its desire for enlightenment; its residing in one place is really undertaking of disciplines and austerities; its reproduction of itself is its attainment of (the fruits of) enlightenment; and its withering and dying is its entry into the state of nirvana. Ryōgen has, it should be noted, taken a four-stage sequence frequently found in Buddhism, namely, that of arising, continuing, changing, and ceasing-to-be, and has interpreted it as the inner sequence and meaning of the process of a plant's life. The result is that he imagines a plant to be a type of Buddhist yogin. When correctly understood, according to him, the life cycle is an enlightenment cycle. And it is certainly not so merely by analogy, for on the basis of this Ryōgen concludes that there exists no reason for refusing to regard plants as belonging to the category of sentient beings.

If we compare the position of Kūkai with that of Ryōgen we can notice that, although both are arguing for the Buddhahood of things within the natural world, Kūkai's position is in reality more radical. As noted above, for the Shingon master, the whole distinction between sentient and insentient is dispensable. Although he argues within the context of the "Buddhahood of Plants" discussions, his position does not, in fact, limit Buddhahood even to the vegetable world but extends it—at least by implication—to any and everything within the phenomenal world. In comparison with this, Ryōgen, although later, is "conservative." He maintains the distinction between what is sentient and what is not, but makes a most forceful argument for inclusion of plants in the category of the sentient. His interpretation of the plant's life cycle as an enlightenment cycle, however, could be seen as something which, while moving trees and plants clearly within the realm of those with the potential of Buddhahood, by implication rules out Buddhahood possibility for natural objects lacking such a cycle—rocks and rivers, for example. This is the kind of distinction which Kūkai's theory seems to have avoided. Finally, Kūkai viewed natural phenomena as already in possession of the Buddha-nature simply by virtue of their being in the phenomenal world; Ryōgen, by comparison, saw Buddhahood as a potentiality only in the case of plants, although it might be argued that, since it was a potentiality that would be actualized in the course of the normal and "natural" life cycle of a plant, it would in fact be present in every plant that reproduced itself and then died.

The difference between these two approaches is in many ways characteristic of the different emphases of the Shingon and the Tendai schools. One hundred and fifty years separate the deaths of Kūkai and Ryōgen, but, in addition, their respective positions demonstrate the Shingon and the Tendai ways of handling this problem. A conflation and harmonization of these two approaches occurred later, and it is with this that the next section is concerned.

Chūjin—Major Changes in the Argument

In twelfth-century Japan the most important discussion of the Buddhahood-of-plants problem occurred in the writing of Chūjin[u]

(1065–1138), a scholar of the Tendai school. He overtly seems only to have summarized the discussions up to this time but, in fact, moved the discussion along by a group of new subtleties and refinements. Chūjin, it should be noticed here, is especially important because he was the principal articulator of this doctrine near the close of the Heian period. He, therefore, stood close in time to the poet Saigyō. His theories were, in fact, being put forth precisely at the time when Saigyō was a young monk and spending time in various Tendai and Shingon temples near the capital city of Heian-kyō.

In his *Kankō Ruijū*[v], Chūjin summarized a group of arguments that had beforehand been advanced for the Buddhahood of plants. He seemed to hold that they cumulatively supported the doctrine. He articulated the following seven arguments:[19]

1. *Shobutsu no kangen*[w]. Trees and plants do not possess Buddhahood in and of themselves, but do so when they are viewed by Buddhas.
2. *Gubōshō no ri*[x]. Trees and plants are in possession of Buddha-nature *(busshō or Buddhatā)*. "Buddha" means "enlightenment." The inner (or mysterious) principle of the Buddha-nature is a purity of original enlightenment *(hongaku)*[y] and has nothing of impurity in it. This is something of which plants and trees are in possession.
3. *Eshō funi*[z]. There is an inner harmony of the achievement of the right reward *(shōbō)*, in this case the Buddha's enlightenment, and all the attendant *(ehō)* circumstances—for example, the earth, etc.—upon which he depends. The enlightenment of him is accompanied by that of all these others. Therefore, plants and trees are already in possession of Buddha-nature.
4. *Tōtai jisshō*[aa]. Of their own nature the myriad things are Buddha, and "Buddha" means enlightenment. In their inner nature the things of the 3,000 worlds are unchangeable, undefiled, unmoved, and pure; this is what is meant by their being called "Buddha." As for trees and plants, there is no need for them to have or show the thirty-two marks (of Buddhahood); in their present form—that is, by having roots, stems, branches, and leaves, each in its own way has Buddhahood.
5. *Hongu-zammi*[ab]. Like all sentient beings, trees and plants have three bodies: the Dharma-body, the Sambhoga-body, and the Nirmāna-body. Therefore, trees and plants can attain Buddhahood as sentient beings can.
6. *Hosshō*[ac] *fushigi*. The self-nature of trees and plants is not capable of being described and, therefore, the Buddha-nature possessed by trees and plants is also ineffable.
7. *Guchūdō*[ad] (Tendai mediation principle) and *ichinen-sanzen*[ae]. The

principle that the 3,000 realms (i.e., all phenomena) are contained in one thought means that mind is all things and all things are mind. Trees-and-plants as well as sentient beings possess all things. This is why sentient beings can conceive of trees and plants. If this were not so, there could be no cognition. The real and original nature of all things *(hosshō* or *dharmatā)* has two aspects. Its quiescent aspect is the one mind and its illuminating aspect is the 3,000 realms of being. The internal unity of these two aspects makes both for knowledge and for the fact that essentially plants and trees have the Buddha-nature.

At first sight it would seem that in the above Chūjin has merely collected and presented seven arguments for the Buddhahood of the botanical realm. However, there are some interesting features in this particular collection of arguments. Ryōgen's argument that the plant's life cycle is an enlightenment process is conspicuous by its absence. Moreover, there seems to be a certain inner coherence in Chūjin's selection. That is, he has chosen arguments which in almost every case present plants and trees as already enlightened and in possession of Buddha-nature. It is for this reason, I would suggest, that Ryōgen's otherwise interesting argument is excluded—in spite of the fact that he too was a Tendai scholar and well known for the position he had taken. Instead of Ryōgen's seeing of an enlightenment *in the process* of a plant's life, Chūjin advances a rather different view in the fourth argument above. There he sees their possession of enlightenment "in their present form" and specifies the *concurrent possession* of roots, stems, branches, and leaves as the mode by which the Buddhahood of plants is shown. In fact, he seems to take pains to state that the Buddhahood of plants need not be conceived in any way upon a *human model;* they have no need to demonstrate any of the ordinarily expected thirty-two marks of Buddhahood.

The significance of this is great and deserves further explication. First, it seems obvious from the above that in the century and a half that passed since Ryōgen had advanced his arguments, the Tendai school no longer felt the need—if we may judge from Chūjin's selection—to argue for the Buddhahood of plants on the basis either of their inclusion in the category of the sentient or on the degree to which their mode of being in the world in some way is assimilable to that of human beings. In a real sense, by this time, it seems that plants and trees are permitted to be what they are, and this in no way throws into jeopardy their potential for Buddha-nature. The whole tenor of Chūjin's arguments suggests an independent arrival at Buddhahood rather than one based upon the degree to which plants demonstrate either characteristics which can in some way be homologized with that of man. Only the first of the seven arguments makes their Buddhahood dependent, but in that case it is dependent upon their being "seen" by Buddhas; and here we can understand that, according to the *Lotus Sutra* image employed there, they are dependent upon the "grace" of the Buddha or Tathāgata in the same way that all other creatures, including ordinary men, are. The impressive common feature of every other one of the arguments advanced is that it lays stress upon the "self-nature" or independent being of trees and plants.

Second, and of equal importance, is the fact that the presentation of the Buddhahood of plants here is much more in terms of something already actualized than in terms of a potentiality. Here his second argument—"The Inner (or mysterious) principle of the Buddha-nature is a purity of original enlightenment [*hongaku*] and has nothing of impurity in it. This is something of which plants and trees are in possession"—is the crux of his position according to my view. It is in many ways an index to a major shift in Tendai thought during the time between Ryōgen and Chūjin. That is, the tendency of the latter to view the enlightenment of plants as a realized actuality rather than a potentiality is ideologically related to a growing tendency in Tendai doctrine to stress "original enlightenment" which was called *hongaku,* over one which had to be initiated and experienced, that is, *shikaku.* Chūjin's use of the term *hongaku* in his second argument is not coincidental; it is part of an important shift in Tendai doctrine, one which deserves further elucidation.

The term *hongaku* refers to the notion that when someone moves from the state of being unenlightened to one of enlightenment *(shikaku)*[af], this occurs only because an already existent and underlying Buddha-nature *(hongaku)* is already present and intrinsic. Historically, *hongaku* grew in importance first in the Japanese Shingon and then in the Tendai school.[20] It increasingly gained preeminence. Because of this underlying and already existent enlightenment, things could be affirmed in the condition in which they existed, since their mode of existence in the world was one of an already enlightened state. This fit especially well into the Shingon emphasis upon the Buddhahood of the phenomenal world in all its forms and as it is.

Because it had an important impact upon the Buddhahood-of-Plants discussion within the Tendai school, this was, in my opinion, crucial. And it was for this reason that the statements and arguments of Chūjin, while on the surface merely a summation of arguments, in fact have within themselves evidence that Chūjin had brought the entire question onto wholly new ground. For him it seems that the Buddhahood of plants was no longer in any sense a possibility to be entertained; it was, rather, an actuality to be accepted. Moreover, when he sees the Buddhahood of plants resident in their mere possession of roots, stems, branches, and leaves, he is affirming their ordinary mode of existence in the world as one which is in itself an enlightened existence and a Buddha-nature. As we have noted above, he does not follow Ryōgen in forcing the members of the plant world into a frame of reference based upon human experience. That is, they are in possession of the Buddha-nature merely by virtue of their existence as plants, not inasmuch as they approximate human experience and norms. In many ways Chūjin disavows the necessity of positing a human model for the understanding of enlightenment and permits these members of the natural world to have their enlightenment in their own way and on their own terms. He adds that this escapes man's capacity for understanding; this is why in his sixth argument he writes, "The self-nature of trees and plants is not capable of being described and, therefore, the Buddha-nature possessed by trees and plants is also ineffable."

It might be expected the Chūjin's position would be the culmination and end of the discussion. But in fact it merely opened up new possibilities. For, although in many ways he presented a way of understanding the Buddhahood of plants (and nature as a whole) without recourse to the human model of enlightenment, he did not simply "naturalize" nature. Inasmuch as he wrote of the "Buddha-nature" of plants and trees, he attributed religious meaning and value to the natural world. He had, in fact, opened up the possibility of a remarkably new type of valorization of nature within the Buddhist context.[21]

Saigyō and a New Shift of Values

In outlining the progression of the Buddhist discussions of the Buddhahood of the natural world in general and of plants in particular, the problem of motivation needs to be addressed. That is, we must ask why it happened that especially in Japan, members of the Buddhist community felt compelled to discuss and present arguments on behalf of the Buddhahood potentialities of the natural world—often in spite of rather tenuous textual support from the Buddhist canon. We have noticed that the trend had been for increasing and growing religious value attributed to nature throughout the centuries of the discussion. Why did this occur in spite of the fact that it seems to have necessitated a rather elastic hermeneutic on the part of those who argued on behalf of the Buddhahood of plants?

The answer to this, I suggest, lies in the fact that Buddhism in Japan especially was forced to accommodate itself to the longstanding and pre-Buddhist attribution of high religious value to the natural world. Thus, the discussions outlined in the foregoing pages were not carried out in a cultural and religious vacuum; they were, in fact, consciously or unconsciously responding to pressures exerted upon them by ancient and deeply ingrained experiences of the Japanese people—experiences especially of nature as a locus of soteriological value. To term this an accommodation of Buddhism to Shintō is an oversimplification, and yet there can be no doubt that the ancient and continuous recognition of the presence of *kami* or divinities throughout the natural world was a prime characteristic of the Japanese religious ethos, and it was necessary for Buddhism to adjust itself to this. The discussions above can be viewed in some sense as the adjustment of theory to this fact of experience. Chūjin's theories, in particular, made it possible from within a Buddhist context to view natural phenomena as already enlightened; this meant that in some sense, at least, things within nature could be seen as Buddhas and, therefore, as approximate equivalents—although within another vocabulary—of *kami*.

But precise political and historical factors contributed to the *emergence* of these valorizations; for, especially in the twelfth century, Japan witnessed the gradual but powerful diminution of the glory, and hence also of the religious significance, of its capital city, Heian-kyō. During this century, the "City of Peace and Tranquility," which for three centuries had seemed perpetual and inviolable, was the scene of battles and intrigue, and, at the end of the century, saw the loss of its possession of the effective ruling powers of Japan. This city, which had been the epitome of Japan's creation of a cultural and civilizational center, and which, therefore, had an important religious meaning and value as well, was suddenly under pressures, both internal and external. We can find in the writings of this century a seemingly sudden awareness that this city, heretofore understood to be virtually perpetual, was itself characterized by "impermanence," the Buddhist teaching of *anitya*—what the Japanese called *mujō*[ag]. It was in such a historical situation, then, that the pendulum of values seems to have swung again, this time very emphatically, in the direction of nature and its capacity to provide solace and some type of "salvation" for individuals looking for a locus of value other than that provided by the city and its style of life.

Therefore, although the general pre-Buddhist religious milieu of Japan moved the *sōmoku-jōbutsu* discussions to new attributions of value to nature within the Buddhist world, the twelfth century and its events added an additional element of coercion, so that some Buddhists began, in fact, to regard nature as the proper locus of salvation. This, it should be noted, went considerably beyond the theory of Chūjin, who wrote early in the century; but Chūjin's theory opened the possibility of this. More exactly, the *hongaku* view of enlightenment made this type of valorization possible. For, although in theory the *hongaku* orientation extended in an existent enlightenment to all things, it retained the notion that man might in fact undergo the experience of *shikaku* or "initial experience of enlightenment." The interesting feature of this is that, in terms of the relative values involved, it grants by implication the natural and phenomenal world an enlightenment which, although basically "possessed" also by man, still seems to require man to appropriate experientially. Therefore, logically, nature is in full possession of what man only still partially possesses.

This means, then, that the implication of the *hongaku* orientation attributed to nature a higher degree of realization than to man. These, it should be noted, were implications which were not, to my knowledge, explicitly drawn out at this period of history but they are rather obviously present and would probably not have been missed during this century, in which men in Japan were claiming to experience in various ways the salvific power of the natural world.

With Chūjin the explicit theory seems to go as far as the Buddhist philosophers would carry it. But the actual religious valorization of nature is not limited to the thoughts and writings of theoreticians. Values can be expressed by others as well, and it is my contention here that the upward valuation of nature goes much beyond Chūjin and that, if we wish to trace it in the twelfth century, we must attend to other writings, especially to the poetry of the Buddhist priest, Saigyō. For the verses of this monk provide the *locus classicus* of the attribution of primacy and soteriological meaning to the natural world. If Chūjin had granted to nature a status equal to that of man, Saigyō seems to have attributed to it an even higher one.[22]

One of his better-known poems, and one included in a later imperial anthology, is the following:[23]

michinobe no	"Just a brief stop"
shimizu nagaruru	I said when stepping off the road
yanagi kage	Into a willow's shade
shibashi tote koso	Where a bubbling stream flows by . . .
tachidomaritsure	As has time since my "brief stop" began.

[SKKS 262; SKS 200; MFM, p.78]

This poem gains some of its unusual degree of artistic finesse from its skillful employment of imagery, especially images of sinuosity: the road, the flowing stream, and the willow, the long and flowing branches of which are visually present even though unmentioned as such. These are all ongoing and flowing in a continuous fashion.

And in this, the structure of the poem corresponds exactly to the experience which the poet is seeking to communicate; for the verse tells us that he merely intended to make a short stop and pause for refreshment at the side of the road on which he was traveling, but that this intended momentary pause was swallowed up by the refreshment itself, and the poet is telling himself that he has already been there a long time. Just as the road, the stream, and the willow's branches are flowing, so too is time. And standing under the willow at the stream, the passage of time goes unnoticed by the poet as he is caught in and carried along by an ongoing reverie within this natural setting.

But the poet here seems eager to suggest that the willow and stream offered him more than a moment's coolness and drink; it offered also this opportunity to lose all sense of time and all concern about pushing on toward a destination. We have no hint in the verse that he is conscience stricken or self-judging in view of his diversion from his progress along the road. Instead, we understand him to be reflecting upon the fact that his moment's pause has in fact lasted much longer, but he intends, it seems, to remain exactly where he is. This is especially interesting inasmuch as most commentators agree that the road he is on is one traversed by him for the sake of a religious pilgrimage. Therefore, it is as if he suggests that his deflection from the "goal" of his pilgrimage is in no way lamentable. Quite the contrary. It is as if, in being drawn into this natural setting, he has been induced into something that has its own sacrality for him. Expressed in the kind of paradoxical language of which Saigyō himself was fond, we might say that it was in going "to the side of the road" *(michi no be)* that he found "the Way." The distant *telos* of his pilgrimage has been sacrificed for one much more proximate and at hand, and Saigyō seems to accept this completely. Here under the willow he finds reverie, a sense of the abeyance of time, and, in some sense, the values of the "sacred" sufficient for himself, values which others might traverse miles to find at a shrine, temple, or other sacred place. He has been drawn into the world of nature, and it—rather than a goal of pilgrimage which is distant and cultically formed—is salvific for Saigyō.

The imagery and emotions of the poem are subtle, but so too is the value attributed in it to nature. The poet has found in the stream and the willow a "given" world of religious meaning. We find in this verse a conception of pilgrimage by implication, but it is one which coheres precisely to that found in other of his poems, one which suggests that the goal of pilgrimage is often found within the natural world through which the pilgrim-poet travels rather than at some distant place deemed and designated as "sacred" by the consensus of the cultus-concerned religious community. We find frequently in his verses the phrase *yukue mo shiranu,* words which mean "and not knowing the destination." In many ways this phrase encapsulates this poet's view of pilgrimage, for he discovers the realm of sacrality along the way rather than at its end. Because of this, his wandering can be comparatively aimless and destinationless. Because in the thought of Mahayana Buddhism the goal of nirvana is to be found within the world of samsara, the postulation of distant goals is, theoretically at least, redundant. Saigyō seems to have translated this principle into a peculiar mode of pilgrimage for himself. In his case, however, it had special value inasmuch as this enabled him to find "the sacred" in natural contexts and phenomena met by him and entered into by him as he went along the road. Although theoretically in Mahayana all things in the samsaric realm are sacred, experientially men find that "although all things are sacred, some things are more sacred than others." In Saigyō's case this was the way in which he experienced the natural world and its forms.

A more overt preference by him of natural over against cultic forms is in the following verse:

hisa ni hete	Long-living pine,
waga nochi no yo o	Of you I ask: everlasting
toe yo matsu	Mourning for me and
ato shinobubeki	Cover for my corpse; here is no
hito mo naki mi zo	Human to think of me when gone.

[SKS 1440; MFM, p. 60]

On the surface this verse might be taken as a lament and as a self-pitying expression of loneliness due to the absence of other human beings. It would seem to be a turning toward the tree to fill a gap created by this absence of fellow men and a request that the tree perform the requisite rites for the poet's own corpse. The principal verbal form here, *toe yo,* is an imperative meaning "say (or chant) a memorial rite!" On this level of interpretation, it is a direct address to the tree and involves a "personalization" of the pine. By the "willing suspension of disbelief" permissible in poetry, it would seem to make a human request of a nonhuman phenomenon of the natural world.

However, a creative ambiguity is placed in the poem by the word *shinobubeki* in the fourth line, for this word is capable of being written with two different characters, each of which carries a different sense. The more immediate meaning would be: "cherish the memory of [someone] afterward." In this context it would mean precisely that the poet laments the fact that no human being would know of his death and engage in a fond recall of his life. But another character could as easily be understood here to give the meaning of "to conceal oneself" or "to be hidden." As such, it applies to the remains or corpse of the poet. If read in this way, the phrase would mean "my corpse which ought to be covered (or concealed from view)."

Therefore, the poet has made a double-leveled request of the pine tree. He seems, on the one hand, to have requested it to be a stand-in for humans who might ordinarily, if they had knowledge of his death, recall his memory and perform rites on his behalf. However, by implication he is suggesting that the pine conceal his body and prevent its exposure to the world. It is not that he wants the pine literally to bury his corpse; rather, he suggests that simply by standing over him forever it will conceal his remains. It is, significantly, a pine, a tree which is always and in every season full of foliage, of which he makes his request. On this level, therefore, he is asking the pine to do nothing extraordinary and unnatural. Simply by existing in its ordinary mode of being as an evergreen tree it can adequately conceal his corpse from the world and the elements. As such, it will perform for him a praiseworthy act of "service." By covering his mouldering corpse with its branches and shed needles it will perform an act of "burial"—but without any violation of its ordinary and usual mode of life and activity. In this sense he entrusts himself to its care.

Although he probably would have had no awareness of historical antecedents to this when composing this verse, it might be said that the movement from the first understanding of this verse to its deeper level of meaning recapitulates the movement of thought from Ryōgen, who saw the plant's enlightenment in a progression like that of man's, to Chūjin, who saw its Buddhahood in its normal and simultaneous possession of roots, stems, branches, and leaves. The difference, however, is that Saigyō makes the natural form of the phenomenon an adequate substitute for man's cultic behavior and, as such, attributes to nature a decided preferability as the locus of the sacred. He shifts the values so that what is a loss to cultic forms becomes nature's gain.

Other aspects and phenomena of the natural world hold for Saigyō a fascination which suggests that his contact with them is of the nature of a religious experience. More specifically, they seem to represent for him the real locus of the Buddhist world of meaning and value. For example, the mist is so celebrated and valued in the following poem:

sora ni naru	A man whose mind is
kokoro wa haru no	At one with the sky-void steps
kasumi nite	Inside a spring mist
yo ni araji tomo	And thinks to himself he might
omoitatsu kana	In fact step right out of the world

[SKS 786, MFM p. 34]

The genius of this verse lies in the simplicity with which the man's activity is presented and the attitude of surprise and wonder registered in his mind. He is portrayed as one who is totally absorbed in "emptiness," for *sora* here suggests both the literal sky above the heads of men and also the Buddhist Void or *śūnyatā*. The dual sense here suggests that the sky is somehow ontologically connected with *śūnyatā* and that, if it is to be taken as a "symbol" of this, it is so in the sense of Kūkai's concept of symbol or *samaya* discussed above. The importance of this is that the man here presented—and it is no doubt the poet himself—is not merely "abstracted," a man lost in a concept of Emptiness or in thoughts of Buddhist ontology. He is, on the contrary, a man whose mind and emotions *(kokoro)*[ah] are unified with the sky-void or, perhaps, with the sky-which-is-the-void. And it is this man who, when he steps into a ground-hugging mist on a spring morning, wonders whether he might not have, in fact, stepped out of the world.

But the intent here is not to present a semiludicrous and "absent-minded" philosopher who mistakes the mist for an extramundane reality. Quite on the contrary, Saigyō, who elsewhere wrote a verse relishing paradox very much akin to Chuang Tzu's delight in the dream about a butterfly's possible dream that he was Chuang Tzu,[24] is doing something similar with this verse. He is asking here whether it might not be possible that the first impression, namely, that he has mistaken the mist for the void, is, in fact, the real illusion. Therefore, the question posed by the verse would be: Is not the "second thought"—that is, the feeling of having been "fooled" into mistaking the mist for *śūnyatā*—the possible delusion here? That is, is it not in fact possible that the mist is actually what it seemed to be in that moment in which the man, whose mind was already united with the void, felt that his body too had entered into Emptiness? And in being in the mist is he not, in fact, in tangible contact with *śūnyatā*? And, if this is so, can it not be said that his entry into the mist was in fact entry into what in Buddhism had ultimate value—with the understanding that in this code of values, such is coterminous with the forms of the natural world?

Kūkai's concept of *samaya* is very instructive here, and in all probability lies within the conceptual background making Saigyō's valorization of nature what it is. Saigyō took Kūkai as a kind of distant mentor, and he identified his own experiences with those of the founder of his order, especially when the poet traveled through parts of Shikoku which hallowed the memory of Kūkai.

Yoshito S. Hakeda articulates the meaning of *samaya* in Kūkai's thought in this way: "In Kūkai's writings the Sanskrit word *samaya* is used in the sense of 'symbol,' 'equality,' 'promise,' or 'vow.' Here [that is, in a text] '*samaya*-body' means 'symbolic body.' For Kūkai any physical symbol has a double structure in that it is an object standing for *X* and at the same time it is part of *X*; e.g., a flower or a *vajra* is a symbol of Mahāvairocana Buddha but at the same time an integral part of Mahāvairocana in terms of the totality of existence. Thus, the four great elements cannot be regarded as 'nonsentient beings' which have nothing to do with Mahāvairocana."[25] The wider application of this and its function as an intellectual foundation for "symbolization" in verse such as Saigyō's results in an intense and complete valorization of physical and natural phenomena as being identical with the religious Reality. In Saigyō's case this means that natural forms are "symbolic bodies" of the Tathāgata and that, in this sense, they are the Tathāgata. In a similar way the sky and the mist are *śūnyatā*.

This is why in Saigyō verse we have a valorization of nature which, in fact, goes beyond that given to trees and plants by Chūjin. Out of the intellectual currents which he received from the times in which he lived, times which—as we have seen—allowed for the harmonization of Tendai and Shingon patterns of thought, Saigyō brought forth a new valorization of the natural world. The degree to which he did this in a self-conscious manner is, of course, problematic. My argument simply is that these things were so much part of the Buddhist milieu in which he at times moved that they can be expected to have shaped and informed his own usage of symbol in verse. He differs from Kūkai, however, in two ways. First, although he takes phenomenological forms as identifiable with Buddhist absolutes, he is selective in what he takes as such; because of his times and his own sensitivity, he has a decided preference for identifying the Tathāgata with forms and phenomena in the natural rather than in the civilizational world. Second, this means that he does not follow Kūkai in placing primary value upon rites, constructed symbols such as mandalas, and cultic patterns of religious expression. For Saigyō, in a very literal way, nature is All.

Nowhere is there a better expression of both Saigyō's dependence upon Kūkai and his partial movement away from his "master" than this verse written while overlooking Japan's Inland Sea:

I was in the province of Sanuki and in the mountains where Kōbō Daishi had lived; when there I stayed in a hut woven out of grasses. The moon was especially bright and, since the sky over the [Inland] Sea was cloudless, I could see it well:

kumori naki	Cloud-free mountains
yama nite umi no	Encircle the sea, which holds
tsuki mireba	The reflected moon:
shima zo kōri no	A view of it there changes the islands
taema narikeru	Into holes of emptiness in a sea of ice.

[SKS 147; MFM p. 59]

There is here, I would suggest, the equivalent of a mandala in nature or, more precisely, nature as mandala. For the progression of visualization and of concentration moves spirally and toward the center of the scene, and there, as if seeing to the inner reality of things, the poet "mistakes" the islands for holes in ice. But again we are faced with the question of whether the "mistake" is really that at all; for the word *taema*, "holes," also means space, and implies the Buddhist notion of Emptiness or *śūnyatā*. That is to say, the poet comes to see—and wants his readers to see, as well—that the island there is really Emptiness itself. Saigyō adeptly patterns the experience after the mandala model provided by his master, but he himself constructs no mandala since nature itself is the absolute. Knowing the extent to which he sought—especially on this pilgrimage to Shikoku—to make Kūkai's experiences his own, we might well ask if he is not here implying that the source of Kūkai's own inspiration to construct mandalas for his disciples was this same natural scene before his own eyes.

This does not mean that religious value is attributed to the concept of nature or to "Nature" *as something abstracted from the phenomena that compose it;* this would be in violation of the idea of *samaya,* the intent of which is to valorize particular phenomena as the Tathāgata. The arc of value returns through the images of Saigyō's poetry to these particular and concrete things in the world of nature.

The natural "images" in Saigyō's poetry are not something which must themselves be transcended and mentally jettisoned once they have served to create a union of the subject and the real object of his "image-ing," that is, the Reality itself. Rather, in total harmony with the view of *samaya* articulated by Kūkai, there is no necessity here of negating the physical and phenomenological world once it has served to point to something beyond itself. For Kūkai and for Saigyō, there is no beyond. The concrete phenomenon—in this case, the sky—is itself both the symbol and the symbolized. It is the absolute which theorists might call "Emptiness," but which is, in fact, nothing other than the phenomenon itself. And because of this, in its own mode of being as concrete and natural, it can fulfill a soteriological role and function for man.

Nature as Soteric

One of modern Japan's greatest thinkers, Ienaga Saburō, in 1944 advanced the idea that nature played a "saving" role for great numbers of people within Japanese religious history. Ienaga notes that a love for nature is evident even in the earliest collection of Japanese verse, the *Man'yōshū* (ca. 759), the poets of which frequently give expression to their feelings about nature with phrases such as, "One never tires of looking at it."[26] But this reflects the attitude of the Nara period (701–781) and of times prior to it; in the subsequent Heian period (781–1191) a change takes place. "During the Heian period a shadow falls across the daily lives of the nobility and gradually a darker one seems to settle into even their consciousness concerning life. But along with this, expectations with respect to the effects of [the world of] nature suddenly become very strong."[27] And, according to Ienaga, these conditions became even more pronounced at the end of the Heian period—that is, in the twelfth century. According to him, it is absolutely essential to understand this historical development if one wishes to comprehend why it is that the twelfth-century poet Saigyō has such a deep longing for nature and regards it as having a "healing power."[28] In such a situation nature takes on the character and role of an Absolute; it unconditionally draws human beings toward itself.

But in Ienaga's opinion, this created a problem for Buddhists of that time. He writes: "Especially for priests or novices who, through their Buddhist faith, were in the process of bringing to completion their own deliverance from the world's bonds of suffering and illusion, now to be drawn into a deeply-rooted delusion because of nature's captivating beauty was something that gave rise to a type of very strange contradiction."[29] And it is in Saigyō primarily that Ienaga sees expression of this inner conflict and contradiction. For instance, as evidence of the poet's awareness of this problem, Ienaga cites the following verse:

> hana ni somu   Why do I, who broke
> kokoro wa ikade   So completely with this world,
> nokoriken   Find in my body
> sutehateteki to   Still the pulsing of a heart
> omou waga mi ni   Once dyed in blossoms' hues?

> [SKS 87, MFM p. 67]

This continued possession of a heart or sensibility that had, according to the metaphor, once been deeply dyed and tinted with the color—that is, the love for—blossoms is regarded by Ienaga as an inevitable impediment to Saigyō's vocation as a Buddhist. But the remarkable thing is the following observation: "[Saigyō] did not try, on account of his Buddhism, forcibly to dispose of his 'flower-and-moon-enchanted' sensibility. On the contrary, it is as though his real peace or tranquility is one which is gained not through Buddhist austerities but by going all the way with his 'blossom-dyed-heart'."[30] On the basis of this he concludes, "It can be said that what really saved Saigyō was not the Tathāgata but was Nature, and in this sense one perhaps ought to refer to him, first of all, as a disciple of Nature rather than as an adherent of Buddhism."[31]

Ienaga then, on the basis of his recognition of nature's role in contexts such as this, thinks that Nature, as an Absolute, has power like that of a Buddha or the Japanese *kami*. In fact, he would regard the aspiration for Nature *as a religion* in Japan's history.[32] This is, according to him, simply to come to recognition the fact that it has really been nature to which many Japanese throughout their history have looked for salvation. But it is something which takes on a special significance in the Heian era; before this, men and women had experienced something of the powers of nature as a savior *(kyūsaisha)* by going out into nature, but in the Heian period nature began to be a place to which one fled in order to escape the "fleeting world" (i.e., the city) and to have one's anxieties removed. It came to stand over against the "passing world" *(ukiyo)*.[33]

And it is then that the *yamazato*[ai] ideal developed, and men went to live in a *yamazato* as a more-or-less permanent retreat from the world. This ideal, which Robert N. Bellah correctly views as an important element in Ienaga's conception of the history of Japan's particular religious development,[34] is well illustrated by Ienaga from Saigyō's verses and from other contemporaneous sources. He then compares Chinese views of nature with this soteric nature discoverable in his Japanese sources in order to isolate the particularity of the latter. He acknowledges the fondness for nature in the verses of Chinese poets such as T'ao Ch'ien, Li Po, and Po Chü-i, as well as the richness of their natural imagery. But, owing to the Chinese insistence upon the importance of human society, the poets of China did not demonstrate "an attitude which comes from an unconditional giving of oneself to nature." For even the greatest nature-poets of China wanted to be civil servants and were unable to free themselves from "a world-view characterized by realism and the desire to 'get on' in the world." There was not in them the Japanese willingness to grant to nature an unconditional importance.[35]

Ienaga finds in the Heian period of Japan multiple instances of Buddhist monks and the group of ascetics known as *hijiri* who developed a distaste for the urban Buddhism of Tendai and Shingon and, in what Ienaga feels to be a reemergence of "Hinayana-like" private pursuit of the goal, left for the mountains to practice what was called "mountain austerities" *(sanrin shugyō)*. Those who did this were drawn both by the quietness of such a location or their disciplines and by the beauty of nature there. Therefore, even within Buddhism a certain harmonization of these two motives was forged in time—especially at the end of the Heian era and in the Kamakura period.[36] In view of this, Ienaga seems to revise what he had written earlier about Saigyō's seeing his love of nature as an obstruction to his aspirations as a Buddhist. If the poet is understood to be secluded in the deep mountains of

Yoshino and in this way forsaking the world, he can be considered to fall within the Buddhist ambit.[37]

But the notion of *yamazato* is indigenously Japanese, and according to Ienaga, something apart both from Chinese thought-forms and from Buddhist ideas. The ideal of the *yamazato* life as a retreat in the mountains, even though shaped in part by Chinese and Buddhist motifs and concepts, is ultimately rooted in the ancient Japanese love of nature; the charm of the *yamazato* depends really upon the amenability of Japanese to be captivated by nature's beauty.[38] He finds in Saigyō and in Kamo no Chōmei, the author of *Hōjōki* [An account of my ten-foot-square hut], the principal expressions of this idea; it is expressed through the image of the mountain retreat which makes nature to be soteric *(kyūsai).*[39]

Ienaga finds something rather different in the poets who compiled the *Shinkokinshū* (completed in 1206), poets such as Fujiwara Teika. These poets did not live in the midst of nature and observe nature as Saigyō had. Therefore, by using natural images they created a world of nature which has a surrealistic quality *(chōgen-jitsuteki shizen),* and it is this world into which they entered in order, somewhat like the thinkers such as Hōnen and Shinran who held to a Buddhist "Pure Land," to find a way of completely cutting off the ephemeral world of everyday life.[40] In this sense, their fabricated world was soteric for them. But it was surreal in spite of the excellence of their verse. As an example Ienaga cites Teika's renowned "Bridge of Dreams" poem, a verse which Robert H. Brower and Earl Miner have translated.[41]

haru no yo no	The bridge of dreams
yume no ukihashi	Floating on the brief spring night
todae shite	Soon breaks off:
mine ni wakaruru	Now from the mountaintop a cloud
yokogumo no sora.	Takes leave into the open sky.

To Ienaga, this verse with its ethereal beauty is something removed from natural phenomena themselves; it celebrates a metaphysical or metapheno-menal existence *(keijijōteki sonzai).*[42]

Ienaga sees this as the establishment of a separate tradition in subsequent Japanese religious history. Here my overview of his detailed discussion is necessarily more brief than the foregoing. But his main point is that these poets of the *Shinkokinshū* era, and the later presentation of natural forms by Zen artists living in the midst of urban settings—for example, in the landscape painting known as *sansui,* in *sumi* painting, and in arts of gardening and flower arrangement—form one strand of development; the *yamazato* ideal as expressed by Saigyō and Chōmei, the *chashitsu* or garden tearoom, and the verse of the seventeenth-century poet Bashō form another strand. According to Ienaga, the difference is that the former group seems to create a nature-beyond-nature and the latter attends to and lives in nature itself.[43] But both conceive of a religious salvation in or through nature, and as such show the diversity of ways in which the Japanese people historically viewed nature as soteric. Ienaga then repeats his major thesis: "If one considers Japanese religious history with the purpose in mind of discovering what things in fact gave salvation to the souls of the Japanese people and then selects only 'Shinto,' 'Buddhism,' and 'Christianity,' and overlooks the salvation provided by Nature—that which, in fact, is much more [inherently] Japanese and extends much farther than these others—then one will not be capable of tracing the real spiritual development of our people."[44] Ienaga closes his study with an ambivalent position. On the one hand, he wonders whether the Pure Land criticism of the *yamazato* idea as too "this-worldly" and ultimately unsatisfying might not be valid,[45] and on other hand, he cannot accept modern criticism of the *yamazato* ideal. For to Ienaga this type of soteric nature and this concept of salvation may have ongoing value and meaning for the Japanese people.[46]

This summary of Ienaga's monograph has, it is hoped, been sufficient to show how at least one interpreter of Japanese history has defined and delineated the religious role and value of nature in that history. Ienaga clearly identifies this role as a soteric one. He, moreover, repeatedly states that Saigyō is a key figure in this development.

But in Ienaga's view Saigyō was a man in conflict with himself, because his experience of the soteric power of nature was at variance with his professed adherence to Buddhism and its traditional soteriology. Ienaga sees this conflict of soteriologies as one which occurred within the mind and sensibility of Saigyō, and one which, therefore, is reflected and expressed in his verse. However, in Ienaga's view the indigenous model of salvation— that is, nature as saving reality—ultimately won the day over the Buddhist one in Saigyō's mind, so that "what really saved Saigyō was not the Tathāgata but was Nature."

However, in my opinion, this is not the best way of interpreting this phase of Japanese religious history. Ienaga completely ignored the long and important "Buddhahood of Plants and Trees" discussion in East Asia, and its significance there. Moreover, implicit in Ienaga's view seems to be the assumption that the soteriology of a religion such as Buddhism is more or less "fixed" and static, so that when in history something else is experienced as soteric, contradiction and conflict are the logical result. But here, in my opinion, is a case where viewing a religion as a symbol system rather than as a single and consistent soteriology facilitates our understanding both the historical facts and the important historical role played by the process of interpretation that accompanies these. Inasmuch as religions such as

Hinduism, Christianity, and Buddhism exist in time and history, what within them is apprehended and interpreted as soteric will not be single, static, or constant. At least in part, the history of a religion is the history of changes in, and the multiplication of, soteric modes within it.

The history of the "Buddhahood of Plants and Trees" discussion in East Asia shows that there was in fact a process within Buddhism by which increasingly higher importance was attributed to the natural world, and that this culminated in granting to nature a saving power and function. A creative and adaptive hermeneutic and a series of reinterpretation brought twelfth-century Buddhism in Japan to the place where someone such as Saigyō was able *as a Buddhist* to attribute the basic soteric role to the natural world.

Therefore, instead of Ienaga's statement that "what really saved Saigyō was not the Tathāgata but was Nature," I would propose the following as fitting the historical facts and situation: "What saved Saigyō was the Tathāgata-which-is-Nature." That is, Saigyō seems to have experienced that natural world as both a soteric reality and as the ultimate Buddhist absolute. His poetry becomes, therefore, the medium through which his apprehension of the fundamental unity of the two is expressed. He is not, then, a man torn by a conflict between incompatible religious values, or someone who, as Ienaga would have it, found his salvation in nature *in spite of* being a Buddhist. Rather, it seems that it was precisely within the sensibility of this twelfth-century Japanese poet that a total identification was forged between nature and the Buddhist absolute; his poetry becomes, therefore, an important "document" in the history of religion in East Asia, since it provides not only insight into the private emotions and thoughts of this man but also what came to be regarded by the Japanese as the "classical" expression in their history of this particular type of soteric mode.

CHARACTER GLOSSARY

a 西行

b 空海

c 草木

d 成佛

e 吉藏

f 湛然

g 大乘玄論

h 無情有性

i 最澄

j 傳敎大師

k 木石佛性

l 拂惑袖中策

m 弘法大師

n 有情

o 無情

p 良源

q 慈慧大師

r 一切皆成佛

s 王姓各別

t 仲算

u 忠尋

v 漢光類聚

w 諸佛の觀

x 具法性の理

y 本覺

z 依正不二

aa 當體自性

ab 本具三身

ac 法性

ad 具中道

ae 一念三千

af 始覺

ag 無常

ah 心

ai 山里

IV

The Buddhist World View

The Jewel Net of Indra

Francis H. Cook

Western man may be on the brink of an entirely new understanding of the nature of existence. The work of classification and analysis which was born from the work of ancient Greek civilization has borne its fruit in the overwhelming success of Western man in manipulating the natural world, including himself. This conquest and manipulation has proceeded without pause, each success engendering new possibilities and successes, and there is reason to believe that this manipulation and exploitation will continue. However, some have begun to wonder if we have not had too much success; the very virtuosity with which we manipulate the natural world has brought us, according to some critics, to the thin line separating success from terrible disaster. Only very recently has the word "ecology" begun to appear in our discussion, reflecting the arising of a remarkable new consciousness of how all things live in interdependence. The traditional methods of analysis, classification, and isolation tended to erect boundaries around things, setting them apart in groups and thereby making easier their manipulation, whether intellectually or technologically. The ecological approach tends rather to stress the interrelatedness of these same things. While not naively obliterating distinctions of property and function, it still views existence as a vast web of interdependencies in which if one strand is disturbed, the whole web is shaken. The ecological viewpoint has not, that is, brought into question the ancient distinctions of property and function which lie behind a brilliant technology. Honey bees and apple blossoms remain what they have always been in our eyes, but added to this way of knowing is another, newer way—the knowledge that these entities need each other for survival itself. This understanding comes to us in the nature of a revelation; an eternally abiding truth has burst upon our consciousness, with an urgent message concerning our life. This new knowledge demands, in fact, a complete reassessment of the manner in which things exist. Perhaps this revelation is not yet closed, and in time we may come to perceive that this interdependency is not simply biological and economic, a matter of bees and blossoms, or plankton and oxygen, but a vastly more pervasive and complicated interdependency than we have so far imagined.

But this essay is not about ecology, at least not directly, and not at all in the sense in which we now use the word. It presents a view of man, nature, and their relationship which might be called ecological in the more pervasive and complicated sense mentioned above, one which we might, in fact, call "cosmic ecology." It is a Buddhist system of philosophy which first appeared in a written, systematic form in China in the seventh century, and it was the characteristic teaching of what came to be known as the Hua-yen school of Buddhism. It is a view of existence which is for the most part alien to Western ways of looking at things, but it is a world view well worth consideration, not only as a beautiful artifact appealing to the esthetic sense, but perhaps as a viable basis for conduct, no less plausible than the traditional Western basis.

We may begin with an image which has always been the favorite Hua-yen method of exemplifying the manner in which things exist. Far away in the heavenly abode of the great god Indra, there is a wonderful net which has been hung by some cunning artificer in such a manner that it stretches out infinitely in all directions. In accordance with the extravagant tastes of deities, the artificer has hung a single glittering jewel in each "eye" of the net, and since the net itself is infinite in dimension, the jewels are infinite in number. There hang the jewels, glittering like stars of the first magnitude, a wonderful sight to behold. If we now arbitrarily select one of these jewels for inspection and look closely at it, we will discover that in its polished surface there are reflected *all* the other jewels in the net, infinite in number. Not only that, but each of the jewels reflected in this one jewel is also reflecting all the other jewels, so that there is an infinite reflecting process occurring. The Hua-yen school has been fond of this image, mentioned many times in its literature, because it symbolizes a cosmos in which there is an infinitely repeated interrelationship among all the members of the cosmos. This relationship is said to be one of simultaneous *mutual identity* and *mutual intercausality*.

If we take ten coins as symbolizing the totality of existence, and examine the relationship existing among them, then, according to Hua-yen teaching, coin one will be seen as being identical with the other nine coins. Simultaneously, coin two will be seen as being identical with the other nine coins, and so on throughout the collection of coins. Thus, despite the fact that the coins may be of different denominations, ages, metals, and so on, they are said to be completely identical. This is said to be the *static* relationship of the coins. If we take these same ten coins again and examine their *dynamic* relationship, then, according to the Hua-yen masters, they will be seen as being totally interdependent or intercausal (depending on point of view). Seen in this way, coin one is said to be the cause for the totality of coins which are considered as being dependent on the first coin for their being. Coin one, that is, is the support, while the total group is that which is supported. Since that particular totality couldn't exist without the support of coin one, that coin is said to be the sole cause for the totality. However, if we shift our attention to coin two and now examine its relationship to the other nine coins, the same can now be said of this coin. It is the sole cause for the existence of the totality of ten coins. From the standpoint of *each* of the ten coins, it can be said that that coin is the sole cause for the whole. However, the cause-result relationship is even more fluid than this, for while each coin can, from the standpoint of the one coin, be said to act as sole cause of the whole, simultaneously the whole acts as cause for the one coin in question, for the coin only exists and has any function at all within the total environment. It can never be a question of the coin existing outside its environment, because since the ten coins symbolize the totality of being, a coin outside the context of the ten coins would be a nonentity. Thus each individual is at once the cause for the whole and is caused by the whole, and what is called existence is a vast body made up of an infinity of individuals all sustaining each other and defining each other. The cosmos is, in short, a self-creating, self-maintaining, and self-defining organism. Hua-yen calls such a universe the *dharma-dhātu,* which we may translate as "cosmos" or "universe" if we wish, with the proviso that it is not the universe as commonly imagined, but rather the Hua-yen universe of identity and interdependence.

Such a universe is not at all familiar to Western people. The Judeo-Christian religious tradition and the Greek philosophical tradition have bequeathed to their posterity a view of existence very much different from that conceived by the Chinese. It differs in several respects. First, it has been, and to some extent still is, a universe which must be explained in terms of a divine plan, with respect to both its beginning and its end. The Hua-yen world is completely nonteleological. There is no theory of a beginning time, no concept of a creator, no question of the purpose of it all. The universe is taken as a given, a vast fact which can be explained only in terms of its own inner dynamism, which is not at all unlike the view of twentieth-century physics. Moreover, our familiar world is one in which relationships are rather limited and special. We have blood relationships, marital relationships, relationships with a genus or species, relationships in terms of animate and inanimate, and the like, but it is hard for us to imagine how anything is related to everything else. How am I related to a star in Orion? How am I even related to an Eskimo in Alaska, except through the tenuous and really nonoperative relationship of species? I certainly do not feel related to these other things. In short, we find it much easier to think in terms of isolated *beings,* rather than one *Being.* Being is just that, a unity of existence in which numerically separate entities are all interrelated in a profound manner. Beings are thought of as autonomous, isolated within their own skins, each independent by and large from all the rest of the beings (both animate and inanimate). The "mystic" who speaks of identity with such things as animals, plants, and inanimate objects, as well as other men, is an object of ridicule. The Hua-yen universe is essentially a universe of identity and total intercausality; what affects one item in the vast inventory of the cosmos affects every other individual therein, whether it is death, enlightenment, or sin. Finally, the Western view of existence is one of strict hierarchy, traditionally one in which the creator-god occupies the top rung in the ladder of being, man occupies the middle space, and other animals, plants, rocks, and so on occupy the bottom. Even with the steady erosion of religious interest in the West, where the top rung of the ladder has for many become empty, there still exists the tacit assumption that man is the measure of all things, that this is his universe, that somehow the incalculable history of the vast universe is essentially a human history. The Hua-yen universe, on the other hand, has no hierarchy. There is no center, or, perhaps if there is one, it is everywhere. Man certainly is not the center, nor is some god.

It must be admitted that the traditional anthropocentric universe has begun to fade under the careful scrutiny of people who are not sentimentalists or who do not childishly seek security in baseless assumptions. A physicist, or a philosopher such as Whitehead, would have to admit that comfortable old concepts such as the distinction of subject and object, or that of agent and act, metaphysical entities such as souls and selves, or even more fundamental notions such as the absoluteness of time and space, are untenable in the light of objective and serious inquiry. The Western world is alive with new ideas, but so far these ideas have not trickled down to the mass consciousness. Most people still have a deep faith in solid substances and believe that their feelings, ideas, and even their own bodies belong to, or inhere in, some mysterious but seemingly irrefutable substance called a self.

It has been said that you cannot kill an idea, but it is even more difficult to see a new idea get a hearing in the human community. Shrinking from a reality which we assume will demean us, we hang on to our old habits of thought, which are really prejudices, just as we clung to our security blankets in our cribs. The anthropocentric bias, particularly, has appeared in one form or another down through Western history. It is of course endemic in the Hebraic and Christian traditions, and it has also given rise to dreadful philosophy for a period of hundreds of years—in Cartesianism, with its affirmation of human consciousness and its view of dead nature; in the "Great Chain of Being" of the eighteenth-century philosophers; and even today among the positivists, in whom one may detect a positivism which shrinks from taking the ultimate step in its positivism. The most ingenious attempts of Western thinkers to erect a satisfying picture of existence has resulted, in short, in a not too surprising conclusion that while we are less than gods, we stand just below the angels, superior to and apart from all other things. One may ask whether this conclusion has not risen out of a pathetic self-deception.

It is a truism that a culture reveals its fundamental assumptions and presuppositions in its art forms, and it is partly for this reason that the study of art is so rewarding. In European art, at least up to the advent of the Romantic movement, a representative, and perhaps dominant, genre has been the portrait. To walk through the rooms of a large art museum is to receive an eloquent testimonial concerning the preoccupation of Western man for the last several hundred years. If we examine one of these paintings, we find that it will be dominated by a face or several faces. The artist has drawn upon every resource of his genius and materials to render the face realistic, lifelike. It is invariably grave and composed, befitting a person who had no doubts as to his worth in the general scheme of things. Are ye not of more worth than many sparrows? Yes, of course! Every quirk of personality is here, along with the warts, bumps, hollows, and spidery lines of much frowning and laughing. The clothes, too, are lovingly painted; we have, in gazing at the portrait, an almost tactile sense of the stiffness and roughness of lace, the suave, warm plushness of velvet, and rich, hard luxury of silk. Rings, brooches, and pendants garnish the figure, glinting weightily with gold and silver. The skillful use of chiaroscuro bestows on the figure the roundness and solidity of life. But there is something else too, though we are in danger of overlooking it in our justified concentration on the grand face and figure dominating the canvas. Over the shoulder of the subject we detect a tiny fragment of world, perhaps seen through the tiny window of the lord's palace. If we do not look sharply, it may not even register on our consciousness, but in its own way, it is an important part of the picture, for it tells us much. It occupies, in some paintings, only a hundredth part of the whole canvas, or, if it fills in the background, the coloring and style are such that the scene serves only as an unobtrusive backdrop for the real focal point of the picture. It is there for several reasons; it helps the painter avoid a dull and unimaginative background for the human foreground; it often contains symbols which help us "read" the meaning of the painting; or it defines and places in its correct context (seventeenth-century Florence, the world, etc.) the true subject. However, all these uses of the natural world add up to one; it serves as a backdrop for the human drama, which is not only what painting is about but what the universe is all about. We still dwell comfortably in the pre-Copernican universe, where the world is a stage created for the most important of dramas, the human one. Even in the nineteenth century, when painters turned their attention to natural scenes as intrinsically valuable, the romantics tended to invest their scenery with human emotions and values and to see the natural only in a human frame of reference. They betray, however subtly, what critics have called the "pathetic fallacy," the tendency to read human values into nature and to sentimentalize it. Whatever Western painters have taken up the brush or chisel, they have revealed this abiding belief in a hierarchical existence in which the human ranks only slightly below the divine.

To see that this is not a universal penchant and to simultaneously see a portrait of the universe as experienced by another part of the human family, we might briefly turn to the Oriental wing of our art museum. In the art of the Far East we see few faces—an empress or two, a few high-ranking Buddhist monks, at most. We see mainly landscapes, done in black ink on silk or paper, for just as portraiture and human events are the dominant Western concern, the landscape is dominant in Oriental art. Yet humans are there in the landscapes, along with their homes, occupations, and diversions. But if one were to walk quickly past the scrolls, these figures would be almost, or completely, overlooked, for they do not stand out in the paintings. In fact, no one part of the scene dominates the others. The scene is one of mountains, trees, a stream or lake, perhaps a small hut barely visible in the trees, and a small human figure or two. The mountains recede into the hazy distance, suggesting great spaces, and while the scene is tranquil and serene, there is nevertheless the strong suggestion of a living vitality, a breathing life. The viewer is struck by a sense of continuity among the various elements of the scene, in which all are united in an organic whole. The humans in the picture, which are almost always there, have their rightful place in this scene, but only their rightful place as one part of the whole. Nature here is not a background for man; man and nature are blended together harmoniously. Even this way of analyzing the scene distorts the situation; we see only being itself in its totality, "man" being merely one isolatable element of no more or less prominence than a tree or a bird. Are ye not of more worth than many sparrows? No.

These two examples of art reveal, I suggest, two different ways of understanding not only man's place in the total scheme of things, but the basic structure of existence in general. The humanistic or anthropocentric orientation of the first painting is clearly in sharp contrast with the landscape, assuming the status of a self-evident presupposition. The humanistic bias of the former also reflects a tacit assumption that being is organized in a hierarchical manner, in which some parts of existence—notably, the divine and human—stand above other parts, with all the rights and privileges pertaining thereof. Historically there has been little doubt on the part of Western people that we do stand apart from, and superior to, all else. When we gaze out at the creation, we see a reality which is primarily broken and fragmented, with none of the continuity and interrelatedness observed in the Chinese landscape; and, of course, this discontinuity, or alienation, exists mainly for us and our confrontation with the other. This would be of merely academic interest were it not for the fact that such a view is said to cause the individual to suffer greatly.

Now, while there seems to be a fundamental difference in the way Western and Eastern people regard experience, let it not be assumed that a Chinese or Japanese is born into the world with a vision of identity and interdependence. Buddhism was founded by an Indian, and the Hua-yen school was a product of Chinese experience; both were taught to help Oriental people, who suffer from the same existential plight that Western people do. Human beings are basically the same in the manner in which they organize experience through recurrent training, learning to make sense out of what William James spoke of as a "blooming, buzzing confusion." However, Buddhism did arise in the East, indicating that there is a *tendency* to see things as described by Hua-yen. Conversely, the *tendency* in the West has been to analyze rather than unify, to discriminate rather than see all as one, to make distinctions rather than see all qualities within each datum of experience. But the truth of the matter is that the universe as described in Hua-yen documents is the world as seen by enlightened individuals, Buddhas, and not by ordinary folk of any race, time, or geographic area. Thus the Hua-yen vision is not at all self-evident, even to a Chinese philosopher. The message of Buddhism is claimed to be universal; since all people suffer in the same basic way, the cure is universally beneficial.

The Chinese landscapes described above can be thought of as plastic duplicates of Hua-yen philosophy, in the sense that both attempt to express a vision of the manner in which things exist. What is clear from both is that there is a great emphasis on the relatedness of things, and as was mentioned, this relationship is the dual one of identity and interdependence. This matter of relationship is extremely important, and perhaps the most important difference between the Hua-yen view of things and the ordinary view is that people ordinarily think and experience in terms of distinct, separate *entities,* while Hua-yen conceives of experience primarily in terms of the *relationships* between these same entities. It is simply a question of fundamental, basic reality; is it separate parcels of matter (or mental objects) or is it relationship? It is interesting in this regard to see that a great number of Western physicists have now drawn the conclusion, based on the implications of Einstein's theories, that relationship is the more fundamental. As one physicist has remarked, if all the matter in the universe less one bundle of matter ceased to exist, the mass of the remaining parcel of matter (and hence its existence) would be reduced to nothing—the implication being that mass is a function of total environment and dependent on it.[1] Nonetheless, in the seventh century, Fa-tsang and other Hua-yen masters taught that to exist in any sense at all means to exist in dependence on the other, which is infinite in number. Nothing exists truly in and of itself, but requires everything to be what it is.

Previously, in examining the relationship existing among ten coins, it was said that any one coin is identical with all the other coins. The reader has undoubtedly heard of this business of identity before. Oh yes, the Mysterious East has this obsession with Identity. We smile to think of the yogi walking through the jungle meditating on the sameness of things and being pounced upon and eaten by a real, unmystical tiger. So much for identity, we say, in the belief that we have disposed of any nonsense about identity. Or, like the cynic in Orwell's *Animal Farm,* we may grant that things are all equal, but some things are more equal than others. Things seem to be very unequal, radically nonidentical. But the Hua-yen masters were not mystics, and while agreeing that there were men and tigers, eaters and eaten, they could insist on identity anyway. Let us turn to another example of identity in an attempt to see in what way things are just what they are and yet identical.

We might take the example of a human body as a kind of organic whole similar to the totality analyzed by Hua-yen. Here too we can agree that there are distinctions in form and function among the constituents of the whole body. My ears do not look like my toes, and I cannot see with my elbow. Ears detect sounds, my stomach digests food, my nose detects odors and helps me to breathe. We do not confuse the parts; we know where everything is and what it does. It is equally evident that what we call the body is an organism made up of all these parts, and normally the parts do not exist apart from the body. If we now look into the relationship between any one part of the body and the whole body, it will be obvious that we are really discussing the relationship between this one part and all other parts, whether considered individually or collectively.

Let us examine the place of the nose, being prominent and, therefore, seeming to offer itself for inspection. In what sense is it identical with my body or with any other part of the body? The Hua-yen argument is really very simple; what we call the whole is nothing apart from the individuals which make up that whole. Thus the nose, in being integrated perfectly into the configuration we call a body, not only acts as a condition without which there could be no body, but in fact becomes or is the body. I can therefore point to my nose and say, "This is my body," and there will be no disagreement, with the possible exception that someone might say, "It is only a part of your body." This is true; it is a part of my body, but at the same time it is my body. To insist that it is *only* a part is to fall into a fallacious view of the whole as an independent and subsisting entity to which parts belong. The bell tower on the Riverside campus of the University of California is not something which is added to an already existent campus. It is the campus.

Thus the part and the whole in this sense are one and the same thing, for what we identify as a part is merely an abstraction from a unitary whole.

But in what way can it be said that the nose is identical with my left elbow? We may understand that in a sense a part is identical with the whole as a whole, but identifying part with part raises difficulties, for the two parts look different, are spatially distinct, and perform different functions. The postulation of identity does not remove these distinctions, and Hua-yen insists that not only are things both identical *and* different, but, paradoxically, that they are identical *because* they are different. In other words, to have the body I now have, I need a nose which is between my eyes and has the office of detecting odors, an elbow which bends in a certain way, allowing me to write and throw, a heart in my chest which pumps blood, and so on. If everything was literally a nose, I would be just one immense nose; in fact, I would not be "me." Thus each individual is required in its own unique form, with its own unique function, to act as a condition for the whole in question. The identity of the nose and the left elbow consists in their identity as *conditions* for the whole. Therefore, while the two are different, they are the same; in fact, they are identical precisely because they are different. Seen in this light, then, when the nose is understood for what it is, the whole body is known; when we know the nature of the body, we know what the nose is. For this reason, Hua-yen can say that ten thousand Buddhas can be seen preaching on the tip of a single hair. In other words, the one truth which is common of all things (ten thousand Buddhas) is evident in the tip of the hair once we know its place in the whole.

The reader is bound, at this point, to interpose in exasperation, "Very well, they are all the same *as conditions,* but nevertheless, life and death don't appear to be the same to me!" Certainly they seem different. One moment the loved one is talking with us, cheeks pink with life, loving and caring, and the next moment he or she lies still, pale in death, never more to laugh, love, or care again. Is there no differences? Does nothing happen when the hard-headed, practical tiger eats the mystical yogi?

Yes, of course something happens, the Hua-yen Buddhist agrees that something does. The yogi really dies and becomes part of the tiger (although this is not the kind of identity insisted upon by Hua-yen). Now, we may go out and shoot the tiger so he will not eat any more people, but we are still left confronting the question of the place of tigers in the world, and our attitude here is going to determine whether our own private existence is going to be a success or a failure. It is the human habit to reject such things as hungry tigers, or their equivalents—cancer, bullets, or the slow, insidious, but equally effective tiger of old age. We would have nothing but sunshine, sweet wine, eternal youth, and endless satisfactory amours. Intellectually we know that tigers are real and do exist, but emotionally we reject them with fear and loathing, and we would rather that they did not exist. They are somehow intruders in the sacred circle of life, foreign agents sent to subvert our happiness. They are antilife. It is the very picking and choosing which brings back upon ourselves anxiety, fear, and turmoil; for by dividing up the one unitary existence into two parts, the good and the bad, we distort the reality which is the one unitary existence. That is, we blind ourselves to the fact that existence in its totality is both life *and* death, success *and* failure, health *and* sickness. Tigers are not foreign intruders but facts of life.

Both life and death are part of the one everchanging process we call being (which is really a "becoming") and thus both are conditions for that being. To see things in a totalistic perspective means to transcend a small, pathetic subjectivity and to see all the pernicious, vexing contraries harmonized within the whole. As D.T. Suzuki said in his commentary on Bashō's *haiku*

> Lice, fleas—
> The horse pissing
> Beside my pillow

the real world is a world of lice as well as butterflies, horse piss as well as vintage champagne, and to the person who has truly realized this, one is as good as the other.[2] To insist otherwise is to make an impious demand of existence which it is unwilling and unable to satisfy. The "ugly" things of life exist, and the only question is how we are to confront them. The romantic hero smashing himself to pieces against the stone wall of necessity has never found favor in Asian literature.

This matter of identity can be explored in more depth if we turn to the matter of interdependence again, for the two relationships are so inextricably related themselves that one cannot be understood without the other. In returning to the nose, let us examine it in its dynamic relationship with the body-totality. Now, this humble organ is, according to Hua-yen, the total cause for the rest of the body. Since, as was pointed out, the "rest" is an assemblage of parts, this means that the nose causes my right elbow, my left knee, and so on. This is, admittedly, a highly unusual way of looking at a nose, and it is true that if in this analysis of cause and result we stopped completely with the assertion that the nose causes the body, this would be a very questionable assertion indeed. Moving from this example to the Hua-yen cosmos, this would be tantamount to saying that a drop of water in the Nile River is the cause for the whole universe. Mysticism indeed! But the issue of one sole causal agent is not being discussed here, and, in fact, part of the function of Hua-yen thought is to destroy the fiction of a sole causal agent. The apparent absurdity of arguing that the nose causes the rest of my body arises from the sheer necessity of examining the relationship of *each* part of the whole to the whole in a linear manner, one part at a time in sequence. If we move to another part of the body, the left index finger, let us say, we can now assert that the finger is the cause for the body. This does not cancel out the causal function of the nose; the reality of the situation is that any part can be said to assume the role of total cause when the relationship is examined purely from the point of view of the one part being examined. At this point, it might be assumed that the Hua-yen masters are making a rather commonplace observance, that a whole is the result of the collaboration of many individual parts each exerting its own partial causal power. However, this is not the case, and Fa-tsang, in his *Hua-yen i-ch'eng chiao i fen-ch'i chang,* says that if this were the case,

> there would be the errors of annihilationism and eternalism. If [each part] does not wholly cause [the whole] to be made and only exerts partial power, then each condition would only have partial power. They would consist only of many individual partial powers and would not make one whole, which is annihilationism. . . . also, if [the part] does not wholly create [the whole], then when one [part] is removed, the [whole] should remain. However, since the whole is not formed, then you should understand that the [whole] is not formed by the partial power [of a condition] but by its total power.[3]

Thus according to the Hua-yen school, the part exerts *total power* in the formation of a particular whole.

When we move to every part of the body, to every organ, limb, cell, or subcellular particle, and in each case analyze the relationship of that part to the whole body, it can be said that that part of the whole is *the* sole cause for the whole. When referring to causality, Hua-yen is not making the naive assertion that first there is, let us say, a nose, and then later the rest of the body comes into existence as a result of the prior condition of the nose. Time is not involved, nor is there a question of production of a result from a cause in a progressive series of events. The real question concerns the relationship existing between simultaneously existing individuals. Whether a totality is composed of two parts, a million parts, or an infinity of parts, causality in the sense meant by Hua-yen refers to a relationship among present entities.

The totality we have been looking at is nothing more than a number of simultaneously existing individuals, and since the relationship of support and supported always exists between any one individual and all other individuals, or the whole, it would seem clear that not only does the individual support the whole but, upon a more complete investigation, what is a cause or support from one point of view is result or the supported from another. The categories of support and supported, or cause and result, are completely fluid and interchangeable, becoming either as the point of view shifts. It is the necessity of point of view which in fact obscures the real status of the individuals which compose the whole. They are all simultaneously cause and result, or support and supported, for this is precisely the picture of existence which Hua-yen hopes to describe: a universe which is nothing but the complete mutual cooperation of the entities which make it up.

It may be well to try to clarify the sense in which Hua-yen uses the term "cause" at this point. The description of the intercausal or interdependent nature of the parts of the body illustrates the magnitude of the relationships as well as the nature of that relationship, but the meanings of "cause," "condition," "support," and other terms have not been discussed at much length. As has already been mentioned, "cause" is not used here in the popularly understood sense of a temporal sequence of events in which if an antecedent event is present, a subsequent event will occur. Perhaps the Hua-yen use of the term will become clearer if we resort to a model of an even simpler kind. Let us take a tripod. If we bind three poles together near one end and then stand the three poles up on outspread legs, the tripod will remain standing. Here the tripod is a whole, which is of course composed of parts. If, now, one of the poles is removed, the other two poles will topple over. This toppling action is not meant, however, to show what happens to the whole when a part is removed, but rather shows that in order to be *that* whole it needs this one pole. Obviously the universe does not collapse when one individual member dies, but it is no longer *that* particular whole it was when the individual survived. Now, if we label the three poles *a, b,* and *c,* and remove pole *a,* the falling of the remaining two poles shows that from the point of view of *a,* it has complete power to form the tripod. However, if we turn our attention to pole *b,* now that pole, from the new point of view, is said to be completely responsible for the whole tripod. What has happened to *a?* Seen from the point of view of pole *b,* it is result, or that which is supported. Since a tripod is three interdependent poles, each of the three parts is simultaneously acting as cause or support for the whole tripod and yet is indubitably part of a whole which is being supported.

It is to be admitted that the term "cause" is being used in an unusual manner in these examples, since what is evident is that these are all examples of what might better be called interdependency or mutual conditionedness. Yet, Fa-tsang and other Hua-yen masters do use the word "cause," and the Hua-yen universe is a universe of self-causation. The traditional term to describe such a situation is *fa-chiai yüan-ch'i,* which seems to be a translation of the Sanskrit *dharma-dhātu pratītya-samutpāda,* translated either as the "interdependent arising of the universe" or, perhaps better, the "interdependent arising which is the universe," since all that exists is part of the one great scheme of interdependency. Bertrand Russell said that the only reasonable definition of cause would be the sum total of all existent conditions, in the sense that any event will occur unless any one of the available conditions fails. It is in this sense that we should understand the Hua-yen use of the word, for in the Hua-yen universe, the individual will *be,* and will perform its function, unless some other individual withdraws its support.

One of the most important implications of such a view is that every single thing in the universe comes to have an important place in the scheme of things. In the "Great Barn," every rafter, shingle, and nail is important, for where can we find a barn apart from these things? This apparently insignificant shingle I see there in the building is a necessary condition for the barn, and in fact, it *is* the barn. Yet, what do we mean by "shingle"? It is not a shingle outside the context of the barn of which it is a part, for "shingle" only has meaning in its proper context. It is true that there is no building without this little shingle, but it is equally evident that "shingle" has neither existence nor meaning outside the barn of which it is a part. They make and define each other.

To make one more analogy in a rather long series of analogies, existence is something like an old-fashioned American square dance. In the square dance, what I am and what I do are completely defined by my inclusion in the square dance, for obviously I am nothing apart from it. My being, and my office, can be seen as being nothing but functions of the dance in which I exist. However, where is the square dance without me, and "I" am every member of the dance? I am the square dance. Thus we have a profound, crucial relationship here; that I am, and that I am defined in a certain way, is completely dependent on the *other* individuals who compose the dance, but this dance itself has no existence apart from the dancer. The Buddhist, in viewing things as being interdependent in this manner, comes to have, ideally, a profound feeling of gratitude and respect for things, however humble they may appear to people who do not share his understanding, for in some manner that eludes the rest of us, he is aware that what he is depends utterly upon them.

Having taken this brief look at the doctrine of interdependence, we may now return to the matter of identity, as perhaps more problematic than the matter of interdependence. Yet, there is finally no real problem, because "identity" is only another way of saying "interdependent"; they are one and the same. The point to the doctrine of interdependence is that things exist *only* in interdependence, for things do not exist in their own right. In Buddhism, this manner of existence is called "emptiness" (Sanskrit *śūnyatā*). Buddhism says that things are empty in the sense that they are absolutely lacking in a self-essence *(svabhāva)* by virtue of which things would have an independent existence. In reality, their existence derives strictly from interdependence. If things possessed essences or substance of a metaphysical nature, then there truly would be real, ultimate differences between things. However, if each experiential datum, whether material or mental, derives its existence and meaning purely through its dependence on everything else, then it is not ultimately unique at all, but must be seen as identical with everything else in its emptiness. Thus to be identical with everything else means to share in the universal interdependence, or intercausality, of all that exists. If one objects that one still perceives a vast difference between good and evil, or Buddhas and ordinary folk, or life and death, one need not be surprised, for to be human means to perceive these differences. However, the Buddha insisted that to be attached to these meanings in such a manner brought disaster to the individual. It is the perennial teaching of Buddhism that such attachment will fill his heart with desire and loathing, make his life a ceaseless hell of turmoil *(duḥkha)*, madden him, and finally send him to his grave confused, bitter, and afraid.

Identity can be thought of as the static relationship among things, while interdependence is the dynamic relationship; they are two sides of the same coin, and both are alternate ways of saying that all is empty *(sarvam śūnyam)*. It is on the basis of this doctrine of emptiness that Hua-yen insists on a totalistic view of things. Totalism has two meanings. First, it means that all things are contained in each individual. The nose, in its identity and interdependence with the rest of the body, takes in the whole body, for whatever is true in the ultimate sense concerning the nose is also true of the whole body. If we know reality in the form of one phenomenon, then we know all of reality. It is for this reason that Hua-yen can make the seemingly outrageous claim that the whole universe is contained in a grain of sand. However, not only does the one contain the all, but at the same time, the all contains the one, for the individual is completely integrated into its environment.

Second, totalism refers to a manner of experiencing events in which room is allowed for all kinds of events, and in which nothing is excluded as alien or "bad," as was discussed earlier. This is difficult to accept for the person unaccustomed to Eastern thought, for it demands that one make room not grudgingly or fatalistically, but joyously and with profound gratitude, for the horse urine and lice that do in fact coexist with fine champagne and beautiful butterflies. The totalistic view sees these as no less real, and no less wonderful, once we have transcended a petty, partial view of existence in which our comfort and unslakable thirst determine what has and has not a right to exist. In the totalistic universe, which is one organic body of interacting parts, it is an act of self-defeating madness to insist on a never-ending diet of vintage champagne, sunshine, and laughter, and to insist vehemently and with no small amount of hubris that urine, darkness, and tears be banished forever. In every contest, there has to be of necessity both a winner and a loser (granting an occasional draw), and all that Hua-yen asks is that we realize, and appreciate, the fact that we cannot ever have one without the other. The partial view would have only one or the other; the totalistic view sees that the two always go together.

The totalistic world as described by Hua-yen is a living body in which each cell derives its life from the other cells, and in return gives life to those many others. Like the human body, the Hua-yen universe is ever changing, for in it there is not one thing which is static and unchanging, unless it is the law of perpetual change itself. It is an incredible stream of activity wherein when one circumstance alters, everything alters with it. "Do I dare to eat a peach?" asks one of T.S. Eliot's characters, and the question of action becomes an extremely delicate one to the individual who sees the fantastic interaction of things. Thus in a universe which is pure fluidity, or process, no act can but have an effect on the whole, just as a pebble tossed into a pool sends waves out to the farthest shore and stirs the very bottom. This is hard to see. We can comprehend how a modification in one small part of our body can affect the total organism, but we find it hard to believe that the enlightenment of one monk under a tree in India somehow enlightens us all, or, conversely, that my own intransigent ignorance is a universal ignorance. However, if we can comprehend that the greater whole of which the body is a part is no less organic, and no less interrelated, such an idea is not so unlikely. At that point, the moral life as conceived by Buddhism becomes possible.

University students today do not find the Buddhist concepts of emptiness and interdependent existence (which are the same thing) difficult to understand, as they might have been a generation ago and more. Much more conversant, if even in an elementary way, with scientific and philosophical trends, they can see fairly easily that the very old Western assumptions about substances, selves, agents, and the like, are no longer tenable, or are at least open to serious doubt. Their intellectual world is a different one from that of even the previous generation. They feel much more at home with such startling concepts as the unified field and the ecosphere. They have begun to appreciate, however dimly, that in some real sense, everything is alive and exerting its influence on everything else, that even dead things are alive.

Faraday, over a hundred years ago, made the startling remark that an electric charge must be considered to exist everywhere, and Alfred North Whitehead, commenting on this statement, paraphrased it by saying that "the modification of the electromagnetic field at every point of space at each instant owing to the past history of each electron is another way of stating the same fact."[4] Faraday, Whitehead, and the Buddhists of the Hua-yen are all, in their own way, making the observation that nature is not at all dead, but rather is most vital. It is certainly not a case of animism or spiritism, but, whatever may be the basis, a realization that even things commonly thought to be dead or inanimate exert a continual, crucial influence on each other.

The work of earlier physicists such as Faraday and Maxwell, and later men such as Einstein, as well as Whitehead with his process philosophy, and others, have all laid the groundwork for an entirely new understanding of the nature of existence, and this understanding is gradually beginning to filter down to the layperson. Thus, as I remarked earlier, the intellectual grasp of such Buddhist concepts as emptiness and interdependence has become much easier and much more prevalent, so that the university student is not absolutely baffled by these ideas. So much that is in the air in Western thought coincides in general outline with Hua-yen cosmology that what might have once passed for bad thinking by Oriental "mystics" can now be discussed seriously.

My concluding point is that intellectual grasp is not enough, according to all that the old Buddhist thinkers have had to say. They did not intend their treatises to be mere theoretical exercises, to be read, understood, and filed away in the great dust bins of the mind. The Hua-yen vision was first of all meant to tantalize the reader and lure him to *realize* (i.e., to *make real* in his everyday experience) what had been only theory. To realize the Hua-yen universe means to go beyond an intellectual grasp of the system to a *lived experience* of things existing in this manner, for the Hua-yen world view is nothing if not a lived reality. To live this reality in turn means to alter drastically one's moral and ethical stance as they relate to the infinite other. Here, in conclusion, a story told by a Buddhist priest may give some idea of what it means to live the Hua-yen vision.

> That I have been able to establish myself as well as I have has been totally because of my teacher's guidance. It was customary for him to visit the shrines of various guardians, placed around the grounds of the temple, every day after the morning service. One morning while he was making his rounds, he discovered a single chopstick in a drain. He brought it back, called me to his room, held out the chopstick to me and asked, "What is this?" I replied, "It is a chopstick." "Yes, this is a chopstick. Is it unusable?" he asked further. "No," I said, "It is still usable." "Quite so," he said, "And yet I found it in a drain with other scraps. That is to say, you have taken the life of this chopstick. You may know the proverb, 'He who kills another digs two graves.' Since you have killed this chopstick, you will be killed by it." Spending four or five hours on this incident he told me how I should practice. At that time I was seven or eight years old. His guidance at that time really soaked in. From that time on, I became very careful and meticulous about everything.[5]

In the Hua-yen universe, where everything interpenetrates in identity and interdependence, where everything needs everything else, what is there which is not valuable? To throw away even a single chopstick as worthless is to set up a hierarchy of values which in the end will kill us in a way in which no bullet can. In the Hua-yen universe, everything counts.

Someone once made the observation that one's skin is not necessarily a boundary marking off the self from the not-self but rather that which brings one into contact with the other. Like Faraday's electric charge which must be conceived as being everywhere, I am in some sense boundless, my being encompassing the farthest limits of the universe, touching and moving every atom in existence. The same is true of everything else. The interfusion, the sharing of destiny, is as infinite in scope as the reflections in the jewels of Indra's net. When in a rare moment I manage painfully to rise above a petty individualism by knowing my true nature, I perceive that I dwell in the wondrous net of Indra, and in this incredible network of interdependence, the career of the Bodhisattva must begin. It is not just that "we are all in it" together. We all *are* it, rising or falling as one living body.

Environmental Problematics

Kenneth K. Inada

In this century, metaphorically speaking, we have witnessed the shrinking of the world to a considerable degree. As rational and concerned beings, it is incumbent upon us to understand the full implications of this shrinkage. The nature of the shrinkage has many dimensions, depending on the perspectives that are drawn, but for our purposes we may point to two principal modes of perception, the conceptual and the ontological, both of which are nonexclusivistic and mutually binding.

On the conceptual side, we may assert that the world is seen in terms of a single entity or concept, that all the lands and peoples of the world and their activities have now come within the sweeping purview of man. On the ontological side, the realm of existence is experienced sensually and physically in terms of which experience a unique nature is felt and in which all the connections and relationships become the basis of what we call reality. In brief, one side is mental (conceptual) and the other corporeal (sensed). Indeed, knowledge attendant to both modes of perception has rapidly advanced and increased because of the marvels of science and technology, and we live literally in an era of instant phenomena, even beyond the confines of the earth, although we must ever be watchful of any scientific lag that may accrue to cause a disruption in our lives. All this is well and good, but the crucial question remains: Are we really at home with the world? Or, turning inward, are we at home with our own existence? Do we really know the real nature of the human condition, the involvement of man with his surroundings, and, were we to know some measure of it, can we properly and successfully relate ourselves to the world at large? The answer may not be had easily, and may not even be forthcoming; this state of apprehension is indicative of the plight in which we presently find ourselves.

Martin Buber once remarked that man not only is born *in* the world but *with* the world. His philosophy of "I and Thou" precluded any dichotomy or separation between the two components. More recently, Paul Weiss has candidly observed:

A philosophy which cannot get beyond personal commitments or a common language, no matter how carefully it speaks or how closely it adheres to current theories, is radically defective. And it will remain so, I think, if it is

231

unable to allow one to affirm that there are animals, birds, trees, hills, rivers, a sun and a moon, even when there are no men, or when they say nothing about these.[1]

These remarks were probably intended for the narrow positivists, analysts, and linguists, but they also address broadly all who have a limited vision of things and who are unable to account for the holistic nature of things beyond their own existence. Conceptually and ontologically, there is no denial today that the total existential realm can be accommodated and related so as to develop a full philosophy of nature, and yet the situation is such that we still lag behind by persisting in our narrow, self-imposed and tradition-bound modes of perception. How then can we best move out of this restrictive mode? This I believe is the question that faces us today, and, without facing it, we may not be able to gather our resources for understanding the makings of an environmental ethics. It is here that I wish to discuss what Buddhist thought can contribute to alleviate the situation and to develop the proper holistic mode of perception: a synoptic vision with a penetrative quality.

The program before us is formidable, and we can only touch upon the initial conceptual stance and relate it vitally to the so-called ontological concreteness of things. By the term, "ontological," I do not refer to any entity, thing, or object which has a separate or independent state of existence or makes reference to substance-oriented philosophy; rather, this refers to the inherently intuitive feel of the total nature of one's existence, something akin to Heidegger's existential being-in-the-world concept. It can be said that the so-called elements of being that we so casually speak of do not in and of themselves describe being itself. This was the basic premise of early Buddhist thought, including that of the historical Buddha, I believe, but it was made prominent later on by Nāgārjuna in his major work, *Mūlamadhyamakakārikā* (Verses in Reference to the Fundamental Middle Doctrine). Systematically castigating all forms of self-existence *(svabhāva)* or inherently existent nature, Nāgārjuna finally exhibited the fact that enlightened existence is completely shorn of the conventionally and ontologically oriented elements of being. In short, he got rid of all so-called elemental ontologies but at the same time he attempted to intimate that a unique form of reality, *tattva* or "thatness" of being, still remains unblemished in the dynamic flow of existence. In this sense, the usual pluralistic ontologies that we attach ourselves to in order to perceive things or life in general were "replaced" by a kind of dynamic, formless ontology. This is not at all to be cryptic, nor is it to move into some indescribable transcendent realm. Nāgārjuna moved, in short, from ordinary ontologies to a supreme form of ontology, and, in this specific vein, I have referred to him as a Supreme Ontologist, much to the displeasure and puzzlement of a few scholars.

Although we live far removed from the days of the historical Buddha, the basic doctrines have been kept remarkably intact, especially in the Theravāda tradition. With the first rise of the neo-Buddhist movement, which gradually came to be known as the Mahāyāna, these doctrines were not abandoned or destroyed but subjected to a sweeping new and revolutionary interpretation. Today, we live in an era where both traditions, Theravāda and Mahāyāna, have met on relatively neutral ground, that is, in the non-Asiatic World, to develop yet another vigorous interpretation of the doctrines. Not only are the doctrines coming under critical scrutiny in terms of Western philosophical and scientific methodology, but the religious confrontation and dialogue are beginning to take interesting shapes. This exchange has especially been initiated from Christian quarters and by those intellectuals who have sought supplementary approaches to life, reflected in the keen interest in Zen and related meditative disciplines. In this novel situation, it is quite natural that another neo-Buddhist movement is subtly emerging from all of this interaction and that new forms of experiential data are rapidly appearing on the scene. Perhaps it would not be remiss to state that the challenge presented by these developments is a two-way street, that other non-Buddhist systems are equally being subjected to a reexamination of their existing doctrines and to the attendant gradual change.

What we are witnessing today in Buddhism is analogous to what transpired in China and Japan, for example, in the creating of their own respective brands of Buddhism, which came to fruition in China during the T'ang dynasty and in Japan during the Kamakura period. Thus the challenge to us today offers prospects that are most promising. In this respect, our serious concern with environmental ethics is forcing us to seek an accommodation with a long-tested and reliable tradition. We must therefore meet the challenge with absolute objectivity, in a spirit of boldness, resolve, and adventure.

The most representative Buddhist doctrines are all familiar to us, namely, suffering *(duḥkha)*, impermanence *(anitya)*, nonself *(anātman)*, *saṃsāra*, *nirvāṇa*, the middle way *(madhyamā pratipad)*, emptiness *(śūnyatā)*, *karman*, relational origination *(pratītya-samutpāda)*, wisdom *(prajñā)*, and compassion *(karuṇā)*. A quick glance at these doctrines will reveal that all focus on the nature of experiential reality. That is to say, every doctrine specifically expands on that nature by revealing either the unenlightened or enlightened character. Buddhism, of course, took over this dyadic treatment of man's nature from its predecessors, Hinduism and Jainism in particular, but it went beyond to develop its own interpretation of the suffering of man and the way out. All the doctrines mentioned above except for nonself, in their normal definition, are pre-Buddhistic, and yet close examination will show that each is given a new twist, a new meaning, as applicable to man's nature. Still, too many scholars in both East and West have tended to seek some sort of an identity for or accommodation to the doctrines and have therefore linked Buddhism directly, albeit indiscriminately and unfairly, with Hinduism and Jainism, treating it as a mere extension, if not an appendage, of these systems. The linkage still persists in some quarters today, for old concepts are hard to replace, especially those burdened by old meanings. No one, to my knowledge, has gone over the Buddhist doctrines singly or *in toto* to bring out the vast differences that developed as a consequence of the Buddha's original enlightenment. Usually it is the other way around; that is, scholars seek to demonstrate the continuity of these doctrines in the whole fabric of Indian philosophical and religious tradition.

Being the children of the intellectual climate of their times, the Buddha and his immediate followers had no alternative but to utilize the existing language to express a new philosophy of life. It was for them an uphill struggle from the start, but they persisted and eventually succeeded despite the linguistic difficulties. They did so because the doctrines that they expounded expressed the awesome spirit and substance of a new dimension in experiential reality. And here I would like to emphasize a principle of being that pervades all the doctrines. I have already referred to the dyadic nature of the enlightened and the unenlightened natures, but this dyadic nature is exhibited in most of the doctrines, for example, in suffering and nonsuffering, wholesome and unwholesome natures, permanent and impermanent natures, and self and nonself. This observation may seem academic or even pedestrian, and it could end at this point with an uncritical acceptance of the dyadic nature. Buddhist doctrines, however, embody a most unique idea, which, while allowing the old concepts to remain as they are, nevertheless revolutionizes them by injecting a new dimension of being into them.

What, then, is this unique idea? For want of a better term, I shall refer to it awkwardly as "the principle of parity of existence" or "the parity principle of existence" or even "the ontological parity of reality." Again, we note that Nāgārjuna crystallized all of Buddhist thought by concluding in his famous verses that there is no difference between the realms of *saṃsāra* and *nirvāṇa*.[2] There is still debate over the correct interpretation of these verses. My interpretation is that *saṃsāra* and *nirvāṇa* fall within the same realm of existence because of the guiding "parity principle." That is, the existential elements relative to *saṃsāra* and *nirvāṇa* are one and the same in form, and their functions have a parity regardless of unenlightened or enlightened status. It should be noted that the parity principle was not discovered by Nāgārjuna or by others in this line; it was specifically included in the original teachings of the Buddha. The Buddha said quite cryptically in reference to the four Noble Truths: "He who sees *duḥkha* sees also the arising of *duḥkha*, sees also the cessation of *duḥkha*, and sees also the path leading to the cessation of *duḥkha*."[3] In the same vein he asserted: "Whatever is of the nature of arising, all that is of the nature of cessation."[4] The rising and falling of activity may be segmented, but these segments find a common source or ground which does not in itself differentiate the segments. Indeed, the common ground of existence is all that each of us has. It is the alpha and omega of all of life's travails and of its resolution, if that resolution is forthcoming at all. In a similar vein, the *Majjhima Nikāya* asserts: "Whoever sees conditioned genesis *(paṭiccasamuppāda)* sees *dhamma* (truth of existence); whoever sees *dhamma* sees conditioned genesis."[5] Furthermore, in the *Itivuttaka*, the Buddha emphatically states: "That monk sees *dhamma*. Seeing *dhamma* he sees me."[6] These statements indicate an odd identity among the terms used here and would seem to suggest that some sort of a mystical union is needed in order to understand and realize the putative equation. Actually, there is nothing mystical here. In both statements the parity principle functions to show that the nature or realm of the terms — *dhamma, paṭiccasamuppāda,* and Buddha — constitutes one and the same function in their mutually inclusivistic natures.

In early Buddhist thought, we also come across the following cryptic but profound statement:

> Monks, there is a not-born, a no-become, a not-made, a not-compounded. Monks, if that unborn, not-become, not-made, not-compounded were not, there would be apparent no escape from this here that is born, become, made, compounded.

> But since, monks, there is an unborn . . . therefore the escape from this here is born, become . . . is apparent.[7]

The passage gives a clear indication that reality has two facets lodged in the selfsame ground of existence. This singular ground of existence is assertible because of the parity principle. The Buddha made it clear from the beginning that experiential reality is in a sense Janus-like — one side is conventionally bound (compounded, conditioned), the other nonconventionally bound (uncompounded, unconditioned); and yet we thrive without knowing or sensing the presence of both sides in tandem or in a mutually supportive sense, because we are predominantly influenced by the one-dimensional, empirical nature of things.

As we move on to the Mahāyāna tradition, we also encounter the parity principle in the *Prajñāpāramitā Sūtras,* especially in the condensed *Heart Sūtra,* containing the oft-quoted "identity" statement with respect to form *(rūpa)* and emptiness *(śūnyatā)*—actually, it is emptiness related to all five *skandhas*, which constitute the basic framework of Buddhist experiential reality. These are later refined into other elements of being *(dharmas)* and consciousnesses *(vijñānas)*, for example, but they all "come home" to the basic framework. The so-called identity of form and emptiness is another refinement of the parity found in the compounded (conditioned) and uncompounded (unconditioned) nature of things in the advancement of the functional framework of the Bodhisattva Ideal, about which we shall have more to say later.

Nāgārjuna, of course, reiterated the parity principle of existence in a more dramatic and systematic way by denying substantive treatment of everything, since all characteristics of that treatment, from naïve perceptions (realism) to sophisticated conscious plays (conceptualism), are unaccountable in any shape or form. Moreover, to account for anything, "something" besides itself is involved in perception that denies the sole presence of the thing. The natural reaction to the statement just made is: "But then, what is that something? Is it not just another form of a substance or a part of the substantive treatment?" The questions are well-put but not well-grounded. Nāgārjuna will not fall into a dialectical regression. He will not accept terms that could lead one away from the experiential reality, the metacenter of total and dynamic process. Thus he will deny any discourse on emptiness, which would lead to nihilism, or on elements, which would lead to substantialism— two of the extremes avoided by the Buddha himself. In one famous verse,[8] he identifies relational origination *(pratītya-samutpāda)* with emptiness *(śūnyatā)* and the middle way *(madhyamā pratipad)*. Here he is exhibiting the fact that experiential reality has three facets, namely, the empirically grounded relational nature of the rise of all perceptions or events, the nonempirical "empty" nature in virtue of the dynamically relational or dependent nature, and the total or holistic nature of an enlightened way of life commonly known as the middle way. Any discourse on any thing belongs only to the first facet, the empirical realm, but there are the other facets with which to contend. Since we are empirically bound from the beginning and must start with this condition, Nāgārjuna concludes the chapter by asserting thus:

> One who rightly discerns relational origination will
> indeed rightly discern the universal nature of suffering,
> its origination, its cessation and the way to enlightenment.[9]

This verse clearly affirms the centrality of relational origination, central in the sense that it permeates our lives from beginning to end as we dedicate ourselves to confront the universal nature of suffering and its resolution.

Elsewhere[10] I have discussed the two strains in Buddhist causality, that is, in reference to relational origination, to indicate the nature of the parity principle, without which the understanding of experience would be unbalanced and would invariably be weighted in favor of the empirical side.

In the highly sophisticated and psychologically oriented system of Yogācāra-vijñānavāda, we find the parity principle in function. The unique eight-*vijñāna* theory seems very complex and even too speculative for the ordinary mind to comprehend, but, in the final analysis, its function is only to express the preservation of the holistic nature of the experiential reality in which all forms of perceptions, images, illusions, and consciousness take place. The theory starts off with ordinary perceptions, turbulent *(pravṛtti)* as they are because of the graspings for the elements of being, which must ultimately be transformed *(parāvṛtti)* by meditative discipline into the purity of perceptions, where the final state of enlightenment is in the recognition of the unique nature of consciousness-only *(vijñaptimātratā)*. For, what has been discriminated in our perceptions *(yad vikalpyate)* is not real; it only seems real to one who attempts to set up the subject in relation to the elements of the so-called outer realm of perception; that is, it is a dichotomous perceptual relation. But this school denies any self-nature *(svabhāva)* that arises in the interaction between subject and object, just as in Madhyamika thought, as there is nothing but illusion in the discriminatory sense *(parikalpita-svabhāva, abhūta-parikalpa)*. Just as in Nāgārjuna, the concept of emptiness is taken over as an epistemic foil to prevent further substantive accounting of perceptual data in the consciousness. As perceptions actually go on in terms of dependent nature *(paratantra),* there is only relational structure and no elements as such, but, ultimately, the true experiential reality *(pariniṣpanna-svabhāva)* is realized by the complete incorporation of all elements of being in a nondiscriminative insight *(nirvikalpajñāna).*[11] This is the final perfected nature of existence, which is sometimes referred to as the accomplishment of the middle way by virtue of consciousness-only; thus we return to the basic Buddhist doctrines. Throughout the perceptual process, discriminative and nondiscriminative, the same ground of existence is sustained to present man with the potentiality for and challenge of excelling himself so as to reach greater realms of being.

Having established the presence and function of the parity principle, our task henceforth should not be too difficult. As intimated earlier, Buddhist doctrines were spawned in the ambience of prevailing doctrines of the various schools of thought, but the meaning of the Buddhist doctrines was given a fresh twist that could not be justified or accommodated by merely resorting to the aid of the prevailing doctrines. In this sense, the whole of Buddhist thought took on a neologistic appearance. For example, the doctrine of nonself *(anātman)* can be singled out as the foremost neologism in Buddhism. No other school, to my knowledge, uses this term within its system.

The nonself concept is not really the logical opposite or the contrary to the *ātman* concept, to be sure, for it belongs to an entirely different category of being, so-called, and to this extent it remains unanalyzable. It can, however, be sensed in the dynamic experiential reality within the complex play of the parity principle, that is, the mutual function of the empirical (conventional) and nonempirical (roughly nonconventional) natures. In these natures, what we see is the empirical side and what we do not is the nonempirical, in an anomalous way. For example, it is said that the grasping phenomenon *(upādāna)* relative to the five *skandhas* issues forth in the nature of a self or subject, while the nongrasping phenomenon indirectly reveals the subtle, unconditioned nature of nonself. One side is constructive in the conventional sense, the other nonconstructive; one side is deterministic, the other nondeterministic. These pairs of terms seem to give the impression of opposition. I contend, however, that the nonself and all other doctrines that "depict the other side" of the empirical nature of things are unique and novel beyond mere diametrical opposition. For, were they antithetical to each other, this would prevent any dialectical movement and preclude their function within the parity of things. In short, the antithetical elements do not in and of themselves produce anything, just as empirics in and of themselves are inane and thoroughly neutral. The acts of the so-called individual are holistic always, and the holistic nature is more than a mere aggregation of the parts or elements of being. Our empirically and rationally oriented logic simply cannot contend with or accommodate such neologistic concepts as nonself or emptiness.

The salient point here is that, though paradoxical in treating the "other side" of the empirical, we are able to speculate on certain traits that may not be extractable from the empirical realm but are nevertheless very much in presence and in force in the experiential reality. I refer to such traits as openness, extensiveness, flexibility, dynamicity, change, and continuity. These traits are seemingly common knowledge to all of us, and yet we fumble in justifying or analyzing them with our undaunted empirico-logical tools. I am sure there will be those who would question or challenge my position, but here I must turn the question around and state that the burden of proof is on them; that is, they must convincingly prove the nonpresence of these traits in our ordinary experience. Historically, even David Hume, working solely within empirical grounds, was at his wit's end in attempting to formulate an adequate answer concerning the nature of causation or the continuity of events in serial order.

It might help at this point to return to the concept of emptiness. The key function of emptiness, as seen earlier, is to foil any empirical and epistemic thrusts made by the unwary or biased mind. Specifically, it serves two purposes: to deny empirics from overpowering the perceptual process, and to deny the epistemic wheel to turn in virtue of the elements based on the empirics or any speculative elements derived thereof. The concept has a cathartic function in this respect, but here I should like to add another dimension to it. It is that at the point of catharsis, emptiness issues forth simultaneously in a release and deliverance from empirical natures—or from nonempirical natures for that matter. Thus, when emptiness is realized, the ordinary self with its pervasive *skandhic* elements becomes more than itself, larger than itself—larger in the sense that all the traits just mentioned are fully manifested and become truly functional. With emptiness, then, the empirical and the nonempirical realms go hand in hand without any dichotomy or interruption. Consequently, openness, extensiveness, continuity, and so on are part and parcel of the life process, and we become cognizant of these traits, but at the same time we know not whence they spring.

When Nāgārjuna, for example, says that he cannot be criticized because he does not maintain a position,[12] he is actually invoking the parity principle to indicate that he is not going to be a party to the empirico-logical game, since there is much more to experiential reality than playing a futile game.[13] He is not able to spell out what is "beyond" because to do so would be to cater to the opponent's methodology and his scheme of things. In short, Nāgārjuna had to avoid the circular, tautological nature that inheres in a scheme once a methodology is introduced and accepted. Truth of existence or the Dharma has an unrestricted character, and no amount of theorizing can bring it down to a manipulable level. This is not to deny the strength of a conceptual scheme. It would be prudent, however, to heed the cautious advice of early Mahāyānists and the later, more dramatic Zennists: "the concept of emptiness itself must also be emptied." This is the only way to prevent an infinite regress into nothingness or toward the sustenance of something. This brings us to the middle way concept.

The middle way has no middle, it is often said. This is, of course, a true statement, for should it have a middle, then automatically it would have the two extremes. The middle way does not lend itself to a dialectical process, either, because all forms of dialectical function involve an interaction of the poles or extremes. It would be permissible for the interaction of entities, physical and otherwise, but that would at once prevent the realization of the *Supremely Ontological* way which possesses neither boundaries nor limits. The middle way, it is said, is "equatable"[14] to relational origination and emptiness. And relational origination in turn is "equatable" to the Dharma and the Buddha, the enlightened nature of things. To be enlightened, using the illustration of a light, is to illuminate in the ten (all or full) directions and to open up and accommodate every element within the ambience of existence. This would be the kind of freedom realizable in *nirvāṇa*, where all forms of ontological attachments have been dissolved.

The central thrust of a recent book by Keiji Nishitani, *Religion and Nothingness,* is to address specifically the nature of ontological parity. For emptiness is now discussed in terms of "being-sive-nothingness," which emphasizes the transcendence of duality, wherein being is being and nothingness is nothingness.[15] Nishitani goes on to assert: "It is here that emptiness, as a standpoint of absolute nonattachment liberated from this double confinement, comes to the fore" and that "being and emptiness are seen as copresent from the start and structurally inseparable from one another."[16] He elaborates that emptiness is "the point at which everything around us becomes manifest in its own suchness."[17]

The above assertions are in line with what I have referred to as the parity principle of existence. They lend support to my view of the nature of emptiness as pivotal to experiential extensiveness. Without emptiness as a key ingredient in experiential reality, experiences cannot move forward or outward to incorporate all elements within the realm. This is another way of describing the temporal and spatial natures of the experiential reality, that is, the vertical and horizontal characteristics of reality in process. This is not to "homogenize" the elements in virtue of emptiness or suchness but rather to understand the undifferentiable aspect of experience which makes way for the absorption and incorporation of those elements without this incorporation being subjected to the usual ontologization and abstractive process. Seen from another point of view, unless such a nature is present in experience, experience itself will forever be dictated by the phenomena of attachment and nonattachment relative to those elements. Eventually, it would be reduced to a narrow mechanical process bereft of such human traits as altruism, sympathy, and love. These traits are made possible because the nature of emptiness opens up experiential reality by shunting off those impetuous empirical elements, preventing them from arising, and simultaneously ties up the whole realm of existence in the presence of those very elements. Things are thus what they are because they are perceived as being under the aegis of suchness or emptiness. In this sense, emptiness is a unifying principle without which the whole experiential process would not be what it is. By this statement I am also suggesting that emptiness is not only in the preserve of the enlightened person but that it could function even within the common or ordinary experience of the unenlightened, although its nature is uncognized for the most part. Emptiness, then, not only gives character to the experiential reality but also stimulates the smooth, open flow of that reality. And thus it has been established that emptiness becomes the basis of all forward, and outward as well as inward, activities and thereby engenders the truly social basis of experience. Emptiness is then the key to all human contacts, not only with fellow human beings but with all beings, sentient and insentient, in the whole realm of nature.

This brings us to the Mahāyāna ideality of existence—the Bodhisattva Ideal. In the *Heart Sūtra,* the opening lines assert strongly that the Bodhisattva in his deep meditative mood saw the realm of experience, the five *skandhas,* as totally empty. This vision came, of course, from the absolutely objective perception of things in their completeness and wholeness. The Bodhisattva, of course is a philosophic myth that depicts the perfected individual who "delays" his entrance into *nirvāṇa* because he is cognizant of the fact that he and others are related or involved in such a way that there is openness on the one hand and extensiveness on the other. It is the perfect model of social concern and action, somewhat akin to what Western religionists allude to as the spirit of ultimate concern. It is at once the perfect model of environmental concern, whereby the social and environmental natures of things are treated together, not in terms of contiguity but in terms of the continuity of reality. This is an area which needs to be explored and worked on seriously, since ordinary minds are incapable of comprehending the continuity and coexistent nature of reality; indeed, the two realms of man and environment are taken to be so vastly different that indifference and even alienation may be the normal response to a raising of this issue. Opponents might not entertain such notions as intimacy, interpenetration, and mutual identifiability and would thus roundly reject them, not knowing that the so-called ontological blinders are self-imposed.

From the Buddhist side, the story is different. There is no problem in accepting such concepts as identity, coexistence, and interpenetration. The Bodhisattva's principal features are based on these concepts, and his unique character has been described as incorporating both wisdom *(prajñā)* and compassion *(karuṇā).* I cannot emphasize strongly enough the fact that these features are, through and through, instances of the parity principle in action, and that acts of wisdom and compassion, though distinct in their own ways, find a common ground of existence. That is to say, each act of wisdom is a manifestation of compassion and, vice versa, each act of compassion is a manifestation of wisdom, and so, in the final analysis, both features collapse into the holistic ground of experiential reality, which is the truly enlightened nature of existence. In the two modes of perception discussed earlier, we may discern certain parallel features, respectively, in terms of the conceptual mode (roughly, the "wisdom" side) and the ontological mode (roughly the "compassionate" side), but, from the standpoint of action, both are one and the same in a "self-surpassing oneness," as Nolan P. Jacobson has persuasively argued.[18]

The acts of Bodhisattva are, then, a graphic exemplification of an experiential reality of a free and open nature, where the conceptual and ontological modes of perception are no longer distinct and different but, rather, mutually supportive and identifiable. This is what we normally refer to as the infrastructural nature of things, and, in Avataṃsaka or Hua-yen thought, it refers to the dynamic and mutually identifiable and penetrative nature of things. Where the Indian Buddhists were highly metaphysical in describing the Bodhisattva's life and perception of the world, as depicted, for example, in the *Avataṃsaka Sūtra,* the Chinese Buddhists were more down-to-earth and practical in their application of that perception of the world, as seen in the various Ch'an (Zen) texts. In all instances, however, there is an emphasis on the continuous and harmonious relationship that exists within the myriad realms of existence, that is, realms that are both allegedly internal and external to the experiencing reality of things—indeed, a relationship that is conversant with both realms, although the terms internal and external are arbitrary, and strictly and ultimately metaphysical. As depicted in the Hua-yen realm of *dharmas (dharmadhātu),* the final complete realm that transcends all specifics and principles of being is at once the realm of ordinary, everyday phenomena, where everything is everything just as it is, without distinction, description, or analysis. Things are what they are because of the total interpenetration of all elements *(dharmas),* but simultaneously they arise by virtue of relational origination, which involves all elements without drawing boundaries, limits, or distinctions. This, in short, is the enlightened view of the mountains as mountains, as the Zennist would affirm.

It was mentioned earlier that the *Supremely Ontological* has no boundaries or limits. It is now apparent, I believe, that the boundless, unlimited nature refers to the Bodhisattva's experiential nature of things and that experience is "thus and so" *(tathatā)* by virtue of its openness in all directions. Thus, I have used the graphic phrase, "open ontology," which is merely another way of asserting the *Supremely Ontological.*[19] Again, this state of dynamic being is potentially realizable, but, for the most part, we are in ignorance of it because we are victims of the empirics which captivate or lure us into forming the basis for the usual conceptual and ontological modes of perception.

We should now examine the nature of ignorance. The normal understanding of this concept is naturally on the purely mental or intellectual plane; that is, one is said to be ignorant when one does not comprehend matters concerning the empirics. Nonempirics—for example, an idea of an empirical datum—may of course fall into the realm of ignorance. This type of understanding is not only naïve but contagious. It is naïve in the sense that it covers only the "surface" elements of total being and thereby skirts the very foundation of their existence. It is contagious in the sense that it is easily adapted and perpetuated due to the persistent attachment to empirics or nonempirics, as the case may be. Consequently, ignorance in the form of not knowing the fullness of being is perpetuated. In more technical terms, *"avidyā"* is literally the "no-vision" (without insight; *a + vidyā*) of true reality. In this respect, the Buddhist interpretation provides a novel twist, compared with the orthodox or traditional Indian views, and I am inclined to expand on it as the "unclarity of true nature of being," which is the antithesis of the *Supremely Ontological*. The "unclarity of true nature of being" can be perceived from another standpoint as the "ontological unclarity of being," a somewhat roundabout way of pointing at the obstacle-ridden state of being that surrounds and obstructs true experiential reality. In sum, then, the nature of Buddhist ignorance is to be a warning against the temptation to construct or condition experiential reality in terms of the empirics and projected nonempirics of existence. However, on a more positive note, there is a "flip side" to this damaging egoistic tendency in man, that is, an openly resilient and expansive nature, which undergirds the very elements to which we are so attached. In accordance with my own terminology, we should then be disciplining our conceptual and ontological modes of perception so that a glimpse, if not the whole open vision, of the *Supremely Ontological* can be developed into a true experiential reality.

This discussion has come to the point where we may draw some conclusions in reference to man and his environment within the Buddhist context.

1. In describing man's place in the environment, we should not treat man or the environment as independent of each other. This is the major premise upon which all concerns for the environment must begin. Although this is a simple premise, it is most difficult to abide by because of man's selfish and aggressive nature, whether that nature is inherent or learned. And there are abundant examples of man's depletion and destruction of our natural resources.

2. In order to stop this wanton depletion and destruction, we must have a new understanding and, most importantly, a new vision of things. Here the original insight of the historical Buddha could come into play. Rather than taking off on some metaphysical flight to explain experience, the Buddha concentrated on man's experiential nature and came up with a startling insight: a vision of the open unity, clarity, and continuity of existence. To involve man's nature is, then, to involve at once his more extensive and unlimited relationship to his surroundings. In other words, man is not alone but thoroughly relational, and the grounds for a relational nature must be found within man's own nature and not in something external, to which he must react on a one-to-one basis. Still, there are those who would argue that man is by nature an independent and nonrelational creature, except on

occasion where it serves his egoistic desires to relate with others, as Thomas Hobbes has so cogently contended.[20]

3. The clue to understanding the relational bind is discovered by seeking a way through man's own nature and uncovering the possibility of an unhindered continuous relationship or, more technically, the existential continuum, or what I prefer to describe more precisely as an open and freely flowing extensive ontology. The Buddha's enlightenment showed the way to the coterminous and coextensive relationality of man and nature; that is, any act by man, however, insignificant it may be within the total context of things, reverberates through the realm that is greater than himself. This possibility is crystallized in the parity principle of existence. This is where the *saṃsāric* nature of things is not alienated from the *nirvāṇic* content, nor is the *nirvāṇic* content aloof from the *saṃsāric* nature of things. Enlightenment or *nirvāṇa* is at once the confirmation and revelation of the parity principle in function.

4. In the Mahāyāna tradition, there has been a further development of the parity principle through a focus on the epistemic nature of things; that is, the dichotomous nature of perception is made apparent, and it is asserted that the real foundation of it is the nature of emptiness. Paradoxically, it is emptiness which gives substance to the perceptual elements themselves and which serves as the ground for the relational function. The alternative, as we are so accustomed to do with indifference, would be to give primacy to the perceptual elements and thereby fall prey to some forms of realism, empiricism, conceptualism, phenomenalism, and so on, all of which would only multiply and complicate the problems that attend the experiential process. The Buddha stood fast with the doctrine of the middle way and did not budge one way or the other with any theory concerning the elements and structural mechanics of the perceptual process.

Concluding Remarks

It should be apparent by now that the problematics in environmental concerns and the establishment of an ethical basis for existence are really the problematics relative to man's understanding of his own experiential process. Man's own constitutive nature in the process is the key to an understanding of the relationality of the total ambience, extending it as far as one would like it to go. There are no boundaries or limits in this respect, for the mutuality of man and the environment in which he finds his place is continuous and kept intact at all times.

The damage already done to our environment undoubtedly will have serious consequences to our own well-being now and in the future. There is no turning back the environmental clock. The mutuality of man and his environment is ever dynamic and the tension between them will inevitably become apparent in signs of "wear and tear" on both sides. We must do our best to slow down the deteriorating conditions, and, if it is at all possible, work judiciously toward the ideal of a healthy balance between the two. The important point is that it is still within man's means to do something about the problem. Science and technology are man's province, and he is still the master of both. Yet, there must be an enlightened approach to solving the problem through reason; at the same time, reason must reach down, so to speak, to become a part of the very basis of man's constitutional makeup in order to help alleviate the situation. This may sound mystical again, but from a Buddhist standpoint, reason is still a relatively small, though vital, component of existence; thus it must not be kept apart from existence but instead must be integrated within the larger experiential nature of things. It should not, in short, stand in the way of the experiential process. This is the Buddhist approach, and, I must admit, it is not easy to comprehend either its implications or the function of its various doctrines, which emerge from the proper understanding of the experiential process, the relational origination of things. We certainly need to reexamine and refocus this process in order actively to be involved in the setting of goals in environmental ethics. Short of this kind of involvement, the Buddhist way will fall on deaf "empirical" ears and be taken as a mere conceptual fantasy. As is often said, Buddhist concepts are nonconceptualizable in the final analysis. But this raises the disturbing possibility that the concepts could remain dormant by default.

Finally, there are environmentalists at work today who are producing much valuable work. For example, I was fascinated by a recent book by Kenneth E. Boulding, *The World as a Total System*.[21] In it, the author discusses the various types of systems perceived by man, with a considerable amount of detailed analysis on each system, including the world as a physical system, a biological system, a social system, an economic system, a political system, a communications system, and an evaluative system. The author's argument is quite persuasive in its systemic style and methodology, but I have misgivings: the conceptions of these various systems, however effective and profoundly applicable they may be to our society, fail to relate to the very basis of man's own perceptual and constitutional makeup. To this extent, the whole work is limited to being another noble attempt at coming to grips with a conceptual world structure and the problems attendant upon it. It does not deal specifically with the whys and wherefores of the systems themselves. In consequence, we are left with substantial and pertinent data, while we are still searching for a philosophy which harmoniously blends man and all of nature.

Toward a Middle Path of Survival

David J. Kalupahana

The question is being tossed round: "Can the East help the West to value nature?" One of the assumptions behind this question seems to be that in some sense the West has failed to appreciate or value nature. In fact, environmental ethics has become a major issue precisely because Western science has permeated human life on Earth, whether it be in the West or in the East, in the Northern Hemisphere or in the Southern Hemisphere. There is no denying that Western science has made life easier, more comfortable, and in some ways more satisfying. However, this satisfaction is gradually turning out to be a dissatisfaction, a nightmare for some people, especially those who have begun to realize the threat to natural phenomena posed by the increasing demands of the so-called technological world.

Because the development of science and technology in the Western world, although contributing to a more satisfying way of life, has simultaneously generated fear and trembling in our minds regarding the destiny of mankind, it is appropriate to examine the broad conceptual structures or paradigms, serving as the basis for scientific inquiries or emerging as a result of scientific explorations, that have been highlighted by the intellectual community, those "lovers of wisdom." One such paradigm that has dominated classical, and to some extent scientific thinking, is the problem of *paired opposition* in nature. For example, we have the binary oppositions recognized by physicists, biologists, meteorologists, and others. Science, while recognizing such paired oppositions nevertheless wants to keep its world view open-ended enough to accommodate future discoveries, especially in the light of its perceptions of other phenomena that demonstrate no such binary oppositions. Thus, problems remain. Even after the complementary opposites are noted and the extreme binary oppositions are resolved, there are still questions regarding the value of these phenomena. For instance, science assumes that its attitude, approach, and methods are so objective and unprejudiced that it can openly claim that nonhuman nature has no value at all.

Neither the Buddha nor his followers can be considered scientists in the strict sense of the term. However, like all scientists and philosophers who formulate their experiences in conceptual terms, the Buddha as well as his followers provided conceptual formulations of what they observed as nature and human life. In these formulations, they carefully avoided three types of solutions to the problem of *paired opposition* referred to earlier, and which were proffered by some of the major philosophers of the East as well as the West.

The first recognizes the substantial reality of the paired opposites such as *yang* and *yin,* male and female, positive and negative, light and darkness, life and death, good and bad, and so on. While assuming that these opposites are substantial, it admits the possibility of their reconciliation in a higher synthesis. According to this view, the sense experiences that provide knowledge of the opposites can still be valid. A more optimistic view of life emerges from this perspective. It resembles the position adopted by the Taoists as well as the thinkers of the earlier and more rationalist *Upaniṣads.* Cartesian dualism, with its emphasis on two distinct substances, mind and matter, along with its recognition of the conception of God as a possible unifying ground, may provide inspiration for such a thesis.

The second assumes the opposites to be less substantial and, therefore, *easily* reconciled or dissolved in a higher synthesis. Sense experience yielding knowledge of the opposites is here looked upon with suspicion. It is misleading and enjoys no significant epistemological status. The Advaita Vedānta school of thought, providing one of the philosophical justifications for the *Bhagavadgītā,* can be classed under this category. Advaita Vedāntins in the modern world have not failed to show their enthusiasm for Hegelianism, thereby indicating a similarity between these two traditions. Common to all these solutions is the recognition of an absolutism of one form or another.

The third type of solution to the paired opposition is similar to the first version referred to earlier in that it recognizes the substantiality of the opposites, but, instead of attempting to reconcile them in a higher synthesis, leaves them as inevitable, though intolerable, phenomena. It wholeheartedly advocates a pessimistic view of life by assuming the incapacity of the human being to resolve this problem, leaving its ultimate solution in the hands of an external power. In the Asian context, the dualistic view of Madhva, which has remained the more popular religious expression, seems to come closer to this form of solution. In the Western world, Kierkegaard embodies a similar way of thinking. The Jaina thinkers in India, while retaining a comparable conception of the opposites, replaced the notion of a supreme being with an extremely deterministic notion of karma which likewise led to a totally pessimistic view of life. The extreme notions of nonviolence *(ahiṃsā)* is an offshoot of this very deterministic theory of karma that leaves all responsibility squarely, yet unfairly, upon the individual.

Most interpretations of Buddhism in the modern world are based upon a conscious or unconscious recognition of one or the other of these paradigms.

A distorted interpretation of the Buddhist conception of life emerged with the medieval Hindu thinkers like Udayana Ācārya, an interpretation that was responsible not only for the disappearance of Buddhism as a distinctive ideology from the Indian scene, but also for a legacy of misunderstandings and misinterpretations regarding this tradition in the Western world. Schopenhauer was one of the first to be misled by the Hindu interpretation of Buddhism, assuming that Buddhism advocates a notion of universal suffering and hence a tragic view of life. The paradigm that contributes to this absolutistic view about suffering was not examined in detail. The paradigm is the irreconcilable substantiality of paired opposites. It gives rise to an absolutistic view of suffering as embodied in the statement, "Everything is suffering" *(sarvaṃ duḥkham)*. Neither such a paradigm nor a similar explanation of suffering can be found anywhere in discourses discovered so far.

Confusion about this point continues even today. For example, Walter Kaufmann, who usually has rare insight into the nature of the Buddha's teachings, has made the following remark about Buddhism and Schopenhauer:

> One might have expected Schopenhauer to realize all of this [some points concerning Hume's theory of tragedy], since he stressed the universality of suffering more than any previous philosopher. But at this point he felt a kinship to Buddhism—the universality of suffering is the first of the first of Buddha's "four noble truths"—and Buddhism and tragedy represent two utterly different responses to suffering.[1]

Since the remark is cryptic and Kaufmann does not elaborate upon his observation, it is somewhat difficult to respond. However, the misunderstanding of Buddha's conception of nature and human life, in this case, seems to stem from the wrong identification of his philosophical standpoint with one or the other of the three paradigms referred to above.

The Buddha's conception of nature and human life carefully avoids the substantialist interpretation of paired opposites. Furthermore, the avoidance of substantialist conceptions of opposites does not mean either their negation or reconciliation in a higher synthesis. The philosophical middle path enunciated by the Buddha judiciously avoids the notions of substantial existence and nihilistic nonexistence in favor of an empirical explanation of the notions of arising and ceasing depending upon conditions.[2] In other words, the conception of paired opposites is retained, not reified. For the Buddha, abstract conceptions of masculin-*ity* and feminin-*ity*, light-*ness* and dark-*ness*, positiv-*ity* and negativ-*ity*, and so on, have no meaning except in the context of the empirical events or phenomena conceptualized as man and woman, day and night, positive and negative, and so forth. To the Buddha, non-substantiality *(anatma)* was a methodological instrument, comparable to a surgeon's scalpel, for dissecting experience and conception in order to get rid of cancerous elements and to preserve the healthy ones. It was neither a butcher's knife nor a scaffold for the dismemberment, destruction, or annihilation of all human experience and conception.

To begin with, the Buddhist explanation of experience does not involve a passive intellect, a *tabula rasa.* Neither does it acknowledge a set of *a priori* categories of intellect or mind. A passive intellect is presupposed in order to recognize the possibility of knowing the object of experience "as it is," in its true and uncorrupted form. This is an extremely substantialist or essentialist approach. Similarly, an admission of *a priori* categories sets the stage for the discovery of laws of thought, which again are believed to be universal and incorruptible. The former tips the scale in favor of the object and the latter highlights the subject. Philosophical discourses based upon such assumptions lead to further paired opposites: realism-idealism, realism-nominalism, determinism-indeterminism, eternalism-annihilationism, and so on. This is the background in which the search for metaphysical entities either in the object or in the subject has been proceeding. Until such discoveries are successfully completed human beings tend to remain in a state of anxiety and uncertainty. Thus, it is the task of the philosopher to satisfy this curiosity of human beings with well-constructed theories. The Buddha was not unaware of this human search and predicament, as is evident from the following statement:

> In this case, monk, it occurs to somebody: "What was certainly mine is certainly not mine (now): what might certainly be mine, there is certainly no chance of my getting." He grieves, mourns, laments, beats his breast, and falls into disillusionment. Even so, monks, does there come to be *anxiety* *(paritassanā)* about something objective that does not exist.
>
> In this case, monk, the view occurs to someone: "This world is this self; after dying I will become permanent, lasting, eternal, not liable to change, I will stand fast like unto the eternal." He hears the doctrine as it is being taught by the Tathagata or by a disciple of the Tathagata for rooting out all resolve for bias, tendency, and addiction to the determination and conditioning of views, for the appeasement of all dispositions, for the relinquishing of all attachment, for the waning of craving, absence of lust, cessation and freedom. It occurs to him thus: "I will surely be annihilated, I will surely be destroyed, I will surely not be." He grieves, mourns, laments, beats his breast, and falls into disillusionment. Thus, monks, there comes to be *anxiety* about something subjective that does not exist.[3]

The conceptualization about something that is not given in experience, merely because it helps us to overcome our anxieties about existence, did not appeal to the Buddha as a long-term solution to the human predicament. This does not mean that he completely discounted all such conceptualizations, for, as a pragmatist, he was not unmindful of some of the immediate benefits that may be enjoyed especially by the "tender-minded" as a result of utilizing some such conceptualization. However, as a "tough-minded" empiricist who was more concerned with immediate than with long-term benefits, he was not willing to admit metaphysical entities either in the objective world or in subjective life as ultimate realities. Substances or essences, permanent and eternal, whether these relate to objectivity or subjectivity could have no lasting value in his empiricist philosophy. He avoided the search for pure and undiluted sense impressions as well as universal and incorruptible concepts. The overcoming of anxiety is not to be achieved by the renunciation of sense experience and conception, but by the relinquishing of the metaphysical search itself.

Relinquishing a metaphysical search does not involve the renunciation of reflection and investigation altogether, for without these, human beings would be like "sessile sea-anemone on the rock"[4] waiting for the waves to bring its nourishment. They need to abandon the search for mysterious causes and conditions and to understand experience in the *historical present* in order to deal with the future. On the basis of such an epistemological approach, the Buddha formulated his understanding of nature as well as human life.

Reflecting on the basis of past experiences, the Buddha maintained that all experienced phenomena, including human life, have dependently arisen (*pratītyasamutpanna*).[5] The use of the past participle to express this experience is significant. This is not an essentialist enterprise. Rather it is an explanation of experience comparable to that offered by a radical empiricist for whom "the flights and perchings" of a bird are equally relevant to an understanding of its movement.[6] Following upon this understanding of nature and human life, the Buddha formulated an abstract principle of explanation,which he referred to as "dependent arising" (*pratītyasa-mutpāda*).[7] This latter, expressed in nominal form compared with the previous use of the past participle, does not represent a "real" in its eternal way. On the contrary, it has to be constantly verified, for it is the product of limited experience, not "omniscience." Being the result of limited human experience, and requiring constant verification and revision, this radical empiricist approach needs to be coupled with a pragmatic method. For this reason, the Buddha looked upon the conception of the fruit, the effect or the consequence (*artha*) defining the conception of a thing or an event or a phenomenon (*dharma*).[8] Hence, he emphasized the idea that a thing is not simply a thing (*dharma*), but a dependently arisen thing (*pratītyasamutpanna dharma*). Even though the term *dharma* came to be used without this qualification, whenever a definition of a *dharma* was called for or was needed, he immediately utilized this pragmatic definition.

Dependent arising is often referred to as *dharmatā,* which is the Buddhist term for *nature.*[9] Thus, the Buddha's discourse begins with an account of the world or the universe *(loka).* It does not presuppose the sharp dichotomy between human life and nature used by others to make the latter an absolutely irresistible force which human beings have to contend with, or an external object created for their pleasure and enjoyment. His was not an absolutistic explanation or theory of nature in which the lines are drawn sharply and distinctly so as to make the human being either a hapless object or the epicenter of the universe. A human being is part of nature. Like everything else in the teeming and dramatic richness of nature, he is dependently arisen or causally conditioned. He comes into being depending upon various conditions, contributes his share to the drama, and makes his exit. He is part of nature, that is, in a constant process of becoming *(bhava),* evolution *(pariṇāma),* and dissolution. This process of becoming or evolution is neither haphazard nor strictly teleological. The world is neither an empirical sand heap nor an ever-elusive absolute. Its dramatic richness lies in its concrete contextual fruitfulness.

This form of qualification has far-reaching philosophical consequences which are at least twofold. In the first place, it enables a person to renounce the search for mysterious substances, subjective as well as objective. Second, it facilitates the dissolution of sharp dichotomies and paired opposites through a process of melting the solidified or reified concepts without having to eliminate them altogether. This includes the royal pair of dichotomies that has dominated most essentialist and intellectualist enterprises throughout human history, namely, the dichotomy between fact and value. It is the dissolution of this solidified distinction between fact and value that will enable us to perceive a significant relationship between nature and human life. Nature is not simply a brute fact to be contrasted with otherworldly human values. Abandon this monstrous solidified conceptual thinking, and soon human life, together with its most sublime moral values, will be seen as an inalienable part of mother nature.

In the Buddhist context, the term *dharma* signifies both fact and value.[10] *Dharmatā* is the dependent *nature* not only of the so-called brute fact, but also of social, political, ethical, or even spiritual "value." It is noteworthy that in the Buddhist discourses the "naturalness" *(dhammatā)* associated with moral and spiritual behavior is illustrated by similes taken from physical nature, such as the healthy growth and development of plant life that receives appropriate nutritive conditions, or the natural behavior of animals,[11] or even the innocence of a little baby lying on its back.[12] These are processes that evolve depending upon various conditions, one of which is "interest."

Ignoring the important part played by "interest" in the evolution of nature as well as human life, intellectuals have very often adopted the perspective of an "onlooker," a perspective that leads to the distortion of the nature of mental life of human beings, not only giving rise to psychological fallacies but also eliminating any possibility of recognizing some form of naturalism in mental life.

William James has the following to say about the perspective of the "on-looker" and the process of evolution:

> Survival can enter into a purely physiological discussion only as an *hypothesis made by an onlooker* about the future. But the moment you bring in a consciousness into the midst, survival ceases to be a mere hypothesis. . . . *Real* ends appear for the first time now upon the world's stage. The conception of consciousness as a purely cognitive form of being, which is the pet way of regarding it in many idealistic-modern as well as ancient schools, is thoroughly anti-psychological, as the remainder of this book will show. Every actually existing consciousness seems itself at any rate to be a *fighter for ends,* of which many, but for its presence, would not be ends at all. Its powers of cognition are mainly subservient to these ends, discerning which facts further them and which do not.[13]

Although James does not hold the view that physical phenomena and animals are possessed of consciousness, what is operative in human consciousness as "a fighter for ends" could not be very different from the so-called "instinct" in animals and "tendencies" in natural events. Another statement of James, furthermore, seems to reduce the sharp dichotomy between animal instincts and human interests:

> Each mind, to begin with, must have a minimum of selfishness in the shape of instincts of bodily self-seeking in order to exist. This minimum must be there as a basis for all further conscious acts, whether of self-negation or of a selfishness more subtle still. All minds must have come, by way of the survival of the fittest, if by no direct path, to take an interest in the bodies to which they are yoked, altogether apart from any interest in the pure Ego which they also possess.[14]

If there is any higher moral nature in human beings which is not found among the animals and physical nature, that moral nature should be founded on the recognition of self-interest, self-instinct, or the fight for survival on the part of man as well as nature. The Buddhist conception of compassion and nonviolence and the Confucian idea of benevolence are both based upon the recognition of such interest or instinct. The excesses of compassion and benevolence, on the contrary, are the results of ignoring the pragmatic outlook in life. The Jaina theory of nonviolence represents such an extremist version of nonviolence.

As mentioned earlier, the Buddha recognized that dependent arising is not the result of omniscience. Rather it is a conceptualization based upon limited human knowledge and understanding. It is the "big blooming buzzing confusion"[15] receiving some form of order and uniformity in the reflective (radical empiricist) and interested (pragmatic) human minds. However, this reflection and interest can be carried beyond their legitimate limits to produce a world that is artificial, rigid and substantial, not only in its conceptualization but also in the actual realization. Thus, more often we find ourselves placed in a world that is "dispositionally conditioned" *(saṅkhata, saṃskṛta)* rather than one in which simple interest prevails. According to Buddhism, it is the former, the dispositionally conditioned, that is the source of most human suffering *(dukkha, duḥkha),*[16] for even the most powerful and compassionate creator cannot keep up with the demands made by human beings. In James' words:

> The best simply imaginary world would be one in which *every* demand was gratified as soon as made. . . . It would need not only a space, but a time of *n*-dimensions, to include all the acts and experiences incompatible with one another here below, which would then go on in conjunction—such as our spending money, yet growing rich; taking our holiday, yet getting ahead with our work; shooting and fishing, yet doing no hurt to the beasts; gaining no end of experience, yet keeping our youthful freshness of heart; and the like.[17]

The Buddhist view of suffering is based primarily upon the realization that human beings crave such an imaginary world. The way out of this suffering does not consist of relinquishing every human interest and need, every form of human demand and every bit of human satisfaction. It is not the adoption of a life of abject poverty and self-mortification. It is only a call for the renunciation of a life of self-indulgence which is the unfortunate transformation of an attitude of "interest" into one of greed, lust, and thirsting. The middle path recommended is the "appeasement of disposi-tions" *(saṅkhāra-samatha, saṃskyāropaśama).*[18] *It is neither the annihilation of interest nor the transformation of interest into a state of craving or thirsting.*

Appeasement of dispositions is synonymous with freedom (*nibbāna, nirvāṇa).*[19] In his very first discourse, the Buddha referred to two extreme forms of life adopted by human beings.[20] The first is self-indulgence which he condemned as low, vulgar, individualist, ignoble, and unfruitful. The second is self-mortification which is painful, ignoble, and unfruitful. Avoiding these two extremes, he recommended a middle path that is both noble and fruitful. Realizing that what is "actually possible in this world is vastly narrower than all that is demanded,"[21] and utilizing such a realization to appease one's dispositions, the Buddha recognized the possibility of overcoming suffering and attaining happiness and tranquility.

Fruitfulness *(artha)* and nobility *(dharma)*[22] are the foundations of this middle path which is recommended for lay people as well as for those who have opted for a more strenuous religious life. Neither fruitfulness nor righteousness is achieved through the simple renunciation of pleasures of sense or of social life, for if that were the case, then Siddhartha could have attained freedom and happiness on the day he left home. His attainment of enlightenment and freedom came only after he realized the nonsubstantiality not only of all experienced phenomena *(dharma)*, but also of views, conceptions, and ideas about such phenomena. Commitment and strict adherence to or grasping after ultimate truths leading to inflexibility in regard to one's beliefs are seen as the primary reason for bondage and suffering. One should be prepared to abandon one's cherished beliefs, whether these relate to physical or social or moral laws, if such beliefs are to cause harm to oneself and others. Revisionism is not a weakness so long as the criterion for it is fruitfulness and righteousness. "Even the ideas about what is good have to be relinquished, let alone those about evil," so declared the Buddha.[23] James struck a similar note when he maintained that "there is always a *pinch* between the ideal and the actual which can be got through by leaving part of the ideal behind."[24]

When abstract ideas are not elevated to the level of absolute truths, when fruitfulness is made a criterion for deciding what is important and relevant, when excessive greed and selfishness are renounced, in short when "possessive individualism"[25] is abandoned, it would not be difficult for human beings to adopt what James called the "moral equivalent to war." If there were to be an element of aggressiveness in nature and human life, it is the responsibility of the most advanced of species, namely, Homo sapiens, to utilize that aggressiveness in order to create an environment where it can survive without destroying itself as well as nature. When the Buddha admonished that "one should take oneself as an example and neither kill nor destroy,"[26] he was not speaking of other human beings only, but was referring to all forms of life *(sabbe)*, that is, life in general, life on earth that is related by way of mutual dependence.

About two and half centuries after the Buddha, the Indian monarch Asoka, who became a Buddhist disciple, adopted this "moral equivalent to war," not in the face of defeat in war, but at the height of success and glory. Even though he gained a convincing victory in the Kālinga war, immediately he renounced his warmongering and pursued a policy that was to lay the foundation for moral reawakening in the Indian continent in which all human beings, irrespective of their caste and creed, and all animal and even plant life were saved from unnecessary and wanton destruction and annihilation. "Live and let live" was the ultimate motto of this monarch. As is well known, it was this monarch that was responsible for the spread of the Buddha's message beyond the confines of the Indian continent leaving lasting impressions in South, Southeast, and East Asian countries. In these regions one rarely heard of environmental problems, except those caused by natural physical events, until the introduction of modern commercialism and the resultant "rape of nature."

If the West has failed to appreciate nature, it is because it has made a determined attempt to retain its past conceptual heritage without paying enough heed to more innovative thinkers like those of the pragmatic tradition. Given the obvious similarities between my interpretation of the early Buddhist tradition and American pragmatism, an interesting alternative to borrowing from the East presents itself. Since an appropriate nonabsolutist philosophy has already been formulated in the West, there is really no reason for a Westerner to rush toward the East looking for answers to his environmental problems: such answers are already available to him right at his doorstep.

V

The Indian World View

A Metaphysical Grounding for Natural Reverence: East-West

Eliot Deutsch

The title of my paper "A Metaphysical Grounding for Natural Reverence: East-West" is problematic or controversial with respect to all three of its key phrases: (1) "a metaphysical grounding," (2) "natural reverence," and (3) "East-West." With the positivist/analytic tradition in contemporary philosophy, according to the testimony of some of its leading exponents, apparently in disarray, it might no longer be necessary to defend metaphysical inquiry as something essential to philosophy; but let me just remark that the basic understanding one has of the nature of reality, the most fundamental way in which we organize and value our experience, does—it seems clear enough to me—inform all of our action, and certainly the manner or style of our interrelationship with physical nature. One of the burdens of this paper, in any event, is to show that this is the case.

It might be argued, as many interested in environmental ethics have done, that a hardheaded pragmatic or no-nonsense utilitarian moral attitude combined with a solid scientific understanding of the way in which natural systems function, in the words of J. Baird Callicott, "through a process of mutual adjustment and evolutionary co-determination,"[1] is sufficient to develop an appropriate environmental ethic—and that talk about "natural reverence" and the like, if not distracting, is irrelevant, at best a bit of harmless sentimentality. I argue, on the contrary, that it is precisely this pragmatic/utilitarian narrowing of the metaphysical and axiological foundations needed for the development of an appropriate environmental ethic which is partly (but very significantly) responsible for the very absence of that ethic in so many peoples of the world today. Without what I am calling "natural reverence" I don't see how it is possible for us to do more than work out temporary, makeshift adjustments in our actual working relations with our natural environment. Although common-sense pragmatism in these matters might be necessary, it is certainly, by all accounts, not sufficient. I don't mean to imply, however, that the entire burden of developing an environmental ethic rests on metaphysical and axiological considerations alone: quite obviously, the political, the economic, and the social are involved at every point. By "natural reverence" I simply mean the attitude, the awareness, of the belonging together of man and nature in freedom—in such a way that allows for a meaningful, creative play in that relationship.

The so-called ecological crisis of today is not, as some might believe, a Western phenomenon alone. Everyone, of course, knows about Japan; but one has only to travel about a short while in both countryside and city of any other Asian country to learn that it too clearly suffers, albeit often in early stages (which are, nevertheless, sometimes the ugliest), from technological mismanagement and from a lack of imagination and creativity—indeed, from a lack of natural reverence. The East today has no more lived up to its highest ideals than has the West. It is, however, also apparent that a great deal of the ecological crisis stems from Western-based technology and the metaphysical and axiological positions that have sustained and nurtured that technology. It is not inappropriate, therefore, that we do turn to the East for metaphysical and axiological inspiration. We don't turn to the East for a better scientific understanding of nature (although many individual Asian scientists might indeed contribute to that understanding), but for different ontological perspectives and moral ideals that might influence our own thinking.

Now there are, of course, many—and very diverse—Asian traditions. I concentrate on Indian thought (namely, Vedāntic), with special attention given, on the one hand, to the idea that there is a radical discontinuity between reality and nature and, on the other hand, to the idea of *karman* as providing the strongest bond of continuity between man and nature.

Before turning directly to a creative response to that one tradition in Indian philosophy, a few things need to be said about our Western thinking—and for this purpose Kant is a useful focal point. Although Kant might seem to be an unlikely choice for a discussion of environmental ethics, certain aspects of his thought seem to typify so clearly a number of basic Western attitudes and, nevertheless, to offer possible connections to some of the basic Indian notions that I discuss.

Kant's treatment of the sublime in his *Critique of Judgment* is hardly at the core of contemporary Kantian studies, but his treatment does, I think, indicate the manner in which much of Western thought about the man/nature relationship gets formulated within the categories of "separation" and "domination"—to which ecologists and environmental ethicists so often refer—and how this thought runs at least one of its courses in our tradition.

According to Kant, when we experience nature's awesome magnitude and/or might, we recognize immediately the disparity between our sensibility and that magnitude or might; indeed, we recognize our very impotence as finite, physical beings. The first recognition or experience of the sublime, however, leads us then to reaffirm our superiority to nature in virtue of our being rational, moral beings, for it is we who harbor the idea of the sublime; it is we who retain our integrity in the face of nature's immensity and power.

With reference both to that immensity (the "mathematically sublime") and that power (what Kant calls the "dynamically sublime" — "Bold, overhanging, and as it were threatening rocks; clouds piled up in the sky, moving with lightning flashes and thunder peals; volcanoes in all their violence of destruction, hurricanes with their track of destruction" — that which has always excited the romantic imagination), it is argued that

> now, in the immensity of nature and in the insufficiency of our faculties to take in a standard proportionate to the aesthetical estimation of the magnitude of its realm, we find our own limitation, although at the same time in our rational faculty we find a different nonsensuous standard, which has that infinity itself under it as a unity, in comparison with which everything in nature is small, and thus in our mind we find a superiority to nature even in its immensity. And so also the irresistibility of its might, while making us realize our own [physical] impotence, considered as beings of nature, discloses to us a faculty of judging independently of and a superiority over nature, in which is based a kind of self-preservation entirely different from that which can be attacked and brought into danger by external nature. . . . Therefore nature is here called sublime merely because it elevates the imagination to a presentation of these cases in which the mind can make felt the proper sublimity of its destination, in comparison with nature itself.[2]

Even in what would initially appear to be experiences that would humble man in relation to nature, according to Kant, we yet assert our superiority over nature (and, by implication, our right to dominion), for nature in its sublimity is only what we represent; it is what occasions our state of mind and elevates our imagination. In fact, sublimity is not part of nature at all; it is a quality of our minds. Kant states explicitly that

> sublimity, therefore, does not reside in anything of nature, but only in our mind, insofar as we can become conscious that we are superior to nature within, and therefore also to nature without us (as far as it influences us). Everything that excites this feeling in us, e.g., the might of nature which calls forth our forces, is called (although improperly) sublime.[3]

But then, somewhat surprisingly, Kant links this idea of the sublime as residing in the mind and not in nature with a cultivated moral consciousness.

> In fact, without development of moral ideas, that which we, prepared by culture, call sublime presents itself to the uneducated man merely as terrible.[4]

And not only is the experience of the sublime reserved for those of an "educated" moral sense, but that very sense is said (contradictorily?) to be developed as a result of that experience.

> The beautiful prepares us to love disinterestedly something, even nature itself; the sublime prepares us to esteem something highly even in opposition to our own (sensible) interest.[5]

It is then in the last analysis the ability of the human being to detach his own interests, purposes, needs from the content of experience which grounds man's superiority over nature. We conquer by our disinterestedness, by our disengaging our physical being from our spiritual subjectivity. Although Kant's idea of detachment does serve, as I argue later, as something of a bridge to Indian thought, notice for now how this spiritual capacity is, for Kant, made the basis not for a way of bringing man into closer harmony with nature, but for elevating him in status over nature as both a rational and moral being. For him, disinterestedness is not—as I argue it should be— brought into the service of creativity and kinship, but in further severing man from his natural world.

There are, I believe, two major ideas developed in Indian philosophy which, although often hinted at in Western thought, are rather unique to that tradition, and may be useful in our thinking about environmental ethics—the metaphysical grounding for natural reverence. The first of these ideas seems initially to be most removed from our central issue, if not capable of undermining the whole idea of natural reverence. This is the idea, put forward in its most conspicuous form in Advaita Vedānta, the nondual school of Vedānta expounded principally by Śaṁkara in the eighth century, that radical discontinuity obtains between reality (Brahman) and everything else in experience. Sureśvara, an early follower of Śaṁkara, put it succinctly.

> Between the world (Existence) and the rock-firm Self (Reality) there is no connection whatsoever except that of ignorance.[6]

Contrary then to someone like Leibniz who argues that "jumps are forbidden not only in motions, but also in every order of truths," the Advaitin argues that the undifferentiated fullness of being—designated as Brahman or Ātman—is utterly incommensurable with all subject/object, time-bound, spatial multiplicity. In fact, when the former is the "content" of consciousness, the latter as such ceases to be. Nature then is *māyā*—the term usually, but oftentimes unfortunately, translated as "illusion." Drawing from Advaita, I argue that rather than undermining the idea of natural reverence, this radical discontinuity provides its surest foundation. Without *māyā*, there cannot, I think, be the creative play that is required for a proper man/nature relationship.

The second idea *karman* is not associated with any particular school of Indian thought, and, indeed, in one form or another is embraced by all of them. It is one of the root ideas of Indian philosophy and religiosity. A great deal has been written about the so-called law of karma, especially in recent years, as a nomic principle of human action. Karl Potter has, however, I think, convincingly shown that *karman* must be understood in its natural language matrix as having to do not with *action*, as this term has come to be used and understood in both everyday language use and in philosophical (action) theory, but rather with "making."

> Whereas "action" means to me various, though not all sorts of doings, . . . in context in Sanskrit philosophical works the use of words stemming from the root *kṛ* carries with it a series of expectations which hang together but which are not the expectations we have when we hear the word "act" or "action" in English. It is much more like the expectations we have when we hear the word "make". . . .[7]

> To "make," that is to *"kṛ"* something is to construct it, to produce it out of some materials one has at hand, to create something. Furthermore it is to take up these materials with a desire, an intention to produce something which will serve a certain function. . . . So making carries with it the implication of a result which is intended by the maker to be useful to someone for some purpose. . . .[8]

When applied to the mental realm,

> since mental acts are notoriously free from any obvious, that is to say, publicly observable products, the metaphor leads Sanskrit speakers to postulate an unobservable product, viz., a *karman* in the form of traces *(saṁskāra).*[9]

Potter then shows how this "making" sense of the term leads to the *theory* of *karman,* for a

> new making is not merely occasioned by the trace of the past making, but is also colored *(vāsita)* by it so that it properly reflects the moral quality of the original making.[10]

The "law of karma" then supposedly ties together everything that one does into patterns of action informed by habits acquired in past experience, and shows the subtle ramifications or consequences of one's makings throughout one's environment. Whereas the notion of radical discontinuity appears to sunder man from nature, the law of karma assuredly binds him into the strongest continuity with natural processes and makes him co-implicate, as it were, with them.

In the *Bhagavadgītā*, a famous teaching is put forth called *karmayoga*. It argues that it is only when we act, when we make, without attachment to the fruits of our makings, that we can act properly and in a state of freedom. The freedom *(mokṣa)* associated with Brahman-realization and everyday acting/making *(karman)* come together then—for, with respect to our environmental theme, the making which is karmic in the man/nature relationship is rightly creative only when it is grounded in just that disinterestedness associated with liberation, self-knowledge, or *mokṣa*. At the phenomenal level, within *māyā*, we can work with nature, without obsessive and thereby finally destructive concern only when we act as *karmayogins*—makers disciplined in attitude and understanding. Let me explain, and thereby develop my main position concerning natural reverence.

When viewed from strictly rational or empirical perspectives, nature has come to be regarded, for the most part, as an indifferent system of either necessary connections or customary regularities, but without intrinsic value or purpose. Nature is "fact," not "value." Nature can become value-laden, it seems to me, only from a spiritual perspective which sees nature either as a manifestation of spiritual being or, Advaitic-wise, as an appearance grounded in a spiritual reality. Freedom, which I believe is required for natural reverence, is in the latter view not to be conceived as the opposite of necessity (from which it would then never escape), but as obtaining on an entirely different level of being—and, in relation to nature, the source of creative making which is a kind of play *(līlā)*. Freedom or *mokṣa* is the only solid ground for that disinterestedness which Kant saw as the basis for the aesthetic, for in freedom there is no ego which needs to be served and catered to. The *karmayogin* is one who acts, who makes, without attachment—and thereby, according to the *Gītā*, acts with skill: yoga, the text says, is "skill in action." One can cultivate and not exploit (and become a victim of that exploitation) only when the value-producing ground, freedom, is realized concretely in consciousness and action. Paradoxically, when nature is seen to be valueless in the most radical way, it can then be made valuable *with* us in creative play. Natural reverence, as here conceived, undercuts then the presupposition that Kant so clearly exhibits, that man stands separate from, over against, subordinate or superior to, some *entity* called "nature" and toward which he is able to take certain attitudes. With *māyā*, with creative play, there is nothing more natural than "natural reverence": it has its own kind of necessity, which is basically "aesthetic" rather than either rational or empirical in character. This "necessity" is concerned with rightness or appropriateness without a predetermined end. It is a working-*with* not a working-*at*: it is creative throughout. And just as an artist, if he is a good one, must have a profound respect for his material (his "medium"), knowing and regarding its limits and possibilities, listening to its inherent rhythm, as it were, to its vitality, so any person, if he or she is to be in creative harmony with nature, must be sensitive to its ordering principles, to its vital integrity. Imagination works within a profound sense of concern, but one that is liberated from narrow ego needs. It thus allows one to be freely with nature and at the same time to be obedient to its needs.

By turning to Asian thought (in this case, Indian Vedāntic philosophy) for inspiration we might yet find a way to bring our scientific understanding of nature's organic complexity into an integral harmony with a spiritual understanding of reality's simplicity. The *Gītā* states laconically: "He who sees inaction in action and action in inaction, he is wise among men, he does all action harmoniously."[11] The *karmayogin,* the *Gītā* insists, must understand the nature of both "the field" and "the knower of the field"—and then couple this understanding with the nonattachment of freedom. A natural reverence then becomes one's most basic attitude with nature—and the rest then depends upon one's creative capacities, which no metaphysics as such can provide.

"Conceptual Resources" in South Asia for "Environmental Ethics"

Gerald James Larson

It is a reasonably simple exercise for a South Asianist to address the subject of this book by setting forth a purely descriptive and/or analytic discussion of traditional South Asian metaethical positions that could be construed as "conceptual resources" for doing "environmental ethics." Such an exercise involves, in my judgment, identifying at least three basic positions.

First, it is possible to identify what a metaethicist might characterize as a perspective of "nonnaturalistic, intuitionist, noncognitivism," or in the indigenous idiom of traditional South Asia, the perspective of Mīmāṁsā, either of the Bhāṭṭa type or of the Prābhākara type. From such a perspective, what is good is not a natural property of the world. The good cannot be defined but is realized directly in intuition, and it cannot be dealt with in terms of the notions of true and false. What is good, rather, has to do with the direct, injunctive prescriptions set forth in the *Veda* about what we should do at certain crucial points in our lives. The Vedas do not tell us anything about the world, but they enjoin us to act in a certain way (or, in other words, the act-deontology of the Bhāṭṭas) or to follow certain rules (the rule-deontology of the Prābhākaras).

Second, it is possible to identify what a metaethicist might characterize as a perspective of "naturalistic, nonintuitionist cognitivism," or, in the indigenous idiom, the so-called "realist" perspectives in traditional Indian philosophy, namely, the Nyāya-Vaiśeṣika, the Jaina, and the early Buddhist positions. From such a perspective, what is good is a natural property of the world. The good can be defined and talked about in terms of the world in which we live, and it can be discussed in terms of what is true and false. Moreover, there are predictable consequences which provide the basic motivation for behaving in a moral way. The cultural trappings for such a position involve psychological hedonism (the *sukha-duḥkha* continuum), *karman* and *saṁsāra,* and *dharma* as a theory of obligation. It is a commonsense point of view given the presuppositions of the South Asian culture frame, and it is the most obvious moral position or moral theory to assume in such a context. As a normative position, it could be tagged as a kind of teleological cognitivism (or what Potter has called "path-philosophy").

Third, it is possible to identify what a metaethicist might characterize as a perspective of "nonnaturalistic, intuitionist a-moralism" (or what I like to call the "wild card" in the Indian deck), or, in the indigenous idiom of traditional South Asia, the perspective of Sāṃkhya, Yoga, Vedānta, and certain varieties of Mahāyāna Buddhist reflection (Mādhyamika and Yogācāra). From such a perspective, there is nothing that is truly or intrinsically good. To be sure, many things appear to be good either in terms of minimizing frustration *(duḥkha),* or in terms of maximizing more favorable rebirths, or in terms of sheer contemplation, or in terms of intellectual reflection. Serious discrimination reveals, however, that all determinate formulations or awarenesses of what is good prove to be temporary, limited, and most important, inextricably allied with dialectical modalities *(sukha-duḥkha-moha)* that undercut the perception, inference, or intuition that *anything* is intrinsically good. There may be some contributory or instrumental (or, in other words, extrinsic) "value" in the world in that it can point one in a certain direction or prepare one for ultimate insight, but, finally, the ultimate experience itself is *not* a moral experience—it is "beyond good and evil," or, putting the matter directly, it is the denial that moral and ethical theorizing has any value at all! As a normative position, one might tag such a perspective with (the admittedly barbaric) expression "gnoseological intuitionism" or the claim that the ultimate experience is a non-moral or a-moral intuition that arises through an extraordinary modality of knowing.

Among these three traditional perspectives in South Asian theorizing, the first perspective, namely, the act-deontology or rule-deontology of Mīmāṃsā, is an unlikely candidate for environmental ethics, since its injunctions are based on a corpus of texts, the Vedas, the authority of which is barely relevant even in orthodox communities in modern India, quite apart from nonorthodox South Asian environments or environments altogether outside of South Asia. This leaves us, then, with the second perspective, or, in other words, the "teleological cognitivism" of the Indian realist traditions (Nyāya, Vaiśeṣika, Jaina, and early Buddhist thought), and the third perspective, or what I have called the "gnoseological intuitionism" of Sāṃkhya, Yoga, Vedānta, and Mahāyāna Buddhist thought. In terms of environmental ethical discussions, I am inclined to agree that the South Asian realist traditions (Nyāya, Vaiśeṣika, Jaina, and early Buddhist thought) could be employed fruitfully as a way of undergirding a "pragmatic" approach to environmental ethics, as David Kalupahana has forcefully argued in his paper "Man and Nature: Towards a Middle Path of Survival."[1] I am also inclined to agree that the South Asian "gnoseological intuitionist" views of Sāṃkhya,

Yoga, Vedānta, and Mahāyāna Buddhist thought could be employed fruitfully as a way of establishing a somewhat new approach to "natural reverence," as Eliot Deutsch has argued in his paper, "A Metaphysical Grounding for Natural Reverence: East-West."[2] Moreover, J. Baird Callicott's critique of Deutsch has a South Asian answer, in my view. Callicott argues that the South Asian notion of Oneness is "substantive and essential . . . and the experience of it homogeneous and oceanic," whereas "in both contemporary ecology and quantum theory at their respective levels of phenomena the oneness of nature is systemic and (internally) relational."[3] Such a basic difference may be said to be valid in terms of Vedānta and Mahāyāna Buddhist accounts of "gnoseological intuitionism," but, as is well known to South Asianists, such a difference would not hold in Sāṁkhya and Yoga accounts. The notion of *prakṛti* as *triguṇa (sattva, rajas, tamas)* is clearly "systemic and (internally) relational" in Callicott's sense, and environmental ethicists could possibly find powerful conceptual resources for developing "organic" and/or "holistic" perspectives on nature within the traditions of Sāṁkhya and Yoga in South Asian thought.

In any case, as mentioned at the outset, from a purely descriptive and/or analytic point of view, it is a reasonably simple exercise to proceed in the manner I have briefly been outlining by finding "conceptual resources" in Asian traditions for doing "environmental ethics." To be sure, we could debate whether I have been sufficiently precise in formulating the various South Asian options, and more than that, whether it is possible to identify additional perspectives as well—for example, one could, I suppose, suggest "conceptual resources" from South Asian theistic, Tantric, or Śākta traditions, and so forth.

Overall, however, I am increasingly troubled and/or frustrated *(duḥkha)* by such purely descriptive approaches to comparative philosophizing as the ones I have been outlining and which are implicit in our work as a whole, and my frustration is both methodological and theoretical. My methodological frustration can easily be pinpointed. We appear to be using, albeit unconsciously, a particular metaphor that, in my view, is methodologically loaded and seriously misleading. If one substitutes the word "natural" for "conceptual" in the expression "conceptual resources," it becomes immediately apparent that we are using an economic metaphor in our undertaking. Since the eighteenth century, European nation-states have been utilizing Asia to supply a variety of resources: spices, tea, cotton, minerals, oil, natural gas, cheap labor, and hosts of other commodities. Now it seems that we are setting out again, only this time we are on the lookout for "conceptual resources." We appear to be using, in other words, an economic metaphor of raw materials. The needed "ideas" for environmental ethics are presumably in short "supply" in our own environment, but we recognize that there is an increasing "demand" for some new intellectual commodities.

What is methodologically loaded and seriously misleading about such an economic metaphor of raw materials is the corollary component of such a metaphor, namely, that we are not really interested in the raw materials in their natural state. We want, rather, to appropriate the raw materials so that we can use them for making what *we* want. We all know full well that the "ideas" and/or "concepts" that we need are not available directly in Asian contexts. They are deeply embedded in culture frames, kinship systems, traditional institutional frameworks, and so forth, from which they must be detached or "dug out" as it were and then imported into our own frameworks. Moreover, if they are to be utilized profitably, these "resources" will have to be processed, manufactured, mass-produced, and, finally, distributed. Of course, we recognize that the market for the eventual product is worldwide or global, and in that sense we can congratulate ourselves that what we are doing will subsequently benefit not only Asia but all people everywhere. This, of course, is exactly the rationale that the British used in India during the Raj. Raw materials were purchased in South Asia at a remarkably cheap price; factories in England then processed and manufactured the raw materials into useful consumer items which were subsequently sold in markets in India and elsewhere for a significant profit (and taxed as well). The rationale for the whole process was that the British were actively developing the Indian economy!

The methodological point for our work is that when we proceed by using an economic metaphor in this fashion, we are committing ourselves to a comparative enterprise of external appropriation. Ideas and concepts come to be construed as "things" or "entities" that can be disembedded from their appropriate frameworks and then processed and made to fit into our own frameworks. Such a method for comparative philosophy is, in my view, one-dimensional, overly selective, forced, anachronistic, sociologically unsophisticated, and, perhaps worst of all, unpersuasive. Surely we can develop more sophisticated methodological approaches in our comparative philosophizing.

As already indicated, however, my frustration *(duḥkha)* is not only methodological but also substantive and/or theoretical. My substantive or theoretical concern can be expressed by referring to some comments made by J. Baird Callicott in his article, "Non-Anthropocentric Value Theory and Environmental Ethics." Callicott suggests that environmental ethics may be thought of in two quite different ways, either (a) a sort of subdivision of applied ethics (on analogy, say, with business ethics), that is to say as "an *application* of well-established conventional philosophical categories to emergent practical environmental problems"; or (b) a creative enterprise that "may be understood to be an *exploration* of alternative moral and even metaphysical principles, forced upon philosophy by the magnitude and recalcitrance of these [environmental] problems." Moreover, says Callicott, if understood in the latter, more ambitious sense, the task of the environmental ethicist "is that of a theoretician or philosophical architect (as in Descartes' self-image)."[4] My substantive concern has to do with Callicott's way of putting the problem, namely, the environmental ethicist as a "theoretician or philosophical architect (as in Descartes' self-image)." To me as a comparativist, this way of putting the matter does not go far enough in identifying what is really at issue. It simply is a paraphrase of the basic problem, or, putting the matter somewhat differently, this very idiom is itself a part of the problem. The notion of the philosopher as a "theoretician or philosophical architect (as in Descartes' self-image)" is itself part of the conceptual framework that emerged in the seventeenth century for the first time and which included the rise of quantitative science, technology, manipulative reasoning, and the political economies of the emerging nation-state. It is a conceptual framework or mind-set that divides, classifies, quantifies, and distinguishes discreet "universes of meaning" (to use Thomas Luckmann's idiom).[5] Modern philosophy itself, in other words, as a distinct, separate discipline that analyzes, explores, and applies concepts, is symptomatic of a world view that causes "environmental pollution, the aesthetic degradation of nature, human overpopulation, resource depletion, ecological destruction and . . . abrupt massive species extinction," according to Callicott.[6] My point here is not an ethical or moral one. I am not regretting what has happened since the seventeenth century, nor am I seeking to assign some sort of blame. My point, rather, is a theoretical one, and I am inclined to express it in the following Zen-like way: We have not understood the environmental crisis until we realize that there is *no* philosophical answer to it. If we seriously think that we can find "conceptual resources" in Asia and then work them into our own philosophizing, *and* that such an effort would have a serious impact on the environmental crisis, then we really have not understood the environmental crisis at all! Put differently, our effort is itself a part of the problem. We are spinning our wheels, and nothing at all will or can change. It is a bit like the Vedānta of Śaṅkara: cleverly tinkering with concepts that deny everything on one level while allowing everything to remain just as it is on another level.

My substantive and/or theoretical frustration, in other words, is that philosophy (including comparative philosophy) as conventionally construed in the modern world since Descartes cannot adequately deal with the environmental crisis. Rather it is part of the crisis and cannot itself be used as a way of dealing with the crisis. This entails, furthermore, that all of the other "divisions" of modern academia, namely, economics, sociology, political science, physics, mathematics, chemistry, the biological sciences, and so forth, cannot as separate "language games" or "universes of meaning" deal adequately with the crisis either. It is this very predilection in European intellectual history since Descartes (and its progeny) to divide and separate intellectual tasks, and, more than that, to isolate and professionalize cognitive pursuits from other dimensions of human functioning (for example, trade, commerce, kinship relations, sexuality, and so forth) that is itself reflective of our current environmental crisis. One way of putting the point is to suggest that what we thought was a Weberian process of "rationalization" (increased efficiency, goal-oriented behavior, and so forth) has turned out to be a Freudian defense-mechanism notion of "rationalization" and that, therefore, what we had anticipated to be a modern, sophisticated, efficient, and civilized world has, in fact, turned out to be yet another highly neurotic world system even more dangerous than earlier ones, since its capacity for self-destruction is global and species-wide. Nor do I think, let me hasten to add, that we can retreat into premodern religious visions or apologetically contrived modernist versions of those same visions. Such visions may provide solace or salvation or "release" from issues such as the environmental crisis, as indeed they always have, but they tend largely to be either question-begging alternatives to dealing with the environmental crisis or else, like philosophy and other isolated cognitive domains, themselves symptomatic of the crisis.

What is needed instead, in my view, is a radical reorientation of the manner in which we might construe the problem, and I would like to call attention to some fundamental considerations that should be kept in mind as we seek to determine a starting point for bringing about such a reorientation. I shall mention three such fundamental considerations which, if taken together, might provide a kind of prolegomenon to a serious discussion of the environmental crisis from the perspective of comparative studies. The considerations are hardly new, nor are they particularly controversial, but they are frequently lost sight of in contemporary discussion.

First, I should like to call attention to what Charles Hartshorne has characterized as "the fallacy of misplaced symmetry," a problem that Hartshorne finds in much of Asian thought (Śaṁkara, Nāgārjuna, and so forth) as well as in European thought (Bradley, Bergson, and so forth). In a recent paper, Hartshorne refers to the fallacy as follows:

> I find a common fallacy in these widely separated thinkers. A relation between two terms is really two relations, the one of A to B, and the one of B to A. Neither Bradley nor Nāgārjuna take this duality into account. . . . Past events are realities, not unrealities. This doctrine is missing both from Bradley's and from Nāgārjuna's account. Hence they clearly begged the

question. . . . They overlooked time's arrow, the asymmetry of temporal relations. They committed the fallacy of misplaced symmetry. Another way to put the matter is, both thinkers refuted only a static view of multiplicity. They spatialized time. . . . Relations of dependence in space are indeed symmetrical, but not those in time.

Do effects depend on causes? Of course. Do we depend on our ancestors? Of course. Do causes depend on effects? Of course not. Do we depend on our descendants? Whatever our descendants turn out to be, we are what we are. But it is absurd to say, whatever our ancestors were, we are what we are. Without them we would not have been, period. But our existing now is absolute fact that no occurrence or non-occurrence in the future can nullify. . . . It is the indispensable foundation of any tenable rationality. All our living implies a real past, immune to alteration, and a merely potential future, whose exact characters are in the process of being created, step by step, beginning now.[7]

Whether one would follow Hartshorne's asymmetry-of-relations argument all the way to his process metaphysics is, of course, debatable; but in this context I wish to press what I take to be a nondebatable claim regarding the environmental crisis, namely, that it is something totally new and that there is an asymmetrical relation between it and all earlier natural crises. The survival of life on earth as we now know it is seriously in jeopardy. To use a Sāṃkhya idiom from South Asia, we have reached the "curds" stage of an earlier "milk" stage in the unfolding of our natural habitat as a species, and we cannot wish away the "curds" stage by arguing for a symmetrical relationship between milk and curds. The curds can only become milk again at the time of the great dissolution *(mahāpralaya)*, but, of course, when that happens, there can no longer be anything alive to enjoy the milk!

Second, I should like to call attention to what might be called the fallacy of disembedded ideas. Philosophy (and comparative philosophy) operates on the level of conceptual analysis, but we have learned from the history of Asian thought (East Asian and South Asian) as well as from much of modern European thought (Marx, Weber, Freud, Wittgenstein, and so forth) that conceptual frameworks are always embedded in larger culture frames insofar as they are vital components for a "form of life." We have learned from Kuhn and Feyerabend that even our most treasured abstractions, that is to say, the conceptual apparatus of our modern science, exists or "has life" only in such environments ("paradigms," frames," and so forth). In our comparative work we have discovered over three thousand languages on our planet and hundreds of "culture frames" and "paradigms." In our scientific work we have discovered that there is a statistical probability that perhaps as many as one million planets in our own galaxy alone are capable of supporting "intelligent life." Yet in view of all of this, we still ask ourselves if archaic notions such as the "Tao," *brahman-ātman,* Allah, God, *dharma,* or whatever, all of which notions are derived from premodern, qualitative-science "frames" or "paradigms," can be disembedded, dusted off, and somehow utilized in dealing with the environmental crisis. It is my inclination to think that we would do better, rather, as comparativists, to inquire into the manner in which ideas and/or concepts function in their respective "frames" and "paradigms" as a way of getting a handle on how our modern "concept clusters" might be generating and are being generated by the contemporary "frames" and "paradigms" in which we live.

Third, I should like to call attention to what might be called the fallacy of "the sovereignty of the subject." I take the expression from Foucault's *The Archaeology of Knowledge,* in which he inquires into the reasons for the difficulty of developing what he calls a "general theory of discontinuity."

> There is a reason for this. If the history of thought could remain the locus of uninterrupted continuities . . . it would provide a privileged shelter for the sovereignty of consciousness. Continuous history is the indispensable correlative of the founding function of the subject: the guarantee that everything that has eluded him may be restored to him; the certainty that time will disperse nothing without restoring it in a reconstituted unity. . . .
>
> In various forms, this theme has played a constant role since the nineteenth century: to preserve, against all decenterings, the sovereignty of the subject, and the twin figures of anthropology and humanism.[8]

I am neither a post-structuralist nor a deconstructionist, but I think that Foucault's point is well taken in any properly framed discussion of the environmental crisis. I mentioned earlier that, using statistical probability, it has been determined that "intelligent life" may be present on as many as one million planets within our own galaxy. Using similar procedures in mathematical astronomy, it has been estimated that there may be as many as ten million planets within our galaxy that are able to support "life" in some sense. Our own planet is about 4.6 billion years old, and there is mounting evidence that some forms of life have been present almost from the beginning. Hominid forms have existed from about five hundred thousand years ago, but "civilized" life (in the sense of animal husbandry, agriculture, polished tools, pottery, some form of social life, and so forth) has only existed since about 6000 B.C.E. (or, in other words, from what is usually called the "Neolithic" period in such areas as the ancient Near East, Mohenjo-Daro, and so forth). Cognitive and affective capacities sufficient to support "civilized" life, in other words, are quite recent from within the perspective of the "history" of life forms on our own planet, and the self-reflective images we have of ourselves as so-called "modern" hominids are a bit over two hundred years old. Remarkable strides have been made recently in such areas as brain physiology, biochemistry, mathematical astronomy, and so on, but similar strides have been lacking for the most part in theoretical formulations of the role and function of self-awareness in the hominid life-form. We still operate with "philosophies" and "psychologies" of self-awareness but have very little grasp of the evolutionary significance of such constructions. Putting the matter another way, we have very little understanding of the human need for or the evolutionary significance of the self-awareness of the human life-form. We have very little sense of the "meaning of meaning," and we appear to be stuck with interpretations of self-awareness that may have long outlived their usefulness. I suspect that future progress in dealing with the environmental crisis will have to address critically the problem of "the sovereignty of the subject" and to avoid the fallacy of assuming that what we think we are is in any sense an adequate, accurate, consistent, or clear measure of what we are.

The fly is still alive and well in the bottle. What I mean by alluding to Wittgenstein in this context is that we have not yet succeeded in framing our problem in a way that allows us to escape from a mind-set that is itself a part of the problem. Comparative reflection is, I think, helpful in enabling us to see this—in enabling us, as it were, to uncork the bottle.

Far be it from me to predict what will happen if the fly gets out of the bottle, but if we take seriously the sorts of considerations I have briefly been describing, namely, "the fallacy of misplaced symmetry," "the fallacy of disembedded ideas," and "the fallacy of the sovereignty of the subject," we as comparativists may well have much to contribute by way of addressing problems related to our present "environmental crisis." Let me conclude by programmatically mentioning at least a few of these contributions.

First, comparativists could be helpful in generating better metaphors for construing the problem. As comparativists, we know full well that an economic metaphor of "conceptual resources" with all of its negative connotations of exploitation and external appropriation, is not at all an apt way of thinking about conceptual frameworks. Conceptual systems or schemes are inextricably a part of a comprehensive way of life, and indeed are frequently symptomatic for helping to uncover the latent or hidden forces and/or processes that are operative in a given culture or society. In this regard, it seems to me, a biological science metaphor along the lines of comparative anatomy comes close to highlighting the problem of the environmental crisis. An arm is not a fin, and a lung is not a gill, but there are nevertheless interesting affinities between these pairs in concrete life forms over time. In a similar fashion, one conceptual framework is not identical to another, nor can simple substitutions be made between them, but nevertheless there can be illuminating comparisons about the manner in which conceptual frameworks or networks operate in larger, concrete social realities. Such a metaphor of comparative anatomy would focus attention on thinking or conceptualization, not necessarily as a *cause* or a *prescription* for a society's or a culture's problems, but, rather, as a *symptom* or a *diagnosis* regarding society's or a culture's self-understanding. Why is it, for example, that we tend to think of the environmental crisis as a "philosophical" or "ethical" problem when it is obviously so much more than that? What do our conceptual frameworks regarding "ethics" tell us about our Western historical experience, our "anatomy," as it were, as a culture or as a set of genetically related cultures? Classical Chinese thought is symptomatic of quite a different "anatomy," as is classical Indian thought, Eskimo thought, Islamic thought, and so forth. I am speaking here, of course, only in terms of metaphor, and I am not arguing for a naturalistic reductionism. I am simply suggesting that as a comparativist I find a biological science metaphor much more to the point of what is at issue in any interesting discussion of the environmental crisis. There are undoubtedly a number of other metaphors which could be helpful, and as comparativists we are nicely positioned because of our training to discuss them.

Second, comparativists could be helpful in encouraging more broadly based cross-cultural and interdisciplinary research in an area such as the environmental crisis. The comparativist in the course of training early along learns that one cannot simply do linguistics, philosophy, religion, anthropology, and so forth, nor can one isolate one's research in only one cultural context. As suggested earlier, in almost every instance, our Western scholarly specializations are little more than heuristic and historical divisions derived from the vicissitudes and power struggles of our own developing social reality. There again, "philosophy" (or any other division in the modern academy) is a symptom of rather than a prescription for the environmental crisis. To look to "philosophy" for solutions to the environmental crisis is to acquiesce in the marginalization of the cognitive life that has been occurring in European and American culture since the seventeenth century. The time has come, perhaps, to criticize such compartmentalization as itself a major symptom of our current environmental crisis and to launch cross-cultural and interdisciplinary inquiries that bring together humanists, scientists, politicians, and the rest—inquiries that do not permit specialists to hide behind their narrowly conceived expertise.

Third, and finally, uncorking the bottle and allowing the fly to escape will surely have some intriguing political implications. If it is the case that conceptual schemes or networks make up part of the "anatomy" of every culture or society, and if it is the case that the "philosopher" must relinquish his privileged (and marginalized) isolation in order to begin to get a handle on the scope of the environmental issue, then this surely means that the conventional centers of power and wealth of our modern way of life will be seriously threatened and, as Marx has taught us, will hardly roll over and play dead. The committees for determining comfortable government grants, private fellowships, and legislative funding for higher education, all of which dispense their largess on the premises of marginalization and the maintenance of the status quo, will undoubtedly not be happy, and yet these structures of modernity are deeply implicated in the environmental crisis and cry out for criticism in any serious treatment of the issues. But by what authority would one issue the criticism or carry out a given program for political action? In the name of Reason? Civility? Justice? Fairness? As comparativists, we know that such notions are construed differently from culture to culture and that one important factor in shaping the differences is the set of power relations that operate in a particular social reality. Hence, to begin rethinking a problem such as the environmental crisis in our modern world is at one and same time to begin reshaping the power relations in that world—in other words, the intellectual work is in an important sense a political act. To some extent, of course, this is a sort of Marxian point with the important difference, however, that unlike the Marxist, the comparativist has no platform of certainty, no "vanguard" status by means of which to pursue a political program. The comparativist is simply one more participant in an ongoing effort to attain some sort of reflexive grasp of what is happening to the human species in our own time.

To put all of this somewhat differently, the truly important task for the comparativist in the environmental debate is not to offer up non-Western, alternative "world views" for possible adoption, but, rather, precisely the opposite, namely, through comparative analysis to come to a more critical understanding of what it means to be human at a time when all of the old certainties of our Western and non-Western traditions have largely collapsed.

Epilogue: On the Relation of Idea and Action

J. Baird Callicott and Roger T. Ames

Eastern traditions of thought represent nature, and the relationship of people to nature, in ways that cognitively resonate with contemporary ecological ideas and environmental ideals; or, many of the scholars contributing to this volume so claim. In his enormously influential environmental critique of the Western intellectual tradition, "The Historical Roots of Our Ecologic Crisis," Lynn White, Jr., casually registered that impression himself and candidly revealed the fundamental pragmatic assumption underlying his analysis: "What people *do* about their ecology [i.e., natural environments] depends on what they *think* about themselves in relation to things around them. Human ecology [i.e., the way people actually live in their natural environments] is deeply conditioned by beliefs about our nature and destiny. . . ."[1] This seems obvious to intellectual historians, philosophers, and all those who live in a world of ideas. And we should expect, accordingly, that the "human ecology" of Asian peoples would be correspondingly different from that of Western peoples. We should expect, more particularly, that, if what our authors in this anthology say is true, Asian peoples would be less inclined to exploit and destroy their natural environments than those in the West.

If we shift, however, from purely theoretical considerations and look for empirical confirmation of our expectations in actual human practice, what we find everywhere in East, Southeast, and South Asia is accelerating environmental deterioration. The effects on human health of eating fish taken from mercury-polluted waters were first discovered in Japan. And the Japanese are notoriously unregenerate slaughterers of the desperately endangered great whales. The rain forests of Southeast Asia are among the most ruthlessly exploited in the world. The world's most infamous nonnuclear industrial accident occurred in Bhopal, India. And many of India's surface waters, including the sacred Ganges, are grossly polluted by municipal and industrial wastes. The only remaining winter refuge of the Siberian crane in China is now threatened by draining and farming. And China suffers from massive soil erosion.[2]

The brute fact that environmental degradation is rampant in much of Asia—indeed, that particularly grotesque instances of wanton environmental behavior are not uncommon in that quarter of the world—would seem to imply that one of the following propositions is false: (a) the claim, made by many of the contributors to this collection, that Asian traditions of thought, each in its peculiar way, emphasize human continuity with other-than-human being and adaptation to natural processes; or (b) the natural assumption, clearly articulated by Lynn White, Jr., that what people think really does substantially affect what they do and how they live.[3]

As editors of this volume we are persuaded by the cumulative weight of evidence provided by its several contributors for proposition (a); and in some broader capacity—as thinking denizens of this planet seeking a responsible future—we also have confidence in the practical efficacy of ideas, that is, in proposition (b). As a first attempt to reconcile both (a) and (b) with empirical observation, we might submit that contemporary environmental misdeeds perpetrated by Asian peoples today can in large measure be attributed to the *intellectual* colonization of the East by the West.

From the mid-fifteenth to the mid-twentieth century, many Western nations openly pursued a policy of naked imperialism—imposing, by force of arms, their common economic, political, administrative, and religious culture on Asian (and African, and Australian, and American) peoples. Granted, most Asian nations are no longer literally Western colonies. But few former victims of Western imperialism have returned to precolonial ways. That would imply, in effect, a return to the past. In a world reduced to a global village by contemporary communications and transportation technologies, multinational corporations, and nuclear arms, a return to the past may not even be a genuine option for any but the most geographically isolated peoples. For most, it is sink or swim in the ineluctable twentieth and (very soon) twenty-first centuries. And in the world as it exists today, "progress" and "development" mean industrialization. And industrialization, even if pursued in a climate of anti-Western rhetoric, entails Westernization nonetheless. All the Asian environmental ills just mentioned, after all, are either directly caused by originally Western technology (e.g., heavy metals pollution) or aggravated by it (e.g., soil erosion).

Technology is not culture-neutral any more than it is value-neutral. To adopt a technology is to adopt, like it or not, the matrix of presuppositions in which the technology is embedded. And "modern technology," for the most part, is embedded in the Bacon-Newton complex of ideas—science as manipulative power over an inert, material, mechanical *res extensa*. Modern technology is embedded, in short, in the dominant Western paradigm. Thus, by attributing the deplorable environmental conditions prevailing in contemporary Asia to Westernization—manifestly in the technological sense and, therefore, *a fortiori* in the cognitive sense as well—we may retain confidence in the assumption that the way people think shapes the way people behave, and also credit the claims detailed in this book about the environmental attitudes and values implicit in Asian *traditions* of thought.

To this line of argument one might reply that if Asian traditions of thought really are more in tune with ecological and environmental ideas and ideals, and if what people think really does substantially shape how they behave, then modern technologies and their inevitably associated Western world view ought to be—contrary to what seems the general rule—adopted with great care and circumspection by their Asiatic hosts. The dialectic of acculturation, however, does not appear to work quite so felicitously— especially where the process is less coercive than seductive. Experience seems to show that new and efficient Western ways of doing things—with heavy machinery, exotic chemicals, and high technology—are, very often, uncritically and unsuspiciously embraced by peoples heretofore innocent of their use; intoxicated by the positive payload, that is, increased productivity and living standard, they disregard the environmental costs. Further, a mood of urgency often seems to pervade the so-called (revealingly) developing nations, a need to catch up and compete with the West, that preempts time and capital-consuming environmental countermeasures—such as pollution abatement and sewage treatment technologies, or selective timber cropping and forest regeneration. Because of its head start and greater wealth, the West can afford the luxury of such environmental emollients—which often appear to policy makers in developing nations as impediments to, rather than as necessary conditions for, economic prosperity. Materialism, in both its ontological and axiological senses, and mechanism seem to be embraced almost as a latter-day enlightenment, paving the way to development and prosperity. Traditional indigenous belief systems, if not swept aside by the popularity of newly acquired Western modes of life, means of production, and habits of thought, may be simply ignored by the new local technological elite or patronized like *objets d'art* from a bygone era.

So, Lynn White, Jr.'s, claim that Western *ideas* have brought on the present environmental crisis, and the corollary claim (explored here for the first time in detail) that Eastern *ideas* may be somehow therapeutic, thus can, after all, be made consistent with the observation that the contemporary environmental crisis is ubiquitous, infecting the East no less than the West. What global environmental distress may prove is only the global reach of essentially Western beliefs about the nature of nature, human nature, and the proper relationship between the two.

Looking a little deeper, however, the present environmental crisis appears to be less a unique, unprecedented historical event than the climactic paroxysm of a malaise as old as civilization itself, perhaps even as old as mankind. The neolithic revolution was characterized not only by the domestication of plants and animals but by deforestation, siltation, erosion, and desertification.[4] And, before that, the slow encroachment of *Homo sapiens* out of Africa, through the forests of Europe, and across the steppes of central Asia grimly correlates with a wave of extinctions of large mammals. The "discovery of America," only some ten to twenty thousand years ago by Siberian big-game hunters was accompanied by an orgy of destruction—including the extinction of two magnificent species of American elephant, an American horse, camel, and long-horned bison, to mention only a few.[5] The precise role of human hunters in these extinctions, both in the New World and the Old, is a matter of dispute; but it can hardly be disputed that spear-wielding, fire-setting primates dramatically changed the face of the land from Southern Africa to Lapland and from Beringia to Tierra Del Fuego.

These considerations put our conundrum concerning Asian environmental thought and environmental action into a more universal human frame. Far Western peoples (American Indians) are also alleged to have expressed, in very different ways from those of the East, an attitude of respect for nonhuman natural entities, and a willing adaptation to natural processes.[6] Yet incontrovertible evidence of the human abuse of nature, prior to infection with European notions, is found in the fossil remains of North and South America. Reflection on the ancient record of human depredation and environmental destruction suggests that the roots of our ecologic crisis reach far beyond the variable topsoil of intellectual history, whether Eastern or Western, into the common substrata of human nature itself.

Geographer Yi-Fu Tuan directly engaged the problematic relation between human thought about nature, and human action in respect to nature, in his "Discrepancies Between Environmental Behavior and Attitude: Examples from Europe and China," published in 1968.[7] Stimulated to critical comment by Lynn White, Jr.'s, paper, which had appeared the previous year, Tuan pointed out that the northeastern Mediterranean environment was deforested with the usual results (flooding, erosion, and eventual climate change) by pre-Christian Greeks and Romans—contrary to what one would expect if White's thesis (which focused single-mindedly on the Judeo-Christian aspect of the Western tradition), and his assumption about the relation of thought and action were true. Tuan concludes that "against [the] background of the vast transformations of the pagan world, the inroads made in the early centuries of the Christian era were relatively modest."[8] And, turning to China, he rehearses episode after episode of wholesale land abuse by the ancient Chinese long before intercourse with Western civilization—indeed, in some cases, long before there was anything that could even properly be called "Western civilization."

Intellectual historians and comparative philosophers concentrate on the symbolic expression of a culture, while the social scientist is disposed to look more immediately at the record of human action written on the face of the land. Writes Tuan, "unlike the Western man of letters the geographer is usually aware of China's frequent mistreatment of nature. He perceives that country, not through the refined statements of Taoist philosophy, Neo-Confucianism, and Oswald Siren, but through the bleak reports of Mallory, Lowdermilk, and Thorp."[9] Yi-Fu Tuan, as we see, does not deny the claim that in China, at least, there existed a tradition of natural philosophy and philosophical anthropology more resonant with contemporary ecological ideas and supportive of contemporary environmental ideals than that characteristic of the Western tradition. That is, he does not side with Western cultural chauvinists and assert that Oriental intellectual traditions are no less anthropocentric and indifferent to the needs of nature than Occidental intellectual traditions—the "pot calling the kettle black" rejoinder. Rather, he seems to concede that Chinese Taoist and Buddhist thought did indeed emphasize "a quiescent and adaptive approach towards nature," but that there simply exist "glaring contradictions of professed ideal and actual practice."[10] As the title of his article suggests, there are intractable discrepancies between environmental behavior and attitude. What people think is less closely related to how people live than we (especially we persons of letters) may uncritically suppose.

Taking a closer look at Yi-Fu Tuan's discussion, however, one finds that he documents almost as many cases of behavior that are consistent with and seem to have been inspired by Taoist and Buddhist ideas as cases of behavior which contradict them—everything from ancient forest conservation to the abandonment of China's first railroad in the name of *feng-shui* geomancy. And he seems to suggest that there was another, countervailing traditional pattern of *thought* in China which has received less play in the West than Taoism and Buddhism, but which has, on the ground in China, exerted considerable influence on patterns of collective cultural behavior. Writing before acute sensitivity to gender-bias emerged—which has made it very impolitic for a male writer to make such claims in just these terms—he suggests that certain intellectual trends in China have encouraged the "masculine" expression of dominance and control over nature.[11] Among these are astronomy and a folk tradition which glorifies the "magnificent deeds" of legendary emperors. According to Tuan, Chinese astronomy, "inspired such masculine attitudes as geometric order, hierarchy, and authoritarian control over earth and men."[12] Tuan, in other words, explains the intermittent tendency of the Chinese to undertake un-Taoist "action contrary to nature" by reference to a certain set of *ideas,* forthcoming in part from reflection on the ways of Heaven. As Tuan himself revealingly queries, "if animistic belief and Taoist nature philosophy lie at the back of an adaptive attitude toward nature, what *conceptions* and *ideals*—we may ask—

have encouraged the Chinese, through their long history, to engage in gigantic transformation of environment—whether this be expressed positively in huge works of construction or negatively in deforested mountains?[13]

China, in Tuan's representation, seems to have been, from time to time and place to place, under the alternate influence of the yin and the yang. When and where the yang was in ascendance, new cities like Ch'ang-an were laid out on a rigid rectilinear grid and old growth forests were burned to deprive dangerous animals and brigands of their coverts. When and where the yin was in ascendance, buildings, roads, and bridges in China were sited in accordance with *feng-shui* (the art of "taking proper note of the forms of hills, and directions of water courses since these are themselves the outcome of the molding influences of winds and waters"), and, even without official compulsion, Chinese peasants were wont to practice "forest care."[14] Tuan's remarks clearly imply, in other words, that it was specifically the alternate influence of *ideas*—astronomical and heroic, on the one hand, and Taoist and Buddhist, on the other—which occasioned the indisputable examples both of gross environmental assault and environmental accommodation and restoration in the progress of Chinese civilization. One might, therefore, fairly infer from Tuan's account, taken as a whole, that had there existed in China no other cognitive constructs than Taoism and Buddhism, the Chinese countryside would have been a good deal less wrecked than it actually was upon the eve of its opening to the West.

Yi-Fu Tuan's discussion of Western environmental destruction prior to "the greatest psychic revolution" in the history of Western culture, "the victory of Christianity over paganism" (as Lynn White, Jr., had luridly described it) is similarly ambiguous.[15] Greek paganism, taken over by the Romans with little more than a change of labels, was hardly biocentric. In sharp contrast to the paganism typical of the wilder northern and western Europeans, and certainly to that of the even wilder American Indians, the Greek divinities were notoriously anthropomorphic and the Greek outlook, correspondingly, anthropocentric.

Moreover, Greek paganism was, to borrow Tuan's controversial representation, "masculine" in character—not merely metaphorically or symbolically, but literally, self-consciously, and self-assertively so. Robert Graves has persuasively advanced the thesis that a much earlier "psychic revolution" took place in the Mediterranean cradle of Western civilization.[16] It began when Greek-speaking pastoralists from the northeast overran the settled agricultural peoples native to the region, and it was completed during the high classical fifth and fourth centuries B.C. The Greek invaders brought with them a male sky/weather god, Zeus, while the indigenous Mediterraneans worshiped the Earth-Mother goddess. The military and political conquest of the lands in and around the Aegean Sea by the Greeks was represented in their own mytho-history as the victory of the Olympic pantheon over chthonic cults *and,* quite explicitly, according to Graves, of the male over the female.

Further still, if an interest in astronomy and geometry leads, as Tuan suggests, to a tendency to impose Heaven's rigid rectilinear order on terrestrial nature—without regard to Earth's natural contours, flows, processes, and biotic relationships—then no culture would exhibit such a tendency more certainly than that of the Greeks (and their Roman imitators and admirers), who were perhaps more singularly devoted to both geometry and astronomy as paradigmatic schemata than any other ancient people.

If the masculine principle is one of top-down "logical" organization and dominance over nature, in contrast to one of emergent "aesthetic" order and an attitude of mutual accommodation, then the fact that Greek and Roman pagans imposed "vast transformations" upon the Mediterranean basin hardly confutes the supposition that environmental attitudes are directly expressed in environmental behavior.[17] From the historical point of view postulated by Graves, Christianity seems less a psychic revolution than the confluence and mutual reinforcement of two pastoral patriarchal legacies—one Greek, one Hebrew.

Two rather simplistic models of the relation of environmental thought to environmental action were explicitly advanced in White's and Tuan's complementary classics of early environmental philosophy. (1) What people do about their ecology depends upon what they think about themselves in relation to things around them; and (2), to the contrary, actual environmental practice often glaringly contradicts professed environmental ideal.

Do our natural (and social) attitudes and values direct our behavior or, on the contrary, are they a sort of muzak of the mind, a mere cerebral gloss, while environmental (and social) behavior proceeds from more primitive visceral sources? Are we, as we like to flatter ourselves, a species liberated from our biological urges and free to act upon conscious information, knowledge, and values; or are we, rather, like so many ants, driven by instinct to behavior we can only observe, not control? So starkly stated, either alternative seems clearly false. Behavior does not flow exclusively from attitudes and values; but neither are attitudes and values simply irrelevant to what people do and how they live. The relationship is more complex than either the sanguine supposition of White or the skeptical conclusions of Tuan. Let us briefly suggest the following model.

All forms of life, plants as well as animals, some more than others, modify their environments. Human beings and their protohuman ancestors, pursuing the survival imperatives shared with all other species, are, in this respect, not exceptional. What is exceptional about the human species is its stratagem for survival and adaptation—culture—which has amplified the environmental impact of our species both in extent and in intensity. The invention of clothing, artificial shelters, and tools (weapons); the domestication of fire; and the storage and transmission of these skills by means of language catapulted *Homo sapiens* into a class by itself—a one-species titantic force of global environmental change.

With language, the *sin qua non* of a complex material culture, there also emerged cognitive culture—systems of symbols, meanings, beliefs, mysteries, magic, mythology, and morality. These emergent semiotic structures overlie and interpenetrate the bare vertebrate sensory representation of the ambient environment to bring into being a variety of "cultural worlds," or "world views." The "world"—experienced, thus, as a structured, meaningful whole—is the theater of human action. It sets, implicitly or explicitly, putative limits on what is possible, and by defining the place and purpose of man in nature, provides a role model for human behavior. World views, like the genes of their carriers, are tested in the crucible of natural selection. They may help or hinder their subscribers in the business of life, and, thus, may themselves spread or shrink in influence. World views grow and change in response to success and failure in praxis, or calcify and die.

For example, the essentially social model of nature and human-nature interaction typical of woodland American Indian peoples might have evolved as a response to the ecologically destructive—and, therefore, ultimately self-destructive—depredations of their Paleo-Indian ancestors (the Siberian big-game hunters newly arrived in the Americas). There may, in other words, have been an essentially Darwinian process of selection operating in North America on the cognitive cultures of the surviving remnants of the immigrant American elephant hunters after they had destroyed their resource base. Subsequent generations of American Indians evolved a mytho-ecological world view and something resembling a land ethic as a cultural response to the wanton ways of their forebears.[18] To suggest that this was an essentially Darwinian process of *selection* among cognitive cultures is to suggest that it was not conscious or deliberate—as if members of a band of hunter-gatherers said to one another, "Look at what happened to our forebears, we had better change our myths so that we won't repeat their mistakes." Rather, those mythic complexes which better mapped ecological exigencies and encouraged restrained exploitation of natural resources and adaptation to natural processes enabled their subscribers to live in equilibrium with their environments, and so themselves survived and spread in influence. Yi-Fu Tuan, incidentally, suggests that a similar process went on in China.

> An adaptive attitude towards nature has ancient roots in China. It is embodied in folklore, in the philosophical-ethical precepts of Taoism, and later,

Buddhism, and it draws support from practical experience: the experience that uncontrolled exploitation of timber, for example, brings hurtful results. Even as early as the Chou period (eighth century [*sic*]-third century B.C.), deforestation necessitated by the expansion of agriculture and the building of cities seems to have led to an appreciation of the value of trees.[19]

The innate aggressiveness that *Homo sapiens* inherited from prehuman omnivorous savanna primates may be either aggravated or tempered by the particulars of a cultural world view, but not stanched altogether. A world view, in other words, may encourage environmental (or, as far as that goes, social) exploitation, or it may discourage it. Translated into these terms, Lynn White, Jr., has suggested that the way nature is represented, in the recently prevailing Western world view—as a divine artifact—and the way mankind is represented, in the same tradition—as God's viceroy on Earth— has aggravated native human aggressiveness and encouraged human exploitation of nature. And translated into the same terms, Yi-Fu Tuan has argued that the human tendency, gradually augmented in power by an evolving human material culture, to transform and consume the surroundings has been dampened rather ineffectually by the belief in guardian *genii loci* in the pre-Christian pagan Mediterranean basin, and by *wu-wei* and by Buddhahood for plants and trees in classical China.

Given the qualifications implicit in his own discussion of discrepancies between environmental attitude and behavior in China and the similar qualifications that a more penetrating analysis of classical Greco-Roman attitudes toward nature introduces, there is less evidence for Tuan's skepticism than for White's optimism about whether environmental ideas and values can exert a significant influence on environmental behavior. But, of course, developing an appropriate philosophic orientation, alas, will not be a panacea for environmental ills. Human beings, to modify Aristotle's classical characterization, are cultural animals. The beast in us impels us to employ our material culture to take the shortest path to the most immediate gratification of the most visceral wants. Our cultural ideas and ideals can expand and complicate our understanding of the workings of the world in which we live; they can redefine our sense of place and purpose in the world; and they can reevaluate the objects of desire. Adapting another of Aristotle's notions, we may observe that *akrasia* is endemic to human nature. People may "know" the good and yet not always act in accordance with it.

Western cognitive culture today appears to be in the midst of a millennial upheaval which, granted, undoubtedly appears more disjunctive from the internal perspective than it may in retrospect. Nonetheless, ideas, inherited from an amalgamated Greco-Roman and Judeo-Christian heritage—about the world, about who we are as human beings in the world, and about what in the world is valuable to have and to hold—seem to have played themselves out, both theoretically and pragmatically.

Theoretically, the objective material *res extensa* has dissolved into an interactive, dynamic plenum. We erstwhile divinely informed and appointed lords of the universe have discovered ourselves to have been molded and imprinted by interaction with our environment and to be precariously dependent upon the exact and very complex ecological conditions which brought us forth. And ironically, in the midst of unprecedented material accumulation, we find that we are in danger of losing the very things which make life most worthwhile.

Pragmatically, the ecologically destructive effects of the hyper-yang Western world view, until recently, have been successfully delayed. Western Europe, as Aldo Leopold has pointed out, has been remarkably resilient in the face of human transformation.[20] Upon finally reaching the ecological limits of their own lands, Europeans spilled out and moved their operations to a vast New World. And, in the course of what must be the world record for continent busting, their rapidly expanding technology managed to stay a jump ahead of resource degradation. But, with the shrinking size of the planet and this relentless march of empire, the ecological limits of the Earth have been stretched and broken. The need to reevaluate the world view that has occasioned such a massive environmental transformation thus becomes increasingly critical. If human ideas do have practical force in shaping our environment, what complex of attitudes can we develop that will optimize the enormous benefits of our technologies, while at the same time preserving and enhancing our ecological viability?

We are persuaded that Asian traditions of thought can help the West reconstruct its world view in the ways suggested in the introduction to this volume. Firstly, they can help along the process of Western self-criticism by providing an alternative place to stand, an outsider's point of view, from which the West can more clearly discern the deeper substrata of its inherited intellectual biases and assumptions. And secondly, if, as some scholars have suggested, the historical dialectic of Western thought is being impelled in what has until now been a predominantly Oriental direction, Eastern traditions, rich in metaphor, simile, and symbol, can help the West articulate, in ways that are culturally assimilable, the very untraditional abstract ideas forthcoming from contemporary theoretical studies of the nature of nature.

Confronting the cost of our industrial success in terms of ecological impoverishment and deformity, it is well that we look back in nostalgia for the lost Eden of our mythic past. It is salving if not comforting to remind ourselves not only that human beings have always changed the world but that the world we have changed has always changed us. The species lost to chain saws and bulldozers today are as unrecoverable as the mastodons and woolly mammoths lost to spears and anthropogenic conflagrations at the end of the Pleiştocene. While it is naive to suppose that the momentum of the ecospasm presently building on the planet can be quelled by comparative philosophy, neither is abject pessimism—about the power of ideas *eventually* to alter the course of history—warranted.

Only the most inveterate materialist or economic determinist could ignore the recent efficacy of the ideas of Galileo, Bacon, Descartes, Newton, Hobbes, and Locke. In a very straightforward sense, the contemporary "real world" is the scion of their thought. And their thought, of course, was intimately linked to the thought of Western antiquity. Living in the hour of a cultural sea change, it is very difficult to know who among our contemporaries will be venerated by later generations as the "fathers" (or "parents" more likely) of the post-modern world, the Age of Ecology (or Integration, or Systems, or whatever it will be called).

Quite apart from the gradual process of cultural redirection and environmental rehabilitation, we must set as an immediate goal the preservation of whatever biotic diversity and biospheric integrity we can. Surely, we can envision an eminently livable, appropriately technological, systemic society well adapted to and at peace and harmony with its organic environment. And it is a humbug to insist that the human community must necessarily be a burden to the rest of nature. On the contrary, human habitation and use of the environment *can* actually enhance the diversity, integrity, stability, and beauty of biotic communities. Biologist René Dubos has argued that Western Europe was, prior to the industrial revolution, biologically richer as a result of human settlement and cultivation.[21] The creation and cultivation of small fields, hedgerows, and forest edges enhanced the diversity, integrity, and beauty of the preindustrial European landscape. The ethnobotanists Gary Nabhan and Arturo Gomez-Pompa have recently drawn similar pictures of the Papago inhabitation of the Sonoran desert and the Maya inhabitation of the Central American rain forest, respectively.[22] Is an irresponsible technological civilization inspired and informed by an obsolete world view—the mechanical paradigm—the only one imaginable? Aren't there alternative technologies and alternative social goals? The critical and speculative discipline of comparative philosophy may help, we believe, to chart a future course that will seek, through an accommodating will, to maximize the creative possibilities of mankind in the environing world.

Notes

Introduction

1. The University of Wisconsin-Stevens Point seems to have implemented the first philosophy course anywhere with this title in 1971.

2. For example, P. Shepard and D. McKinley, eds., *The Subversive Science: Essays Toward an Ecology of Man* (New York: Houghton Mifflin, 1969); R. Disch, ed., *The Ecological Conscience: Values for Survival* (Englewood Cliffs, NJ: Prentice Hall, 1970); and I.G. Barbour, ed., *Western Man and Environmental Ethics: Attitudes Toward Nature and Technology* (Reading, MA: Addison-Wesley, 1973).

3. Richard Routley's "Is There a Need for a New, an Environmental Ethic?" (*Proceedings of the Fifteenth World Congress of Philosophy* I [Sophia: 1973]: 205–10) was a ground-breaking essay. Also seminal was Holmes Rolston, III's, "Is There an Ecological Ethic?" (*Ethics* 85 [1975]:93–109). Somewhat less venturesome, but nevertheless significant, were the essays by the philosophers William T. Blackstone, Joel Feinberg, Charles Hartshorne, Walter H. O'Brient, Nicholas Rescher, and Robert G. Burton, in Wm. Blackstone, ed., *Philosophy and Environmental Crisis* (Athens, GA: University of Georgia Press, 1974).

4. *Environmental Ethics: An Interdisciplinary Journal Dedicated to the Philosophical Aspects of Environmental Problems,* founded by Eugene C. Hargrove, editor-in-chief.

5. J. Baird Callicott, "Non-Anthropocentric Value Theory and Environmental Ethics," *American Philosophical Quarterly* 21 (1984):299.

6. Thomas E. Hill, Jr., review of Robert Elliott and Arran Gare, eds., *Environmental Philosophy, Environmental Ethics* 6 (1984):367.

7. The most widely quoted and reprinted is Lynn White, Jr., "The Historical Roots of Our Ecologic Crisis," *Science* 155 (1967):1203–7.

8. The most thorough discussion may be found in A.L. Herman, "The Genesis of Pollution" (unpublished manuscript).

9. Ian L. McHarg, *Design with Nature* (Garden City, NY: Doubleday and Company, Inc., 1969), p. 26. Of course, this sort of assault provoked a massive apologia. Francis A. Shaeffer, *Pollution and the Death of Man—The Christian View of Ecology* (Wheaton, IL: Tyndale House Publishers, 1971) represents the Protestant reply; Albert J. Fritsch, S.J., *Environmental Ethics: Choices for Concerned Citizen,* (Garden City, NY: Anchor Books, 1980), a Catholic reply; and John Passmore, *Man's Responsibility for Nature: Ecological Problems and Western Traditions* (New York: Charles Scribner's Sons, 1974), a historical-philosophical rejoinder.

10. Cf. J. Donald Hughes, "Ecology in Ancient Greece," *Inquiry* 18 (1975):115–25; *Ecology in Ancient Civilizations* (Albuquerque: University of New

Mexico Press, 1975); "The Environmental Ethics of the Pythagoreans," *Environmental Ethics* 2 (1980):195–213. See also, John Rodman, "The Other Side of Ecology in Ancient Greece: Comments on Hughes," *Inquiry* 19 (1976):108–12. For a somewhat programmatic outline of a critique of the Greek philosophical legacy, see J. Baird Callicott, "Traditional American Indian and Western European Attitudes Toward Nature: An Overview," *Environmental Ethics* 4 (1982):292–318.

11. Thomas S. Kuhn, *The Copernican Revolution: Planetary Astronomy and the Development of Western Thought* (Cambridge, MA: Harvard University Press, 1957), succinctly comments that "early in the seventeenth century atomism experienced an immense revival. . . . [A]tomism was firmly merged with Copernicanism as a fundamental tenet of the 'new philosophy' which directed the scientific imagination" (p. 237).

12. Cf. David L. Hall and Roger T. Ames, *Thinking Through Confucius* (Albany, NY: SUNY Press, 1987).

13. Ian McHarg, *Design with Nature,* p. 24.

14. Hwa Yol Jung, "Ecology, Zen, and Western Religious Thought," *Christian Century* 88 (1972):1153. A more circumspect discussion may be found in Hwa Yol Jung, "The Ecological Crisis: A Philosophic Perspective, East and West," *Bucknell Review* 20 (Winter 1972):25–44.

15. Lynn White, Jr., "Historical Roots," p. 1206. However, see the sobering discussion of Yi-fu Tuan, "Discrepancies Between Environmental Attitude and Behavior: Examples from Europe and China," *The Canadian Geographer* 12 (1968):176–83.

16. Gary Snyder, "Smokey the Bear Sutra." We quote from a typeset broadside Callicott received from the author after a poetry reading at Wisconsin State University-Stevens Point ca. 1970. No indication of who published it may be found. Instead, in the spirit of the times, at the end of the poem there is written in parentheses, "may be reproduced free forever." It has been recently reprinted in *Working the Woods, Working the Sea: An Anthology of Northwest Writing* (Port Townsend, WA: Empty Bowl, 1985). There Snyder explains the circumstances of its composition and circulation.

17. Harold J. Morowitz, "Biology as a Cosmological Science," *Main Currents in Modern Thought* 28 (1972):151–57.

18. William R. LaFleur, "Saigyō and the Buddhist Value of Nature," *History of Religions* 13 (1973–74):93–128, 227–48.

19. Roderick Nash, *Wilderness and the American Mind* (New Haven: Yale University Press, 1967), pp. 20–21, 192–93.

20. Huston Smith, "Tao Now: An Ecological Testament," in I.G. Barbour, ed., *Earth Might be Fair: Reflections on Ethics, Religion, and Ecology* (Englewood Cliffs, NJ: Prentice-Hall, Inc., 1972), pp. 66, 68–69.

21. A notable exception is Eliot Deutsch, "Vedanta and Ecology," in T.M.P. Mehadevan, ed., *Indian Philosophical Annual* 16 (1970): 1–10. Deutsch, however, does not appear to be directly or consciously responding to the suggestions in the environmental ethics literature.

22. Chung-ying Cheng, "Model of Causality in Chinese Philosophy: A Comparative Study," *Philosophy East and West* 26 (1976):12, 18.

23. The most recent of these has been edited by two of our contributors. See, Gerald James Larson and Eliot Deutsch, eds., *Interpretation Across Boundaries: New Essays in Comparative Philosophy* (Princeton, NJ: Princeton University Press, 1988).

24. For an introduction to the fundamental presuppositions of the Asian philosophic traditions, as we have here organized them, see the following resources. For China: David L. Hall and Roger T. Ames, *Thinking Through Confucius;* Richard J. Smith, *China's Cultural Heritage* (Boulder, CO: Westview Press, 1983); Tu Wei-ming, *Confucian Thought: Selfhood as Creative Transformation* (Albany, NY: SUNY Press, 1985). For Japan: Hajime Nakamura, *The Ways of Thinking of Eastern Peoples* (Honolulu: East-West Center Press, 1964); T.P. Kasulis, *Zen Action/Zen Person* (Honolulu: University of Hawaii Press, 1981); D.T. Suzuki, *Zen and Japanese Culture* (Princeton: Princeton University Press, 1959). For Buddhism: David J. Kalupahana, *Buddhist Philosophy: A Historical Analysis* (Honolulu: University of Hawaii Press, 1976); T.R.V. Murti, *The Central Philosophy of Buddhism* (London: George Allen & Unwin, 1955). For India: Karl H. Potter, *Presuppositions of India's Philosophies* (Englewood Cliffs, NJ: Prentice Hall, 1963); Ninian Smart, *Doctrine and Argument in Indian Philosophy* (London: George Allen & Unwin, 1964).

25. Holmes Rolston, III, "Can the East Help the West to Value Nature?" *Philosophy East and West* 37 (1987):172–90.

26. Lynn White, Jr., "Historical Roots," p. 1206.

Pacific Shift

1. Keiji Nishitani, *Religion and Nothingness* (Berkeley: University of California, 1982), p. 285.

2. See Russell Schweickart, "No Frames, No Boundaries," in *Earth's Answer: Explorations of Planetary Culture at the Lindisfarne Conferences* (New York: Harper and Row/Lindisfarne, 1977), pp. 3–13.

3. See Gregory Bateson, "Effects of Conscious Purpose on Human Adaptation," in *Steps to an Ecology of Mind* (New York: Ballantine, 1972), pp. 440–47; and *Mind and Nature: A Necessary Unity* (New York: Dutton, 1979), p. 32.

4. See James Lovelock, *Gaia: A New Look at Life on Earth* (New York and Oxford: Oxford University Press, 1979).

5. See Francisco Varela, "Living Ways of Sense-Making: A Middle Path for

Neuroscience," in *Disorder and Order*, ed. P. Livingstone, (Stanford: Stanford University Press, 1985).

6. See Humberto Maturana and Francisco Varela, *El arbol de conscimento* (Santiago, Chile: Editorial Universitaria, 1984), p. 89.

7. The material that is merely sketched here is treated in greater detail in my book, *Pacific Shift* (San Francisco: Sierra Club Books, 1986), chapter 3.

8. For a discussion of the relation between Carnot and Turner, see Michel Serres's brilliant essay, "Turnet traduit Carnot," in *Hermes III: La Traduction* (Paris: Edition de Minuit, 1974), pp. 233–44. For a discussion the narratives of evolution and the English novel, see Gillian Beer's *Darwin's Plots* (London: Routledge & Kegan Paul, 1983).

9. See John de Francis, *The Chinese Language,* (Honolulu: University of Hawaii Press, 1984).

10. See Lewis Thomas, "At the Mercy of Our Defenses," in *Earth's Answer,* pp. 156–69.

11. See Immanuel Wallerstein, *The Modern World-System: Capitalist Agriculture and the Origins of the European World-Economy in the Sixteenth Century* (New York: Academic Press, 1974), p. 347.

12. As quoted in Nishitani's *Religion and Nothingness,* p. 107.

Biology as a Cosmological Science

1. J.D. Bernal, "Molecular Structure, Biochemical Function, and Evolution," Chapter 5 of *Theoretical and Mathematical Biology,* edited by T.H. Waterman and H.J. Morowitz (New York: Blaisdell Publishing Co., 1965).

2. The general viewpoint on Spencer comes from an essay by P. Medawar in his book, *The Art of the Soluble* (London: Methuen, 1967).

3. From "The Hollow Men," by T.S. Eliot.

4. See *The Two Cultures and the Scientific Revolution,* by C.P. Snow (Cambridge University Press, 1959).

5. I am indebted to Dr. E. Broda, who pointed out to me this quotation from Boltzmann and provided the English translation given here.

6. H.J. Morowitz, *Energy Flow in Biology* (New York: Academic Press, 1968).

7. P. Teilhard de Chardin, *The Phenomenon of Man* (New York: Harper & Row, 1959).

8. W. Elsasser, *Atom and Organism* (Princeton, NJ: Princeton University Press, 1966).

9. Morowitz, op. cit.

10. F.S.C. Northrop, *The Meeting of East and West* (New York: The Macmillan Co.).

11. P. Dahlke, *Buddhism and Science* (London: Macmillan and Co., 1913).

The Metaphysical Implications of Ecology

1. See for example, E.A. Burtt, *The Metaphysical Foundations of Modern Science* (Garden City, NY: Anchor Books, 1954); and Ernest Nagel, *The Structure of Science* (New York: Harcourt, Brace and World, 1961).

2. The term "New Ecology" was first used in H.G. Wells, with Julian Huxley and G.P. Wells, *The Science of Life* (New York: Garden City Publishing Co., 1939) p. 961, to characterize ecology after the quantifiable "ecosystem" model was developed by Arthur Tansley in 1935. See Warwick Fox, "Deep Ecology: A New Philosophy of Our Time?" *The Ecologist* 14 (1984):194–200; and J. Baird Callicott, "Intrinsic Value, Quantum Theory, and Environmental Ethics," *Environmental Ethics* 7 (1985):257–75, for a discussion of the convergence and complementary characteristics of the New Physics and New Ecology.

3. John Gribbin, *In Search of Schrodinger's Cat: Quantum Physics and Reality* (New York: Bantam, 1984), claims that while "Newton had it [atomism] in mind in his work on physics and optics, atoms only really became a part of scientific thought in the latter part of the eighteenth century when the French chemist Antoine Lavoisier investigated why things burn" (p. 19). But, according to Thomas Kuhn, *The Copernican Revolution: Planetary Astronomy and the Development of Western Thought* (Cambridge, MA: Harvard University Press, 1957), whose historical point of view is somewhat broader than Gribbin's, "early in the seventeenth century atomism experienced an immense revival. . . . Atomism was firmly merged with Copernicanism as a fundamental tenet of the 'new philosophy' which directed the scientific imagination" (p. 237).

4. "Primary" and "secondary" qualities were terms given to Galileo Galilei's distinction between putative actual and nonactual qualities of the elements by John Locke, *Essay Concerning Human Understanding* (New York: E.P. Dutton and Co., Inc., 1961). Locke attempted to ground the distinction empirically rather than theoretically, the futility of which was subsequently demonstrated by Berkeley. The revealing terms, "the full" and "the empty," are attributed to the fifth-century atomists by Aristotle, *Metaphysica,* 985b4.

5. See G.S. Kirk and J.E. Raven, *The Presocratic Philosophers: A Critical History with a Selection of Texts* (Cambridge: Cambridge University Press, 1962); and E.A. Burtt, *The Metaphysical Foundations of Modern Science.*

6. Ibid.

7. See Ernst Nagel, *The Structure of Science.*

8. Ibid.

9. For Democritus's materialistic psychology, see W.K.C. Guthrie, *A History of Greek Philosophy,* vol. 2 (Cambridge: Cambridge University Press, 1965); for Lucretius's, see Titus Lucretius Carus, *De Rerum Natura,* trans. Robert Latham (Harmondsworth: Penguin, 1951); and for Hobbes's, see Thomas Hobbes, *Leviathan* (New York: Collier Books, 1962). For Pythagoras's dualism, see W.K.C. Guthrie, *A History of Greek Philosophy,* vol. 1 (Cambridge: Cambridge University Press, 1962); for Plato's, see especially "Phaedo" in *Plato I: Euthyphro, Apology, Crito, Phaedo, and Phaedrus With an English Translation by Harold Fowler North* (London: William Heineman Ltd. for The Loeb Classical Library, 1914); and for Descartes's see *Meditations on First Philosophy,* in E.S. Haldane and G.R.T. Ross, trans., *The Philosophical Works of Descartes,* vol. 1 (Cambridge: Cambridge University Press, 1911).

10. There is remarkable unanimity of thought on this head among Pythagoras, Plato, and Descartes, the West's most influential dualists.

11. See Thomas Hobbes, *Leviathan.*

12. See Immanuel Kant, *Foundations of the Metaphysics of Morals* (New York: Bobbs-Merrill Co., Inc., 1959).

13. See especially Plato, *Parmenides* and *Phaedo.*

14. See Aristotle, *De Partibus Animalium* and *Politicus.*

15. Ibid.

16. Anthony Quinton, "The Right Stuff," *The New York Review of Books* 32 (Dec. 5, 1985):52.

17. See Ernst Haeckel, *Generelle Morphologie der Organismen,* 2 vols. (Berlin: Reimer, 1966); and Carl Linnaeus, "Specimen Academicum de Oeconomia Naturae," *Amoenitates Academicae II: Holmae* (Lugdoni Batavorum: Apud Cornelium Haak, 1751).

18. Donald Worster, *Nature's Economy: The Roots of Ecology* (Garden City, NY: Anchor Books, 1979).

19. See Gilbert White, *The Natural History of Selborne* (New York: Harper, 1842).

20. See John Burroughs, "The Noon of Science" in *The Writings of John Burroughs,* vol. 17: *The Summit of the Years* (Boston: Houghton Mifflin and Company, 1913); and Frederick E. Clements, *Research Methods in Ecology* (Lincoln: University Publishing Co., 1905).

21. See R. Tobey, *Saving the Prairies: The Life Cycle of the Founding School of American Plant Ecology, 1895–1955* (Berkeley: University of California Press, 1981); and Robert P. McIntosh, *The Background of Ecology: Concept and Theory* (Cambridge: Cambridge University Press, 1985).

22. See Charles Elton, *Animal Ecology* (New York: Macmillan Co., 1927).

23. See Arthur G. Tansley, "The Use and Abuse of Vegetational Concepts and Terms," *Ecology* 16 (1935):292–303.

24. Donald Worster, *Nature's Economy,* p. 303.

25. Ibid., p. 332.

26. See Aldo Leopold, *A Sand County Almanac and Sketches Here and There* (New York: Oxford University Press, 1949).

27. See Aldo Leopold, "Some Fundamentals of Conservation," *Environmental Ethics* 1 (1979):131–48.

28. Aldo Leopold, *A Sand County Almanac,* p. 216.

29. Paul Shepard, "A Theory of the Value of Hunting," *Twenty-Fourth North American Wildlife Conference* (1957):505–6.

30. Harold J. Morowitz, "Biology as a Cosmological Science," *Main Currents in Modern Thought* 28 (1972):156.

31. Arne Naess, "The Shallow and the Deep, Long-Range Ecology Movement. A Summary," *Inquiry* 16 (1973):98.

32. Ibid., p. 95.

33. Werner Heisenberg, *Physics and Philosophy: The Revolution in Modern Science* (New York: Harper and Row, 1958), remarked: "[W]e may say that all elementary particles consist of energy. This could be interpreted as defining energy as the primary substance of the world. . . . The elementary particles are certainly not eternal and indestructible units of matter, they can actually be transformed into each other. . . . Such events have been frequently observed and offer the best proof that all particles are made of the same substance: energy" (pp. 70–71).

34. Gary Snyder, "Song of the Taste," in Gary Snyder, *Regarding Wave* (New York: New Directions Publishing Corporation, 1967), p. 17.

35. See Naess, "The Shallow and the Deep, Long-Range Ecology Movement."

36. Eliot Deutsch, "Vedanta and Ecology," in T.M.P. Mehederan, ed., *Indian Philosophical Annual* 7 (Madras: The Center for Advanced Study in Philosophy, 1970):1–10.

37. Paul Shepard, "Ecology and Man: A Viewpoint," in P. Shepard and D. McKinley, eds., *The Subversive Science: Essays Toward an Ecology of Man* (Boston: Houghton Mifflin Co., 1967), p. 3.

38. Fritjof Capra, *The Tao of Physics: An Exploration of the Parallels Between Modern Physics and Eastern Mysticism* (Boulder: Shambala, 1975), pp. 30–31.

39. Eliot Deutsch, "Vedanta and Ecology," p. 4.

40. See Kenneth Goodpaster, "From Egoism to Environmentalism," in K. Goodpaster and K. Sayre, eds., *Ethics and Problems of the 21st Century* (Notre Dame: University of Notre Dame Press, 1979), 21–35.

41. Paul Shepard, "Ecology and Man: A Viewpoint," p. 2.

42. See Alan Watts, *The Book on the Taboo Against Knowing Who You Are* (New York: Pantheon Books, 1966).

43. Holmes Rolston, III, "Lake Solitude: The Individual in Wilderness," *Main Currents in Modern Thought* 31 (1975):122.

44. Paul Shepard, "Ecology and Man: A Viewpoint," p. 4.

45. See Paul Shepard, *Thinking Animals: Animals and the Development of Human Intelligence* (New York: The Viking Press, 1978).

46. See Jonathan Powers, *Philosophy and the New Physics* (London: Methuen, 1982).

47. See J. Baird Callicott, "Intrinsic Value, Quantum Theory, and Environmental Ethics."

48. See Kenneth Goodpaster, "From Egoism to Environmentalism."

49. Aldo Leopold, *A Sand County Almanac with Essays on Conservation from Round River* (New York: Ballantine Books, 1966), p. 197.

50. John Seed, "Anthropocentrism," Appendix E in Bill Devall and George Sessions, *Deep Ecology: Living as if Nature Mattered* (Salt Lake City: Peregrin Smith Books, 1985) p. 243.

The Continuity of Being

1. Frederick W. Mote, *Intellectual Foundations of China* (New York: Alfred A. Knopf, 1971), pp. 17–18.

2. Ibid., p. 19.

3. For a thought-provoking discussion on this issue, see N.J. Girardot, *Myth and Meaning in Early Taoism* (Berkeley: University of California Press, 1983), pp. 275–310.

4. For a suggestive methodological essay, see William G. Boltz, "Kung Kung and the Flood: Reverse Euphemerism in the *Yao Tien*," *T'oung Pao* 67 (1981):141–53. Professor Boltz's effort to reconstruct the Kung Kung myth indicates the possibility of an indigenous creation myth.

5. Tu Wei-ming, "Shih-t'an Chung-kuo che-hsüeh chung te san-ko chi-tiao" [A preliminary discussion on the three basic motifs in Chinese philosophy], *Chung-kuo che-hsüeh shih yen-chiu* [Studies on the history of Chinese philosophy] (Peking: Society for the Study of the History of Chinese Philosophy) 2 (March 1981):19–21.

6. Mote, *Intellectual Foundations of China,* p. 20.

7. Ibid.

8. See Jung's Foreword to the *I Ching (Book of Changes),* translated into English by Cary F. Baynes from the German translation of Richard Wilhelm, Bollingen Series, vol. 19 (Princeton, N.J.: Princeton University Press, 1967), p. xxiv.

9. Needham's full statement reads as follows: "It was an ordered harmony of wills without an ordainer; it was like the spontaneous yet ordered, in the sense of patterned, movements of dancers in a country dance of figures, none of whom are bound by law to do what they do, nor yet pushed by others coming behind, but cooperate in a voluntary harmony of wills." See Joseph Needham and Wang Ling, *Science and Civilisation in China,* vol. 2 (Cambridge: Cambridge University Press, 1969), p. 287.

10. Actually, the dichotomy of spirit and matter does not feature prominently in Chinese thought; see Tu, *Chung-kuo che-shüeh shih yen-chiu,* pp. 21–22.

11. Wing-tsit Chan, trans. and comp., *A Source Book in Chinese Philosophy* (Princeton, N.J.: Princeton University Press, 1969), p. 784.

12. Ibid.

13. For a notable exception to this general interpretive situation in the People's Republic of China, see Chang Tai-nien, *Chung-kuo che-hsüeh fa-wei* [Exploring some of the delicate issues in Chinese philosophy] (T'ai-yuan, Shansi: People's Publishing Co., 1981), pp. 11–38; 275–306.

14. For a general discussion on this vital issue from a medical viewpoint, see Manfred Porkert, *The Theoretical Foundations of Chinese Medicine: Systems of Correspondence* (Cambridge, Mass: MIT Press, 1974).

15. Tu, "Shih-t'an Chung-kuo che-hsüeh," pp. 19–24.

16. A paradigmatic discussion on this is to be found in the *Commentaries on the Book of Changes.* See Wing-tsit Chan, *Source Book in Chinese Philosophy,* p. 264.

17. See Chang Tsai's "Correcting Youthful Ignorance," in Wing-tsit Chan, *Source Book in Chinese Philosophy,* p. 501.

18. For this reference in the *Chou I,* see *A Concordance to Yi Ching,* Harvard-Yenching Institute Sinological Index Series Supplement No. 10 (reprint; Taipei: Chinese Materials and Research Aids Service Center, Inc., 1966), 1/1.

19. The idea of the "dynastic cycle" may give one the impression that Chinese history is nondevelopmental. See Edwin O. Reischauer and John K. Fairbank, *East Asia: The Great Tradition* (Boston: Houghton Mifflin Co., 1960), pp. 114–18.

20. Chuang Tzu, chap. 7. See the Harvard Yenching Index on the *Chuang Tzu,* 20/7/11.

21. See William T. de Bary, Wing-tsit Chan, and Burton Watson, comps., *Sources of Chinese Tradition* (New York: Columbia University, 1960), pp. 191–92.

22. Wing-tsit Chan, *Source Book on Chinese Philosophy,* pp. 500–1.

23. Ibid., pp. 262–66. This idea underlies the philosophy of change.

24. Ibid., sec. 14, p. 505. In this translation, *ch'i* is rendered "material force." The words *yin* and *yang* in brackets are added by me.

25. Ibid., pp. 698–99.

26. Ibid., p. 496.

27. Wu Ch'eng-en, *Hsi yu chi,* trans. Anthony C. Yü as *Journey to the West,* 4 vols. (Chicago: University of Chicago Press, 1977–), 1:67–78.

28. Ts'ao Hsüeh-ch'in (Cao Xuequin), *Hung-lou meng* [Dream of the Red Chamber], trans. David Hawkes as *The Story of the Stone*, 5 vols. (Middlesex, England: Penguin Books, 1973–), 1:47–49.

29. For two useful discussions on the story, see Fu Hsi-hua, *Pai-she-chuan chi* [An anthology of the White Snake story] (Shanghai: Shanghai Publishing Co., 1955), and P'an Chiang-tung, *Pai-she ku-shih yen-chiu* [A study of the White Snake story] (Taipei: Students' Publishers, 1981).

30. P. Ryckmans, "Les propos sur la peinture de Shi Tao traduction et commentaire," *Arst Asiatique* 14 (1966): 123–24.

31. Teng Shu-p'in, "Shang-ch'uan ching-ying-yü te i-shu" [The finest essence of mountain and river—the art of jade], in *Chung-kuo wen-hua hsin-lun [New views on Chinese culture]* (Taipei: Lien-ching, 1983), Section on Arts, pp. 253–304.

32. Wing-tsit Chan, *Source Book in Chinese Philosophy,* p. 463. This translation renders *ch'i* as "material force."

33. Ibid.

34. Ibid.

35. Ibid., p. 530.

36. Wang Ken, "Yü Nan-tu chu-yu" [Letter to friends of Nan-tu], in *Wang Hsin-chai hsien-sheng ch'üan-chi* [The complete works of Wang Ken] (1507 edition, Harvard-Yenching Library), 4.16b.

37. Wing-tsit Chan, *Source Book in Chinese Philosophy,* p. 98.

38. Ibid., p. 699

39. *Menicus,* 7A4.

40. Wing-tsit Chan, *Source Book in Chinese Philosophy,* pp. 699–700.

41. For example, in Chu Hsi's discussion of moral cultivation, the Heavenly Principle is clearly contrasted with selfish desires. See Wing-tsit Chan, *Source Book in Chinese Philosophy,* pp. 605–6.

42. Ibid., p. 539.

43. For a suggestive essay on this, see R.G.H. Siu, *Ch'i: A Neo-Taoist Approach to Life* (Cambridge, Mass.: MIT Press, 1974).

44. Roman Jakobson, "Two Aspects of Language and Two Types of Aphasic Disturbances," in Roman Jakobson and Morris Halle, *Fundamentals of Language* (Gravenhage: Mouton, 1956), pp. 55–82. I am grateful to Professor Yu-kung Kao for this reference.

45. *Chuang Tzu,* chap. 4. The precise quotation can be found in *Chuang Tzu ying-te* (Peking: Havard-Yenching Institute, 1947). 9/4/27.

46. *Chuang Tzu, cap.* 2 an *Chuang Tzu ying-te,* 3/2/8.

47. For a systematic discussion of this, see Yu-kung Kao and Kang-i Sun Chang, "Chinese 'Lyric Criticism' in the Six Dynasties," American Council of Learned Societies Conference on Theories of the Arts in China (June 1979), to be included in *Theories of the Arts in China,* eds. Susan Bush and Christian Murck (Princeton, N.J.: Princeton University Press, forthcoming).

Human/Nature in Nietzsche and Taoism

1. Friedrich Nietzsche, *Thus Spoke Zarathustra,* Subsequent references to Nietzsche's works will be made mostly within the body of the text, by means of the following abbreviations and the section or aphorism number:

AC - *The Antichrist*
BGE - *Beyond Good and Evil*
HA - *Human, All-too-human*
GS - *The Gay Science*

While I have in most cases consulted the available English translations, the translations of the quotations are my own—for the sake of preservation of the imagery—from the *Kritische Studienausgabe (KSA)* of Nietzsche's *Werke,* edited by Colli and Montinari (Berlin: de Gruyter, 1980).

2. *Chuang-tzu* 17 (*IC* 149). In quoting from the *Chuang-tzu,* I refer to the chapter number and also to the partial translation by A.C. Graham, *Chuang-tzu: The Inner Chapters* (London: George Allen and Unwin, 1981), abbreviated as *IC,* followed by the page number. The bulk of the discussion is based on the seven "Inner Chapters," which are generally agreed to be from the hand of Chuang-tzu himself, though there will be occasional reference to passages from the Outer Chapters which are in harmony with the core of the work. References to the *Tao Te Ching,* will be to

the number of the chapter; I have used the translation by D.C. Lau, *Lao Tzu: Tao Te Ching* (London and New York: Penguin Books, 1963), and also Ch'en Ku-ying, *Lao Tzu: Text, Notes and Comments,* translated by Rhett W. Young and Roger T. Ames (San Francisco: Chinese Materials Center, 1977). For a comparison of Nietzsche's idea of the dance and Chuang-tzu's notion of "free and easy wandering" *(hsiao yao yu),* much of which is relevant to the themes of the present essay, see Graham Parkes, "The Wandering Dance: *Chuang-tzu & Zarathustra," Philosophy East and West* 33, no. 3 (1983).

3. Other relevant terms are: *te,* or "power," which refers to the "natural potency" a being gets from *t'ien* and/or *tao; hsing,* meaning the "nature" of a being (and especially of the human being); *chen jen,* the "genuine, authentic, or true person;" and *tzu-jan,* meaning "spontaneous activity" or, more literally, "self-so-ing." These last two terms are characteristically Taoist, making their first appearance in the *Lao-tzu* and *Chuang-tzu.*

4. "On the Future of our Educational Institutions," lecture 4. For an interesting selection of very early (unpublished) writings by Nietzsche on his love of nature, see Alwin Mittasch, *Nietzsche als Naturphilosoph* (Stuttgart: Kröner, 1952), chapter 2. "The Young Nietzsche's Feeling for and Sense of Nature."

5. "On Truth and Lie in the Extra-Moral Sense," a translation of which can be found in Daniel Breazeale, ed., *Philosophy and Truth: Selections from Nietzsche's Notebooks of the Early 1870s* (Atlantic Highlands, N.J.: Humanities Press, 1979). One is reminded of the numerous passages in *Chuang-tzu* which transpose the reader into the perspectives of various kinds of animals; and also of William Blake's lines concerning "Energy [as] Eternal Delight":

How do you know but ev'ry Bird that cuts the airy way
Is an immense world of delight clos'd by your senses five?

"The Marriage of Heaven and Hell"

6. *On the Genealogy of Morals,* Essay III, 9.

7. See, in particular, *Lao-tzu* 18, 38; and *Chuang-tzu* 2, 6, 13, 14 (*IC* 60, 91–92, 128–29).

8. Zarathustra III, 4. References to *Zarathustra* will be to the book and chapter numbers—the most useful convention, even in the absence of numbered chapters in the original.

9. *Chuang-tzu* 1, 4, 20 (*IC* 47, 72–75, 121). For a discussion of this theme in *Chuang-tzu* with reference to Heidegger's ideas about *Zuhandenheit* and the utilitarian standpoint, see my "Thoughts on the Way: *Being and Time* via Lao-Chuang," in Graham Parkes, ed., *Heidegger and Asian Thought* (Honolulu: University of Hawaii Press, 1987).

10. *Chuang-tzu* 2 (*IC* 58). Compare the "daemonic man" in chapter 1, who

"sucks in the wind, drinks the dew [and] rides the vapour of the clouds" (*IC* 46), and the one in chapter 6 who is able "to climb the sky and roam the mists" (*IC* 89).

11. A fine treatment of Chuang-tzu's idea of responding in full awareness can be found in A.C. Graham's "Taoist Spontaneity and the Dichotomy of 'Is' and 'Ought'," in Victor H. Mair, ed., *Experimental Essays on Chuang-tzu* (Honolulu: University of Hawaii Press, 1983).

12. For a more detailed discussion of this theme, see Graham Parkes, "The Overflowing Soul: Images of Transformation in Nietzsche's *Zarathustra*," *Man and World* 16 (1983).

13. *Zarathustra* II, 10 and IV, 11. The tree of life needs the darkness of the earth, the death of winter, and the decay of foliage in order to be able to extend its life up into the heights and light.

14. In "The Wandering Dance," loc. cit.

15. *Chuang-tzu* 2, and 17 (*IC* 61, 123). Compare the rather Zarathustrian passage in chapter 6 in which Confucius says to Yen Hui: "You dream that you are a bird and fly away in the sky, dream that you are a fish and plunge into the deep. There's no telling whether the man who speaks now is the waker or the dreamer. Rather than go towards what suits you, laugh; rather than acknowledge it with your laughter, shove it from you" (*IC* 91). It is a little-known—and intriguing—fact that Heidegger was quoting the story of the minnows in discussions of empathetic intersubjectivity as early as 1930; see the Prologue to "Thoughts on the Way," loc. cit.

16. For an account of the history of the idea of participation in the Western tradition, see Owen Barfield, *Saving the Appearances* (New York: Harcourt, 1965); and for a helpful articulation of the distinctions among the notions of animism, anthropomorphism, and personification from a depth-psychological perspective aligned with Nietzsche's, see chapter 1 of James Hillman, *Revisioning Psychology* (New York: Harper, 1976).

17. *GS* 57, which it is important to read in connection with aphorisms 54 and 56–59. One is reminded in this context of Freud's ideas about archaic inheritance and Jung's discussions of the productions of the collective unconscious.

18. This theme is especially prominent in Nishitani's extended treatment of Nietzsche in his 1949 text *Nihirizumu*. See *The Self-Overcoming of Nihilism*, trans. Graham Parkes with Setsuko Aihara (University of California Press, forthcoming).

19. This distinction is made in section 398 of *The Will to Power,* where Nietzsche goes on to characterize breeding as "a means by which the forces of humanity are stored up monumentally, so that races can build upon the work of their ancestors—not only outwardly, but inside, growing organically out of them . . ."

20. Again, this is a major theme in Nishitani's treatment of Nietzsche in *The Self-Overcoming of Nihilism*.

On Seeking a Change of Environment

1. For a more elaborate employment of this culturalogical method, see my *The Uncertain Phoenix* (New York: Fordham, 1982), chap. 1, "Speculation and Foresight."

2. I have discussed First and Second problematic thinking in my *Eros and Irony* (Albany, New York: SUNY Press, 1982), pp. 114–23.

3. See ibid., pp. 123–48.

4. The attempt by Martin Heidegger to uncover a new language for philosophy has recently been renewed by Jacques Derrida, who seeks to employ a language of *difference* that avoids the apparent necessity to reference objects which cannot in fact be made present by the traditional language of metaphysics.

5. For the development of such a theory of language, see David L. Hall and Roger T. Ames, *Thinking Through Confucius* (Albany, New York: SUNY Press, 1987), chap. 5. This work considers the subject of language within the context of Confucius's thinking, but much of what is developed there is relevant to the consideration of philosophical Taoism as well.

6. Witness the wildly ad hoc (and, therefore, broadly irrelevant) attempts on the part of twentieth-century mathematicians and logicians to resolve the Zenonian paradoxes.

7. See Hall, *The Uncertain Phoenix,* chaps. 5 and 6, for a detailed discussion of the relevance of certain of these Taoist concepts to an interpretation of future developments in technological society.

Putting the Te Back into Taoism

1. J. Baird Callicott, "Non-Anthropocentric Value Theory and Environmental Ethics," *American Philosophical Quarterly* 21 (1984):299.

2. Friedrich Nietzsche, *Beyond Good and Evil,* par. 211.

3. To be fair to Callicott, in his more recent paper entitled "Conceptual Resources for Environmental Ethics in Asian Traditions of Thought: A Propaedeutic," *Philosophy East and West* 37 (1987), p. 115, he states explicitly: "Environmental ethics, in other words, begins with the assumption that traditional metaphysics and moral theory are more at the root of the environmental problems than tools for their solution."

4. See the descriptions of Lao Tzu and Chuang Tzu in the last chapter of the *Chuang Tzu.*

5. This term was coined by David L. Hall for our *Thinking Through Confucius* (Albany, NY: SUNY Press, 1987).

6. Po-Keung Ip, "Taoism and the Foundations of Environmental Ethics," *Environmental Ethics* 5 (1983):335.

7. J. Baird Callicott, "Conceptual Resources for Environmental Ethics."

8. See J. Baird Callicott, "The Metaphysical Implications of Ecology," passim.

9. What follows here is summarized from the introduction to our book, *Thinking Through Confucius,* and from an earlier paper of mine, "The Meaning of Body in Classical Chinese Thought," *International Philosophical Quarterly* 24, no. 1 (1984):39–53.

10. David Keightley has recently been doing some reconstructive philosophical work on the oracle bones that suggests a notion of conceptual polarity dating back at least as far as the early Shang period.

11. See statements on this distinction in such divergent sources as the Confucian *Analects* 13/23 and A.N. Whitehead, *Modes of Thought* (New York: MacMillan, 1938), pp. 60ff. For David L. Hall's development of this distinction, see especially *Eros and Irony: A Prelude to Philosophical Anarchism* (Albany, NY: SUNY Press, 1982).

12. See Stephen C. Pepper, *World Hypotheses* (Berkeley: University of California Press, 1942), pp. 162ff.

13. As we shall see below, a particular in this context is to be understood as a relational "focus" rather than an essentialistic, atomistic "thing."

14. See K.C. Chang, *Food in Chinese Culture* (New Haven: Yale University Press, 1977), introduction.

15. See *Lü-shih ch'un-ch'iu pen-wei-p'ien*[dk] (Peking: Shang-yeh Press, 1984), pp. 7–8.

16. See, for example, M. Loewe, *Life and Death in Han China* (London: George Allen Unwin, 1982), p. 63; K. Schipper, "The Taoist Body," in *History of Religions* 17 (1978), p. 371; D.L. Hall, *Eros and Irony,* pp. 246–49; Tu Wei-ming, *Centrality and Commonality: An Essay on Chung-yung,* (Honolulu, University Press of Hawaii, 1976), pp. 118–19.

17. The former belongs to Schipper, ibid.: "And it is a fact that in China, as in our society, the female sexual and reproductive functions have been much more tabooed than the male ones. I cannot help wondering if this taboo could not also help to explain the almost total denial of this creation myth in Chinese classical literature." The latter is Hall's. See his paper, "Process and Anarchy: A Taoist Vision of Creativity," *Philosophy East and West* 28 (1978):271–85, and *Eros and Irony.*

18. Hall, *Eros and Irony.* This same point is made by David Loy in his definition of *wei wu-wei* as nondual action. Loy suggests that *wu-wei* action is nondual in the sense that it does not allow a final distinction between subject and object. He concludes that "if the universe is whole . . . and if . . . each particular is

not isolated but contains and manifests that whole, then whenever 'I' act it is not 'I' but the whole universe that 'does' the action or rather *is* the action. If we accept that the universe is self-caused, then it acts freely whenever anything is done. Thus, from the nondualist perspective, complete determinism turns out to be equivalent to absolute freedom." See *"Wei-wu-wei*: Nondual action," *Philosophy East and West* 35 (1985), p. 84.

19. The character, *chen,* is revealing of the way in which truth and reality were perceived in this tradition. First, this character means both true and real, and second, it is constituted by and classified under the radical for transformation, *hua.*

20. The historian, Michael Loewe, goes so far as to assert that for the classical Chinese context, "in neither mythology nor philosophy can there be found the idea of *creatio ex nihilo*." See Loewe, *Life and Death in Han China,* p. 63.

21. Joseph Needham uses *Hsün Tzu* 9/13a (Dubs, trans., p. 136) to suggest that there is an Aristotelian distinction between living and nonliving substance in this tradition. While the *Hsün Tzu* passage is quite explicit, it might reflect a Confucian preoccupation with the human being that is not representative of the tradition, and must be measured against the fact that *hsing* in the earliest sources meant not only "human nature," but the fundamental nature of all things. For example, in a text as early as the *Shu-ching* (Chün-ch'en), where *sheng* is being used for *hsing,* it states that "the masses have an abundance of *sheng,* and shift their ground in response to things."

22. See D.C. Lau, trans., *Chinese Classics: Tao Te Ching* (Hong Kong: Chinese University Press, 1982), p. 156, for a discussion of the dating of these two texts. On the basis of taboos, Lau determines that the so-called A text dates from before the death of Kao Tsu in 195 B.C., and the B text from before the death of Emperor Hui in 180 B.C.

23. Ibid., which also contains the original translation, p. ix.

24. Ibid.

25. Ibid., p. xv.

26. Ibid., p. xxxiv.

27. *Shih-chi* PNP 130:4b.

28. W.T. Chan, *A Source Book in Chinese Philosophy* (Princeton: Princeton University Press, 1963), p. 136.

29. See *Shih-chi* (Peking: Chung-hua, 1962), p. 3288.

30. See, for example, Donald Munro, *The Concept of Man in Ancient China* (Stanford: Stanford University Press, 1969), p. 147.

31. Their argument is that *sheng* also means "to climb" as does *teng*[dl], and that idiomatically in the Ch'i dialect, *teng* can mean "to get" (*te*). Therefore, *sheng* here *really* means "to get."

32. My colleague, Graham Parkes, suggests a resonance here with Heidegger's meditations on the pre-Socratics' use of *physis,* defining it as *"das waltende Aufgehen":* "powering arising."

33. B. Karlgren, "Glosses on *Book of Documents,*" *Bulletin of the Museum of Far Eastern Antiquities* 20–21 (1948–49:120).

34. The *Shuo-wen* gives the graph with "tree" *(mu*[dm]*)* as a constituent element, as an archaic form of *chih* in the small seal script.

35. In the human context, this might account for the *Shuo-wen* definition of *te* as "getting from oneself within and from others without *(wai te yü jen, nei te yü chi yeh*[dn]*)."*

36. *Chuang Tzu* 64/23/70ff. See Burton Watson, trans., *The Complete Works of Chuang Tzu* (New York: Columbia University Press, 1968), p. 259: A.C. Graham (trans.), *Chuang-tzu: The Seven Inner Chapters and other Writings from the Book Chuang-tzu* (London: George Allen & Unwin, 1981), p. 190.

37. *Tao-te-ching* 34.

38. Ibid., 51.

39. Ibid., 28.

40. Ibid., 55.

41. *Han Fei Tzu* 95:8 and *Tao-te-ching* 38.

42. *Chuang Tzu* 14/5/47, Graham translation, p. 81.

43. *Chuang Tzu* 2/1/32 and 12/5/8.

44. *Chuang Tzu* 19/6/89ff.

45. *Analects* 12/10 and 12/21.

46. *Tao-te-ching* 79.

47. *Chuang Tzu* 7/3/4ff.

48. *Chuang Tzu* 19, passim.

49. See P. Boodberg, "Philological Notes on Chapter One of the *Lao Tzu,*" *Harvard Journal of Asiatic Studies* (1957):598–618. He also argues for the primacy of the verbal *tao*.

50. Here are four such occurrences. See J. Legge, *The Chinese Classics* (London, 1865), vol. 3. pp. 99, 102, 113, 119.

51. See, for example, Holmes Rolston, III, "Can We and Ought We to Follow Nature?," *Environmental Ethics* 1 (1979):7–30.

52. W.T. Chan, *The Way of Lao Tzu* (New York: Bobbs-Merill, 1963), p. 9.

53. T. Izutsu, *A Comparative Study of the Key Philosophical Concepts in Sufism and Taoism II* (Tokyo: Keio Institute of Cultural and Linguistic Studies, 1967), p. 91.

54. Yü Ying-shih, "The 'Philosophical Breakthrough' and the Chinese Mind" in *Che-hsüeh nien k'an* [Bulletin of the Chinese Philosophical Association] (1983):171.

55. Joseph Needham, *Science and Civilisation in China* (Cambridge: Cambridge University Press, 1954–), 2:36–37. Needham describes the *tao* in these terms while at the same time asserting: "We believe that the Chinese mind throughout the ages did not, on the whole, feel the need for metaphysics; physical Nature (with all that implied at the higher levels) sufficed. The Chinese were extremely loath to separate the One from the Many or the 'spiritual' from the 'material.' Organic naturalism was their *philosophia perennis*" (p. 37). While this particular statement would seem to have an affinity with our interpretation of *tao,* Needham is not always consistent with his important insights, and certainly could be clearer.

56. *Tao-te-ching* 42.

57. Ibid., 55.

58. For a justification for reading *chih*[do]—most often translated as "knowing"—as "realizing," see my paper, "Confucius and the Ontology of Knowing," in *Interpreting Across Boundaries,* eds. Eliot Deutsch and Gerald Larson: 265–79.

59. *Chuang Tzu* 51/20/6; cf. Graham translation, p. 121.

60. Robert C. Neville, *The Tao and the Daimon* (Albany, NY: SUNY Press, 1982), p. 137.

61. For the relationship between these two terms in the *Tao-te-ching* itself, see chapter 37 where *tso* seems to mean *wei*[cz].

62. See Bernhard Karlgren, *Grammata Serica Recensa* (Stockholm: Museum of Far Eastern Antiquities, 1950).

63. The "one-sidedness" of this kind of activity is suggested by a phonological relationship with *pei*[dp], passive indicator from "to be covered,"[dq] "one-sided = insincere," *pi*[dr], "they, that."

64. David L. Hall, *The Uncertain Phoenix: Adventures Toward a Post-Cultural Sensibility* (New York: Fordham University Press, 1982), p. 249.

65. See also *Tao-te-ching* 2, 10, 37, 43, 48, and 63. I translate *chih che*[ds] (Ma-wang-tui texts just have *chih*) as "erudite" here to convey the negative sense of this category. "Erudition" rather than "wisdom" suggests the imposition of predetermined structures on experience, and is a source of distortion rather than edification. Because these structures mediate one's own personal experience, they inhibit participation. "Erudition" thus contrasts with "proper order"—order that is "made one's own" through participation. I deliberately choose the term proper to describe order *(chih)* because of its root meaning "to make something one's own," as

in "property" or "appropriate." The kind of order suggested here is, from a human perspective, always personal and participatory.

66. Ibid., 2, 10, and 51.

67. Joseph Needham, *Science and Civilisation,* pp. 59–61, also p. 164. For the citations of a legion of such commentators and a sustained argument against this interpretation, see my "Taoism and the Androgynous Ideal," *Historical Reflections/ Reflections Historiques* 8, no. 3 (1981):21–46, and "The Common Ground of Self-cultivation in Classical Taoism and Confucianism," *Tsinghua Journal of Chinese Studies* 30 (1986).

68. David L. Hall, *Phoenix,* p. 249.

69. A.C. Graham, "Taoist Spontaneity and the Dichotomy of 'Is' and 'Ought,' " in *Experimental Essays on Chuang-tzu,* ed. Victor H. Mair (Honolulu: University of Hawaii Press, 1983), p. 8.

70. Ibid., pp. 7, 11.

71. Lynn White, Jr., "The Historical Roots of Our Ecologic Crisis," in *Ecology and Religion in History,* ed. David and Eileen Spring, (New York: Harper & Row, 1974), p. 28.

72. *Tao-te-ching* 13.

The Japanese Concept of "Nature"

1. *Nippon Kokugo Daijiten* [Japanese Dictionary] (Tokyo: Shogakukan, 1972).

2. Martin Heidegger, *Einführung in die Metaphysik* (Tubingen: Niemeyer, 1953), p. 10.

3. Ibid, p. 11.

4. Loc. cit.

5. At best one can find an echo in the *natura naturans* of the late Middle Ages (Averroes).

6. B. Kimura, "Schulderlebnis und Klima" (Fuhdo), *Nervenarzt* 37 (1966):394–400.

7. *Shōbōgenzō,* 20th Book: Being-Time, 1240.

8. *Zen no Kenkyū* (Tokyo, 1911), Preface.

9. *Essays,* V (Tokyo, 1944).

The Japanese Experience of Nature

1. The term "cultivation" designates a complete commitment to training and practice. The term *shugyō* is often used to describe the rigors of monastic life.

"Keiko,"[bo] meaning "practice," is a more tame expression and is characteristic of the training of a lay person or secular forms of self-improvement.

2. By "Being" I mean personal development in an ontological sense. Referring to Martin Heidegger, for example, Being or *Dasein* refers to the full sense of a person's participation in this world. Heidegger distinguishes between ontic beings *(Seindes)*, being itself *(Sein)*, and "Being" as it refers to humans *(Dasein)*. The Japanese sense of *shugyō* includes social being and being-in-nature (Heidegger's *mitsein)* as well.

See Watsuji Tetsuro's *inrigaku*[bp] [*Ethics*], in vols. 10 and 11 of his *Zenshū* [Complete Works] (Tokyo: Iwanami Shoten, 1978), 2nd ed., for an elaboration of the role of *mitsein* as a necessary prerequisite for a person's ethical development.

3. For example, see Ienaga Saburo, *Nihon Shishōshi ni Okeru Shūkyōteki Shizenkan no Tenkai* [The Development of a Religious View of Nature in the History of Japanese Thought] (Tokyo, 1944); and Watsuji Tetsurō, *Fūdo: ningengakutei na kōsatsu* (Tokyo, Iwanami Shoten, 1935), trans. J. Bownos, entitled *Climate and Culture: A Philosophical Study,* for UNESCO Japan (Tokyo: Hokuseidō Press, 1971); Watsuji Tetsurō, "The Japanese Spirit," in *Studies in Japan's Spiritual History, Continued* (Tokyo: Iwanami Shoten); and E.G. Seidensticker, "In Praise of Shadows: A Prose Elegy of Tanizaki," *Japan Quarterly* 1 (1954):16–52.

4. See David Edward Shaner, "Biographies of the Buddha," *Philosophy East and West* 37 (1987): 306–22.

5. Yuasa Yasuo, *Kamigami no Tanjō* [Birth of Kami] (Tokyo: Ibunsha, 1977). Similar themes are developed in his "Religious Tradition in Japan," Proceedings of the National Culture and World Peace Conference, Seoul, Korea, 1976. See also, Ishimoda Tadashi, *Japan's Ancient State* (Tokyo: Iwanami Shiten, 1971); Veda Masaaki, *Japanese Myths* (Tokyo: Iwanami Shinsho, 1970); Masuda Katsumi, "Island of Mystery," in *Bungaku* 4–6 (1971); Tsuda Sōkiei, "Kami and *mikoto*," in *Studies of Japanese Classics, Part Two* (Tokyo: Iwanami Shoten, 1950); Matsumura Takeo, *Studies of Japan's Myths*, vol. III (Baifūkan); Kobayashi Yukio, *Ancient Mirrors* (Tokyo: Gakuseisha, 1965); Harada Toshiaki, *Japan's Ancient Religion* (Tokyo: Chūō-Korōnsha, 1969).

6. Alicia and Daigan Matsunaga, *Foundation of Japanese Buddhism*, vol. I, *The Aristocratic Age* (Los Angeles-Tokyo: Buddhist Books International, 1976), p. 171. For an additional insightful discussion of Kūkai's personal history, see Yoshita S. Hadeka, trans., *Kūkai: Major Works* (New York: Columbia University Press, 1972), pp. 1–60.

7. Yuasa Yasuo, *The Body: Toward an Eastern Mind-Body Theory,* trans. T.P. Kasulis and Shigenori Nagatomo (Albany, NY: SUNY Press, 1988). See also Joseph M. Kitagawa, *Religion in Japanese History* (New York: Columbia University Press, 1966), esp. chapter two.

8. Kitagawa's phrase.

9. For sharing Kitagawa's insight, and developing the concept further, I am indebted to Professor Masatoshi Nagatomi, Harvard University (Fall 1985).

10. The soteriological value of this "love" has been discussed in William LaFleur, "Saigyō and the Buddhist Value of Nature," in *History of Religions* 13, no. 3 (1974). For a similar theme related to the *Kojiki* and *Nihongi*[bq], see John C. Pelzel, "Human Nature in Japanese Myths," in Takie Sugiyama Lebra and William P. Lebra, eds., *Japanese Culture and Behavior* (Honolulu: University Press of Hawaii, 1974).

11. Yuasa Yasuo, "Religious Tradition in Japan" (from the manuscript of a lecture on "Natural Culture and World Peace" delivered at Seoul, Korea, 1976), p. 8.

12. Kūkai was one of the most progressive intellectuals of his age. Even though theory and study were less important than practice, his gifted intellectual analytic abilities enabled him to systematize Shingon doctrine and to excel in his studies of Chinese, Sanskrit, calligraphy, and numerous other artistic endeavors. In addition to this archaic and intellectual blend, Kūkai was extremely energetic. His achievements as the founder of the monastic center on Mt. Kōya led to such impressive accomplishments that it is difficult today to distinguish his actual contributions from the myriads of legends spread by his wandering priests *(kōya-hijiri)*[br].

13. Alicia and Daigan Matsunaga, *Foundations of Japanese Buddhism,* vol. I, p. 180.

14. *Dharmakāya* as *Mahāvairocana* is one of the three Buddha bodies *(trikāya): Dharmakāya, Sambhoghakāya,* and *Nirmānakāya.* For a more detailed discussion of the relationships within the *trikāya* theory, see Hakeda, *Kūkai: Major Works,* pp. 84, 151; Hisao Inagaki, trans., *Kūkai's Principle of Attaining Buddhahood with the Present Body* (Ryūkoku Translation Pamphlet Series 4) (Kyoto: Ryūkoku Translation Center, Ryūkoku University, 1975), p. 25; Alicia and Daigan Matsunaga, *Foundations of Japanese Buddhism,* vol. II, *The Mass Movement: Kamakura and Muromachi Periods* (Los Angeles-Tokyo: Buddhist Books International, 1976), p. 52; and Shōzui Makoto Toganoo, "'The Symbol-System of Shingon Buddhism (2),'" *Mikkyō Bunka* (Koyasan: The Esoteric Buddhist Society, December 1971), p. 53.

15. For an account of Kūkai's mission to China, see Robert Borgen, "The Japanese Mission to China, 801–06," *Monumenta Nipponica,* 37 (1982):1–25.

16. See Tu Wei-ming, "The Continuity of Being: Chinese Visions of Nature," in Leroy S. Rouner, ed., *On Nature,* Boston University Institute for Philosophy and Religion, Vol. 6 (Notre Dame, Indiana: Notre Dame University Press, 1984).

17. I have argued this point in greater depth in chapters three and four of my *Bodymind Experience in Japanese Buddhism* (Albany, NY: SUNY Press, 1985).

18. Yuasa, *The Body,* manuscript p. 83 (brackets mine). Yuasa articulates four meanings of *"kairitsu"* (see chapter seven). I have indicated that the meaning of *"kairitsu"* as *samādhi* is in keeping with the developed sense of intentionless, prereflective, and dynamic "natural experiences."

19. In the *Benkenmitsu nikyō ron* (Treatise on the Difference Between Exoteric and Esoteric Buddhism), Kūkai distinguishes four salient features of each. First, the exoteric doctrine is preached by the *nirmānakāya* (historical Buddha-body) and is geared for his audience's level of understanding. In contrast, the esoteric doctrine is preached by the *Dharmakāya* Buddha *(Dainichi Nyorai)* for his own enjoyment without the use of instructional techniques, that is, it typifies his innermost enlightened experience. Second, the exoteric doctrine states that this experience of enlightenment is mystical and transcends linguisitic description. However, esoteric doctrine states that such a linguistic description is possible via "true words" or *mantras* (Jp. *shingon*). Third, in the exoteric tradition it is believed that enlightenment is gradual process taking aeons of lifetimes to achieve. In the esoteric tradition, proper practice enables a person to "instantly unite with the *Dharmakāya* Buddha and attain enlightenment." And finally, in the exoteric tradition sentient beings are classified according to their spiritual capability. In the esoteric tradition, all sentient beings are able to realize enlightenment. Such a realization may be aided not only by "true words" but also by works of art and various mental and physical practices.

20. For a discussion of this dynamism in the Taoist contest, see Shigenori Nagatomo, "An Epistemic Turn in the *Tao te Ching*: A Pheńomenological Reflection," *International Philosophical Quarterly;* in the context of Dōgen, see my "The Bodymind Experience in Dōgen's *Shōbōgenzō,*" *Philosophy East and West,* 35 (Jan. 1985):17–35.

21. For a relevant discussion of this sort of assimilation, refer to the doctrine of *honji-suijaku*[bs] in Alicia Matsunaga, *The Buddhist Philosophy of Assimilation* (Tokyo, Japan: Charles E. Tuttle Co., 1969), esp. chapters 7, 8, and 9.

22. See Wilbur M. Fridell, "Notes on Japanese Tolerance," *Monumenta Nipponica* 27 (Autumn 1972):253–72.

23. See J. Baird Callicott, "Conceptual Resources for Environmental Ethics in Asian Traditions of Thought: A Propaedeutic," *Philosophy East and West* 37, (April 1987), pp. 124–25, 127, and n. 31. Callicott does not cite specific page numbers in Arthur Herman's book *An Introduction to Buddhist Thought* (Washington, D.C.: University Press of America, 1983). In Herman's defense, I have checked his first descriptions of the Buddhist concept of suffering (Sk. *duhka*) and found that he correctly emphasizes that the Buddhist concept of suffering, anxiety, and unsatisfactoriness should *not* be interpreted as an indication of a pessimistic, negative, or world-denying attitude. On p. 58 Herman summarizes a fifth point on this matter by saying "the very fact of *nirvana* as a condition beyond pain means that, to the Buddhist, life is not ultimately painful; hence, life cannot be characterized as always 'painful.' To argue otherwise would make non-sense of this ultimate optimism of Buddhism." *Nirvāṇa* is also not a condition of escaping via a cessation of feeling and perception *(saññāvedayitanirodha)*. On p. 60 Herman emphasizes suffering is not an intrinsic property of this world; it is rather an intentional condition due to excessive desire, covetousness, and craving. Herman correctly states that by clarifying one's intentions, which clutter an otherwise originally clear mirror-like mind, one participates fully with others and the natural world. Accordingly, Herman says the

Buddha "emphasizes the promise and optimism of the Buddhist way" (p. 61). Indeed, cultivating a way of living that encourages selfless participation with others makes possible the development of a moral life.

24. For an entire book dedicated to clarifying the common misconception concerning relative versus absolute nothingness in Mahayana Buddhism, see Keiji Nishitani's *Religion and Nothingness* (Los Angeles: University of California Press, 1982). The life-affirming character of *nirvana* in Early Buddhism is underscored by David J. Kalupahana, in his *Buddhist Philosophy: A Historical Analysis* (Honolulu: The University Press of Hawaii, 1976), his *Causality: The Central Philosophy of Buddhism* (Honolulu: The University Press of Hawaii, 1975), and his *The Principles of Buddhist Psychology* (Albany, NY: SUNY Press, 1987).

25. Thomas P. Kasulis (from an unpublished manuscript of a lecture delivered at the Honolulu Concert Hall, Honolulu, April 1978).

26. Hakeda, *Kūkai: Major Works,* p. 78.

27. Tamaki Koshirō, "On the Fundamental Idea Underlying Japanese Buddhism," *Philosophical Studies of Japan,* vol. XI (Tokyo: Japan Society for the Promotion of Science, 1975), p. 26.

28. William Theodore de Bary et al., *Sources of Japanese Tradition* (New York and London: Columbia University Press, 1971), p. 141; Hakujū Ui, "A Study of Japanese Tendai Buddhism," *Philosophical Studies of Japan,* vol. I (Tokyo: Japan Society for the Promotion of Science, 1959), p. 36–37; Tamaki "On the Fundamental Idea," p. 26.

29. Hakeda, *Kūkai: Major Works,* pp. 77, 235. For two fine etymological analyses of *kaji,* see Inagaki, *Kūkai's Principle,* pp. 11–12, 27–28; and Shozui Makoto Toganoo, "The Symbol-System of Shingon Buddhism (3)," *Mikkyō Bunka* (Koyasan: The Esoteric Buddhist Society, June 1972), pp. 74–79.

30. Hakeda, *Kūkai: Major Works,* p. 234; Toganoo, *Mikkyō Bunka* (3), p. 65, 78–79.

31. Inagaki, *Kūkai's Principle,* pp. 11–12; Toganoo, *Mikkyō Bunka* (3), p. 64.

32. Yuasa, "Religious Traditon," pp. 9–10; Toganoo, *Mikkyō Bunka* (3), p. 64.

33. It should be noted that Dōgen is not the first to hold such a view. The following statement taken from the *Lotus Sutra* captures this notion: *Sōmoku kokudo shikkai jōbutsu,*[bt] "the grass, trees, earth and natural surroundings all possess Buddhahood" [unpubl. translation by Hajime Nakamura—personal communication November 5, 1979 (Tokyo, Japan)]. Professor Nakumura emphasizes that this is an important theme for understanding "The Way of Japanese Thinking"; its relevance for an environmental ethic is apparent. Cf., William LaFleur's essay on Saigyō contained in this volume.

34. See Kosen Nishiyama and John Stevens, trans., *Shōbōgenzō: The Eye and Treasure of the True Law,* vol. I (Sendai, Japan: Daihokkaikaku, 1975), p. 103.

35. See Dōshū Ōkubo, ed., *Dōgen Zenji Zenshū*, vol. I (Tokyo, Chikuma Shobō, 1969), p. 206.

36. Nishiyama and Stevens, *Shōbōgenzō*, pp. 104–5.

37. The relation is best represented using the Japanese *soku* function cited previously—"communication *soku* communion" describes more accurately their mutual interpenetration.

38. Matsunaga, *Foundation*, vol. II, p. 239. In this work it is suggested that *shinjin datsuraku* is peculiarly Japanese and would be a most unlikely phrase for Nyojō,[bu] Dōgen's teacher, to utter. It is interesting to note that some scholars hypothesize that Nyojō most likely used "dust" (Jp. *jin*,[bv] Ch. *ch'en*[bw]) rather than "body" (Jp. *shin*,[bx] Ch. *shen*[by]). In other words, Nyojō may have said, "cast off the dust of mind," which has been a typical Zen idiom since the days of Enō[bz] (Ch. Hui-neng[ca]). Dōgen's possible deliberate misconception, typical of his manner of interpretation, serves only to underscore the importance of bodymind oneness with respect to the enlightenment experience.

39. The theme of intimacy in the Japanese tradition has been pursued in depth by T.P. Kasulis (manuscript forthcoming). See also Eliot Deutsch, "Knowingly Religiously," in Leroy S. Rouner, ed., *Knowingly Religiously* (Notre Dame, Indiana: Notre Dame University Press, 1985).

40. For an exposition of the bodymind concept, see David Edward Shaner, "The Bodymind Experience in Dōgen's *Shōbōgenzō*: A Phenomenological Perspective," *Philosophy East and West* 35 (1985):17–35, and *The Bodymind Experience in Japanese Buddhism* (Albany, NY: SUNY Press, 1985).

41. For a clear rendering of the terms *shōakumakusa* and *genjōkōan*, and their significance for Dōgen's ethical scheme, see T.P. Kasulis, *Zen Action/Zen Person* (Honolulu: The University Press of Hawaii, 1981), pp. 93–103.

42. See David Edward Shaner, "The Rectification of Names," *Biology and Philosophy* 3 (1987):347–68.

43. For a parallel argument concerning the application of Western standards of moral theory to Confucian philosophy, which similarly emphasizes character development, see Henry Rosemont, "Against Relativism," in *Interpreting Across Boundaries*, Eliot Deutsch and Gerald Larson, eds. (Princeton, New Jersey: Princeton University Press, 1987), pp. 36–70. See also the *Analects* of Confucius Book II, verse 4. This famous passage emphasizing personal development has served as an organizing theme for Roger Ames's and David Hall's interpretation of cultivation according to Confucius; see *Thinking Through Confucius* (Albany, NY: SUNY Press, 1987). The role of character development as the most important feature of Dōgen's ethical scheme can thus be interpreted as one in concert with themes in both Confucian and Aristotelian ethics.

44. Alasdair MacIntyre, *After Virtue* (Notre Dame, Indiana: University of Notre

Dame Press, 1981), p. 140. For another communitarian perspective see Michael J. Sandel, *Liberalism and the Limits of Justice* (Cambridge: Cambridge University Press, 1982).

45. Edward O. Wilson, *Biophilia* (Cambridge: Harvard University Press, 1984), p. 1.

46. For a discussion of themes related to this point, see my "The Cultural Evolution of Mind"; Edward O. Wilson's "The Evolutionary Origin of Mind"; and Marvin Minsky's "The Society of Mind"; *The Personalist Forum* 3 (Spring 1987): 33–69, 4–18, and 19–32, respectively.

47. The most famous Japanese philosopher of the modern era is Nishida Kitarō (1870–1945). Nishida was strongly influenced by the ecocentric and empiricist orientation of Japanese Zen Buddhism and was the founder of the famous Kyoto school of philosophy. In his early work *A Study of Good* (Jp. *Zen no Kenkyū*) published in 1911, Nishida borrowed the term "pure experience" from the writings of Harvard philosopher William James. Although the theme of pure experience captures indigenous Japanese attitudes, the specific concept had its origins in the intellectual climate of Cambridge, Massachusetts, not the Orient.

William James's influence upon Nishida has been mentioned in, for example, Gino K. Piovesana, *Contemporary Japanese Philosophical Thought* (New York: St. John's University Press, 1969), pp. 95–96; David D. Dilworth, "The Range of Nishida's Early Religious Thought: *Zen no Kenkyū*,"[cb] *Philosophy East and West* 19 (1969), pp. 413, 419; R. Wargo, *The Logic of Basho and the Concept of Nothingness in the Philosophy of Nishida Kitarō,* The University of Michigan, Ph.D. dissertation (Ann Arbor, Michigan: University Microfilms, 1972), p. 66; David A. Dilworth, "Nishida's early pantheistic voluntarism," *Philosophy East and West* 20 (1970), p. 36; David A. Dilworth, "The Initial Formulations of Pure Experience in Kitarō Nishida and William James," *Monumenta Nipponica* 24 (1969), pp. 93–111; and Thomas P. Kasulis, "The Kyoto School and the West," *The Eastern Buddhist* (New Series 25 (1982), p. 128.

48. Particularly instructive, in this regard, are letters written to his parents dated: Sept. 10, 1861; Sept. 16, 1861; Dec. 25, 1861–63?; [Cambridge, 1862 (fragment)]; Mar. 31, 1865?; April 21, 1865; Aug. 23, 1865?; Sept. 12, 1865; Oct. 21, 1865; and [Nov. 1865?]. For a relevant and instructive letter to Alice James, see Nov. 6, 1865. All dated designations are from James, William. 1861–1865. Personal correspondence. William James Collection. Houghton Library. Harvard University, Cambridge.

49. A text of the letter is provided in Gay Wilson Allen, *William James, A Biography* (New York: Viking Press, 1967), p. 84.

50. Nishida himself cites James's *The Principles of Psychology,* vol. I, chaps. VII and XV, and *A World of Pure Experience* as he develops the concept of "pure experience" (Jp. *junsui keiken*)[cc] in the first pages of his *Zen no Kenkyū* (A Study of Good). *"Zen no Kenkyū"* is included in *Nishida Kitarō Zenshū* ["Collected Works of

Nishida Kitarō"] vol. I (Tokyo: Iwanami Shoten, 1965–66). For an English translation see V.H. Viglielmo's *Nishida Kitarō: A Study of Good* (Tokyo: Japanese Government Printing Office, 1960).

51. See, for example, E.G. Seidensticker, "In Praise of Shadows: A Prose Elegy of Tanizaki," *Japan Quarterly* 1 (1954):16–52.

52. Learning to see detail is the trademark of a great scientist. Consider the following examples. On August 23, 1865, during the Thayer expedition, James writes that "Agassiz found 46 new species of fish in four days!" Likewise Edward Wilson uses his monocular vision to great advantage when classifying ants; he can detect, without a magnification aid, subtle morphological differences, even hairs, in individual specimens. Developing an eye for detail is also important for excavations of fossil remains. Stephen Jay Gould describes this acquired skill in "Empire of the Apes," *Natural History* 96 (1987):20–25.

53. Actually this perspective was not uncommon among nineteenth-century biologists. In particular, taxonomy and systematics were considered by many to be fields that had considerable theological value. Given the popularity of the proof for the existence of God by the argument of design (à la Archbishop Paley), the work of collectors and field biologists was frequently discussed in terms of theories concerning the nature of God's mind as revealed by His vast creation. Each new species that was discovered and classified added splendor to the vast diversity of God's creation.

Much of the original opposition to Darwin's *On the Origin of Species,* including Agassiz's opposition, centered upon the nonteleological character of explanations for the transmutation of species contained therein. Without positing the fixity of species, which also implied their simultaneous creation, doubt would be cast upon God's direct "design" and perpetual involvement in the natural world. Recent study of Darwin's personal notebooks suggests that Darwin's famous "delay" in the writing of the *Origin* was due to his being wholly cognizant of the radical philosophical and theological ramifications that his thesis implied.

Documentation concerning Agassiz's theological commitments include: Edward Lurie, *Louis Agassiz: A Life in Science* (Chicago: The University of Chicago Press, 1960); Edward O. Wilson, *Biophilia* (Cambridge: Harvard University Press, 1984), p. 45; Stephen Jay Gould, "Uniformity and Catastrophe," in *Ever Since Darwin* (New York: W.W. Norton & Co., 1977), pp. 147–52; Stephen Jay Gould, "Agassiz in the Galapagos," in *Hen's Teeth and Horse's Toes* (New York: W.W. Norton & Co., 1983), pp. 107–19; Ernst Mayr, "Agassiz, Darwin, and Evolution," in his *Evolution and the Diversity of Life* (Cambridge: Harvard University Press, 1976), pp. 251–76; and Louis Agassiz, *Contributions to the Natural History of the United States of America,* vol. 1 (Boston: Little, Brown, 1857).

Supporting documentation concerning Darwin's delay and the importance of his notebooks includes: Stephen Jay Gould, "Darwin's Delay," *Ever Since Darwin,* pp. 21–27; Sihran S. Schweber, "The Origin of the *Origin* Revisited," *Journal of the History of Biology* 10 (1977):229–316; Frank J. Sulloway, "The *Beagle* Voyage and Its Aftermath," *Journal of the History of Biology* 15 (1982):325–96; Charles Darwin,

Metaphysics, Materialism, and the Evolution of Mind: Early Writings of Charles Darwin, transcribed notebooks, annotated by Paul H. Barrett with Commentary by Howard E. Gruber (Chicago: University of Chicago Press, 1974); and Michael Ruse, *The Darwinian Revolution* (Chicago: The University of Chicago Press, 1979).

54. Edward O. Wilson, *Biophilia,* p. 119.

55. See, for example, W.D. Hamilton, "The Genetical Evolution of Social Behavior," *Journal of Theoretical Biology* 7 (1964):1–52; Edward O. Wilson, *Sociobiology: The New Synthesis* (Cambridge: Belknap Press of Harvard University Press, 1975); and Charles J. Lumsden and Edward O. Wilson, *Genes, Mind, and Culture* (Cambridge: Harvard University Press, 1981).

56. It should be noted that the seeds of this conceptual approach in post-Darwinian biology, contrary to Thomas Henry Huxley's (Darwin's "bulldog") more popular interpretation of a Darwinian world "red in tooth and claw," are at least as old as the works of Petr Kropotkin, *Mutual Aid: A Factor of Evolution* (New York: McClure Phillips and Company, 1903), and *Ethics: Origin and Development* (New York: Benjamin Blom, 1924).

Interestingly, the position of Huxley's grandson is in accord with Kropotkin's; see Sir Julian S. Huxley, "Cultural Process and Evolution," in A.A. Roe and G.G. Simpson, eds., *Behavior and Evolution* (New Haven: Yale University Press, 1958), pp. 437–54, and "The Emergence of Darwinism," in Sol Tax, ed., *The Evolution of Life,* vol. 1 (Chicago: The University of Chicago Press, 1960), pp. 1–21.

57. It may be interesting to note that the concept of group selection does have a Japanese counterpart, albeit issuing from an entirely different context. See Watsuji Tetsuro, *Rinrigaku (Ethics),* in vols. 10 and 11 of his *Zenshu* [Complete works] (Tokyo: Iwanami Shoten, 1978), 2nd ed., chapter 1, "Ningen no gaku to shite no Rinrigaku no igi," (The Significance of Ethics as the Study of Man"), David Dilworth, *Monumenta Nipponica* 26 (1971):389–413; Tanabe Hajime, "The Logic of the Species as Dialectics," trans. David Dilworth and Taira Sato, *Monumenta Nipponica* 24 (1969):273–88; Watsuji Tetsuro, "Yokyoku ni arawareta rinri shiso: Japanese Ethical Thought in Noh Plays of the Muromachi Period," trans. David Dilworth, *Monumenta Nipponica* 24 (1969):467–98; Richard B. Pilgram, "Intervals (Ma) in Space and Time: Foundations for a Religio-Aesthetic Paradigm in Japan," a paper delivered at the "Interpreting Across Boundaries" Conference, sponsored by the Society for Asian and Comparative Philosophy, Honolulu, Hawaii, 1984; and Imanishi Kinji, "A Proposal for *Shizengaku:* The Conclusion to the Study of Evolutionary Theory," *Journal of Social and Biological Structure* 7 (1984): 357–68.

58. For a more detailed discussion of the role of neoteny as it may apply to cultural evolution and comparative philosophy, see David Edward Shaner, "The Cultural Evolution of Mind."

59. Edward O. Wilson, *Biophilia,* p. 119.

Saigyō and the Buddhist Value of Nature

1. Apart from primary sources cited below, I am principally indebted to an article entitled *"Sōmoku kokudo jōbutsu no busshōrontei igi to sono sakusha"* [The authorship and significance as a theory of the Buddha-nature of the phrase "Plants, Trees, and Earth, All Become Buddha"] by Miyamoto Shōson in *Indogaku Bukkyōgaku Kenkyū [Journal of Indian and Buddhist Studies]* 9 (March 1961):672–701 and an article in English entitled "On the 'Attainment of Buddhahood' by Trees and Plants," by Yukio Sakamoto is in the *Proceedings of the IXth International Congress for the History of Religions* (1958), Japanese Organizing Committee for the IXth, I.C.H.R. Science Council of Japan (Tokyo: Maruzen, 1960), pp. 415–22. Donald H. Shiveley has written about the appearance of features of this discussion at a later date and in certain Nō dramas in his "Buddhahood for the Nonsentient: A Theme in No Plays," *Harvard Journal of Asiatic Studies* 20 (1957):135–61. He concentrates largely on the Muromachi period.

2. Miyamoto, "Sōmoku" pp. 695–96.

3. On the importance of Chan-jan for Buddhism, see Miyamoto, pp. 696, 683–85; Kenneth Ch'en, *Buddhism in China,* (Princeton, NJ, 1964), p. 313. Fung Yu-lan, *A History of Chinese Philosophy,* trans. Derk Bodde (Princeton, NJ, 1953), 2:384–86; and Sakamoto, p. 416.

4. Fung Yu-lan, *History* p. 385.

5. Ibid., p. 386.

6. Ibid.

7. Miyamoto, "Sōmoku" p. 696.

8. *Kūkai: Major Works. Translated with an Account of His Life and a Study of His Thought,* Yoshito S. Hakeda (New York and London, 1972), p. 254. The original of this passage is in Kūkai, *Kōbō Daishi Zenshū,* ed. Mikkyō Bunka Kenkyūjō (Tokyo, 1964), 1:53.

9. *Kōbō Daishi Zenshuū,* vol. 2, p. 37.

10. This quotation is from Hakeda's translation, pp. 229–30. The original is in *Kōbō Daishi Zenshū,* vol. 1, pp. 111–112.

11. For the importance of Kūkai's concept of *samaya,* see below. It is also this particular concept of the "symbol" that seems to shape Saigyō's diction. I am especially indebted to Professor Joseph M. Kitagawa for showing me the importance of Kūkai's notion of symbolization for Saigyō poetry.

12. Miyamoto, "Sōmoku" p. 696.

13. Nakamura Hajime, ed., *Shin Bukkyō Jien* [New dictionary of Buddhism] (Tokyo, 1962), pp. 540–41.

14. Miyamoto, "Sōmoku" p. 675.

15. Ibid., pp. 675–76.

16. Miyamoto, "Sōmoku" p. 676; see also Sakamoto, "'Attainment'" p. 417.

17. Ch'en, *Buddhism* p. 307. See also Leon Hurvitz, "Chih-i" *Mélanges chinois et bouddhiques,* vol. 12 (Brussels, 1962).

18. See Leon Hurvitz's translation of this chapter on *Scripture of the Lotus Blossom of the Fine Dharma (The Lotus Sutra)* (New York: Columbia University Press, 1976), pp. 101–19.

19. My translations of his arguments are summaries of the main points of each of the seven. The complete section of the *Kankō Ruijū* dealing with this problem is in *Dai Nihon Bukkyō Zensho* [Complete collection of Japanese Buddhist writings], 40:68–69, new edition (Tokyo, 1971). My version varies considerably from the seven arguments as presented by Yukio Sakamoto in his article "On 'The Attainment of Buddhahood' by Trees and Plants" (p. 418), but I have used his version of argument number 5 as he gives it (see also Miyamoto, "Sōmoku" pp. 679–81).

20. It should be noted that in many of his writings, Ryōgen demonstrates a *kongaku* orientation. My argument here is that by the time of Chūjin this was much more the basic orientation of the whole of Tendai thinking and that, especially in his articulation of the meaning of the Buddhahood of plants, Chūjin demonstrates greater consistency in the application of this orientation to the specific problem under question.

21. For a presentation of the importance of the *hongaku* orientation for later but Tendai-influenced thinkers such as Nichiren and Dōgen, see Nakamura Hajime, *Ways of Thinking of Eastern Peoples* (Honolulu, University of Hawaii Press, 1964), pp. 351ff.

22. The question of the degree to which Saigyō was aware of topics debated in Buddhist circles is not easily answered. In the years immediately after his entry into the priesthood, he visited and, apparently, resided in or near a number of Tendai and Shingon temples in the vicinity of Heian-kyo. I think it reasonable that, given his interest in the natural world, he would have become conversant with the concurrent views of *sōmoku jōbutsu,* for example. The impression that Saigyō was merely a "simple" monk may be largely the result of the fact that his verse was intelligible and accessible to the "masses" relatively soon after Saigyō's death. Furthermore, his own statement to Yoritomo as recorded in the *Azuma-kagami,* namely, "I know nothing about 'depths' in the composition of poetry," is highly ambiguous and cannot be taken as indicative of a lack of interest in intellectual issues of his day. See William R. LaFleur, *Mirror for the Moon: A Selection of Poems by Saigyō (1118–1190),* translated with an Introduction (New York: New Directions, 1978), p. xxiii.

23. In citation of Saigyō's verses, I have listed them as numbered in Itō Yoshio's edition of the *Sankashū* or "Mountain-Home Collection," Saigyō's own collection of his verse. Itō's edition is in the *Nihon Koten Bungaku Taikei* edition (Tokyo: Iwanami Shoten, 1958), vol. 28, ed. Hisamatsu Sen'ichi, Yamazaki Toshio,

and Gotō, Shigeo. Translations are as in my *Mirror for the Moon* (see n.22 above), used by permission,and abbreviated as *MFM* and page number.

24. Saigyō's poem to which I am here referring is the following:

usutsu o mo	Since the "real world" seems
utsutsu to sara ni	To be less than really real,
oboeneba	Why need I suppose
yume o mo yume to	The world of dreams is nothing
nanika omowan	Other than a world of dreams?
	[SKS 1606; MFM, p. 68]

25. Hakeda, *Kūkai,* p. 89, n. 26.

26. Ienaga Saburō, *Nihon shisōshi ni okeru Shūkyōteki Shizenkan no Tenkai* [*The Development of the Concept of Religious Nature in Japanese Thought*] (Tokyo, 1944). For a summary of Ienaga's argument and the place of this important monograph in the context of Ienaga's intellectual development, see Robert N. Bellah, "Ienaga Saburō and the Search for Meaning in Modern Japan," in *Changing Japan: Attitudes toward Modernization,* ed. Marius B. Jansen (Princeton, NJ, 1965), pp. 369–423. Bellah's consideration of this essay is on pp. 389–94. I am grateful to Professor Bellah for reading an earlier draft of my present essay and for providing critical commentary on it. Ienaga, p. 6.

27. Ienaga, *Nihon shisōshi* pp. 9–10.

28. Ibid., p. 11.

29. Ibid., p. 14.

30. Ibid., p. 16.

31. Ibid.

32. Ibid.

33. Ibid., p. 18.

34. Ibid., pp. 20ff. See Bellah, *Changing Japan* pp. 391ff.

35. Ienaga, *Nihon shisōshi* p. 26.

36. Ibid., p. 33.

37. Ibid., p. 34

38. Ibid., pp. 34–35.

39. Ibid., p. 39.

40. Ibid., p. 46.

41. Robert H. Brower and Earl Miner, *Japanese Court Poetry* (Stanford, CA, 1961), p. 262.

42. Ienaga, *Nihon shiōshi* p. 46.

43. Ibid., p. 83.

44. Ibid., p. 85.

45. Ibid., pp. 87–88.

46. Ibid., pp. 89–90.

The Jewel Net of Indra

1. Mendel Sachs, "Space, Time and Elementary Interaction in Relativity," *Physics Today* (February 1969):59. "The derived mass field depends upon the curvature of space-time. The latter geometrical property is, in turn a manifestation of the mutual coupling of all the matter within the closed system. Thus, if the rest of the universe should be depleted of all matter, the mass of the remaining electron, say, should correspondingly go to zero. The derived field relationship is then a quantitative expression of the Mach principle because here the inertial mass of any amount of matter is indeed a well defined function of its dynamic coupling with all of the other matter within the entire closed system."

2. Daisetz T. Suzuki, *Zen and Japanese Culture,* Bolligen Series, vol. 64 (Princeton: Princeton University Press, 1971), p. 237.

3. T. 1866, p. 508c.

4. Alfred North Whitehead, *The Concept of Nature* (Cambridge: Cambridge University Press, 1971), p. 146.

5. Sōgaku Harada Roshi, "On Practice," *Journal of the Zen Center of Los Angeles* (Winter 1973):7.

Environmental Problematics

1. John B. Cobb, Jr., and Franklin I. Gamwell, eds., *Existence and Actuality: Conversations with Charles Hartshorne* (Chicago, Illinois: University of Chicago Press, 1984), p. 116.

2. Nāgārjuna, *Mūlamadhyamakakārikā,* XXV, 19, 20.

3. Walpola Rahula, *What the Buddha Taught* (New York: Grove Press, 1974), p. 27.

4. Ibid., p. 31.

5. I.B. Horner, trans., *The Middle Length Sayings (Majjhima-nikāya),* 1, The First Fifty Discourses (London: Luzac & Co., Ltd., 1954), p. 237.

6. F.L. Woodward, trans., *The Minor Anthologies of the Pali Canon,* part 2, *Itivuttaka: As It Was Said* (London: Geoffrey Cumberlege, 1948), p. 181.

7. Ibid., part 1, *Udāna: Verses of Uplift,* p. 98.

8. Nāgārjuna, *Mūlamadhyamakakārikā,* XXIV, 18.

9. Ibid., XXIV, 40.

10. Kenneth K. Inada, "Two Strains in Buddhist Causality," *Journal of Chinese Philosophy* 12 (1985):49–56.

11. For a brief analysis of the eight-vijñāna theory, see D.T. Suzuki, *Studies in the Laṅkāvatāra Sūtra* (London: George Routledge & Sons, Ltd., 1930), pp. 169–201. See also Triṃśikā (Thirty verses), verses 20, 21, 22.

12. Nāgārjuna, *Vigrahavyāvartanī,* 29.

13. This may remind the reader of Wittgenstein's frustration, expressed in his preface to the *Philosophical Investigations,* that he could not bring the stray aphoristic notes together into a unified system and has left that work for others to do. For his part, he did his best to leave us with an insightful system of thought—however unfinished it may have been; indeed, that may well be his greatest gift. From the Buddhist point of view, I suspect that he was hinting at the reality of things along Buddhist lines, but ultimately he could not find an opening for a solution to the linguistic game because he could not rise above the game in an interpenetrative sense. He simply could not grasp either the nature of emptiness in the Buddhist sense or the parity principle that functions all along in the experiential nature of things—language, logic, and empirics included.

14. I am tempted to substitute other rarely used terms such as isomorphism or homomorphism. The similarity or parallel is there, but, again, one must be extremely careful, for one may be treading on thin ice when making such substitutions. At best, all terms are guide posts or symbols of the reality intended.

15. Keiji Nishitani, *Religion and Nothingness,* trans. with an introduction by Jan van Bragt (Berkeley, California: University of California Press, 1982), p. 97.

16. Ibid.

17. Ibid., p. 90.

18. Nolan P. Jacobson, *Buddhism & the Contemporary World: Change and Self-correction* (Carbondale, Illinois: Southern Illinois University Press, 1983). See especially the last chapter on "The Self-surpassing Oneness," pp. 151–63.

19. It should be made clear that Supremely Ontological or Supreme Ontology, though capitalized, is not a metaphysical principle. It is not the First or Final Cause with a sweeping deductive connotation, as seen in many religious doctrines. It is radically supreme in its openness and resiliency, but such features are neither definable nor describable by resorting to a so-called object language. But where all

forms of objective conditions are removed or detached, there will emerge instantly in its natural (neutral) habitat the pure, bright, full *Ontological* nature. The search for the riddle of existence must start somewhere, to be sure, but I am inclined to believe that the Buddha's solution focuses on this key area: the problematics and dynamics of the conceptual-ontological modes framed within the potentially wider and open texture of experiential reality.

20. Thomas Hobbes, *Leviathan,* ed. Michael Oakeshott (New York: Collier Books, 1962). See especially part 1, where he develops his theory of man's nature and the necessity for a covenant.

21. Kenneth E. Boulding, *The World as a Total System* (Beverly Hills, California: Sage Publications, Inc., 1985). Previously, Boulding published a brilliant work, *Ecodynamics: A New Theory of Societal Evolution* (Sage Publications, Inc., 1978, 1981), which has had a great impact on environmental concerns and developments. This present work of his is an extension of the earlier one.

Toward a Middle Path of Survival

1. Walter Kaufmann, *Tragedy and Philosophy* (Princeton: Princeton University Press, 1968), p. 339.

2. *Saṃyutta-nikāya* (PTS) 2.17.

3. *Majjhima-nikāya* (PTS) 1.139.

4. William James, *Some Problems of Philosophy* (Harvard University Press, 1979), p. 39.

5. *Saṃyutta-nikāya* 2.25.

6. William James, *The Principles of Psychology* (New York: Henry Holt, 1908), 1:243.

7. *Saṃyutta-nikāya* 2.25.

8. *Majjhima-nikāya* 1.395.

9. *Aṅguttara-nikāya* (PTS) 5.313.

10. Ibid.

11. *Majjhima-nikāya* 1.324.

12. Ibid.

13. James, *The Principles of Psychology,* 1:141.

14. Ibid., 1.323–24.

15. James, *Some Problems of Philosophy,* p. 32.

16. *Majjhima-nikāya* 1.228; *Saṃyutta-nikāya* 3.133; 4.401, etc. See also David

Kalupahana, "The Notion of Suffering in Early Buddhism Compared with Some Reflections of Early Wittgenstein," *Philosophy East and West,* 27 (1977):423–31.

17. William James, "The Moral Philosopher and the Moral Life," in *Essays in Pragmatism,* ed. Albury Castell (New York: Harper, 1948), p. 78.

18. *Majjhima-nikāya* 1.167.

19. Ibid.

20. *Saṃyutta-nikāya* 5.421.

21. *Essays in Pragmatism,* p. 78.

22. *Dīgha-nikāya* (PTS) 1.155.

23. *Majjhima-nikāya* 1.135.

24. James, *Essays in Pragmatism,* p. 78.

25. See C.B. MacPherson, *The Political Theory of Possessive Individualism* (Oxford: Oxford University Press, 1962).

26. *Dhammapada* 129–30.

A Metaphysical Grounding for Natural Reverence: East-West

1. J. Baird Callicott, "Conceptual Resources for Environmental Ethics in Asian Traditions of Thought: A Propaedeutic," *Philosophy East and West* 37:115–30 (1987).

2. Immanuel Kant, *Critique of Judgment,* sec. 28.

3. Ibid.

4. Ibid., sec. 29.

5. Ibid.

6. Sureśvara, *Naiṣkarmya Siddhi,* trans. A.J. Alston (London: Shanti Sadan, 1959).

7. Karl H. Potter, "Metaphor as Key to Understanding the Thought of Other Speech Communities," in Gerald James Larson and Eliot Deutsch, eds., *Interpreting Across Boundaries: New Essays in Comparative Philosophy* (Princeton: Princeton University Press, 1988), p. 25.

8. Ibid.

9. Ibid., p. 29.

10. Ibid., p. 30.

11. *Bhagavadgītā,* IV, 18.

"Conceptual Resources" in South Asia for "Environmental Ethics"

1. David J. Kalupahana, "Man and Nature: Toward a Middle Path of Survival" (this volume).

2. Eliot Deutsch, "A Metaphysical Grounding for Natural Reverence: East-West" (this volume).

3. J. Baird Callicott, "Conceptual Resources or Environmental Ethics in Asian Traditions of Thought: A Propaedeutic," *Philosophy East and West* 37 (1987):124.

4. J. Baird Callicott, "Non-anthropocentric Value Theory and Environmental Ethics," *American Philosophical Quarterly* 21 (1984):299.

5. See Peter Berger and Thomas Luckmann, *The Social Construction of Reality: A Treatise in the Sociology of Knowledge* (Garden City, N.Y.: Anchor/Doubleday, 1967).

6. Callicott, "Conceptual Resources," p. 116.

7. Charles Hartshorne, "Śaṅkara, Nāgārjuna, and Fa Tsang," in Gerald James Larson and Eliot Deutsch, eds., *Interpreting Across Boundaries: New Essays in Comparative Philosophy* (Princeton: Princeton University Press, 1988), 104–5.

8. Michel Foucault, *The Archaeology of Knowledge,* tran. A.M. Sheridan Smith (New York: Pantheon Books, 1972), p. 12.

Epilogue: On the Relation of Idea and Action

1. Lynn White, Jr., "The Historical Roots of Our Ecologic Crisis," *Science* 155 (1967):1205 (emphasis added).

2. See D. Bandhu, ed., *Environmental Management* (New Delhi: Indian Environmental Society, 1981); T.N. Khoshoo, *Environmental Concerns and Strategies* (New Delhi: Indian Environmental Society, 1984); Norman Myers, "The Present Status and Future Prospects of Tropical Moist Forests," *Environmental Conservation* 7 (1980):101–14; and V. Smil, *The Bad Earth: Environmental Degradation in China* (Armonk, N.Y.: M.E. Sharp, Inc., 1977), for recent systematic discussions of environmental problems in Asia.

3. Philip Novak, "Tao How? Asian Religions and the Problem of Environmental Degradation," *Revisions* 9 (Winter/Spring 1987), is a recent, and differently cast, discussion of the central problem with which this epilogue is concerned.

4. See Carl O. Sauer, *Agricultural Origins and Dispersals* (New York: American Geographical Society, 1952), for a classic account.

5. See Paul S. Martin, "The Discovery of America," *Science* 179 (1973):969–74.

6. Claims for and against an American Indian land wisdom are reviewed and discussed in J. Baird Callicott, "Traditional European and American Indian Attitudes Toward Nature: An Overview," *Environmental Ethics* 4 (1982):293–318.

7. Yi-Fu Tuan, "Discrepancies Between Environmental Attitude and Behaviour: Examples from Europe and China," *The Canadian Geographer* 12 (1968):176–91.

8. Ibid., p. 179.

9. Ibid., p. 184.

10. Ibid., pp. 181, 188.

11. Feminist authors have, of course, made similar claims. For example, see Carol Gilligan, *In a Different Voice: Psychological Theory and Women's Development* (Cambridge: Harvard University Press, 1982); Alison Jagger, *Feminist Politics and Human Nature* (Totawa, NJ: Rowan and Allenheld, 1983); Nel Noddings, *Caring: A Feminine Approach to Ethics and Moral Education* (Berkeley: University of California Press, 1984).

12. Tuan, "Discrepancies," p. 185.

13. Ibid., p. 184.

14. Ibid., pp. 182 and 183.

15. White, "Historical Roots," p. 1206.

16. Robert Graves, *The Greek Myths* (Baltimore: Penguin Books, 1955). See also Merlin Stone, *When God Was a Woman* (New York: Harcourt Brace Janovich, 1976); and Charlene Spretnak, *Lost Goddesses of Early Greece: A Collection of Prehellenic Myths* (Boston: Beacon Press, 1981).

17. For a fuller explanation of the terms "logical" and "aesthetic" order, see David L. Hall and Roger T. Ames, *Thinking Through Confucius* (Albany, NY: SUNY Press, 1987).

18. See J. Baird Callicott, "American Indian Land Wisdom?: Sorting Out the Issues," in J. Baird Callicott, *In Defense of the Land Ethic: Essays in Environmental Philosophy* (Albany, NY: SUNY Press, 1988), pp. 203–219.

19. Tuan, "Discrepancies," p. 182. The traditional dates for the Chou are ca. 1100–221 B.C..

20. Aldo Leopold, *A Sand County Almanac and Sketches Here and There* (New York: Oxford University Press, 1949).

21. René Dubos, *The Wooing of the Earth* (New York: Charles Scribner's Sons, 1980).

22. Gary Nabhan, *The Desert Smells Like Rain: A Naturalist in Papago Country* (San Francisco: North Point Press, 1982); Arturo Gomez-Pompa, lecture to the Fourth World Wilderness Congress, Estes Park, CO, September 1987.

Index

absolutism, 248
Advaita Vedānta, 248, 260–265, 268, 269, 271
aesthetic order, 105–106, 116–119
Agassiz, Louis, 175, 177–179, 314
Aihara, Setsuko, 302
Allen, Gay Wilson, 313
American Indians, 28
Ames, Roger T., 19, 113–144, 292, 293, 301, 302, 303, 313, 324; and J. Baird Callicott, ix–xii, 1–21, 279–289
Analects, 306, 312–313
anthropocentrism: Chuang Tzu's rejection of, 86; dissolution of, 87–92, 216; justifications for, 104–105; Nietzsche's rejection of, 82–85; as pathetic fallacy, 217–218; as "sovereignty of the subject," 274–275; and Western art, 217; and Western philosophy, 216–217
applied ethics: as distinguished from environmental ethics, 1–2, 270–271
architecture, Japanese, 166
Aristotle, 45, 54, 102, 156, 163, 175–176, 287, 295, 296, 305, 313
ars contextualis (aesthetic cosmology), 19, 113–114, 119–120, 141
art: Western and Oriental contrasted, 217–219
artha (consequence), 251, 254
Asoka, 255
asymmetry-of-relations, 272–273
atomism, 5, 52–53, 148, 292, 295
axiology: *see* value

Bacon, Francis, 280, 289
Bandhu, D., 323
Barbour, I.G., 291, 292
Barfield, Owen, 302
Bashō, 206, 222
Bateson, Gregory, 25–29, 32, 293
Baynes, Cary F., 298
Beer, Gillian, 294
"being-time" (Jp. *uji*), 170–171
Bellah, Robert N., 205, 318
Berger, Peter, 323

Bergson, Henri, 272
Berlin, Isaiah, 14
Bernal, J.D., 37, 294
Bhagavadgītā, 248, 264, 322
Bhopal, 27, 279
biology: in conflict with physics, 40–41; cosmological, 37; defined, 37; and field theory, 56; as a model for Chinese ontology, 70; and physical chemistry, 42–43
biophilia (love of nature), 165, 176–178; *see also* Wilson, Edward O.
Blackstone, William T., 291
Blake, William, 301
bodhisattva, 236
Boltz, William G., 298
Bolzmann, Ludwig, 40, 294
Boodberg, P., 306
Boulding, Kenneth E., 245, 321
Bownos, J., 308
Bradley, F.H., 272
Brahman, 61, 262, 264, 273
Breazeale, Daniel, 301
Broda, E., 294
Brower, Robert H., 206, 318
Buber, Martin, 231
Buddhahood: *see* enlightenment
Buddhism, 9, 26, 27, 32, 47, 74, 95, 157; causality in, 172, 220–225, 237; cosmology of, 169; detachment in, 171; Esoteric, 167–168, 187; Hua-yen, 19–20, 214–229, 242; misunderstandings of, 169, 249; origins of Japanese, 163, 166; as a radical empiricism, 163–165, 249–250, 254; Saigyo and, 183–208 *passim*; San-lun school of, 184; Shingon, 165; Sōtō, 168, Tantric, 269; Theravāda, 233; T'ien-t'ai (Jp. Tendai) school of, 184–185; transformation of 25, 233; Zen, xiii, xiv, 7–9, 16, 17, 30, 141, 160, 271
Burroughs, John, 55, 296
Burton, Robert G., 291
Burtt, E.A., 294, 295
Bush, Susan, 300

Callicott, J. Baird, 18, 51–65, 113, 115,

169–170, 259, 269–271, 291, 292, 295, 297, 302, 310, 322, 323, 324; and Roger T. Ames, ix–xii, 1–21, 279–289
Capra, Fritjof, 17, 61, 297
Carnot, Sadi, 38, 293
causality, Buddhist: see pratītyasamutpāda; Buddhism, causality in
cause, 225
Ch'en, Kenneth, 316
Ch'eng Hao, 75–76, 77
ch'i (vital force), 18, 121, 299; defined, 68–70
Chan, Wing-tsit, 68, 123, 132–133, 298, 299, 300, 305, 306
Chang Tsai, 69–70, 72–74, 299
Chang, Tai-nien, 298
Chang, K.C., 304
Chan-jan, 184–185
chen (transformation), 121, 304
Chen, Ku-ying, 301
Cheng, Chung-ying, 10–11, 292
Chih-i, 190
Chi-tsang, 184
Chou Tun-i, 75, 146
Christianity, 28, 34, 207, 208, 282, 284–285; Nietzsche on, 84–85; Reformation of, 25, 28, 33; transformation of, 25, 233
Chu Hsi, 300
Chuang Tzu, 77, 80, 82, 114, 122, 140, 299, 300–302, 303, 305–306; on anthropocentrism, 86; on forgetting, 88; on forming concepts, 86–87; and Saigyo, 201; on *te,* 126, 129–131; wife of, 146
Chūjin, 191–197, 200, 317; argument for the Buddhahood of plants, 192–193
Chūzan, 189
Clausius, Rudolf, 38–39
Clements, Frederick, 55, 296
Cobb, John B., Jr., xv–xvi, 319
conceptualism, 236, 244
Confucianism, 74, 124, 129, 130, 148–149, 253; Japanese, 163, 166
continuum view of reality, 45–46
Cook, Francis H., 19–20, 213–229
cosmetic order, 118
cosmogony, 67, 118
cosmological order, 106
cosmological perspectivism, 106
cosmos, 118

creatio ex nihilo, 119–120
creation myth, in the Chinese tradition, 67–68, 298, 304; in the Japanese tradition, 166–167; in the Western tradition, 216
crisis, in philosophy, 101, 276–277
cultivation: see *shugyō*
cybernetics, 26, 28, 32

Dahlke, P., 47, 294
Dainichi (Jp. Great Sun), 167
Dainichikyō, 167–168, 172
Darwin, Charles, 31, 37–38, 44, 48, 71, 180, 286, 314, 315
de Francis, John, 294
de Bary, William T., 299, 311
Democritus, 17, 52–53, 105, 295
Derrida, Jacques, 302
Descartes, René, 113–114, 271–272, 289, 295
detachment, Buddhist, 171
Deutsch, Eliot, 20, 60–61, 259–265, 269, 292, 293, 297, 306, 312, 322, 323
Devall, Bill, 297
Dharma (dhamma) (esoteric truth, individual things), 172–174, 235, 236, 242, 251–252, 255, 267, 273
Dharmakāya (Buddha-body), 167, 172–173, 186–187, 310
dharma-datu (Hua-yen universe), 215, 224, 242
Dilworth, David A., 313, 315
Disch, R., 291
disinterestedness, 262
Dōgen, Zenji, 25, 36, 159, 168, 178, 310, 312, 313, 317; and "being-time" (Jp. *uji*), 170; on enlightenment, 172–174; on ethics, 174–175
Dōshū Ōkubo, 312
dualism, conceptual, 119–121, 248, 295
Dubos, René, 289, 324
Dubs, H.H., 68
duhkha (suffering), 169–170, 226, 233, 235, 248, 254, 267, 268, 269–270, 310–311

ecocentrism, 163, 165, 179–180; and Oriental art, 218
ecology, 18, 25–26, 28, 30, 74, 213–214, 279; age of, 289; cultural, 32, 34, 43, 45, 51–64; and "deep ecology," 58–59; and ecosystem, 56, 60, 63; and ethics, 106; as

field theory, 56; origins of, 55, 294–295; and physics, 51–52, 56–57, 59–61, 63
Einstein, Albert, 219, 228
Elassaer, Walter, 44
Eliot, T.S., 227, 294
Elsasser, W., 294
Elton, Charles, 56
emptiness (Jp. *kū*), 170, 200–203, 225, 236, 238–241, 244; see also *śūnyatā*
enlightenment (Jp. *satori*), 168, 173–174, 236, 239–240; analogy with biological life cycle, 190–193; of trees and plants, 184–208; see also *hongaku, shikaku, nirvāṇa*
Enlightenment, European, ix
entropy, 38–39, 41
environmental crisis: as an international phenomenon, 260, 279–282; the problems defining the, 3, 247, 271, 279; rationalization of, 272
Environmental Ethics, xi, xii 1
environmental philosophy: as comparative, 12, 276; conflict between East and West in, xviii; history of, xiii; role of Eastern thought in, xiii–xxi
environmental ethics: as art, 114; Buddhist approaches, 244–246; as distinguished from applied ethics, 1–2; and Taoism, 141–143
environmental attitudes and values: effectiveness and ineffectiveness of, xix–xx; Greco-Roman roots of Western, 4–6, 28, 213, 282, 284–285, 287; in Japanese Buddhism, 183–200; Judeo-Christian roots of Western, xiv–xv, xxi, 3–4, 141, 215–216, 282, 284, 287; in Taoism, 141–143
equilibrium, 41–42
ethics: ecological, 106–107, 147, 149; as aesthetics, 110; communitarian, 174–175, 180; Dōgen on, 174–175; as *ethos*, 131, 135; Taoist perspective on, 110–111
ethos (character), 175; *see also* ethics, Taoism
evidences, sources of novel, 100

Fairbank, John K., 299
Faraday, Michael, 227–228
Faulkner, William, 111
Fa-tsang, 219–220, 223

Feinberg, Joel, 291
feng-shui (geomancy), 283–284
Feyerabend, Paul, 273
Foucault, Michel, 274, 323
Fox, Warwick, 295
Francis of Assisi, xiv, xv
freedom, 161
Freud, Sigmund, 272, 273
Fritsch, Albert J., 291
Fu, Hsi-hua, 299
Fujiwara Teika, 206
Fung, Yu-lan, 185–186, 316

Galileo, 31, 289, 295
gardens, Japanese and English contrasted, 158
Genji, Tale of, 179
George, Stefan, 160
Gilligan, Carol, 324
Giradot, Norman, 298
gnoseological intuitionism, 268–269
Goethe, Johann Wolfgang von, 55, 156–157, 181
Gomez-Pompa, Arturo, 289, 324
Goodpaster, Kenneth, 62, 297
Gould, Stephen Jay, 314, 315
Graham, Angus, 139–140, 301, 302, 305–307
Graves, Robert, 284–285, 324
Gribbin, John, 295
Guthrie, W.K.C., 295

Haeckel, Ernst, 55, 296
Hakeda, Yoshito S., 201 202, 309, 311, 316, 318
Haldane, E.S., 295
Hall, David L., 18, 20, 99–111, 115, 119–120, 137, 292, 293, 302–303, 304, 313, 324; power/creativity distinction, 138
Halle, Morris, 300
Han Fei Tzu, 306
Hargrove, Eugene C., xiii–xxi, 291
harmony, see *ho*
Hartshorne, Charles, 272–273, 291, 323
Hawaii, 29
Heart Sūtra, 235–236, 241
Heaven, in Chinese philosophy, see *t'ien*
Hegel, G.W.F., 55, 248
Heidegger, Martin, 25, 115, 153–154, 158–159, 232, 301–302, 303, 308

Heisenberg, Werner, 297
Heraclitus, 5, 62–63, 85, 86, 115
Herman, A.L., 169, 291, 310–311
hermeneutics, x, 79, 115, 190, 195
Hill, Thomas E., 2, 291
Hillman, James, 302
Hinduism, 25, 61, 169, 208, 233–234, 248
ho (harmony), 118, 134, 145–149, 298;
    Japanese conception of, 166
Hobbes, Thomas, 53, 55, 244, 289, 295,
    296, 321
hōben (Sk. upāya, expedient means), 173
holographic model, 108, 110
hongaku (original enlightenment), 194,
    196–197, 317
Horner, I.B., 319
hosshin seppō "the Dharmakaya expounds
    the dharma"), 172–173
Hsiao Kung-chuan, 124
hsing (nature), 301, 305
Hsün Tzu, 305
Huai Nan Tzu, 122
Hua-yen Buddhism: see Buddhism
Hughes, J. Donald, 291
Hui-kuo, 167
Hume, David, 102–103, 175, 238
Hurvitz, Leon, 317
Huxley, Julian, 40, 294, 315
hylozoism, 115

I Ching (Book of Change), 121
icchantikas (nonbelievers), 185–186, 189
ideas, efficacy of, 279–289
identity, 221
Ienaga Saburo, 203–207, 308, 318
ignorance (avidya), 242–243
imperialism, 280
impermanence (Sk. anicca, Jp. mujō),
    169–170, 196, 233; see also Mu-joh
Inada, Kenneth K., 20, 231–245, 320
individuality, 46
Indra, jewel net of, 214
industrialization, 25–28, 280–281
interest, 253
internal relations, 60
Intersectarian Debate, 188–189
Ip, Po-Keung, 114–115, 303
Ishimoda Tadashi, 308
Izutsu, T., 133, 306

Jacobson, Nolan P., 242, 320
Jagger, Alison, 324
Jainism, 9, 169, 233–234, 248, 267, 268
Jakobson, Roman, 300
James, William, 177–179, 219, 253–255,
    313, 314, 321, 322
Japan, 25, 28, 29, 33, 164
Jefferson, Thomas, 27, 33
Ji-Ko (self), 160–161
Ji-nen (Jp. nature): see nature
Jung, Carl, 298, 302
Jung, Hwa Yol, 7, 292

Kaibara Ekken, 177
Kalupahana, David J., 20, 247–256, 268,
    293, 311, 322, 323
Kant, Immanuel, x, 20, 53, 55, 84–85,
    102–104, 110, 176, 260–262, 264, 296,
    322
Kao, Yu-kung, 300
Karlgren, Bernhard, 125, 305, 307
karma, 60
karman, 233, 260, 263–264, 267
karmayoga (detached acting/making),
    264–265
karuṇā (compassion), 233, 241
Kasulis, Thomas P., xii, 293, 309, 311,
    312, 313
Kaufmann, Walter, 249, 321
Keightley, David, 304
Kepler, Johannes, 31
Khoshoo, T.N., 323
Kierkegaard, Sören, 88, 102–103, 160, 248
Kimura, Bin, 19, 153–162, 308
Kirk, G.S., 295
Kitagawa, Joseph M., 309, 316
Kojiki, 179
kokoro (mind and emotions), 201
Kuhn, Thomas, 273, 292, 295
Kūkai, Kōbō Daishi, 165, 166, 167,
    171–174, 177, 183, 186–188, 201–203

LaFleur, William R., 9, 10, 19, 183–209,
    292, 309, 312, 317
language, as "nonreferential," 106
Lao Tzu: see Tao-te-ching
Larson, Gerald James, 19, 20–21, 267–277,
    293, 306, 312, 322
Latham, Robert, 295
Lau, D.C., 122–123, 301, 305

Lavoisier, Antoine, 295
Lebra, Takie, 309
Lebra, William, 309
Legge, James, 306
Leibniz, G.W., 31, 262
Leopold, Aldo, xvi, 57–58, 59, 64, 288, 296, 297, 324
Leucippus, 52–53, 105
li (principle), 146
Li Po, 205
līlā (play), 263–265
Linnaeus, Carl, 44, 54, 55–56, 296
Livingstone, P., 293
Locke, John, 26–27, 113–114, 289, 295
Loewe, Michael, 304
logical order, 116–119; see also rational order
Lotus Sutra (Saddharma-Puṇḍarīfika), 7, 189–190, 194
Lovejoy, Arthur O., 133
Lovelock, James, 293
Loy, David, 304
Luckmann, Thomas, 271, 323
Lucretius, 295
Lü-shih ch'un-ch'iu, 118, 304

ma (Jp. interval), 166
MacIntyre, Alasdair, 175–176, 178, 313
MacPherson, C.B., 322
Mādhyamika, 268
mahāpralaya (great dissolution), 273
Mahāvairocana (Dharmakāya): see *Dharmakāya*
Mahāvairocana Buddha, 187, 201–202
Mahāvairocana Sutra see *Dainichikyō*
Mair, Victor H., 302
Majjhima Nikāya, 235
Man'yōshū, 154, 165, 179, 203
Martin, Paul, 323
Marx, Karl, *see* Marxism
Marxism, 25, 28, 30, 32, 33, 70, 103, 273, 276–277
Masuda Katsumi, 308
materialism, 25–28, 29; atomic, 52–53; in Chinese philosophy, 69
Matsunaga, Alicia, 309, 312
Matsunaga, Daigan, 309, 312
Maturana, Humberto, 293
Maxwell, James, 228
māyā (discontinuity), 262–264

Mayr, Ernst, 177–178, 314
Ma-wang-tui, 122–123
McHarg, Ian, 4, 291, 292
McKinley, D., 291, 297
McLuhan, Marshall, 29–32
Medawar, P., 294
Mencius, 300
metaethics, 267–268
metaphor, 106, 276, 288
metaphysics: grounding of, 259; as science of first principles, 114, 117
methodology, comparative, 270, 276–277
mikkyō (Jp. esoteric practices), 167
Mīmāṁsā, 267, 268
Miner, Earl, 206, 318
Mittasch, Alwin, 301
Miyamoto Shōson, 188, 316
Mizukara (Jp. nature) 154–155, 159
mokṣa (freedom), 264
mono no aware (sensitivity to things), 179
Morowitz, Harold, 8–9, 10, 17–18, 37–49, 58, 59, 292, 294, 296
Mote, F.W., 67, 71, 73, 124, 298
Motoori Norinaga, 177, 179
Munro, Donald, 305
Murck, Christian, 300
Murti, T.R.V., 293
Mu-joh (nothing permanent), 158–159; *see also* impermanence
Myers, Norman, 323

Nabhan, Gary, 289, 324
Naess, Arne, 58–59, 296, 297
Nāgārjuna, 20, 232–234, 236–237, 239, 272, 319, 320
Nagatomo, Shigenori, 309–310
Nagel, Ernest, 294, 295
Nakamura, Hajime, 293, 312, 316, 317
Nash, Roderick, 9–10, 292
natural reverence, 259
nature: Buddhist valorization of, 183–208; as a Chinese term, 81, 153; as *dharmatā*, 252; as Divine, 161–162; domination of, 260–261; in European languages, 153; as a Japanese term, 153–162; as *māyā*, 262; as *Mu-joh* (nothing permanent), 158–159; as *natura*, 153; as "outside," 155, 157; as *physis*, 153–154; as religion, 205; and self, 155; as soteric, 203–208; as Tathāgata, 207–208; voice of, 156

Needham, Joseph, 68, 72, 133, 298, 305, 306–307
neoteny (holding onto use), 180–181
Neo-Confucianism, 68, 77, 146, 163, 164, 283
neo-Marxism, x
neo-pragmatism, x
Neville, Robert C., 19, 136, 145–149, 306
Newton, Isaac, x, 17, 31, 53, 54, 280, 289
niche, 56, 60
Nietzsche, Friedrich, 18, 79–97 passim, 114, 115, 300–302, 303; and anthropocentrism, 82–83; distinguished from primitivism, 92–97; on forming concepts, 86–87; on Greek attitudes toward nature, 84, 153–154; and herd mentality, 80; and imagery, 89–92; and Übermensch, 87–88; "unmasking" of moral judgements, 85–86
nihilism, 249
Nihongaku ("Japanology"), 164
nirvāna, 170, 233–234, 241, 244, 254, 311
Nishida Kitarō, 161, 178, 313, 314
Nishitani, Keiji, 25, 27–29, 95, 240, 293, 294, 302, 311, 320
Nishiyama, Kosen, 312
Noddings, Nel, 324
nonviolence (ahiṃsā), 248
non-equilibrium theory, 42–44
North, Harold Fowler, 295
Northrop, F.S.C., 45, 294
nothingness (Jp. mū), 170
Novak, Philip, 323
no-self, doctrine of, (Sk. anātman, Jp. muga), 170, 172, 233, 238
Nyāya-Vaiśeṣika, 267, 268

O'Brient, Walter H., 291
Onozukara (Jp. nature) 154–155, 159–160
Onsager, Lars, 42
ontologia generalis, 114
ontology: Chinese, 67
Orwell, George, 220
Ouspensky, P.D., 57
overman: see Übermensch

P'an, Chiang-tung, 299
paired oppositions, 247–249
paradigms, 273–274
Parinirvāṇa Sūtra, 186
paritassanā (anxiety), 250–251

parity principle, 234, 236–237, 240, 244
Parkes, Graham, 18, 79–97, 301, 302, 305
Passmore, John, xv–xvii, xxi, 291
pathetic fallacy: see anthropocentrism
Pepper, Stephen C., 304
perceptions, ontological, 231–232
perceptions, conceptual, 231–232
personal identity, 147–148
perspectivism, 105–107, 109
philosophia perennis, 111
philosophy, comparative, 275–277
Philosophy East and West, xi, xii, xviii
physis (Gk. nature), 153–155
Plato: x, 15, 53, 70, 85, 180, 295, 296; and categories, 44, 133; on human nature, 5–6, 102; as transcendent formist, 6, 14, 31, 54, 116–117
Po Chü-i, 205
polarity, conceptual, 119–121
Porkert, Manfred, 299
post-modernism, x
Potter, Karl, 263, 268, 293, 322
Powers, Jonathan, 297
pragmatism, 20, 255–256, 259
Prajñāpāramita Sūtras, 235
prakṛti, 269
pratītyasammutpāda (paticcasamuppāda) (co-dependent arising), 20, 172, 214–215, 220–225; 233, 236, 251
psychology: of modern science, 53; moral, 61–62
Pythagoras, 5, 13, 31, 32, 53–54, 115, 295

quantum physics, 59, 61
Quinton, Anthony, 54–55, 296

Ramsey, F.P., 107
rational order, 105–106; see also logical order
rationality, the contemporary critique of, 101–104; and ethics, 102–104, as a factor in anthropocentrism, 105–106
Raven, J.E., 295
reality: as becoming, 168–169; as Brahman, 262; as units of harmony, 146, 298
Reischauer, Edwin O., 299
relationality, 220–221
Rescher, Nicholas, 291
rights, 27, 33, 175
Riverine Mentality, 30, 32–34

Rodman, John, 291
Rolston, Holmes III, xvii–xviii, 16, 62, 291, 293, 297, 306
Rosemont, Henry, Jr., 312
Ross, G.R.T., 295
Rouner, Leroy, 310, 312
Routley, Richard, 291
Russell, Bertrand, 224–225
Ryckmans, P., 299
Ryōgen (Jiei Daishi), 188–191, 193–194, 200, 317

Sachs, Mendel, 319
Saichō, 167–168, 186
Saigyō (Satō Norikiyo), 183–208 *passim*; and Buddhist doctrine, 317; and Chūjin, 200; and Kūkai, 201–203; poetry of, 197–203; and Ryōgen, 200
Sakamoto, Yukio, 317
Śākta, 269
Śākyamuni, 187–189
samadhi (Sk. meditation), 168
samaya (symbol), 187–188, 201–203, 316
Śaṁkara, 262, 271, 272
Sāṁkhya, 268, 269, 273
saṃsāra, 233–234, 244, 263, 267
Sauer, Carl O., 323
Sayre, K., 297
Schipper, K., 304
Schopenhauer, Arthur, 249
Schweickart, Russell, 293
Schweitzer, Albert, xv
scientia universalis, 114
Seed, John, 64, 297
Seidensticker, E.G., 308, 314
self, relational concept of, 61–64
sentient/insentient distinction, 184–187
sentimentality, 259
Serres, Michel, 294
Sessions, George, 297
Shaeffer, Francis A., 291
Shaner, David Edward, 19, 163–182, 308, 312, 315
Shepard, Paul, 57–58, 59, 62–63, 291, 296, 297
Shih-chi (The Records of the Grand Historian), 305
shikaku (initial experience of enlightenment), 194, 196–197

shinjingakudō (bodymind awareness), 174–175
Shintō, 163–166, 168, 196, 207
Shively, Donald H., 316
Shi-zen (Jp. nature): see nature
Sho/Sei (nature), 161
shōji (Jp. paper walls), 166
shugyō (Jp. cultivation), 163, 166, 174, 190, 308
Siren, Oswald, 283
Siu, R.G.H., 300
skandhas, 236, 238–239, 241
Smart, Ninian, 293
Smil, V., 323
Smith, Richard J., 293
Smith, Huston, 10, 292
Smith, Adam, 25
Snow, C.P., 39, 294
Snyder, Gary, 7–8, 10, 59, 292, 297
sōmoku (plants and trees), 184
Spencer, Herbert, 37–40, 44, 55
Spretnak, Charlene, 324
Spring, Eileen, 307
Spring, David, 307
Ssu-ma T'an, 123
Stevens, John, 312
Stevenson, C.L., 102
Stone, Merlin, 324
sublime, 260–262
substantialism, 248–250
Sun Chang, Kang-i, 300
śūnyatā, 95, 200–203, 225, 233, 236
Supremely Ontological, 239, 242–243, 321
Sureśvara, 262, 322
Suzuki, D.T., 178, 222, 293, 319, 320

t'ai chi ch'uan (exercise), 146
t'ai-hsü (great void), 70
T'ao Ch'ien, 205
t'ien (heaven/sky), 76–77; defined, 80
t'ien-hsing (the course of heaven), 70
Tamaki Koshirō, 311
Tansley, Arthur, 56, 295, 296
tao, 19, 136, 272; distinguished from laws of nature, 132–135; as epistemic and ontological, 168; etymology of, 131–132; as the Great Harmony, 72; interpreted as field, 131–135; metaphors for, 134; as natural order, 81–82; 306; and *te*,

121–123, 124, 127, 128; as the *That Which*, 108
Tao Chi, 74
Taoism, 9–11, 18–19, 20, 35, 67, 71, 74, 79–97 *passim*, 101, 113–144 *passim*, 283–284, 286; and action, 109; biological language of, 149; and Confucianism contrasted, 83, 85, 129; and consanguinity, 164; cultural aesthetic of, 146, 148; and desire, 109; and discriminative consciousness, 80, 307; as distinguished from primitivism, 92–97; and environmental "*ethos*," 141–143; and first problematic thinking, 107; and knowledge, 109; as non-hierarchical, 109; as a primordial utopia, 82; and spirituality, 143; and the water image, 89
Tao-sheng, 185
tao-te (field and focus), 108–109
Tao-te-ching: 81–82, 85, 108, 114, 119, 120, 122, 153, 154, 301, 303, 305–307, 310; as the classic of *tao* and *te*, 122–123; on *tao*, 133–134; on *te*, 127–128, 130; on *wu-wei*, 137–138
Tathāgata, 187–188, 190, 202, 204, 207–208, 250
tathatā (thus and so), 242
ta-hua (great transformation), 70
ta-t'ung (great unity), 72
te (particular focus, virtue) 19, 91, 108–110, 136, 301; interpreted as insistent particularity, 121–131; philological analysis, 125–126; as tally, 130; as *tao*, 127–130
technology, 260, 263, 280–281, 288, 302
Teilhard de Chardin, Pierre, 29, 294
Tellenbach, Hurbertus, 19, 153–162
Teng, Shu-p'in, 299
theoria/praxis distinction, the consequences of, 99–100
thermodynamics, 48; second law of, 40–41
thinking, 99
Thomas, Lewis, 294
Thompson, William, 38
Thompson, William Irwin, 17, 25–36
time: in Japanese Buddhism, 170–171
Ts'ao, Hsüeh-ch'in, 299
tsao-wu che (creator), 67
Tu, Wei-ming, 18, 67–78, 293, 298, 299, 304, 310

Tuan, Yi-Fu, xvii, 282–287, 292, 324
tzu-jan (self-so, spontaneity, self-creativity), 19, 71, 81, 109–110, 120, 125, 129, 132, 135, 139, 154, 301

Übermensch (overman), 87–88
Udayana Ācārya, 249
ukiyo (passing world), 205
Unamuno, Miguel, 107
Upaniṣads, 248

Vajrasekhara Sūtra (Jp. *Kongōcho-kyō*), 168
value: as achievement, 147–148; as altered by changes, 145; an axiological conception of, 145; a cosmological conception of, 145; and environmental systems as pattern within process, 147
van Bragt, Jan, 320
Varela, Francisco, 26–28, 31, 32, 293
Vedānta, *see* Advaita Vedānta
Vedas, 267, 268
Viglielmo, V.H., 314
vijñaptimātratā (consciousness-only), 237

Wa (Jp. harmony), 166
waka (verse), 183
Wallerstein, Immanuel, 294
Walpola, Rahula, 319
Wang, Ling, 298
Wang, Ch'eng-en, 299
Wang Fu-chih, 69, 73, 76–77
Wang Ken, 76, 300
Wargo, Robert, 313
Waterman, T.H., 294
Watson, Burton, 299
Watsuji, Tetsurō, 156, 308, 315
Watts, Alan, 62, 297
Weber, Max, 272, 273
Weiss, Paul, 231–232
Wells, H.G., 294
White, Lynn, Jr., xiv–xvii, 4–5, 7, 10, 16, 115, 141, 279–282, 284, 287, 291, 292, 293, 307, 323, 324
White, Gilbert, 55, 296
Whitehead, A.N., 105, 115, 216, 227–228, 304, 319
Wilhelm, Richard, 298
Wilson, Edward O., 175–179, 313, 314, 315, 316
Wittgenstein, L., 273, 275, 320

Woodward, F.L., 319
world orders, 105; and *tao,* 108
world view: American Indian, xv, 286–287;
  Chinese, xv; development of, 286;
  Japanese ecocentric, 163
Worster, Donald, 56–57, 296
wu-chih ("no-knowledge"), 19, 108, 110–111
wu-wei ("non-assertive action"), 19, 89,
  109–110, 121, 135, 304; and anarchism,
  136–137; philosphical analysis of,
  136–137; and *yu-wei,* 136–140
wu-yü ("objectless desire"), 19, 109–110

yamazato (mountain retreat), 205–207
yin-yang, 119–121, 123, 146, 248, 299
Yoga, 268, 269
Yogācāra-vijñānavāda, 237, 268
Young, Rhett W., 301
Yü, Anthony C., 299
Yü, Ying-shih, 133, 306
Yuasa Yasuo, 164–168, 173, 308–311
yu-wei, 121, 136–139

Zarathustra, 87–92
Zeno, 31